Movies and Meaning
An Introduction to Film

Third Edition

Stephen Prince
Virginia Polytechnic Institute
and State University

PEARSON

Boston ▪ New York ▪ San Francisco
Mexico City ▪ Montreal ▪ Toronto ▪ London ▪ Madrid ▪ Munich ▪ Paris
Hong Kong ▪ Singapore ▪ Tokyo ▪ Cape Town ▪ Sydney

For my parents

Series Editor: *Molly Taylor*
Editorial Assistant: *Michael Kish*
Marketing Manager: *Mandee Eckersley*
Editorial Production Service: *Chestnut Hill Enterprises, Inc.*
Manufacturing Buyer: *JoAnne Sweeney*
Cover Administrator: *Kristina Mose-Libon*
Electronic Composition: *Omegatype Typography, Inc.*

For related titles and support materials, visit our online catalog at
www.ablongman.com.

Between the time Website information is gathered and then published, some
sites may have closed. Also, the transcription of URLs can result in typographical
errors. The publisher would appreciate being notified of any problems with
URLs so that they may be corrected in subsequent editions.

Library of Congress Cataloging-in-Publication Data
Prince, Stephen,
    Movies and meaning : an introduction to film / Stephen Prince.—3rd ed.
      p.   cm.
    Includes bibliographical references and index.
    ISBN 0-205-38112-X
    1. Motion pictures.   I. Title.

  PN1994.P676   2004
  791.43—dc21   2003040316

Printed in the United States of America

10 9 8 7 6 5 4 3 2 1   RRD-IN   08 07 06 05 04 03

Contents

④ Adaptation

⑥ Documentary

☑1 Film Structure   1

②√2 Cinematography   46

3 Production Design and Performance Style   83

4 Editing: Making the Cut   126

5 Principles of Sound Design   171

6 The Nature of Narrative in Film   213

7 Modes of Screen Reality 261

8 Hollywood International 299

⑦
Brazil

Preface to the Third Edition

The most extensive update to this new edition of *Movies and Meaning* lies in the film examples and photo illustrations used throughout the text. I have incorporated new examples and pictures to illustrate fundamental concepts and terminology. As in previous editions, I have aimed to use films that are, for the most part, familiar to student readers of the book and that, for the most part, were released in the years since the previous edition was published.

Many of the case studies that appear in the book have been revised and new ones have been added. In the previous edition, for example, one of the case studies illustrating narrative structure focused on *The Sweet Hereafter.* That case study now focuses on *Memento,* a film that has much greater salience for student readers. A new *Lord of the Rings* case study appears in the chapter on production design. The *Wayne's World* and *Austin Powers* case study, illustrating comic self-reflexivity in Chapter 7, now focuses on *Austin Powers* and *Charlie's Angels.*

One of the most important developments now underway in the film industry is the takeover by video production processes of the traditional film domain. I've expanded coverage of this issue and, in Chapter 2, spend some time clarifying the differences between the appearance of images captured on film and those captured on video. Also in Chapter 2, new to this edition, I take up the issue of "fake widescreen," which derives from the pervasive use of the Super-35 format and its tendency to create images that ultimately conform to 4:3 television composition.

In the first edition of *Movies and Meaning,* the chapter on narrative appeared as Chapter 6, following discussion of all the filmic elements of audiovisual design (cinematography, editing, sound, and so on). After experimenting in the second edition with the chapter on narrative placed at the head of the book, I have returned it to its original position in this new edition, as Chapter 6. The concepts involved in the study of narrative are more advanced and somewhat more abstract than those of audiovisual design and are more easily grasped by students who have the command of cinematic structure derived from the first five chapters.

The author wants to thank the following reviewers for their insightful comments: Paul Helford, Northern Arizona University; Stephen A. Schrum, University of Charleston; and Tom Sobchak, The University of Utah.

Preface to the Second Edition

Movies and Meaning provides a comprehensive introduction to the motion picture medium. The text is organized around three basic questions: How do movies express meanings? How do viewers understand those meanings? How does cinema function globally as an art and a business?

Most introductory film textbooks concentrate on the first question and tend to minimize or disregard the other two questions. A special feature of this book is the attention that it gives to the ways that viewers understand and interpret the elements of film structure and the attention that it gives to cinema as a global business as well as an art. To fully understand the medium of cinema, the reader needs to know what filmmakers do with the tools of their craft, how viewers respond to the designs those tools create, and how the art and business of film are interrelated. Film is an art form, but it is also a business enterprise. These two domains are not separate; they map onto each other, and knowing one requires knowledge of the other.

These three core questions frame the essential attributes of cinema. The first question—How do movies express meaning?—asks what filmmakers do and how they do it. The basic tools of filmmaking include cinematography, production design, the actors' performance, editing, sound design, and narrative structure. Each of these areas contributes to the organizing design of a film, and, by manipulating these tools, filmmakers are able to express a range of meanings.

To look only at what filmmakers do to create meaning, though, is to leave out a crucial part of the picture. One also needs to know what viewers do with the movies they watch because, without viewers, there are no meanings in film. The medium of cinema depends on a contract between filmmaker and viewer. Together, they co-create the film experience.

Thus, the second core question—How do viewers understand film?—asks what viewers do when watching movies. How do viewers interpret the audiovisual designs that filmmakers have created? How do filmmakers anticipate in their work the likely ways that viewers will react to certain kinds of stories and audiovisual designs? What makes movies understandable to viewers in the first place? How can filmmakers facilitate the viewer's ability to understand and interpret the images and sounds on screen?

Viewers respond to film, and understand it, by applying significant aspects of their real-life visual, personal, and social experience as well as their knowledge of motion picture conventions and style. The upcoming chapters emphasize both aspects of this response: the mapping of real experience onto the screen and the knowledge of medium-specific codes and style. This dual response is a function of the medium's own duality, its ability to *document* visual reality and to *transform* it. These functions receive special emphasis throughout the chapters because they are fundamental to much of what the cinema does and how.

The third question—How does cinema operate as an art and business on a global scale?—asks about the medium's capacity as a business enterprise and a vehicle of creative expression. An account that emphasized the cinema only as an art form would be inadequate and incomplete, and it would fail to grasp some of the medium's essential features, namely, the remarkable interrelation between art and commerce that has defined cinema since its inception. Filmmakers today work in a medium that faces grave economic problems, and these problems are affecting the kinds of films that get made. Furthermore, commercial filmmaking operates as part of a global communications industry, which exerts considerable influence on film content and style. At the same time, the global context carries with it considerable diversity, with filmmakers representing a range of countries, cultures, and styles. Although these issues of art and commerce, of cultural diversity and homogenization, are complex, no comprehensive examination of the medium should ignore them.

Movies and Meaning focuses on narrative filmmaking, and on fictional narratives in particular, because this is the most popular and pervasive form of filmmaking, seen by the largest audiences, and what most people mean when they talk about "the movies." Throughout the text, boxes extend the major topics of discussion into more specialized areas and supplement film examples with brief profiles of major directors. The reader will gain a more comprehensive understanding of cinema by exploring these boxed discussions. Each chapter ends with a few suggested readings to direct the interested reader's attention to more intensive treatments of basic issues. Boldface terms throughout the text designate items defined in the glossary.

◻ ABOUT THE PHOTOGRAPHS

The photographic illustrations utilize production stills and frame enlargements. An on-set photographer makes production stills during the course of a film's production, and they only *approximate* the actual shots and compositions in a film. To exactly reproduce the actual images that viewers see when watching a film, frame enlargements must be used. All frame enlargements in the text are labeled as such. The reader will note that, in general, the production stills look sharper and richer than the frame enlargements, which tend to be softer and grayer. But for the purposes of teaching, where an exact reference to a film's images is necessary, frame enlargements are required, and they are used here in that context. The reader seeing a frame enlargement can be confident that, with respect to all matters of camera perspective, she or he is seeing the exact frame as it appears in the film.

☐ ABOUT THIS EDITION

For this new edition of *Movies and Meaning,* I have updated the film examples and photographic illustrations used throughout the text, and I have expanded, or added to, the discussion of core areas: the history of sound technology; film stock and aspect ratio in cinematography; digital production methods used in film editing, sound design, and special effects, the actor's performance in relation to issues of depth of field, lighting, lenses, and visual effects; and the Hong Kong cinema as a relatively contemporary example of national new wave filmmaking.

At the organizational level, the reader will notice one significant change. The chapter on narrative is now at the front of the book. Because *Movies and Meaning* deals with narrative filmmaking, and because a film begins with a script that formulates a story, it is appropriate to begin the book with an examination of the nature of narrative in cinema. The discussion of film genres, located elsewhere in the previous edition, is now situated within the chapter on narrative.

Aside from this change, the book's plan of discussion proceeds as before. The initial chapters examine the basic elements of creative design in cinema: narrative, the camera, cinematography, production design, the actor's performance, editing, and sound.Chapter 1 examines the nature of narrative in film. What is narrative, what are its elements, how do filmmakers organize those elements so as to create a narrative structure, and how do viewers contribute to the narrative experience?

Chapter 2 explains the concept of film structure and how filmmakers use camera position, angle, lens, and movement to create visual design and meaning. Chapter 3 extends this discussion of the camera by exploring cinematography, the ways that filmmakers use light, color, and composition, and how viewers interpret those effects.

Chapter 4 examines the areas of production design (this includes costume design, set design, and the use of mattes and miniature models) and acting, considered in terms of the unique cinematic characteristics of film performance and how the actor becomes part of a film's total visual design.

Chapter 5 examines film editing. What is editing, what are the principles of continuity editing (the most commonly used system in filmmaking), and what are some alternatives to continuity editing? How do viewers draw inferences and interpretations across shots?

Chapter 6 discusses an often overlooked filmmaking tool, sound design. How do filmmakers design their soundtracks, how do they manipulate sound, and how does sound combine with images in artistically expressive ways? How do viewers interpret sound in relation to images?

These six chapters closely examine the basic tools of the filmmaker's art and how viewers respond to the audiovisual designs those tools create. The focus of Chapters 7 through 11 expands to cover larger issues of cinematic design, of art and business in a global context, and of film criticism and theory.

Chapter 7 looks at how films construct different types of "reality" on screen. The representation of screen reality—the ways movies persuade viewers that what they are seeing is "real"—varies considerably across different categories of film and involves differing kinds of manipulations by filmmakers and assumptions by viewers. Four basic types of screen reality are explored.

Chapters 8 and 9 examine motion pictures in the global context. Chapter 8 studies the impact of popular U.S. commercial filmmaking on world markets and the ways the U.S. industry is organized to compete aggressively in overseas markets. It also traces the connections between blockbuster films (so important in today's industry) and the world market.

Chapter 9 examines international alternatives to Hollywood's model of popular commercial moviemaking. These alternatives are discussed in terms of *auteur* directors and national, new wave film styles.

Chapters 10 and 11 discuss film criticism and film theory. These areas are the logical end-point of an introduction to film. Chapter 10 explores the nature of film criticism, what it is and what it does, and how film critics construct that criticism. Chapter 11 examines theories about the nature of cinema, surveys the most important theories, and discusses their strengths and weaknesses.

When readers have finished *Movies and Meaning,* they will have a comprehensive understanding of the central issues of film study: (1) how filmmakers achieve their effects; (2) how viewers make sense out of what they see on screen; and (3) how cinema operates as an art and a business in a global context. Above all, it is the author's hope that the reader will finish this book having grown not only wiser about the cinema, but with greater affection for it, affection strengthened by knowledge of its secrets.

◻ ACKNOWLEDGMENTS

Writing a book of this size and scope presents numerous challenges. The chief issue is to find the right approach for an introduction to a medium as rich and complex as the cinema and that now encompasses a century of creative development. The approach adopted here aims to be accessible for the reader and easy to understand while honoring the complexity of the medium. Without oversimplifying the medium or the issues involved in its study, considerable effort has been spent to make the writing style appropriate for the general reader.

For their valuable assistance in helping me find the right blend of topics, concepts, relevant film examples, and style of presentation, I must thank my careful editors who helped guide this text toward completion. The project began at the prompting of Kevin Davis at Macmillan who was very enthusiastic about producing a new film textbook and urged me forward despite my initial hesitation over what seemed a daunting task. I must also thank Macmillan's excellent development editor, Linda Montgomery. In addition, I thank the following reviewers of this edition who made insightful comments: Donald Larsson and Richard Terrill, Minnesota State University at Mankato, Blake Wood, Franklin Pierce College, and Paul Helford, Northern Arizona University.

At Allyn and Bacon, Joe Opiela helped steer the text toward completion. Joe was an especially good interpreter of the readers' reports. He made valuable suggestions for bringing the text into line with their recommendations. His support is greatly appreciated. And thanks to Karon Bowers, who continues Joe's work. The photo program is a key feature of this text. My thanks go to Terry Geeskin of the Museum of Modern Art's Film Stills Archive and to the staff at Jerry Ohlinger's Movie Material Store.

Most of the photos in this text are frame enlargements from the actual films under study. Edd Sewell kindly taught me how to use a darkroom. My thanks to Gerry Scheeler for the loan of lights and camera equipment and thanks also to Carl Plantinga and Richard Dillard for their support. A special thanks to Eric Poe Miller and Grant Corley for designing the figures used in the text.

Quotations from Pauline Kael's review of *Last Tango in Paris,* originally published in *The New Yorker,* are used with permission of E. P. Dutton, publisher. Quotations from "*Dead Again* or A-Live Again: Postmodern or Postmortem?" are used with permission of University of Texas Press, publisher. A special thanks to the essay's authors, Marcia Landy and Lucy Fischer, for their kind permission to reprint portions of their essay.

As always, Bob Denton, my former department chair, came through with whatever resources or support I requested. His help and friendship have been a great boost to my scholarship.

Thanks, also, to Teresa Darvalics for her valuable manuscript assistance and to Elizabeth Thomas for her help. Finally, special thanks to Marjorie Payne, my editorial and production editor, for a close and careful reading of the manuscript and for the outstanding visual design she gave the book. She took exceptionally good care of the author's work.

Chapter 1

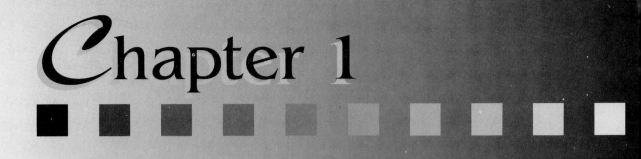

Film Structure

Chapter Objectives

After reading this chapter, you should be able to:

- explain the nature of film structure and its relation to the ways movies express meaning

- describe the production process and its relation to film structure

- describe the relation between film structure and the cinema's properties of time and space

- distinguish the three basic camera positions and their expressive functions

- describe how camera position can clarify the meaning of an actor's facial expression and gestures

- distinguish the three basic camera angles and describe the ways they influence viewer response

- differentiate telephoto, wide-angle, and zoom lenses and explain their optical effects

- explain the basic categories of camera movement and their expressive functions

- explain how a film's structural design is shaped by a filmmaker's choices about how to use the tools of style

- describe the relation between the camera's view of things and human perception

- explain how the camera creates images that both correspond with, and transform, the viewer's visual experience

Key Terms and Concepts

camera position
composition
director
producer
feature film
structure
running time
story time
internal structural time
frame
long shot
medium shot
close-up
normal lens

telephoto lens
wide-angle lens
zoom lens
focal length
angle of view
depth of field
motion perspective
motion parallax
pan and tilt shot
rack focusing
dolly or tracking shot
boom or crane shot
flicker fusion

beta movement
perceptual correspondence
preproduction
production
postproduction
establishing shot
canted angle
emulsion
deep focus
dolly
shutter
persistence of vision
perceptual transformation

The shark in *Jaws* (1975) and the digital characters in *Shrek* (2001) thrilled and amused moviegoers throughout the world. Audiences have embraced films as diverse as *Crouching Tiger, Hidden Dragon* (2001), *A Beautiful Mind* (2001), and *Spider Man* (2002). Each of these pictures provided its viewers with a strong cinematic experience, crafted by filmmakers using the elements of film structure: camerawork, lighting, sound, editing. To understand how movies express meanings and elicit emotions, one must begin by understanding their structural design. This chapter explains the concept of film structure, the camera's role as an element of structure, and the relation between the camera's method of seeing and a viewer's understanding of cinema.

☐ ELEMENTS OF FILM STRUCTURE

Structure refers to the audiovisual design of a film and the particular tools and techniques used to create that design. A convenient way to illustrate this concept is to make a distinction between structure and content. Consider the average newspaper movie review. It provides a description of a film's story and a paragraph or two about the characters and the actors who play them. In addition, the reviewer might mention the theme or themes of the film. These descriptions of story, character, and theme address the content of the movie.

Now, instead of thinking about content, one could ask about those things that help create the story, give shape to the characters, illustrate and visualize the themes. These are questions about the elements of cinema—the camera, lights and color, production design, performance, editing, sound—and their organization in a given film.

The Production Process

A helpful way of understanding film structure—and the material presented in upcoming chapters—is to map its components according to their place in the production process. When does production design occur? Cinematography? Editing? Filmmaking involves three basic steps or stages. **Preproduction** designates the planning and preparation stage.

Titanic (Paramount/20th Century Fox, 1997)
Titanic's production design evokes a now-vanished Victorian world of early twentieth-century Europe. Meticulously detailed costumes and sets are an essential part of the film's structural design.

PREPRODUCTION	PRODUCTION	POSTPRODUCTION
Script	Shooting & Sound Recording of Scenes	Editing of Sound & Image
—optioning		Foley
—writing	Music Scoring	ADR
—revisions		Digital Effects
Hiring of Cast and Crew		Color Timing (Digital/Lab)
Design of Sets and Costumes		Release Prints
Plan Style of Cinematography		
Rehearsals		

Figure 1.1: The production process.

It typically involves the writing of a script, hiring of cast and crew, production design of sets, costumes, and locales, and planning the style of cinematography. Set design and camera style are both previsualized using software programs that enable filmmakers to "see" in advance how camera setups and lenses will look on the sets that are planned. Preproduction also sometimes includes a brief period of rehearsal for the actors. **Production** designates the work of filming the script (cinematography) and sound recording of the action. The director may request a temp track, a temporary musical score that is similar to the one that will be created for the film. **Postproduction** involves the editing of sound and image, composition and recording of the music score, additional sound recording for effects (Foley) and dialogue replacement (ADR), creation of digital special effects (these may also occur during production), and color timing to achieve proper color balance in the images. This may be done digitally (known as digital grading) or using traditional lab methods. Copies of the film are then made for exhibition, either as prints (on film) or as digital video.

Because filmmakers apply the elements of structure at different points in the production process, these elements can be used to modify or influence one another. A director might realize that a scene as filmed lacks emotional force and may turn to the composer for music to supply the missing emotion or to the editor to sharpen its dramatic focus. A cinematographer in postproduction may alter the image captured on film by using digital grading to adjust color, contrast, and other elements.

The Role of the Director

A wide range of creative personnel design picture and sound on any given production. While filmmaking is a collaborative enterprise, one individual has chief artistic authority, and this is usually the **director.** The director coordinates and organizes the artistic inputs of other members of the production team, who generally subordinate

The Immigrant (Mutual Film Corp., 1917)
Charles Chaplin was the complete filmmaker. He wrote, directed, performed in, edited, and composed the music for his films. Many said that,
were it possible, he'd have played all the characters as well. He rarely
worked from a completed script. He preferred to build a set, dress it with
props, and then explore its comic possibilities, making up gags as he went
along. Performance, not camerawork, was the centerpiece of his films.
Here, Charlie and his companion (Edna Purviance) have no cash to pay
for the meal they've just eaten. The hulking waiter (Eric Campbell) suspects the worst. Frame enlargement.

their artistic tastes or preferences to a director's stated wishes or vision. The director,
in turn, answers to the **producer** who generally has administrative control over a production (e.g., making sure the production stays on schedule and within budget). In
practice, though, many producers hold more than administrative authority and are
actively engaged with the director's creative decisions, especially if the producer is a
powerful figure in the industry.

Great variety exists in the working methods of directors. Some directors, such as
Robert Altman (*Gosford Park*, 2001; *The Player*, 1992), welcome input from other pro-
duction team members in a spirit of shared collective artistry. Other directors, such as
Alfred Hitchcock or Charles Chaplin, tend to be more autocratic and commanding in
their creative approaches. Some directors, such as Woody Allen (*Hollywood Ending*, 2002;
Deconstructing Harry, 1997), Steven Spielberg (*The Lost World*, 1997; *Saving Private
Ryan*, 1998), and Stanley Kubrick (*Full Metal Jacket*, 1987; *Eyes Wide Shut*, 1999),
take an active role in the editing of their pictures. Most directors place special emphasis on the quality of the script, believing a polished script to be essential to making a good

STANLEY KUBRICK

During his 46-year career, Stanley Kubrick made only twelve feature films. Despite the relatively small body of work that he left, however, he had an extraordinary impact on the medium and is recognized as one of it major filmmakers. A director of legendary stature, he was renowned for spending years planning a film and years more shooting it and working on postproduction. Famous for doing many takes of each shot and for the precision of his visual designs, Kubrick honed a style that is unique and unmistakable, and his films offer bleak but compelling visions of human beings trapped and crushed by the systems—social, military, technological—they have created.

Kubrick's reputation was that of an intellectual director, keenly interested in a range of subjects and whose films explored issues and ideas, yet he never finished high school. At age 17 he dropped out and began work as a photographer, working at *Look* magazine for several years before completing two documentary shorts for the March of Time newsreel company (*Day of the*

Fight [1951] and *Flying Padre* [1951]). Borrowing money from family and friends, he then completed his first two features as director, *Fear and Desire* (1953) and *Killer's Kiss* (1955). In a move that announced his conviction that cinema was a medium of personal artistry and that he would control his own work, Kubrick produced, wrote, directed, photographed, and edited these films.

After another crime film, *The Killing* (1956), Kubrick made *Paths of Glory* (1958), a powerful drama of World War I and the first of his films to pursue what would be his great theme, the domination of people by the systems they have created (envisioned in this film as the machinery of war and the pitiless chain of command). Influenced by the moving camera of director Max Ophuls, Kubrick's sustained tracking shots became a signature element of his style.

Kubrick's next film, *Spartacus* (1960), was a production on which he, uncharacteristically, did not have complete authority (the picture belonged to its star–

The Shining (Warner Bros., 1980); **Eyes Wide Shut** (Warner Bros., 1999) Kubrick made some of the most imaginative and precisely designed films in cinema history. His passion for design led him to shoot thirty and forty takes of a shot until he had what he wanted. The results were mysterious, haunting, poetic, and included Jack Nicholson's spectacular madness in *The Shining* and nocturnal landscapes of the mind in *Eyes Wide Shut*. Frame enlargements.

producer Kirk Douglas), and as a result, Kubrick was careful to work as his own producer on all subsequent films. He next went to England to film *Lolita* (1962), from the controversial Vladimir Nabokov novel, and he then settled there, using English production facilities for most of his ensuing films. He was becoming a filmmaker whose work transcended national boundary.

Dr. Strangelove (1963) is a modern classic, a shrewd and superb satire of the Cold War and the policy of nuclear deterrance aptly named MAD (Mutual Assured Destruction). Kubrick's startling marriage of baroque imagery and popular music (detonating atom bombs accompanied by the sentimental ballad "We'll Meet Again") became one of his trademarks, used famously in *2001: A Space Odyssey* (spaceships pirouette to the Blue Danube waltz) and *A Clockwork Orange* (lurid violence set to Beethoven's "Ode to Joy").

With *Strangelove*, these two films solidified Kubrick's reputation as a social and cinematic visionary. *2001* (1968) is a visual feast whose startling effects are married to a mystical and mind-bending narrative that takes humankind on a cosmic journey from the dawn of the apes to the era of space travel. Controversial for its violence, *A Clockwork Orange* (1971) depicted a brutal vision of future society where the state learns to control the violent impulses of its citizens. Kubrick said, "The central idea of the film has to do with the question of free will. Do we lose our humanity if we are deprived of the choice between good and evil?" By making the main character a thug and a menace to society, Kubrick aimed to give the question resonance.

With dazzling Steadicam shots of a labyrinthine hotel, Kubrick explored the effects of space on the mind in *The Shining* (1980), which depicts the hotel's sinister influence on a mentally unstable caretaker and his family and ends with one of the director's bleakest images of futility and alienation.

Kubrick extended his pessimistic visions of human failure to eighteenth-century Ireland in *Barry Lyndon* (1975) and the battlefields of Vietnam in *Full Metal Jacket* (1985). His untimely death followed comple-

tion of *Eyes Wide Shut* (1999), a haunting and mysterious evocation of erotic fantasy and its emotional consequences.

Kubrick never made the same kind of film twice. Each picture is uniquely different, uniquely resonant, and must be seen more than once before it begins to yield up its treasures. Kubrick dedicated his life to making films, and he believed that cinema was an art. Few filmmakers gain the authority to pursue this conviction without compromise. Kubrick's achievements in this regard place him in very select cinematic company. By showing filmmakers what the medium can achieve, Kubrick's work remains a continuing inspiration.

film. Two of Clint Eastwood's best films as director, *Unforgiven* (1993) and *The Bridges of Madison County* (1995), feature exquisitely written scripts.

Most directors maintain enduring relationships with key production personnel. As these relationships deepen over the course of several productions, the creative, collaborative work that results becomes richer. Steven Spielberg, for example, has used cinematographer Janusz Kaminski for *Minority Report* (2002), *AI: Artificial Intelligence* (2001), *Saving Private Ryan,* and other films. Oliver Stone has regularly collaborated with Robert Richardson, on *Salvador* (1986), *Platoon* (1986), *Wall Street* (1987), *Talk Radio* (1988), *Born on the Fourth of July* (1989), *JFK* (1991), *Natural Born Killers* (1994), and *U Turn* (1997). Woody Allen invariably relies on editor Susan E. Morse, as does Martin Scorsese with editor Thelma Schoonmaker. George Lucas has relied on Ben Burtt as the sound designer for all of the *Star Wars* films (five so far). The continuities established by these professional relationships are vitally important to a director's ability to get what he or she wants on the screen.

Time and Space in Cinema

The elements of cinematic structure, organized by directors and their production teams, help shape distinctive properties of time and space in a film. A convenient way of thinking about the arts is to consider the properties of time and/or space that they possess. Music, for example, is primarily an art of time. Its effects arise through the arrangement of tones in a musical composition that has some duration or length. Movies, by contrast, are an art of time as well as space.

The time component of movies has several aspects. **Running time** designates the duration of the film, the amount of time it takes a viewer to watch the film from beginning to end. Most commercially released films are called **feature films,** which means that they typically run from 90 to 120 minutes. Some films, however, are much longer. *The Lord of the Rings* (2001), in its theatrical release, was three hours long, and the director's extended version on DVD is even longer.

Story time designates the amount of time covered by the narrative, and this can vary considerably from film to film. In Fred Zinnemann's Western, *High Noon* (1952), the story spans 1.5 hours, roughly equivalent to the running time of the film itself. Story time, on the other hand, can span many epochs and centuries, as in Stanley Kubrick's *2001: A Space Odyssey* (1968), which goes from the dawn of the apes well into the age of space travel. Filmmakers may also organize story time through the use of flashbacks so that it becomes fragmented, doubling back on itself, as in Orson Welles's *Citizen Kane* (1941), in which the story of Charles Foster Kane is told largely through the recollections of friends and associates who knew him.

Internal structural time, a third distinct aspect of cinematic time, arises from the structural manipulations of film form or technique. If a filmmaker edits a sequence so that the lengths of shots progressively decrease, or become shorter, the tempo of the sequence will accelerate. A rapid camera movement will accelerate the internal structural time of a shot. Regardless of the shot's actual duration on screen, it will seem to move faster. (The term *shot* designates the basic building block of a film. During production, a director creates a film shot by shot. In this context, a shot corresponds to the amount of film footage exposed by the camera from the time it is turned on until it is turned off. Films are composed of many shots that are joined to-

The Road to Perdition (DreamWorks/20th Century Fox, 2002)
and **Mission Impossible 2** (Paramount, 2000)
In *Road to Perdition,* Depression-era gangsters, Paul Newman and Tom Hanks, contemplate
their sins. The slow pace and long running time of *Road to Perdition* help give the film an
introspective, meditative, and reflective tone. Snappy editing and a fast pace would be as ill
suited to this material as a leisurely pace would be for contemporary action films, such as
Mission Impossible 2. Frame enlargements.

gether in the process of editing. In a completed film, a shot is the interval on screen
between edit points.)

In *Dances with Wolves* (1990), the editing imposes a slow pace on the story by letting many shots linger on screen for a long time. Director Kevin Costner felt a slow pace
suited this stately epic about an era when horse and wagon were major modes of trans-
portation. By contrast, contemporary action films like *Lara Croft: Tomb Raider* (2001)
race at breakneck speed, rarely pausing long enough for an audience to catch its breath.

A film's internal structural time never unfolds at a constant rate. It is a dynamic
property, not a fixed one. Filmmakers modulate internal structural time to maintain
viewer interest by changing camera positions, the lengths of shots, color and lighting
design, and by altering the volume and density of the soundtrack.

Viewers experience internal structural time as a series of story events held in dynamic relations of tension and release. Viewers often describe films as being fast or slow moving, but in fact the pacing of any given film typically varies, as filmmakers use strucure to create narrative rhythms that alternately accelerate and decelerate. While internal structural time results from a filmmaker's manipulations of cinema structure, viewers experience this type of time subjectively, and their responses often vary greatly. One viewer may love the dramatic intensity and emotional lyricism of *The Bridges of Madison County* (1995) or *Monster's Ball* (2001), while another may find the overall pacing of these films to be too slow.

Cinema is an art of time *and* space. The spatial properties of cinema have several components. One involves the arrangement of objects within the **frame** (the dimensions of the projected area on screen; the term also refers to the individual still image on a strip of film). This is the art of framing or **composition,** which is discussed in the next chapter as it is a part of the cinematographer's job.

The spatial properties of the cinema, though, go beyond the art of framing. Cinema simulates an illusion of three-dimensional space on a flat screen. To do so, it corresponds in key ways with the viewer's experience of physical space in daily life, and filmmakers create these correspondences in the design of their films. Cinematographers control the distribution of light on the set to accentuate the shape, texture, and positioning of objects and people. Film editors join shots to establish spatial constancies on screen that hold regardless of changes in the camera's position and angle of view. Sound designers use the audio track to convey information about physical space. The spatial properties of cinema are multidimensional and can be expressed through many elements of structure. This chapter and succeeding chapters explain these spatial properties and how filmmakers manipulate them.

▢ STRUCTURE AND THE CAMERA

Let us begin our understanding of film structure by discussing the fundamentals of camera usage. These must be grasped before more complex issues of cinematography can be examined in the next chapter. The camera's position, angle, lens, and the camera's movement have a major impact on the visual structure of every film. The reader seeking to understand cinema should begin with a clear sense of the relationship among these characteristics and the differences between them.

Camera Position

The most basic way of classifying camera usage is in terms of **camera position.** This refers to the distance between the camera and the subject it is photographing. Obviously, the camera-to-subject distance is a continuum with an infinite series of points from very close to very far. In practice, however, the basic positions are usually classified as variations of three essential camera set-ups: the **long shot,** the **medium shot,** and the **close-up.** Each of these positions has its own distinct expressive functions in the cinema.

Filmmakers typically use the long shot to stress environment or setting and to show a character's position in relationship to a given environment. In *Titanic* (1997), the majesty of the ship's enormous size is conveyed with a series of long shots that

An American in Paris
(MGM, 1951)
Longer, full-figure framings in the dance sequences of classic Hollywood musicals showcase the beauty of the dance. The longer framing allows the viewer to see the performer's entire body in motion. By contrast, contemporary filmmakers "cheat" when they film dance, using fast editing and close-ups to create the impression of a dance performance without showing the real thing. Here, Gene Kelly dances in an elaborate production number designed around the styles of Impressionist painting. Frame enlargement.

contrast the huge ship with the tiny passengers that crowd its decks. When they are used to open a film or begin a scene, long shots may be referred to as **establishing shots.** Many detective films, for example, begin with a long shot of the urban environment, often taken from a helicopter.

In contrast to the long shot, the medium shot brings viewers closer to the characters while still showing some of their environment. In *Ocean's Eleven* (2001), a comfortable

Ocean's Eleven (Warner Bros., 2001)
Medium-shot compositions can stress the relationship among characters while integrating them into their environment. Tess (Julia Roberts) and Danny Ocean (George Clooney) share an intimate moment inside the Las Vegas Bellagio Casino. The two-shot framing illuminates the characters and preserves details of the setting. Frame enlargement.

medium-shot framing allows Tess (Julia Roberts) and Danny (George Clooney) to converse while revealing aspects of the Bellagio Casino that surrounds them. Sometimes medium shots are labelled according to the number of characters who are present within the frame. Accordingly, this shot from *Ocean's Eleven* could be termed a two-shot. A three-shot, and a four-shot, would designate medium shots with larger numbers of people.

By contrast with long and medium shots, the close-up stresses characters or objects over the surrounding environment, usually for expressive or dramatic purposes, and it can be an extremely powerful means for guiding and directing a viewer's attention to important features of a scene's action or meaning. In *Bridget Jones's Diary* (2001), poor, love-starved Bridget (Renée Zellweger) has a crush on her boss (Hugh Grant), a heartthrob whose specialty is chasing women. When he moves in for a kiss, Bridget is overjoyed, and an extremely tight close-up captures this warmly romantic moment. The tight framing conveys the intimacy and emotional intensity of the moment.

The fact that filmmakers can choose among different camera positions illustrates a basic difference between cinema and theater. In theater, the spectator views a play from a single fixed vantage point, a position in the auditorium, usually from a distance. By contrast, in film, viewers watch a shifting series of perspectives on the action, and their ability to understand the story requires synthesizing the shifting points of view as the filmmaker moves from one camera position to another, from shot to shot. How viewers make sense of changing views of a scene supplied by different camera positions is a major issue to be examined in the chapter on editing.

Camera Position, Gesture, and Expression

By varying the camera-to-subject distance, the filmmaker can manipulate the viewer's emotional involvement with the material in complex ways. What the camera sees is

---

Bridget Jones's Diary (Universal, 2001)
Bridget Jones (Renée Zellweger) and Daniel Clever (Hugh Grant) share their first kiss. Note how the close-up framing crops off portions of Zellweger and Grant's faces. Because it is so tight, the framing concentrates on the characters with special emphasis, accentuating the intimacy of the moment. The out-of-focus background eliminates all distraction from the shot's most important content, the faces of the lovers. Frame enlargement.

what the spectator sees. As the camera moves closer to a character, viewers are brought into the character's personal space in ways that can be very expressive and emotional.

People express emotion and intention in ways that go beyond the words they speak. Posture, gesture, facial expression, eye contact, and vocal inflection express feelings and help define relationships. These signals vary by culture, but all members of a society learn how to read the expressions and gestures of other people as a way of inferring what they are thinking or feeling. By varying camera placement, filmmakers can call attention to significant expressions and gestures and thereby help viewers understand the meaning of the relationships and situations depicted on screen.

When a filmmaker cuts to a close-up, the director can emphasize and clarify a character's reaction, as well as bring viewers into the action and the personal emotional space of the character. Depending on how the viewer feels about that character, this can give rise to either positive emotions (e.g., compassion, empathy) or negative ones (e.g., fear, anxiety).

In George Cukor's *A Star Is Born* (1954), James Mason plays a tragic Hollywood actor, Norman Maine. With his acting career destroyed, the alcoholic Maine collapses into despair and considers suicide. He begins to cry. The camera draws in to a medium close-up, and director Cukor keeps the shot on screen for a surprisingly long time. Cukor said, "To see that man break down was very moving. All the credit for that goes to James [Mason]. He did it all himself. What I did was to let him do it and let it go on and on, let the camera stay on him for an eternity." The shot is designed to elicit the viewer's empathy by revealing an intimate glimpse of a man's private hell.

Facial expressions do not have to be realistic to express emotion or intention. Close-ups in *The Mask* (1994) emphasize the magical face of the main character, rendered with special effects. These effects *transform* normal human reality but also *correspond* with real facial cues. The bulging eyes and open mouth accurately convey the character's startled, alarmed response to a woman pointing a gun at him, but they do so with exaggeration.

The application of digital tools in filmmaking has made great progress in little over a decade, with digital artists learning to represent a great variety of images and lighting conditions. A breakthrough in the representation of water, for example, made possible *The Perfect Storm* (2000), with its convincing, digital ocean. (Compare the tidal wave in that film with the one in *The Abyss* [1989], a decade earlier.) But the emotional richness and complexity of facial expression has not yet been among these breakthroughs. The startle response in *The Mask* or the facial reactions of digital characters in *Shrek* (2001), *Monsters, Inc.* (2001), or *Toy Story* (1995) are conveyed in broad strokes rather than subtle ones.

A rare effort to digitally create photo-realistic faces in *Final Fantasy* (2001) achieved mixed results—faces with finely detailed skin and hair texture but a relatively blank emotional tone. Compare the level of detailing in the sets and physical environments with the characters' faces. The environments are extraordinarily rich in visual detail, but not the faces. Someday soon, digital methods will achieve convincing photo-realistic facial expression. Their failure to do so thus far says much about how complex and rich the human face is as a medium of communication.

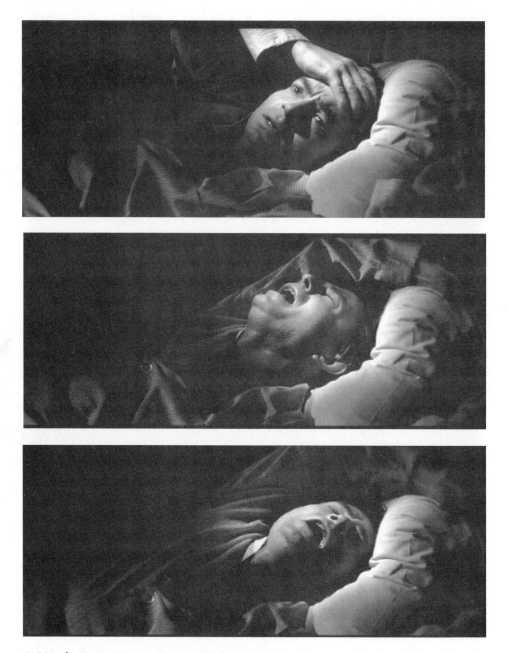

A Star is Born (Warner Bros., 1954)
Changing facial expressions in a single, extended shot from *A Star is Born* convey the despair of Norman Maine (actor James Mason). As a photographic medium, the cinema is especially powerful in its ability to capture and emphasize the smallest details of human facial expression as signs of emotion. The face is one of cinema's most profound channels for emotional expression. (Frame enlargements.)

The Mask (New Line, 1994)
Unreal faces in fantasy films can still have a special expressive power. Bulging eyes and gaping mouth accurately convey a fright response, though with unrealistic exaggeration. Frame enlargement.

Final Fantasy (Columbia, 2001)
To date, most digitally created facial close-ups have involved cartoon or non-human characters because their expressions can be rendered in broader terms. A rare exception is this film, which aimed to create realistic human facial expressions with photographic realism. The results were mixed. To date, digital software hasn't quite cracked the complexity of the human face in motion. Frame enlargement.

Case Study: Charles Chaplin

Few filmmakers understood the emotional implications of camera position better than Charlie Chaplin. Chaplin used a formula to guide his camera placements: long shot for comedy, close-up for tragedy. He understood that the long shot was best suited for comedy because it allowed viewers to see the relationship between Charlie the tramp and his environment, particularly when he was causing chaos and confusion, as he might when tackling a waiter carrying a tray of food or stepping on a board with a brick on one end, causing it to catapult onto the head of a policeman. Laughter depended on seeing these relationships and having sufficient emotional distance from the character. The long shot helped provide viewers with that emotional distance. By contrast, Chaplin knew that the close-up, by emphasizing a character's emotional reaction, could invite tears rather than laughter. Aiming for the heartstrings of his audience, he used his close-ups sparingly so that they would have exceptional dramatic intensity.

The ending of *City Lights* (1931) illustrates this quite well. Charlie has been courting a blind flower girl who believes that he is a millionaire. Charlie happily plays along. At the end of the film, the flower girl regains her eyesight, chances upon Charlie, the disreputable tramp, and realizes with disappointment who he is. At this moment, Chaplin shows Charlie's extraordinary expression in close-up, a mixture of hope, love, fear, embarrassment, and humiliation. This is one of the most perfect close-ups in film history. It emphasizes the complex feelings between the characters, magnifies the emotions on screen, and intensifies them for the film's viewers.

The examples thus far have elicited positive emotions from viewers. Obviously, though, many films and genres, like horror, appeal to viewers by eliciting such negative emotions as fear, disgust, and anxiety. Within the safe confines of a fictional film world, these negative emotions can be pleasurable to experience. In this context, a strategically placed close-up can be disturbing and frightening if it brings the viewer into a relationship of proximity and spatial intimacy with a terrifying or dangerous character, as in this scene from *The Exorcist* (1973).

The effects of camera position, then, are context-dependent, a matter of how a given position is related to the dramatic or emotional content of a shot or scene. By using camera position, filmmakers can enhance or inhibit the viewer's emotional involvement with a character or situation and can elicit both positive and negative emo-

City Lights
(United Artists, 1931)
Chaplin's sublime expression in the final image of *City Lights*. Chaplin intuitively understood the emotional implications of camera position, and he reserved the close-up for special moments of pathos and sentiment. His extraordinary face, the tentative gesture of his hand, the rose it clutches—these emphasize his romantic yearning and his pained embarrassment at being revealed as a tramp and not a millionaire. Frame enlargement.

close up

The Exorcist
(Warner Bros., 1973)
Facial close-ups can be a very powerful way of eliciting negative emotion from viewers. When the possessed Regan (Linda Blair) stares into the camera, as here, it is difficult to avoid flinching. The camera's proximity to a dangerous or frightening character can generate in viewers a sense of being threatened. Frame enlargement.

tions. Good filmmakers are intelligent in their choice of camera position, understanding when to cut in to close-up and when to pull back to long shot. Each position gives the viewer a unique perspective on the action, and filmmakers understand that the effects of these positions can be enhanced by a careful choice of camera angle.

Camera Angle

The camera's angle of view typically varies from shot to shot. Camera angles are classified as variations of three essential positions: low, medium (or eye-level), and high. Low- and high-angle positions are usually defined relative to what the camera is filming. A low-angle shot in *Blade* (1999) shows the main character looking at another

Blade (New Line, 1998)
Camera angle can help visualize point of view. This low-angle shot shows Blade (Wesley Snipes) looking down at a woman who has been knocked to the ground by a monster. The low camera position simulates her point of view as she lies on the ground. Frame enlargement.

Ocean's Eleven (Warner Bros., 2001)
Terry Benedict (Andy Garcia) is the powerful and dangerous owner of the Bellagio Casino in
Las Vegas. As he arrives for work at his casino, the low angle framing enhances his stature
and dramatically reveals the ornate ceiling of the casino's entryway. The low angle composition gives him an impressive command of the frame. Frame enlargement.

character on the ground. The low camera position simulates the point of view of that
character on the ground.

Filmmakers use camera angles for a variety of expressive purposes. These include
conveying information about a character's view of the world and accompanying emotions. In *Citizen Kane,* director Orson Welles uses camera angle to evoke young Charlie Kane's boyhood feelings of bewilderment and powerlessness in his new foster home.
Charlie's imposing guardian gives him a sled for a Christmas present. To magnify Charlie's feelings of helplessness, Welles shoots the man towering above him, from the boy's
point of view, using an extremely low camera angle that forces viewers to look up to
this figure, much as Charlie has to do.

Camera angle can also complicate emotional responses by playing against the visual relationships viewers want to have with characters, as Hitchcock does in his use of
high angles during moments of extreme emotional crisis. In *Psycho* (1960), he used
one of these extremely high angles as a way of solving a dramatic and narrative problem and of working at cross-purposes with the viewer's desired response. A first-time
viewer believes that the psychopathic killer in the film is the deranged mother of motel
owner Norman Bates. In the film's climax, Norman is revealed as the killer. The mother
has been dead for many years, and Norman has kept her alive in his mind, keeping her
body in the house, even dressing up like her and speaking in her voice. Hitchcock's narrative problem was to keep the audience from realizing midway through the film—
when Norman moves her body from the upstairs bedroom to the basement—that the
mother was dead.

Hitchcock attached his camera to the ceiling and filmed from directly overhead
as Norman carries the corpse down to the cellar. The extremely high angle, coupled
with the jostling movement as Norman goes down the stairs, prevents the audience
from realizing he is carrying a corpse. The viewer is even fooled into thinking that
the mother is kicking in protest.

High Angle

Psycho (Paramount
Pictures, 1960)
Hitchcock solves a narrative
problem in *Psycho* by using this
high camera angle. The bizarre,
distorting perspective conceals
the fact that Norman's mother
is dead as he carries her down
to the fruit cellar. Frame
enlargement.

Hitchcock's use of the high angle in this scene is an ingenious solution to his narrative problem. It introduces a bizzare, distorting perspective into the scene that plays against the viewer's desired visual relationship with the characters. Because of the questions that the narrative has raised about this mysterious figure, viewers want to see Norman's mother clearly and up close, not from the odd angle Hitchcock provides. But, by delaying the desired response, Hitchcock builds considerable suspense, and when the payoff finally comes at the end of the film—a close-up of the mother's skeletal face—it is heart-stopping.

Other Angles   The **canted angle,** involving a tilted camera leaning to one side or the other, can be an effective way of making the world look off-kilter, often to express a character's anxieties or disoriented, disorganized frame of mind. In *Starship Troopers,* director Paul Verhoeven uses a tilt to convey the stress of pilot Carmen Ibanez

Tilt shot

Starship Troopers
(Columbia Tri-Star, 1997)
A tilted camera angle catches the
urgency and anxiety with which
Carmen (Denise Richards) pilots
her starship around an oncoming
obstacle. The camera angle turns
the light fixtures in the background into sharp diagonals,
accentuating the compositional
instability. Frame enlargement.

ALFRED HITCHCOCK

Alfred Hitchcock was a consummate showman and entertainer and a serious artist who used film to explore dark currents of human thought and behavior. He thrived in the classical Hollywood studio system because his films were popular with audiences and enjoyed considerable critical respect. As a result, Hitchcock became one of the most powerful Hollywood directors and one of the few known to the public by name.

Born into a Catholic family in the East End of London in 1899, Hitchcock grew into a solitary boy possessed of an active imagination and fascinated by crime. Uncommonly anxious, he believed his many fears motivated his preference for making films about innocent characters suddenly caught up in an unpredictable whirlpool of danger, madness, and intrigue. "I was terrified of the police, of the Jesuit Fathers, of physical punishment, of a lot of things. This is the root of my work."

In 1920, Hitchcock entered the British film industry as a scriptwriter, set and costume designer. In 1924–1925, he worked as an assistant director, and then director, in Germany on several British–German coproductions. He studied and absorbed the style of German Expressionism, and in all of his subsequent films he relied on expressionistically distorted images to suggest an unstable world.

Hitchcock rose to the peak of the British industry with a cycle of elegant spy thrillers—*The Man Who Knew Too Much* (1934), *The 39 Steps* (1935), *The Lady Vanishes* (1938). Seeking greater creative freedom and technical resources, Hitchcock left Britain for Hollywood and completed his first U.S. film, *Rebecca*, in 1940. An auspicious debut, it won an Academy Award for Best Picture. In the years that followed, Hitchcock rapidly consolidated his reputation as a leading director and defined his unique screen world.

Using suspense as his method for drawing the audience into the fictional screen world, Hitchcock concentrated on stories of crime, madness, and espionage in which ostensibly innocent characters confront their

Vertigo (Paramount Pictures, 1958)
James Stewart portrays a detective terrified of heights in *Vertigo*, Hitchcock's most passionate and poetic film. Stewart's pose here is a classic Hitchcock image of the individual haunted by the darkness in his mind and beset by chaos in the outer world. Hitchcock's darkest films offer no places of safety. Frame enlargement.

(Denise Richards) as she maneuvers her spacecraft to avoid a collision, and off-kilter angles make visual the disturbed world of *Natural Born Killers*.

Angle in Context While camera angles are capable of eliciting some of the kinds of emotional responses from viewers described here, it is important to remember that

guilt and complicity in unsavory or villainous activities. In *Shadow of a Doubt,* a psychopathic serial killer (Joseph Cotton) visits his sister in a small California town, and his idealistic young niece discovers his secret and the many ties that bind her to him. In *Notorious* (1946), two U.S. spies (Cary Grant and Ingrid Bergman) fall in love while manipulating and emotionally betraying one another. In *Strangers on a Train* (1951), a charming psychopath (Robert Walker) proposes an exchange of murders to a celebrity tennis player. "You do mine, I do yours," he tells the shocked but intrigued athlete.

Hitchcock reached the height of his powers, and the zenith of his career, in the 1950s with a series of now classic films. In *Rear Window* (1954), about a wheelchair-bound photographer intent on proving one of his neighbors is a murderer, Hitchcock explored the theme of voyeurism, applying it both to characters in the narrative and to audiences watching the film.

To Catch a Thief (1955) was a classy, witty Technicolor romp on the Riviera, and *The Man Who Knew Too Much* (1956) was a glossy, big-budget remake of his 1934 British hit. *Vertigo* (1958), a complex tale of detection, murder, and madness, was Hitchcock's most intensely personal, romantic, and poetic creation. Widely regarded as his masterpiece, it is hypnotic, dreamlike, with a remarkable depth of feeling and an uncompromisingly bleak ending. Disappointed with *Vertigo*'s commercial performance, Hitchcock made *North by Northwest* (1959), a fast, witty, hugely entertaining summation of the espionage and chase thrillers he had perfected in his 1930s British career.

Hitchcock's next film, *Psycho* (1960), proved to be his most influential. This story of murder, madness, and perversion at a seedy roadside motel was a calculated exercise in audience manipulation in which Hitchcock wanted only to make his viewers scream. He succeeded brilliantly. In its coldness, its savage bru-

tality and violence, and its merciless attitude toward the audience, *Psycho* anticipated, and introduced, the essential characteristics of modern horror.

Hitchcock had one more hit in the 1960s—*The Birds* (1963)—and then began a period of decline. *Marnie* (1964), *Torn Curtain* (1966), and *Topaz* (1969) were critical and commercial disappointments. The industry and the modern audience were changing, and Hitchcock could not adapt. The old studio system was dead, and many of the stars (Grace Kelly, Cary Grant, James Stewart) who were essential to Hitchcock's films had retired or were now too old for the parts he needed to fill. The brutality and cynicism of modern film, which Hitchcock had helped inaugurate with *Psycho,* swept by him. Hitchcock had relied for his best effects on suggestion and implication and felt unable to relate to a world in which, and to a public for whom, extraordinary acts of violence were becoming increasingly commonplace.

Hitchcock achieved a brief popular comeback with *Frenzy* (1972), a hit about a British serial killer. Movie censorship had fallen, and Hitchcock included horrific and distasteful scenes of explicit violence, inadvertently demonstrating how creatively beneficial Hollywood censorship had been for him. His last film, *Family Plot* (1976), was an entertaining but unremarkable thriller. Hitchcock's declining health prevented completion of additional films, and he died on April 29, 1980.

Hitchcock's genius for self-promotion (realized through his cameo appearances in films and his witty introductions on his television show, which ran from 1955–1965) and his brilliance at frightening viewers made him one of the most popular and famous directors in screen history. But he was also a serious and sophisticated artist who made brilliant use of cinema as a vehicle for expressing the forces of darkness and chaos in human life.

all of these responses are context-dependent. The information they convey depends on the emotional content and action of a given scene. They must be carefully matched by filmmakers to the material of the scene. In other contexts, other scenes, low, high, and canted angles may have other effects than those mentioned here.

Natural Born Killers
(Warner Bros., 1994)
Unstable, tilted camera angles
help establish the nightmarish,
off-kilter world of serial killers
in Oliver Stone's *Natural Born
Killers.* Stone purposely created
a wildly chaotic visual design to
give the film a psychotic tone.
Frame enlargement.

Japanese director Yasujiro Ozu, for example, used low camera positions and angles extensively, but they are not correlated with any of the effects discussed here. To a large extent, they are motivated by the action of the films, which feature characters sitting on tatami mats while conversing (as is the custom in traditional Japanese homes). The camera gets closer to the ground to film them. One critic has suggested that these low positions and angles work to include the viewer in the world of the film, like a guest sitting on a tatami mat. To assess the function of camera position and angle, then, one must bear in mind their potential for structuring emotional response and also consider the expressive requirements of the scene. What are its dramatic, comedic, emotional, or cultural requirements, and how is their expression facilitated by camera position and angle?

Camera Lens

Besides position and angle, a third factor defines the relationship between the camera and what it photographs. This is the type of lens used in each shot. The lens is the device that gathers light and brings it into the camera to a focused point on the film, thereby creating an image that is recorded on the light-sensitive surface of the film, called the **emulsion.** A filmmaker's choice of lens can drastically affect the look of the image in terms of (1) the apparent size of objects on screen, and (2) the apparent relationships of depth and distance between near and far objects. Camera positions are generally defined by the amount of distance between the camera and what it is photographing, but, without knowing something about the lenses employed, a viewer is liable to misjudge the camera's position. Certain lenses, for example, can make the camera seem much closer to what it is photographing than it really is.

Focal Length and Depth of Field

When the lens is focused on a distant object, the distance between the film inside the camera and the optical center of the lens is known as the **focal length.** The properties of different lenses are understood in relation to their respective focal lengths. A focal length of 50mm conventionally designates a **normal lens** for 35mm film, which

Monster's Ball
(Lion's Gate, 2001)
Changing the lens's focal plane within a shot (a technique called **rack focusing**) can make a dynamic contribution to the composition. It creates a kind of editing within the frame, as the filmmaker racks focus instead of cutting to a new shot. In a long, uninterrupted shot, Hank Grotowski (Billy Bob Thornton) talks with his ailing father, and the changes in focal plane bring first one, then the other, character into focus. Frame enlargements.

is the film format used in commercial theaters. Lenses with focal lengths greater than the normal range are **telephoto lenses** or long focal-length lenses. Those with focal lengths less than normal are **wide-angle lenses** or short focal-length lenses.

The focal length of a lens is directly related to how much it sees, termed the **angle of view.** At a shorter focal length, the angle of view increases, allowing filmmakers to

O Brother, Where Art Thou (Universal/Touchstone, 2000)
The Cyclops (John Goodman) eavesdrops on the conversation behind him between diners Ulysses McGill (George Clooney) and companion. The deep focus composition, achieved with a wide angle lens, emphasizes the separation of foreground and background elements. This kind of extreme deep focus is relatively rare in contemporary film. Frame enlargement.

film a wider area. At longer focal lengths, the angle of view decreases, limiting film-makers to photographing a more narrow area.

Also varying with the focal length of the lens is the **depth of field,** the amount of area from near to far that will remain in focus. A wide-angle lens can capture much greater depth of field than a telephoto lens. With a wide-angle lens, the distance be-tween near objects in focus and distant objects in focus can be very great. By contrast, a telephoto lens will tend to give filmmakers a shallow depth of field, an inability to hold near and far points in focus.

These issues of depth of field are connected to important aesthetic traditions in cinema. Using **deep focus,** filmmakers like Orson Welles (*Citizen Kane*) and Jacques Tati (*Playtime,* 1967) created complex compositions featuring a rich interplay of fore-ground and background detail. By shooting in deep focus and extending the dura-tion of their shots, these filmmakers work with an aesthetic that respects the wholeness of time and space, that is, the playing area of each shot is extended in time (the shot's long duration) and space (depth of field). This is a distinct stylistic alternative to the use of editing to carve up space into many brief shots. The deep-focus tradition is covered in more detail in the section on Realism in Chapter 11.

Yet another characteristic differentiating wide-angle from telephoto lenses is the abil-ity of telephoto lenses to make distant objects appear much closer than they really are. In this respect, the effects of the telephoto lens can overwhelm the impression of true

---

Touch of Evil (Universal, 1959)
Orson Welles was the master of wide angle filmmaking, as practiced in *Citizen Kane* and subsequent films, like this one about a corrupt sheriff in a Mexican border town. Filming on a small set during this police interrogation scene, Welles fills the camera's wide angle of view with numerous characters and gives them a dynamic staging in deep focus. Note the strategic positioning of characters at four planes of distance from the camera. Frame enlargement.

camera position. What might appear to be a close-up can, in fact, be shot using a telephoto lens with the camera in a long-shot position. In these two portraits of the wooden bridge, the bridge is the same size in each photo, but in one case the size is due to a close camera position while in the other it is due to the magnifying effects of a telephoto lens. Viewers will have developed a sophisticated eye for cinema if they can tell when object size on screen is due more to camera position or to the choice of lens.

In sum, wide-angle lenses have a greater angle of view and depth of field than telephoto lenses. Unlike wide-angle lenses, telephoto lenses will magnify distant objects and make them seem closer than they are.

Zoom Lenses   In addition to normal, wide-angle, and telephoto lenses, a fourth category of lens is important in the cinema. This is the **zoom lens.** The zoom is a lens with a variable focal length. It can shift from wide-angle to telephoto settings within a single shot. This can create the appearance of camera movement, making it seem as if the camera is moving closer to or farther from its subject. In fact, however, the camera in a zoom shot remains stationary. Viewers with a sophisticated cinematic eye can discriminate zoom shots from true moving camera shots. In a moving camera shot, perspective changes, that is, the spatial relationship of the camera to the objects around it shifts because the camera is moving through three-dimensional space.

In a zoom shot, by contrast, perspective does not change because the camera does not move. Zooming in will magnify all objects on screen evenly. Zooming out will shrink all objects evenly. This is what produces the impression of camera movement. As objects in the shot enlarge, the viewer has the impression of moving closer to them. Whereas the zoom shot provides simple magnification, the moving camera provides a series of changing spatial relationships produced by movement and known as **motion parallax** or **motion perspective.** The absence of motion perspective in a

Two portraits of the same subject, one taken a few yards away with a normal (55mm) lens and the other at a much greater distance using a telephoto (205mm) lens. Which composition is a function of camera position and which is a function of lens focal length?

shot where the camera seems to be moving is a clear sign that the shot is a zoom and not a true moving camera shot.

Filmmakers sometimes use zoom lenses as alternatives to camera movement, especially if they are filming on a low budget and a quick schedule. Zoom lenses, though, can be used for sophisticated effects. In *McCabe and Mrs. Miller* (1971), director Robert Altman and cinematographer Vilmos Zsigmond employ a zoom to create a moment of dramatic emphasis when the hero realizes a gang of gunmen has come to kill him. Altman and Zsigmond rapidly zoom in on the gang, conveying the hero's sense of anxiety and the rush of excitement he feels. The optical effect suggests these emotional reactions.

Using Lenses

Filmmakers often employ the telephoto lens when they are filming a scene on city streets in which the characters are engaged in conversation and surrounded by real pedestrians. A realistic impression depends on the pedestrians being unaware of the camera and the actors. Filmmakers can hide the camera by placing it at some distance from the action and then use the telephoto lens to bring the characters into the medium shot or close-up framing suitable for the dramatic content of the scene. Telephoto lenses can also facilitate the staging of stunts. When Tom Cruise runs across a busy city street in *The Firm* (1993), viewers jump when a car nearly crashes into him. The car's apparent proximity, though, is an illusion created by a telephoto lens.

Viewers acquire greater cinematic sophistication when they become sensitive to the effects produced by different lenses used in the shots of a given scene. Just as filmmakers change camera positions and angles throughout a scene, they change lenses as well, fitting these to the unfolding dynamics of the dramatic action. In a shot with extreme depth of field, where near and distant objects are in focus, the lens is likely

---

Lara Croft: Tomb Raider (Paramount, 2001)
Wide angle lens perspective makes this shot of Lara Croft (Angelina Jolie) in gun blazing action look more dramatic. The lens exaggerates the size of her guns and makes her arms look longer than they otherwise would. The perspective distortion thrusts the action out at the screen and toward the viewer. Frame enlargement.

Red Beard (1965)
Japanese director Akira Kurosawa preferred the telephoto lens. He also liked to film scenes
with multiple cameras, creating occasional problems of perspective when he cut between
telephoto and non-telephoto shots. In this case, he cuts between two cameras whose lines of
sight form a 90-degree angle. The first camera set-up uses a telephoto lens and makes the
characters seem very close together, whereas the second set-up reveals their true positioning.
The perspective change between the two shots is very striking. Frame enlargements.

---

to be a wide angle. If, on the other hand, depth of field looks very shallow, with a com-
pression of distance so an object that definitely is very far off looks close, the lens is
likely to be a telephoto.

Some filmmakers are closely identified with certain types of lenses. Orson Welles,
Martin Scorsese, and Tim Burton tend to favor wide-angle lenses, while Akira Kurosawa,
Robert Altman, and Sam Peckinpah favor the telephoto. In *Touch of Evil,* his last
U.S. picture, made for Universal Studios in 1958, Orson Welles filmed his gargantuan
detective hero, Hank Quinlan, with extremely short lenses to exaggerate and enhance
his huge and grotesque dimensions. Evaluating a filmmaker's choice of lenses requires
that one be sensitive both to structure—in this case, the visual properties of lenses—

and to the requirements of the scene or shot. Consider the lead-in to the gunfight at the OK Corral in *Tombstone* (1993), when Wyatt Earp, his brothers, and Doc Holiday make their fateful walk down the town's streets toward the corral. A building blazes behind them for dramatic effect. The camera shoots them head-on, as they stride toward it. The long lens isolates the heroes in a shallow plane of focus, giving them an unequivocal visual dominance in the frame. By excluding the fire from the plane of focus, the filmmakers ensured that it would not distract unduly from the foreground drama of the heroes' determination. As an out-of-focus object, the fire is a subordinate element in the frame, but its presence is nevertheless dramatic, serving to prefigure the violence to come. Assessed in these terms, the telephoto framing is an effective one. By contrast, a wide-angle lens would have increased depth of field and thereby eliminated the concentrated visual focus on the heroes.

Camera Movement

The camera's perspective not only changes from shot to shot, but it can shift and move within the shot. The camera can move in virtually any fashion through space. To simplify things, this discussion will focus on three basic categories of camera movement: (1) **pan and tilt,** (2) **dolly** or **tracking,** and (3) **boom** or **crane.** All these types of camera movement shift the boundaries and coordinates of the frame. Moving the camera creates a fluid perspective, unlike a static shot with its fixed framing.

Pan and Tilt

A pan shot produces lateral movement on screen. The camera head rotates in a horizontal fashion from side to side on top of the tripod, which remains stationary. By contrast, in a tilt the camera pivots vertically, up or down. If a filmmaker were shooting a skyscraper, she or he could start with a camera focused on the bottom of the building and then tilt slowly up to the top to reveal, perhaps, King Kong swatting at airplanes. The accompanying diagrams illustrate the action of panning and tilting.

   Pans and tilts tend to establish linking movements, which filmmakers often use to connect objects or establish relationships between them, or to call attention to new areas of the scene. Pans may also be used to readjust the frame to accommodate character movement. If a character crosses the room to open a door, the camera operator might pan to follow the movement. An early example of this use of the pan occurs

Tombstone
(Buena Vista, 1993)
Telephoto lens perspective used to isolate, emphasize, and intensify a point of dramatic climax. Frame enlargement.

Figure 1.2: Pan.   **Figure 1.3:** Tilt.

in Edwin S. Porter's *The Great Train Robbery* (1903). When the robbers make their daring escape from the train after holding it up, they go down an embankment and across a stream to get to their horses. As they do this, the camera operator pans left and tilts down to follow them. It is done a bit sloppily, however, because the robbers get almost out of frame at one point before the camera operator picks them back up again.

In most instances, pans are brief, with the camera only pivoting a small degree. However, its physical design permits the camera to rotate an entire 360 degrees on the mounting attached to its tripod. Nothing, therefore, except for conventional usage, prevents filmmakers from executing a fully circular, 360-degree panning shot. These tend to be

The Great Train Robbery
(Edison, 1903)
After holding up the train, the robbers run for their horses to escape. In the next moment, as they turn left and run down a hill, the camera operator will pan and tilt to follow the action. Frame enlargement.

rare, but they do occur. In *Easy Rider* (1969), when the heroes Wyatt (Peter Fonda) and Billy (Dennis Hopper) visit a hippie commune and its members gather in a circle to pray for their harvest, cameraman Haskell Wexler uses a 360-degree pan across the faces of all the characters, who are grouped in a circle. The camera's movement brings each character's face into frame, creating a symbolic image of unity and completeness.

Dolly, Track, and Boom

Unlike the pan and tilt, in dolly, tracking, and boom or crane shots, the camera, along with its tripod or base, physically travels through space. As a result, these shots produce motion perspective, unlike pans and tilts. A **dolly** is simply a wheeled platform used for mounting the camera in a tracking shot. Sometimes these are called dolly shots because of their platform mount. In tracking, or dolly, shots, the camera may move briefly toward or away from an object, such as a character's face, or it may describe more extended and elaborate movements. In the latter case, a tracking shot may follow a character who is moving. As Rocky sprints along the streets of south Philadelphia to train for his big fight, the camera tracks with him. The rapid track helps visualize Rocky's power and adds energy to the shot.

Tracking or dolly shots generally move in a direction parallel to the ground. By contrast, boom or crane shots execute elaborate movements up or down through space. They take their name from the apparatus—boom or crane—on which the camera is mounted. A famous boom shot occurs in *Gone With the Wind* (1939), during the scene where Scarlet O'Hara visits wounded confederate soldiers at the railroad station. The shot begins with a full-figure framing of Scarlet. The camera then pulls back and booms up to a high angle that shows Scarlet surrounded by a huge field of the dead and dying. This change of perspective creates a powerful dramatic effect by revealing the scale of the carnage surrounding Scarlet, a scale that the initial framing of the shot had concealed.

Functions of Moving Camera Shots

This is a common and powerful function of camera movement: to reveal dramatic information by enlarging the viewer's field of view. A complementary function is to narrow

Figure 1.4: Tracking shot.

Gone With the Wind
(MGM, 1939)
Camera movement can work to reveal details and vistas by enlarging perspective. This famous crane shot begins with Scarlet (Vivian,Leigh) in a relatively tight framing that shows only a few of the Civil War wounded. The boom then reveals the true dimensions of the war's carnage. Frame enlargements.

and focus attention on significant objects or characters. As a director, John Ford rarely moved his camera, but when he did it had tremendous effect, as in *The Searchers,* where a dolly in to John Wayne's face emphasizes the character's intense and pathological hatred of Indians. Note the difference of emphasis between the opening and closing frames of the dolly as pictured in the photos on page 32.

In addition to revealing action or concentrating the viewer's attention, moving camera shots can serve other purposes. One extremely common function is to express

The Searchers
(Warner Bros., 1956)
Camera movement can work to concentrate the viewer's attention on dramatically important objects or details. John Wayne's character in this John Ford Western has an intense racial hatred for Native Americans, and Ford uses a dolly shot to emphasize the depth of this animosity. Pictured here are the beginning and ending frames of the shot. Notice how the dolly brings Wayne's face forward, emphasizing his extraordinary expression. Frame enlargements.

a dynamic sense of movement that makes a shot or scene more sensuous and dramatically exciting. In *The Ghost and the Darkness* (1996), when Val Kilmer and a companion race to kill a pair of marauding lions, cinematographer Vilmos Zsigmond follows their movements with a series of breathtaking tracking shots. The travelling camera plunges the viewer into the scene's frenzied action. Japanese director Akira Kurosawa is a master of sensuous camera movements that add extraordinary dramatic and visual impact to his scenes. In films such as *Seven Samurai* (1954) and *Throne of Blood* (1957), where characters on foot or horse race through a dense forest, Kurosawa tracks the camera rapidly with them, darting in and out of trees, over streams and under branches, plunging the viewer into dense foliage and expressing in the most visually convincing manner the sensation and experience of flight.

U.S. directors Martin Scorsese (*Taxi Driver*, 1976; *Gangs of New York*, 2002) and Brian De Palma (*The Untouchables*, 1987) are masters at using sweeping, sensuous camera movements. In *Goodfellas* (1990), Scorsese uses a handheld camera in a single shot to follow the main character, a New York gangster, as he gets out of

The Ghost and the Darkness (Paramount, 1996)
The tracking camera races with Val Kilmer and a companion as they try to head off a pair of marauding lions. Because the camera moves at the same speed as the two characters, they remain in focus, while stationary objects and several characters running in the opposite direction are subject to motion blur. Cinematographer Vilmos Zsigmond's tracking shot is exceptionally fluid. Frame enlargement.

his car, crosses the street, enters the side door of a nightclub, winds through narrow hallways and a crowded kitchen, and walks into a ballroom filled with hundreds of people and a stand-up comic in mid-routine. In *Snake Eyes* (1998), De Palma used a handheld camera for a 20-minute moving camera shot that follows Nicolas Cage as he walks through a sports arena filled with a capacity crowd. This was a deceptive sequence, however, because it was composed of several shots. These were joined at hard-to-see edit points when a wall or a person passed closely in front of the camera. Another bravura moving camera shot—9 minutes long—opened Robert Altman's *The Player* (1992) as a way of letting the audience know that this would be a very self-conscious film. In the shot, characters discuss their love for the elaborate opening tracking shot of Orson Welles's *Touch of Evil*, as Altman essentially repeats the famous Welles shot.

Filmmakers also use moving camera shots to visualize important thematic ideas. In such cases, the camera's movement is metaphoric and symbolic, its motion correlating, as a visual design, with important issues in a film's narrative. In *Seven Samurai* (1954), for example, to suggest the developing friendship and unity between samurai and peasants, Kurosawa groups them in a circle and tracks the camera around its periphery. In *We Were Soldiers* (2002), to suggest the Vietnamese enemy closing in on an Army Lt. Col. (Mel Gibson) and his men, the cinematographer did an inwardly spiraling tracking shot that loops around and in on Gibson.

Some of the most unique and carefully conceived moving camera shots occur in the films of French director Jean-Luc Godard. Godard's structural designs are extremely self-conscious, that is, they call attention to the technique at work. *Week-end* (1967) is Godard's dark, savagely funny satire of the barely repressed violence of an absurd, Americanized consumer society. In the film, an amoral couple, Corrine and Roland, travel by car to Oinville where they plan to murder Corrine's mother so they might claim the family inheritance. On the way to Oinville, they are caught in a traffic jam. On a narrow country road, a long line of vehicles impedes their progress. Anxious to get past the stalled line, Roland impatiently edges his car along the shoulder of the road, past the other vehicles.

Godard films the sequence in a single, unbroken tracking shot that lasts over 7 minutes. The camera tracks along the road and the line of stalled vehicles, keeping pace with Roland as he inches his way forward. The camera frames the scene slightly to the rear, preventing viewers from seeing what lies ahead. The effect of this maddening and funny sequence depends on the length of the shot—lasting an extremely long time—as well as the slow, methodical progress of the camera along what seems an endless line of stalled vehicles. The tracking shot becomes a metaphor for the experience of being stalled in traffic and enables the filmmakers to subject the audience to that oppressive experience.

These examples of camera movement point toward an important conclusion. Whether a filmmaker uses it to reveal detail, to convey the sensory experience of motion or to symbolically express thematic and narrative ideas, camera movement provides filmmakers with an essential means of shaping and organizing the visual space of a scene. Camera movement gives structure and meaning to the composition of a shot.

Technological Components of Film Art

Technological developments in recent years have made camera movement especially easy to achieve. The design of the Steadicam, a gyroscopically stabilized camera mount that can be strapped to the camera operator's body and used to create a handheld moving camera shot, has revolutionized the ease with which professional-looking camera movement can be obtained. The capabilities of the Steadicam were first displayed

---

Weekend (New Yorker Films, 1967)
Godard's tracking camera slowly travels the length of a line of stalled cars. The framing prevents a view of what lies ahead, deliberately frustrating the viewer. Finally, after several minutes, the camera reveals the cause of the accident. Frame enlargements.

in the sequence in *Rocky* (1976) where Rocky runs up the steps of the Philadelphia Museum of Art, accompanied by the camera operator. The Steadicam shot has a completely fluid, smooth movement with no noticeable jostle. The elaborate camera moves in *Snake Eyes* and *Goodfellas* were achieved with the Steadicam, as were the sweeping camera moves during the climactic battle in Terrence Malick's *The Thin Red Line* (1998).

Malick's film also benefitted from the use of an Akela crane for scenes showing U.S. soldiers hunting their Japanese foes through waist-high grass. These grassy fields on the Australian location (subbing for Guadalcanal in the Solomon Islands where the story was set) were dense, with rocks and holes underneath, an impossible terrain for a camera operator to move about. But the Akela could be securely positioned on solid ground and the camera extended on its 72' arm into the grassy areas that were vital to the story. On the crane, the camera could execute sweeping moves through the fields. In *Ali*, a film biography of boxer Muhammad Ali, Michael Mann used a "lipstick" camera—as tiny as its name implies—that he could hold in his hand as he moved between the boxers in order to film the fight scenes from unconventional angles.

Camera moves can also be digitally simulated today. Computer-effects shots in *Panic Room* (2002) create effortless camera moves through floors in a house, through air vents, and other impossible objects. This is animated footage that imitates the appearance of a camera move.

Obviously, filmmakers in earlier decades did not have the luxury of such devices. When viewing older films, therefore, one must be aware of the physical resources available in earlier periods. Sometimes filmmakers had to struggle with clumsy or cumbersome equipment, and it is often their ingenuity at devising solutions to these technical problems that is a mark of their talent.

During production of *The Last Laugh* (1924), for example, F. W. Murnau experimented with many different ways of producing camera movement. The camera was attached to a ladder, to scaffolding, to a rubber-wheeled trolley, and to the stomach of cameraman Carl Freund while he rode a bicycle. So impressed was Hollywood with the work of Murnau and Freund in *The Last Laugh* that it sent a telegram to Ufa, the German studio that produced the film, inquiring about the special camera that had been used to take the shots, adding that in the United States there was apparently no such device. Robert Herlth, the set designer for *The Last Laugh* and several other Murnau films, remarked that what the Americans didn't know was that "we had discovered new methods with only the most primitive means at our disposal."

Technical sophistication, by itself, provides a misleading yardstick for measuring the quality of films. Film equipment is so advanced today that filmmakers of only moderate talent (a category that does *not* include Malick, Mann, Scorsese, or De Palma) can produce images with a sophistication that the early masters—Renoir, Murnau, D. W. Griffith—could only dream of. Technology without intelligence, however, is just mechanics. It must be balanced by artistic vision and ingenuity.

◻ STRUCTURAL DESIGN AND CREATIVE CHOICE

A film's structural design results from the creative choices made by filmmakers, who confront a range of options as a project moves into production. There is no single, right way to film a scene. Where to position the camera, from what angle, which lens to use, whether to employ camera movement, how to light the set, how to choreograph the actors on screen, how to record the sound and balance dialogue, music, and sound effects, a filmmaker wrestles with all of these decisions. How they are resolved defines the style or structure of a given film.

Case Study: *Saving Private Ryan* and *A.I.: Artificial Intelligence*

Steven Spielberg and cinematographer Janusz Kaminski have collaborated on half a dozen films and in each case have come up with carefully considered structural designs. *Saving Private Ryan* begins with a startlingly graphic depiction of the D-Day invasion of the Normandy beaches, a battle that helped turn the tide of World War II in June 1944. In a harrowing 25-minute sequence, Spielberg depicts the carnage on Omaha beach, where the Allied forces suffered their greatest casualties under withering fire from German troops barricaded on high ground overlooking the beach.

Spielberg wanted the violence in *Saving Private Ryan* to have a chaotic quality that would correspond to the subjective experience of the men on the beach, knowing that death could come at any time, regardless of how one tried to avoid it.

He and Kaminski used the documentary footage shot by combat cameramen on the Normandy beaches as a model. They aimed to emulate the striking features of

Saving Private Ryan (DreamWorks, 1998)
The ferocious intensity of this film's battlefield sequences resulted from highly stylized manipulations of cinema technique. In cinema, there is no one "right" way to shoot a scene. Structural design results from the creative choices made by filmmakers. Frame enlargement.

this footage, much of which was shot in color and had a flat look, with reduced contrast. Accordingly, they decided to film in color, in contrast to their previous World War II collaboration, *Schindler's List* (1993), shot in black and white in order to correspond with much of the historical footage of Nazi atrocities.

They used two techniques—flashing and ENR—to render the colors more monochromatic and to reduce contrast. When film is flashed, the negative is exposed to a small amount of light prior to filming. This has the effect of desaturating color and reducing the density of shadows, allowing more detail to come through in shadow areas. ENR (named after the technician, Ernesto N. Rico, who helped develop the process) is a somewhat complementary process and has been widely used in recent films (*Evita*, 1996; *Amistad*, 1998; *Bulworth*, 1999). ENR retains a portion of the silver in film emulsion, which is normally removed during developing. This has the effect of making shadows blacker, desaturating color, and highlighting the texture and edges of surfaces. As a result of ENR, the patterns on the uniforms in *Saving Private Ryan* grew more vivid, as did the edges of helmets and guns and the reflective surface of the water, heightening the physical effect Spielberg was after. To darken the blood so it would stand out amid the desaturated colors, the effects crew added dyes to make it more blue.

Because the lenses used by combat cameramen were inferior to what a modern filmmaker would use, Kaminski and Spielberg ordered that the protective coating be stripped from some of their lenses. This gave the photographed images a sharp but cloudy appearance, with reduced contrast. To heighten the sense of chaos, they shot scenes with cameras using mismatched lenses, with and without the coating, to give the resulting footage a disjointed and disconnected feel.

To accentuate this off-kilter feeling, they manipulated the camera's shutter (a device that regulates how light reaches the unexposed film) to create strange, memorable effects in some shots. They threw the shutter out of synch to create a streaking, teary effect from top to bottom of the image and set the shutter at unusual angles to give the action a stroboscopic appearance. (*Pearl Harbor* [2001] copied this effect.) To create a disturbed, visually unsettled perspective, they used handheld cameras and employed a Clairmont Camera Image Shaker to vibrate camera perspective both horizontally and vertically.

Through all of these choices about technique, Spielberg and Kaminski aimed to capture the jarring experience of being inside combat. As Spielberg said, the film's style is hard and rough. "We were attempting to put fear and chaos on film. If the lens got splattered with sand and blood, I didn't say, 'Oh my god, the shot's ruined, we have to do it over again,' we just used it in the picture. Our camera was affected in the same way that a combat cameraman's would be when an explosion or bullet hit happened nearby."

The film's design has its visual point of origin in combat photography, even though many of the techniques they used had no basis in such photography. Their design choices—rendering a monochromatic look, emulating the visual qualities of the documentary footage of the invasion, creating a subjective view of the battle—led them to elaborate technological manipulations to achieve these ends.

Spielberg and Kaminski's next collaboration was *A.I.: Artificial Intelligence* (2001), based on a concept for a film that Stanley Kubrick had intended to make before his

A.I. Artificial Intelligence (Warner Bros./DreamWorks, 2001)
By retaining a high amount of silver in the film negative, ENR increases the illuminated appearance of reflective surfaces, such as the countertop here. The positioning of actor Haley Joel Osment, with his vivid reflection, makes the character (a mechanical boy) look more strange and alien. In its first narrative section, the film's compositions stress David's disconnection from the family that has adopted him. Frame enlargement.

untimely death. Spielberg, a friend of Kubrick's, was moved to bring it to the screen in a manner that would honor Kubrick's role and also be true to Spielberg's own style.

Spielberg and Kaminski based the film's look on storyboards and on hundreds of drawings that had been prepared for Kubrick, incorporating their imagery into the film. The picture has three parts, each with its own unique visual design. The Kubrick influence is strongest in the first part, which portrays the adoption of an artificial, mechanical boy (Haley Joel Osment) by a couple grieving for the loss of their real child.

Kubrick liked to film scenes in master shots with wide-angle lenses, and that's how Spielberg and Kaminski work in the first section. The compositions are wide and very controlled, and the color design is cool and blue. They use ENR to add contrast and sharpness to the images and make the colors paler, accentuating the coldness of the shots. ENR also makes shiny steel or glass surfaces look more reflective, as hard as diamonds. All of these manipulations of lighting, composition, color, and image processing (ENR) help create a cold visual tone and an emotional distance that is characteristic of Kubrick's work.

Then, when David arrives and bonds with the mother, the colors become warmer and Kaminski uses smoke to diffuse the light and make the images much softer and less cold and hard. This change moves the film closer to the emotional warmth and immediacy that is typical of Spielberg's work (in contrast to Kubrick's). The controlled, clean, and open compositions of the first section grow cluttered and dense in the second, action-oriented part of the movie, which features David on the run, separated from his family. The third and final section—when David becomes a real boy and gets to meet his mother again after a long separation—repeats the warm colors, intimate framings, and soft lighting that appeared earlier when David first bonded with her. The Spielberg style is strongest in this third section.

The film's unusual design blends the style of two directors—Kubrick and Spielberg—whose work and artistic sensibilities are very dissimilar. The film's structural design proceeds in a different direction than that of *Saving Private Ryan* because the overall creative goal—finding a way to integrate the styles of the two filmmakers—dictated a fresh approach.

Structural design results from a filmmaker's inevitable need to choose one or more sets of techniques and tools, based on an organizing design concept. The many potential ways to film a scene are narrowed to a single approach as filmmakers decide how to organize the tools of filmmaking. Decisions about where to place the camera, whether to move it, and what type of lenses to use must be integrated with other decisions about lights, color, sets, costumes, editing, and sound in order to arrive at a coherent and expressive audiovisual design.

THE CAMERA AND HUMAN PERCEPTION: CINEMA'S DUAL CAPABILITY

The camera records screen action through a changing series of positions, angles, lenses, and movements, and as they make their creative decisions, filmmakers need to anticipate how viewers will see and make sense of their images. To what extent does the camera's way of "seeing" approximate the viewer's customary habits of viewing the world? Is there a relationship between the appearance of images on the movie or television screen and the appearance of real-world objects and things in the viewer's mind's eye? These issues are relevant for comprehending how film structure operates and how viewers understand films.

Transforming Visual Reality

Obviously, both camera and human eye can see color, texture, movement, and the location of people and things in three-dimensional space. Motion pictures seem very lifelike, and even impossible objects, like Godzilla, can be rendered with apparent photographic realism. The camera, though, can see selectively in ways the human eye cannot. In other words, it has the property of **perceptual transformation,** the ability to show things in ways that differ from ordinary visual experience. Telephoto and wide-angle lens perspectives have no counterpart in human vision. The eye cannot magnify the size of distant objects, as a telephoto lens can, or increase the apparent distance between near and far objects, as a wide-angle lens can. A cinematographer who cranes up to a high-angle long shot employs a unique cinematic technique that the viewer's eye cannot duplicate, as does an editor who cuts among shots taken from different camera positions and angles, and with different lenses, to provide a shifting series of perspectives on the action. Viewers quickly learn that motion picture images and stories can define their own rules of representation. Stylized films like *The Crow* (1994) or *The Matrix* (1999) take viewers on imaginary journeys to screen worlds that differ remarkably from the one they inhabit in daily life. Viewers accept the unusual images, characters, and stories established in these films as a representational reality that is true on its own stylized terms.

HOW MOVIES CREATE THE IMPRESSION OF MOTION ON SCREEN

Viewers see only *apparent* motion on screen. As a strip of film runs through the projector, each frame is projected individually. Inside the projector is a device called the **shutter,** which blocks the light for a fraction of a second while the next frame is pulled down into place. The projector thus emits light in a pulsating beam that turns on and off. In the theater, viewers see a series of still frames projected on the screen and sit in alternating periods of light and dark.

The illusions of cinema—the viewer's impressions of movement and of a continuously illuminated screen—are due to several factors of perception. The retina of the eye retains an image for a fraction of a second after the source is gone (a phenomenon called **persistence of vision**). If a light source is switched on and off rapidly enough, a threshold is reached where **flicker fusion** occurs, a blending together of the individual pulses of light. Twenty-four frames per second, the projection speed of sound film, is adequate to sustain retinal after-images and produce flicker fusion. At 24 frames per second, viewers cannot see the pulsing light that the projector is emitting. (A popular nickname for the movies is *flicks*. This term dates from the silent era when slower projection speeds were used, enabling spectators to see a flicker effect, produced by the pulsing light from the projector. Hence the term *flicks*.)

Retinal after-images and flicker fusion explain why viewers fail to perceive the projector's pulsating light. They do not, however, explain why viewers see moving objects on screen. Motion perception is a complex phenomenon, and under the right conditions spectators will see apparent motion when no real movement has occurred. If a series of closely spaced light bulbs are illuminated in rapid sequence in a darkened room, a spectator will see a single light source moving across

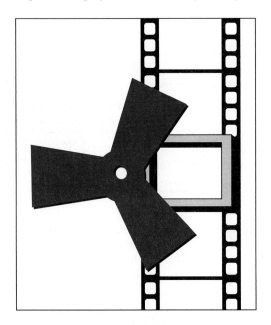

Figure 1.5: Intermittent motion
at 24 frames per second.

Corresponding with Visual Reality

But the camera, and other elements of film structure, do not simply alter and transform the viewer's experience of people, places, and physical environments. Cinema also has the capability of **perceptual correspondence,** the ability to show things in ways that reference and correspond with the viewer's visual and social experience. Close-

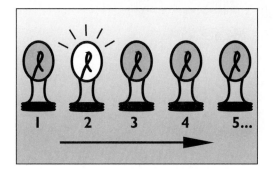

Figure 1.6: Successive events perceived as apparent motion.

television frame is equivalent to a complete scanning of all 525 lines and is composed of two "fields." Odd-numbered lines are scanned first (one field), then the even-numbered lines (one field). The TV image runs at 30 frames (60 fields) per second. This is above a critical fusion threshold. (In addition, the viewer sees a continuously illuminated screen because the eye cannot resolve or perceive the very small spaces between the phosphorus dots that make up the unilluminated portions of the screen image.)

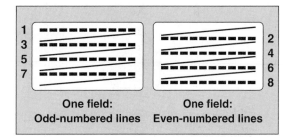

Figure 1.7: The video frame consists of two fields.

the room rather than a series of lights illuminated one after another. This phenomenon has been called **beta movement.** If the intervals between a series of illuminated lights, or the positions of a galloping horse captured in a series of film frames, are small enough, the eye's motion detectors encode this information as movement. The viewer sees a single travelling light or a galloping horse on screen.

Many viewers today watch movies by renting video-tapes and playing them back on television screens. The mechanics of image generation on television are somewhat different than in film. The television image is created by the illumination of red, blue, and green phosphorus dots or pixels, arranged on 525 lines of vertical resolution. The television image is produced by scanning the visual information contained in these lines. As each line is scanned, its pixels are illuminated. One

In these ways, the most fundamental features of cinema—the appearance of continuous light and motion—are built on shared characteristics of perception common to all viewers. These features are automatic. Viewers do not have to make any effort to bring them into play. The cinema activates universal perceptual abilities held by all members of its audiences. This fact underlies the medium's great appeal and accessibility.

ups, for example, emphasize facial expressions. Social experience has taught viewers how to interpret these as signs of a person's thoughts, feelings, and intentions.

Eric, the murdered artist who returns to life seeking vengeance against his killers in *The Crow,* has superhuman powers and wears heavy, ghoulish makeup to accentuate his ghostly appearance, but his face is still key to much of what happens in the narrative because it reveals his reasons for acting. Viewers study it for clues to his personality

The Matrix (Warner Bros., 1999)
A wide-angle lens alters normal visual reality by stretching and exaggerating perspective in this shot of Keanu Reeves. The optics of the lens has transformed the ordinary appearance of things. The effect is motivated by the action of the scene—he's dangling from an office building high off the ground, and the effect is meant to convey his distress. Frame enlargement.

and emotions and interpret it by using skills that are routinely employed in everyday life. Moreover, while viewers understand that *The Crow* is primarily a revenge story that will follow the conventions of this kind of tale, they nevertheless relate these conventions to their knowledge of human behavior and measure the credibility of Eric's actions in the film with a socially derived understanding of motive, intent, and behavior. Eric may be a ghost with super powers, but his anguish, the ruthlessness as well as the tenderness he displays during his quest for vengeance, must correspond with the viewer's understanding of human behavior and feeling. Otherwise, the story and its flamboyant stylistic transformation of reality will lose credibility.

The Crow (Miramax, 1994)
Even in highly stylized films, facial expression corresponds with the viewer's understanding of behavior and personality. Viewers of *The Crow* delight in the special effects fantasy while studying the ghostly face of Eric (Brandon Lee) for clues to his feelings and motives. Frame enlargement.

Among the most powerful correspondences that cinema can establish with the viewer's experience are perceptual ones. On the movie screen, the viewer sees depth, distance, and motion in ways that seem remarkably lifelike. A fully three-dimensional world comes to life on the flat two-dimensional screen. When Eric flies through the darkened city as a crow, the viewer experiences the sensation of gliding through space because of the highly detailed and emphatic motion perspective that has been built inside the computer-generated flying shots. But movement and depth on screen are both visual illusions. Neither really exists.

The camera captures the same information about light, shadow, color, texture, motion, and location in space that viewers use in perceiving and responding to the real three-dimensional world. Movies build this information into shots in ways that emphasize the three-dimensionality of the image appearing on the flat screen. This opens the door to tricks of all kinds in cinema. In *The Matrix*, some of the most memorable visual effects are the high-speed moving camera shots that envelop the characters in scenes of fast action. But during production these shots did not involve *any* camera movement. Keanu Reeves and the other performers were photographed by a series of still cameras arranged into the circuit that the nonexistent moving camera would travel. Computer software interpolated the missing pictures to fill out the orbit of a continuous camera move. Moreover, Reeves and the others were photographed against a blank background (a "greenscreen") and were then digitally inserted into computer-animated environments. The filmmakers jokingly referred to their work as "virtual cinematography." Neither the interactions of character and location nor the moving camera that the viewer "sees"

The Matrix (Warner Bros., 1999)
The illusion of high-speed moving camera shots in *The Matrix* was created without any actual camera movement. Sophisticated digital software supplied the motion perspective that created the effect. Because the 3D motion cues in the images were realistic, viewers found the effect credible. Frame enlargement.

in *The Matrix* in fact existed. But because the perceptual cues in the shots about movement and space seemed true, the illusions were credible and compelling.

Cinema, then, has a dual capability: It corresponds with, and also transforms, the viewer's visual and social experience. These functions—correspondence and transformation—establish a very complex relationship between movies and viewers. To understand how filmmakers design their work, one needs to grasp how those structures build on and connect with the viewer's perceptual skills and how they can go beyond these as well. The first condition furnishes the grounds that make film intelligible, while the second underlies much of the delight that the medium provides. We will have more to say about these issues in upcoming chapters.

Hitchcock's *Vertigo* (1958) has a main character who is afraid of heights. To visualize the character's dizziness, Hitchcock films a city street from an extremely high angle and combines a zoom and track in opposite directions to suggest the feeling of falling through space. The resulting image deforms normal visual reality, but viewers readily accept this in the interest of style and for the delight that it provides.

SUMMARY

Film structure or style results from the ways a filmmaker chooses to manipulate the camera, editing, light, sound, and color. This chapter has explained the fundamentals of the camera, specifically the factors of position, angle, lens, and movement, and how these factors affect the way a viewer perceives the content of a shot or scene. By understanding the range of creative choices filmmakers confront, and by appreciating their options in resolving those choices, one begins to understand a film's structural design.

Camera positions are variations of three basic set-ups: the long shot, the medium shot, and the close-up. While long shots typically stress landscape or environment over character, close-ups usually privilege character over environment. By varying the camera-to-subject distance, the filmmaker manipulates the viewer's emotional involvement with the scene or character in complex ways. Camera position can emphasize facial expressions as signs of a character's inner emotional life or can even work at cross-purposes to a viewer's desired relationship with a scene or character.

Camera angles are variations of low, medium (or eye level), or high angles. Like camera position, camera angle can be used to manipulate the viewer's reactions. Camera angles can represent a character's point of view and emphasize a character's strength or, conversely, his or her insignificance. Angles can be consistent with, or play against, a viewer's desired relationship with a scene or character. As with camera position, the effects of camera angle are always dependent on the emotional context and action of a given scene.

Camera lenses supply distinctive optical characteristics to shots. Telephoto lenses reduce depth of field and angle of view, while wide-angle lenses enlarge these. Zoom lenses can substitute for camera movement, although they will not produce motion perspective as does a moving camera.

Camera movement includes pan and tilt shots, dolly or tracking shots, and boom or crane shots. Pans and tilts create linking movements, connecting objects or establishing relationships between them. Tracking and crane shots can add a dynamic sense of movement to a shot or express thematic ideas.

The camera, and the structural designs it helps create, both record and transform the outward appearance of things, the way they look. The cinema has a fundamental connection with the viewer's perceptual skills and experience. The viewer's impressions in film of continuous light, apparent motion, and spatial depth all derive from this fundamental connection. What makes the cinema such a rich imaginative experience is the way it builds on and creatively enhances this connection. Style, then, can be understood as a kind of creative response by filmmakers to the tendency of the motion picture camera to reproduce the surface appearance of the objects it photographs. By intervening stylistically—by choosing to use a wide-angle lens or a high camera angle—a filmmaker can creatively shape the material of the shot and the world of the film to the dimensions of the imagination.

SUGGESTED READINGS

Geoff Andrew, *The Director's Vision: A Concise Guide to the Art of 250 Great Filmmakers* (Brooklyn, NY: Lawrence Hill, 1999).

David Breskin, ed., *Inner Views: Filmmakers in Conversation* (Winchester, MA: Faber and Faber, 1997).

John P. Frisby, *Seeing: Illusion, Brain, and Mind* (New York: Oxford University Press, 1980).

E. H. Gombrich, *Art and Illusion* (Princeton, NJ: Princeton University Press, 1984).

Eve Light Honthaner, *The Complete Film Production Handbook* (Boston, MA: Focal Press, 1996).

Steven D. Katz, *Film Directing Shot by Shot: Visualizing from Concept to Screen* (Boston, MA: Focal Press, 1991).

Sidney Lumet, *Making Movies* (New York: Alfred A. Knopf, 1995).

Ken Russell, *Directing Films: The Director's Art from Script to Cutting Room* (London: B. T. Batsford, 2000).

Chapter 2

Cinematography

Chapter Objectives

After reading this chapter, you should be able to:

- describe the work of previsualization
- describe what the cinematographer contributes to a film's visual design
- explain how cinematographers work with film stock, lenses, and aspect ratios
- differentiate between realist and pictorial lighting designs
- describe the creative challenges of light source simulation
- explain why pictorial lighting designs work especially well for creating visual symbolism
- differentiate between hard and soft light and explain their expressive functions
- explain the differences between high- and low-key lighting set-ups
- explain the principles of lighting continuity
- explain the differences between lighting for color and lighting for black and white
- describe how color design establishes symbolic meaning, narrative organization, and psychological mood and tone
- explain the relationship between cinematography and digital effects
- explain how visual conventions help establish representational reality and how filmmakers may "quote" from other films

Key Terms and Concepts

mise-en-scène
cinematography
production design
performance style
previsualization
wavelength
hue
saturation
intensity
gray scale
additive
subtractive
film stock
aspect ratio
widescreen ratio
soft-matted

open matte
letterbox
hard-matted
pan-and-scan
anamorphic
Super 35
realistic lighting design
practical (light)
pictorial lighting design
rear projection
hard light
soft light
fall-off
contrast
film noir
high-key lighting

low-key lighting
key light
fill light
back light
digital video
high-definition video
digital grading
visual effects supervisor
live action
digital effect
compositing
motion control
greenscreening
(CGI) computer-
    generated imagery
convention

During production, a film's visual design results from the way that filmmakers arrange elements before the camera—sets, costumes, actors, props, light, and color. *Titanic* (1997), for example, featured extremely detailed sets and costume design, and the film's meticulous re-creation of that vanished historical world held extraordinary fascination for audiences. Viewers responded to the romance at the center of the film's narrative, but also to the luxuriance of its imagery. The term **mise-en-scène** is sometimes used to designate a film's overall visual design and to refer to all of the elements placed before the camera to be photographed.

Filmmakers also control the visual design of their work through editing, but this occurs during postproduction, after they have implemented the designs achieved through light, color, production design, and performance. Accordingly, we will examine editing after considering these other elements of production proper.

Cinematography, examined in this chapter, pertains to the use of light and color. **Production design** involves the creation of sets, locations, costuming, and all visual environments that are depicted on screen. **Performance style** deals with the actor's contribution to the film and how filmmakers incorporate actors as visual elements within the frame. A filmmaker's use of actors can be quite realistic or extremely stylized and pictorial. Chapter 3 examines the areas of production design and performance.

☐ COLLABORATION AND PREVISUALIZATION

The director, cinematographer, and production designer work together in close collaboration to create an effective visual design. Production designers and cinematographers translate the director's vision into the terms of their respective crafts, and, in practice, they subordinate their own artistic inclinations to the director's wishes. Production designer Mel Bourne, whose credits include Woody Allen's *Annie Hall* (1977) and *Manhattan* (1979) and Adrian Lyne's *Indecent Proposal* (1993), characterizes the creative partnership necessary to plan the visual design of a film by stressing that the production designer and cinematographer should be working on the same wavelength, which, in turn, comes from the director.

During preproduction, the cinematographer and production designer consult with the director to discuss and define the film's design. This work is called **previsualization** because it is an initial attempt to formulate the basic features of how the film will look. As aids to previsualization, the director, cinematographer, and production designer will often look for references in such visual fields as architecture, painting, and photography. To visualize J. R. R. Tolkien's Middle Earth, the filmmakers of *The Lord of the Rings: The Fellowship of the Ring* studied the book covers and the watercolor paintings used to illustrate the novels and hired two of the illustrators to serve as conceptual artists on the film. To design *L.A. Confidential* (1997), director Curtis Hanson and cinematographer Dante Spinotti used photographer Robert Frank's 1958 book, *The Americans*. This collection of Frank's work showcased the visual elements they wanted in their film—high intensity light that "burns out" in the photos, high contrast, and the incorporation of light sources within the photo—as well as a 1950s time period that coincided with the film's narrative. Even comic books might supply inspiration, as Japanese *manga* did for the directors and cinematographer of *The Matrix* (1999).

Other motion pictures are a common source for previsualization. To plan the lighting for *Insomnia* (2002), cinematographer Wally Pfister studied modern film classics distinguished by their moody lighting, *The Godfather Part III* (1990), *Apocalypse Now* (1979), *Seven* (1995). To previsualize the Mel Gibson Vietnam war film, *We Were Sol-*

American Beauty (DreamWorks, 1999)
The relationship between the director and cinematographer is a crucial one on any production, and it can vary considerably depending on their talents and personality. Many first-time directors lack the aptitude for strong visual design and depend on their cinematographer's choices about lighting and camera placement. By contrast, Conrad Hall, *American Beauty*'s cinematographer, found first-time director Sam Mendes to be a strong visual stylist with very precise ideas about framing, lighting, and camera placement. Stimulated by Mendes's ideas and cinematic talents, Hall produced work that won the 1999 Academy Award for Best Cinematography.

diers, cinematographer Dean Semler studied the classic war films *All Quiet on the Western Front* (1930) and *Pork Chop Hill* (1959). In shooting Steven Spielberg's *The Lost World* (1997), cinematographer Janusz Kaminski drew from *King Kong* (1933), *Godzilla* (1954), *Gorgo* (1961), and *The Beast from 20,000 Fathoms* (1953).

☐ THE ESSENTIALS OF CINEMATOGRAPHY

The cinematographer creates the images that viewers see on screen, manipulating their elements to establish a unified and memorable design. Memorable compositions result from the careful control of image elements and their balancing within the frame. Such compositions can vividly express a film or scene's underlying emotional dynamics or themes. These compositions from *The Deep End, AI: Artificial Intelligence, The Score,* and *A Beautiful Mind* strongly convey their film's organizing themes.

How does a cinematographer organize visual elements to produce such images? Working with the director, the cinematographer determines the film stock on which the picture will be shot, the aspect ratio, the lenses and camera positions used in filming scenes, and the lighting and color design of the scenes.

The Deep End (20th Century Fox, 2001)

Refracted through the beveled glass of a front door, the face of a mother (Tilda Swinton) appears to split apart, and the filmmakers hang on this image. The mother has been thrust into a nightmare world when she tries to protect her son from gangsters and murder. The fracturing of her image helps to visualize the stress and anxiety of her predicament. Frame enlargement.

A.I.: Artificial Intelligence (Warner Bros./Dreamworks, 2001)

A family who adopts a mechanical boy is deeply unsettled by his nonhuman personality and programmed responses. This composition visually describes the emotional alienation between David and his "parents." This extreme high angle shot stresses his oddness. He is surrounded by a ceiling lamp, isolated in his own space, cut off from his adoptive family. Frame enlargement.

The Score (Paramount, 2001)
The compositions in this film fully exploit the anamorphic 2.35:1 frame. These are compositions for cinema, not television. To suggest the tension between a pair of quarreling lovers (played by Robert De Niro and Angela Bassett), the composition places them at opposite edges of the frame. Furthermore, the camera is at some distance from the actors, a visual strategy that works well on the big cinema screen but not on the smaller TV frame. Frame enlargement.

A Beautiful Mind (Universal/DreamWorks, 2001)
Russell Crowe plays John Nash, a gifted mathematician afflicted with schizophrenia. Mathematics enables Nash to express his intelligence and creativity, but his obsession with numbers and their predictable relationships is also a sign of his madness. In this scene where Nash writes a formula on a library window, the composition suggests the darker side of his attraction to math. Like the bars on the window, the numbers wall him off, imprisoning him in his own private, mental world. Frame enlargement.

WHAT IS LIGHT AND COLOR?

Light and color are the tools of the cinematographer's art. In addition to planning camera set-ups and movements, the cinematographer organizes the lighting design of scenes, and the placement of color gels to augment or enhance certain colors on screen.

Light is a form of radiant energy, a part of the total electromagnetic spectrum. Light is visible only at its source or as it is reflected off of another object. Colors are visible when white light is broken down into its component **wavelengths.** Colored objects reflect or transmit their color values, depending on whether they are solid objects or translucent. A rose appears red because it absorbs all visible wavelengths with the exception of red light, which it reflects. A bottle of green dishwashing liquid looks green because the liquid transmits only green light and acts as a filter to block out all other colors.

In the cinema, colors can be created on the set by using these processes of reflectance and transmission.

Lighting a blue object on the set will increase its ability to reflect blue to the camera. Using a red gel or filter over a white light source will cause that source to transmit only red light.

Properties of Color

Three properties of color are important. **Hue** refers to the color itself. Red, blue, green, and yellow are hues. These four hues are unique. They do not resemble one another. By contrast, pink, a derivative of red, is not a unique hue. **Saturation** refers to the strength of a color. Red is more highly saturated than pink.

Intensity or brightness refers to how much light a given colored object reflects. In respect of this property, the viewer makes certain assumptions that influence the way colors are perceived. For example, a viewer will judge a red cloth seen at high noon and again at dusk as the same color, but its intensity will vary. Seen at high noon, it will appear much brighter than at dusk. In this regard, perceptions of hue and intensity do not always correspond. Viewers assume color constancy while correcting for perceived variations in brightness.

The Gray Scale

Until the 1960s, black and white was a common film format. Since the 1960s, by contrast, black and white has been used rarely but with powerful artistic effect. Steven Spielberg shot his film about the Holocaust, *Schindler's List* (1993), in black and white because it would give his film a harsher, stark look appropriate to its grim subject matter.

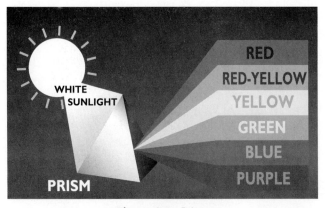

Figure 2.1: Prism.

Film Stocks, Lenses, and Aspect Ratios

Cinematographers work with a variety of **film stocks,** which are identified by their manufacturer and stock number (e.g., Kodak 5298). Selecting one or more stocks for

Black-and-white film and television cameras see only degrees of brightness, ranging from white to black through intermediate shades of gray. This spectrum is known as the **gray scale,** and it determines which colors are used or avoided in costumes and sets during filming. Different colors have the same degree of brightness. In black-and-white cinematography, this creates a problem. Objects of different colors but the same intensity, or gray scale value, will blend together on screen. Black-and-white film will not distinguish them.

In color film, hues will naturally separate objects. Shooting in black and white, cinematographers must separate objects by their degrees of brightness. Cinematographer Laszlo Kovacs (*Easy Rider* [1969], *Ghostbusters* [1984]) points out that in color a brown head will separate naturally from a beige wall, but in black and white the two may run together. The cinematographer has to keep in mind not only how the human eye will see the colors in a scene, but how the black-and-white camera will read the brightness values of those colors.

Additive and Subtractive Color Mixing

The earliest color systems in film history were **additive.** By adding varying proportions of red, green, and blue light (achieved through the use of filters to convert the white projector light into these hues), they produced a diverse range of colors on screen. Adding green and red, for example, will produce yellow. Additive systems in film, though, were soon replaced by **subtractive** color mixing, which removes various wavelengths from white light. To accomplish this, subtractive color filters are used. These colors are magenta, yellow, and cyan. They are contained as layers of dye in the strip of raw, unexposed film, and as white light enters the camera, they filter and transmit only those few wavelengths needed for subtractive mixing.

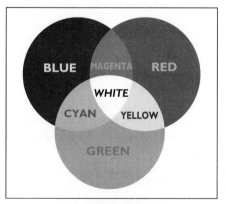

Figure 2.2: Additive mixing.

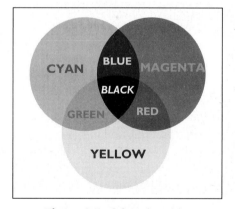

Figure 2.3: Subtractive mixing.

a production enables the cinematographer to control a large number of image characteristics. Film stocks vary in terms of their sensitivity to light, color reproduction, tolerance for diverse lighting conditions, amount of grain (grain is visible as tiny specks or dots within the image), contrast levels, sharpness, and resolving power (the ability to

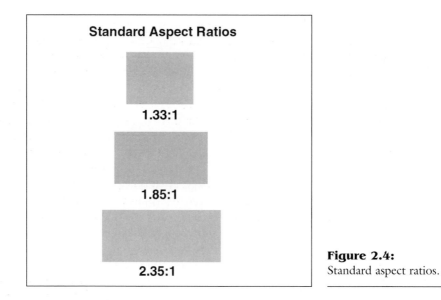

Figure 2.4:
Standard aspect ratios.

discriminate fine detail). A cinematographer will select a given stock depending on how it handles these characteristics and its suitability for the design of a given production.

Cinematographer Darius Khondji, for example, shot all of the nighttime scenes for *Seven* (1995), a dark thriller about a serial killer, on Kodak 5287 because this stock gave him exceptionally dark blacks, suitable for the film's mood and theme. To accentuate this effect even more, Khondji used ENR to restore silver to the negative, increasing the density of its blacks. To create the off-kilter visual style of *Natural Born Killers* (1994), Oliver Stone and cinematographer Robert Richardson intermixed five 35mm stocks, four 16mm stocks, and three 8mm stocks to create vivid changes in color, contrast, grain, and resolution. In *U Turn* (1998), during an argument and fight between two principal characters, Stone and Richardson switched film stocks in mid-scene to create glaring changes of color and grain. These were intended to visualize the scene's volatile emotional swings.

Filmmakers often emulate the inspiring innovations of other directors and cinematographers. On Spike Lee's *Clockers* (1995), cinematographer Malik Sayeed employed a stock never before utilized in a motion picture, Kodak 5239, which was manufactured for use by NASA and the Air Force. The grain structure of the stock made its images look extremely raw—suitable for this grim film about urban drugs and violence—and it vividly rendered primary colors, making reds and blues glow on screen and leap out of the frame. (See Color Plate 12.) The unusual look of *Clockers* impressed Oliver Stone and Robert Richardson, who used the stock in *U Turn* to create selectively lurid color effects. Spike Lee again employed 5239 on *Summer of Sam* (1999). Since then, the "cross-processing" of a raw, grainy stock has come into general use. Recent examples include the dream sequences in *From Hell* (2001), the Hughes brothers's film about Jack the Ripper, and the 1950s flashback scenes in *Blow* (2001), which starred Johnny Depp as a drug dealer.

Cinematographers select their lenses to give images the visual properties that will express a film's underlying themes or the dramatic requirements of given scenes. *Pleasantville* (1998) is a fantasy about a 1950s-style sitcom whose characters become progressively more modern in their outlook. To suggest this change at a visual level, the cinematographer began shooting with shorter lenses that corresponded with those used in 1950s films and then, as the story progressed, began moving to the longer focal lengths characteristic of contemporary filmmaking. In a subliminal fashion, this gave the images an evolving historical look and context. To suggest a world in which everything was for sale, the cinematographer of *The Truman Show* (1998) used the extreme wide-angle perspectives often seen in television advertising. To capture a 1970s look for scenes in *The Velvet Goldmine* (1998) occurring in that time period, the cinematographer used zoom lenses rather than camera movement. Zooms were featured prominently in films of that era, and the cinematographer liked the way the zoom emphasized surfaces (because it merely magnifies an image) rather than depth and perspective, as true camera movement does.

When choosing an **aspect ratio** (the dimensions of the screen image), cinematographers must balance several considerations. Which of the available ratios is best suited for the themes or action of the film? *Memento* (2000) was shot in anamorphic widescreen (2.35:1) because the shallow-focus lenses typically used in that format could be used to isolate the main character (who is confused and suffering from memory loss) from his surroundings.

A second critical consideration involves the consequences of converting a film exhibited theatrically in widescreen to home video and conventional television monitors. During the classical Hollywood period of the 1930s and 1940s, frame size remained fairly standard, with an aspect ratio (width to height) of 1.37:1. (The frame enlargements from *Brute Force, Strangers on a Train,* and *Singin' in the Rain* appearing in Chapter 6 illustrate this ratio.) This was a nearly square ratio and one that is well suited to home video presentation since it closely approximates the dimensions of conventional television screens.

Since the 1950s, however, **widescreen ratios** have been standard. Today, viewers see films projected in ratios of 1.85:1 or 2.35:1. These ratios are wider, more rectangular, than the classical Hollywood ratio. Accordingly, cinematographers must be careful to compose their shots in ways that make best use of the chosen aspect ratio. A 2.35:1 ratio, for example, facilitates compositions utilizing the horizontal axis of the frame more effectively than the vertical axis as the frame enlargement from *The Score* demonstrates. Filmmakers working in this ratio can spread things out across the frame, but the ratio is not good for depicting tall objects. Because of this, Janusz Kaminski shot *The Lost World* in a 1.85:1 ratio to give the dinosaurs more headroom than a 2.35:1 ratio would supply. The latter ratio however, is well suited for epics, Westerns, and historical dramas and has been used extensively in such pictures.

In choosing an aspect ratio, filmmakers must take into account the video releases of their work and the changes introduced into widescreen films by the conversion to video. The television monitor has a nearly square, 4:3 ratio, which requires that the widescreen film be reformatted for its video release. Many filmmakers will shoot in a 1.85:1 ratio because video conversion will introduce minimal changes in their framing. Martin Scorsese filmed *Casino* (1995) and *Kundun* (1997) in a 1.85:1 ratio for

Raging Bull
(MGM/UA, 1980)
Compositions in the theatrical
1.85:1 ratio are generally transferred open matte to video. Note
the extra information at the top
and bottom of the unmatted
frame. Frame enlargements.

this reason. Shooting in 1.85:1, a cinematographer will compose the shot for both
ratios, theatrical and television. The frame enlargements from Scorsese's *Raging Bull*
(1980) demonstrate the dual composition. For theatrical release, the film will be **soft-
matted**: An aperture matte in the projector will mask the top and bottom of the image,
producing the 1.85:1 ratio on the theater screen. When converting the film for video
and television's 1.33:1 ratio, the film may be transferred **open matte,** that is, full
frame with no matting. The frame enlargements from *Raging Bull* show the open
matte 1.33:1 frame and the cropped 1.85:1 (theatrical) framing. Although both

a

b

Dirty Harry
(Warner Bros., 1971)
Films shot in a 2.35:1
ratio undergo more severe
alterations during video
transfer. Compare the full
widescreen framing with
the pan-and-scan counter-
part that turns the
two-shot into the framing
of a single character. *Dirty
Harry* was shot in ana-
morphic widescreen,
which squeezes a wide
angle of view onto the
film frame. The image is
unsqueezed during pro-
jection to restore its
widescreen ratio. Com-
pare the unsqueezed full
frame with the squeezed
image as it is recorded on
film. Frame enlargements.

c

compositions are similar, only the cropped image corresponds with the way the film appeared when exhibited in theaters.

Warner Brothers' DVD releases of Stanley Kubrick's films generated controversy because of this disparity between the matted and unmatted ratios. Kubrick shot his films in a 1.85:1 ratio yet, apparently, he never formally approved the use of image cropping ("letterboxing") for their home video release. Thus, when Warners released the "Stanley Kubrick Collection" on DVD, the films were transferred open matte. The packaging of *Eyes Wide Shut* (1999), for example, contains the disclaimer, "This feature is presented in the full aspect ratio of the original camera negative, as Stanley Kubrick intended." The labelling is a little misleading—no film today is exhibited theatrically full frame (the full ratio of the original camera negative). As we have seen, soft matting crops the top and bottom of the frame, producing the 1.85:1 ratio. DVDs typically present films in their correct aspect ratios. In light of this, Warners' DVDs generated controversy because they carried this great director's films in a different ratio than the way the pictures had been presented theatrically.

If a filmmaker chooses to work in a 2.35:1 ratio, it may entail severe problems for video conversion. Such a film will either be letterboxed or panned-and-scanned. The frame enlargements from *Dirty Harry* (1971) demonstrate the differences between these formats. If **letterboxed,** a film will be **hard-matted** for video, that is, frame bars will mask the top and bottom of the television monitor, producing a wider-ratio picture in the center of the screen (and without eliminating anything from the top and bottom of the image). Viewers of a letterboxed video get to see proper, or nearly proper, screen ratio, but the trade-off is a shrunken image that lacks the majesty and power of its big screen counterpart. Many viewers dislike having only a small and narrow picture area in the center of their television screen.

Panning-and-scanning produces a video image that fills the television monitor but in an incorrect aspect ratio (*Dirty Harry* series, photo b). The entire 2.35:1 image cannot fit on a television screen except via letterboxing. As an alternative, therefore, a panned-and-scanned conversion reproduces only part of the wide-screen frame. A technician handling the video transfer decides where the center of interest lies in a 2.35:1 shot and that portion is transferred to video. However, the transfer engineer can also electronically pan or cut from one side of the widescreen frame to another in order to follow action. Thus pan-and-scan transfers appear to have more camera movement and editing than, in fact, exists in the film original. This is a severe alteration of the integrity of a cinematographer's work. (Photo c in the *Dirty Harry* series shows the **anamorphic** image as it appears on the strip of film. The anamorphic process produces the 2.35:1 screen ratio by squeezing a widescreen image onto a square frame of film and then unsqueezing it during projection to create the widescreen ratio. Photo a is the unsqueezed result derived from photo c.)

Super 35 is a popular nonanamorphic widescreen format that enables filmmakers to matte their compositions for a variety of viewing ratios, from 1.33:1 to 2.35:1. They carefully frame the action so that it will play in a 1.33:1 ratio for television and home video and in a 1.85:1 or 2.35:1 ratio in theaters. *Gladiator* (2000), *The Lord of the Rings* (2001), *Panic Room* (2002), and *In the Bedroom* (2001) were all shot in Super 35 and matted for a 2.35:1 ratio.

Harry Potter and the Sorcerer's Stone (Warner Bros., 2002)
Super 35 enables filmmakers to matte their compositions for theatrical exhibition in 2.35:1 and
for home video in 1.33:1. These frame enlargements from *Harry Potter* show both compositions. Unfortunately, it is the 1.33:1 television composition that filmmakers often have most in
mind due to the fact that films have a longer life on video than in theaters. As a result, the
widespread use of Super 35 in films today creates many "fake widescreen" movies. Frame
enlargements.

Unfortunately, filmmakers working in Super 35 often decide to "split the difference," clustering important picture information in the center of the frame to avoid picture loss when the image is reformatted on video for full-screen televisions. This creates a kind of "fake widescreen" that is very common today because so many films are shot in Super 35. The frame enlargements from *Harry Potter and the Sorcerer's Stone* (2002) demonstrate that, though the film was shown theatrically in 2.35:1, the compositions have been designed so that they will play in full frame 1.33:1. This is not the case with our examples from *The Score* (or *Red Beard* in the previous chapter), whose shots are designed exclusively for widescreen cinema, not full-frame television. In this respect, Super 35 represents a blurring of the boundaries between cinema and television.

The aspect ratio selected will often influence the lenses employed during production. Many cinematographers dislike shooting wide-angle in anamorphic 2.35:1 because of the curvature the lens introduces into the composition during moving camera shots. If they are committed to working at the shorter focal lengths, they will often shoot 1.85:1 or on Super 35.

Having decided on the film stock, lenses, and aspect ratio, the cinematographer determines with the director the camera's placement for each shot in a given scene and how the shot will be lit. Camera placement and lighting are interconnected issues: The lighting of each shot is a function of where the camera is positioned.

Lighting Design

Depending on the style and subject matter of a given film, and the dramatic requirements of the scene, the cinematographer may employ a realistic or a pictorial lighting design or some combination of each approach.

Realistic Lighting

A lighting design that distributes light to simulate an explicit source on screen, whether it be the sun or a table lamp indoors, is a **realistic lighting design.** It suggests that the light on-screen is cast by one or more specific sources. If it is an exterior scene, the light source is usually, by implication, the sun. If it is an interior scene, then the table lamps, overhead ceiling lights, or street lights visible through windows become the implied source lights. These are "effect" lights because the cinematographer uses them to convey the effect that they are casting the visible light in the scene. This may or may not actually be true. If the table lamp in the set is rigged to be a real source of lighting for the camera, then it is called a **practical** because it is a visible light source on the set that actually works for exposure of the film. In other cases the actual lights for exposure may be off-screen. Lights for effect, then, may be distinct from the lights for exposure. In the case of those lights termed *practicals,* the light source that creates the effect and the exposure is the same.

In Joel and Ethan Coen's *Fargo* (1996), police chief Marge Gunderson (Frances McDormand) and her husband share an early-morning breakfast. Cinematographer Roger Deakins supplied a realistic lighting design. It is motivated by a visible effect light—the hanging kitchen lamp—which, the viewer understands, is supposed to be casting the visible light in the scene. Notice, however, the even level of illumination throughout the room and the relative absence of shadows. It is unlikely that the naked light bulb in the hanging lamp could produce these qualities. Deakins lit the

Fargo (PolyGram, 1996)
Light source simulation in a
realistic design, whose effect is
that the hanging lamp is casting
the visible illumination. Frame
enlargement.

scene using off-camera sources to envelop the actors and set with an even level of illumination. Notice also that the naked bulb in the hanging lamp has "burned out," that is, it is highly overexposed. This is because the camera is exposing for the light levels on the characters and set rather than for the practical light source.

"Burnout" effects may sometimes be an important part of a realistic design. The term refers to an overexposed portion of an image in which details are lost. Much of the action of *The English Patient* takes place in the Sahara Desert. To convey the heat of that landscape, cinematographer John Seale photographed the film's characters by exposing on their shadowed faces and letting the sunlit areas of the desert burn out with overexposure. This made the desert look hotter.

Cinematographer Michael Ballhaus devised a very creative approach to simulating light sources in Francis Ford Coppola's *Bram Stoker's Dracula* (1992). There were no electric lights in Dracula's time, all light being supplied by candles or lanterns, oil lamps or torches. The light these instruments cast was flickering and unsteady. To simulate this, Ballhaus placed his electric lights on flicker boxes, which created wavering, flickering

**The Man Who Wasn't
There** (USA Films, 2001)
Cinematographer Roger Deakins
created this striking, realistic
lighting design by using only
one practical, the lamp on top of
the piano. Frame enlargement.

Traffic (USA Films, 2001)
Burnout effects are common in contemporary cinematography, but decades ago they were considered to be unacceptable errors of lighting. Director-cinematographer Steven Soderbergh adds considerable tension to this courtroom scene by burning out the window in this extravagant way. Frame enlargement.

illumination. Coppola's film is a gaudy and stylized fantasy. *Realism* is not the sort of term that one would apply to such a film. Nevertheless, the filmmakers sometimes observed realistic principles of light-source simulation.

Pictorial Lighting

Pictorial lighting design stresses purely pictorial or visual values that may be unrelated to strict concerns about source simulation. Realistic and pictorial approaches are not rigid categories, and many films may utilize both approaches. *Bram Stoker's*

Bram Stoker's Dracula (Columbia Pictures, 1992)
Pictorial lighting designs suggest purely visual effects unconnected to issues of realism. Dracula's shadow disengages itself from the vampire Count, advances on Jonathan Harker (Keanu Reeves), and begins to strangle him. The effect is pictorial and poetic. Frame enlargement.

The Silence of the Lambs (Orion, 1990)
After a long scene with subtle, restrained lighting, the filmmakers suddenly
switch to this extravagant design for a shot showing one of serial killer
Hannibal Lecter's victims. The lighting is completely unmotivated in that it
has no connection to any sources established within the dramatic action of
the scene. With no attempt to hide them, the cross lights and backlights
are visible in the frame. The effect is purely pictorial, a visual flourish
designed to give impact to this moment of horror. Frame enlargement.

Dracula includes many scenes in which the lighting design is governed by extravagantly pictorial considerations. When Dracula (Gary Oldman) meets with real estate
representative Jonathan Harker (Keanu Reeves), who has journeyed by train and coach
to the vampire's remote Transylvanian castle, Coppola and Ballhaus achieve one of
their most striking pictorial effects.

Harker shows Dracula the portrait of Mina, the woman he is engaged to marry.
Dracula realizes that she is the reincarnation of his own true love lost many centuries
ago. Wanting to possess Mina as his own beloved, Dracula feels murderous rage toward Harker. As the two converse, Dracula's shadow, which had been cast on the
back wall, disengages itself from the vampire. The shadow advances on Harker and
begins to strangle him.

The effect is not only visually striking but surprising and uncanny. Coppola and
Ballhaus creatively violate the logic of shadow phenomena. Shadows are either attached to or cast by the object to which they belong, but in neither case do they behave independently of that object. Coppola violates the perceptual regularities governing
cast-shadow behavior, shocking viewers and guiding their interpretations toward ideas
of supernatural power. It is a purely pictorial (and physically impossible) moment in
the scene.

The effect was created by shooting part of the scene live and part of the scene with
rear projection. Dracula's cast shadow on the wall is not a true shadow at all but
was created by a dancer working in sync with actor Gary Oldman's movements. The
dancer was placed behind the "wall," which was actually a screen onto which the

dancer's shadow was projected. When the "shadow" disengages itself from Dracula, the effect is created by the dancer breaking sync with Gary Oldman and pantomiming the act of strangulation.

Pictorial Lighting for Thematic Symbolism

Filmmakers often employ pictorial designs to visually symbolize the thematic content of a scene or film. Pictorial designs do this far more successfully and explicitly than realistic designs because filmmakers can manipulate light and color in ways that are unfettered by concerns about realism and that can directly relate to the underlying social, psychological, or emotional themes of a scene. Pictorialism enables filmmakers to use light and color to visually embody the underlying significance of a given scene or film.

Case Study: *Apocalypse Now*

Cinematographer Vittorio Storaro's pictoral designs for Francis Ford Coppola's *Apocalypse Now* (1979) create a precise visual statement of the existential moral issues at the heart of the film. The Vietnam War drives a renegade U.S. soldier named Kurtz (Marlon Brando) insane, and the military brass sends an assassin named Willard (Martin Sheen) upriver to Kurtz's compound to murder the colonel. Most of the narrative takes place during Willard's trip upriver and raises the question about what Willard will do when he finally meets Kurtz. Will he kill him as he has been instructed, or, because both men are equally murderous and bestial, will he join Kurtz instead?

To suggest the psychological and spiritual bond between the two characters, Storaro employed a strikingly similar lighting design for each man. Kurtz is filmed with

---

Seven (New Line, 1995)

Filmmakers often create pictorial effects by showing and filming a light source within the scene. Investigating a murder scene, police inspector Morgan Freeman cradles his flashlight on his forearm. The dust suspended in the hazy air reflects in the flashlight beam to make it visible. Director David Fincher's film portrays a world of absolute moral and spiritual darkness for which the flashlight's inability to illuminate the room becomes a potent metaphor. Frame enlargement.

FRANCIS FORD COPPOLA

Along with Martin Scorsese, George Lucas, and Brian De Palma, Coppola belonged to a young generation of university-trained film students-turned-directors who established careers in the early 1970s. His earliest films (*Dementia 13*, 1963; *Finian's Rainbow*, 1968) are undistinguished and do not hint at the talent that suddenly burst forth in *The Godfather* (1972), the most successful example of epic narrative filmmaking produced by a major studio since *Gone With the Wind* (1939). Starring Marlon Brando and Al Pacino, *The Godfather* offers a richly romanticized and harshly brutal portrait of the rise to power of the Corleone crime family. Feeling he had oversentimentalized the Corleones in the first film, Coppola set out to destroy them in the harsher, bleaker sequel, *The Godfather, Part II* (1974), which many critics consider superior to its predecessor.

Between these two epics, Coppola made *The Conversation* (1974), an edgy, sophisticated portrait of the psychological disintegration of an electronics wizard and domestic spy (played by Gene Hackman). An extraordinarily stylized and ambiguous work, *The Conversation* avoids the formulaic features of the bigger budgeted *Godfather* films.

These three films remain Coppola's greatest achievements as director. His subsequent career is checkered with grandly conceived but incompletely realized ambitions. Seduced by a huge budget and ballooning ambitions, Coppola released *Apocalypse Now* (1979), a visually spectacular but conceptually muddled account of the Vietnam War. For much of its length it is undeniably hypnotic, but, after the precision and clarity of his previous three films, its diffuseness is disappointing.

The Godfather
(Paramount Pictures, 1972)
Coppola brilliantly integrated masterful storytelling with an ambitious visual design in *The Godfather*, an enduring modern classic. Marlon Brando's performance as Don Vito Corleone, the mafia Godfather, was so vivid and remarkable that it inspired a generation of mimics and comic impersonators.

His next films, *One from the Heart* (1982), *Rumble Fish* (1983), *The Cotton Club* (1984), *Peggy Sue Got Married* (1986), *Gardens of Stone* (1987), and *Tucker* (1988), generally failed to connect with critics or public and often seemed more conventional than visionary. Part of Coppola's problem was a faltering economic base. He attempted to establish his own studio by creating Zoetrope Studios in 1980, but *Apocalypse Now* saddled him with huge debts, and the disastrous box-office performance of *One from the Heart* compounded his problems. The more conventional films that followed are partly a result of Coppola's efforts to extricate himself from a mountain of debt by crafting less audacious and more commercial products.

Coppola returned to epic form with *The Godfather, Part III* (1991), a compelling but uneven conclusion to the saga of Michael Corleone, and *Bram Stoker's Dracula* (1992), a controversial but genuinely visionary and audacious adaptation of the Stoker novel. The latter film is one of Coppola's most ambitious and artistically successful works.

Coppola remains a powerful force in contemporary U.S. films. His up-and-down career is marked by an unresolved tension between grandiose artistic ambitions and the budgetary limitations and need for box-office success inherent in studio-financed productions. Unlike Woody Allen, who works successfully and well on limited resources, Coppola often requires huge budgets for his visions and has had difficulty accommodating the inevitable compromises such budgets entail.

Apocalypse Now
(United Artists, 1979)
Pictorial lighting for thematic symbolism: the faces of Kurtz (Marlon Brando) and Willard (Martin Sheen). Cinematographer Vittorio Storaro's lighting design stresses the moral conflict between good and evil within each character and suggests an essential equivalence between both men. Frame enlargements.

his face half in and half out of shadow to convey the character's cruelty and moral darkness and the inner struggle between good and evil that has driven him insane. After Willard kills Kurtz, the same lighting design is used to make him look Kurtz-like. Willard's face is partially eclipsed, half in the light, half in the shadow. The lighting tells the viewer that Willard has become Kurtz. Postproduction editing of the film, however, weakened the visual and thematic force of this pictorial statement. After early test screenings indicated that the original ending did not work for audiences, Coppola added a different conclusion in which Willard rejects Kurtz's kingdom and leaves.

Coppola's original ending was more ambiguous. In both the original and revised endings, Willard kills Kurtz, but in Coppola's original version, Willard remains behind on the steps of Kurtz's compound facing Kurtz's army, his face lit to look like Kurtz. Coppola's preferred version ended here. He wanted the film to conclude with the question of whether Willard has become Kurtz, and Storaro's lighting clearly implied that he has. The way this ending was changed—by showing Willard leaving Kurtz's compound—undermined the meaning established by Storaro's lighting design, and this made the film thematically less coherent.

Types of Light: Hard and Soft Light

Once the cinematographer and director decide on the overall balance of realistic and pictorial elements, they further specify their lighting design in terms of the proportions of **hard** and **soft light.**

Hard and soft lighting differ in terms of **fall-off** and **contrast.** Hard lighting typically creates high contrast and fast fall-off. The boundaries between the illuminated areas and the areas in darkness or shadow are sharply defined. The rate of fall-off, or change between light and dark, is rapid. This creates a high contrast between light and dark areas as they are distributed throughout the frame. Another way of understanding contrast is in terms of shadow definition. High-contrast lighting produces very strong shadow definition, as in the shot from *Out of the Past* (1947), a **film noir** made during a period when high-contrast black-and-white cinematography was very popular.

By manipulating fall-off and contrast, cinematographers enhance the three-dimensional appearance of film images. Notice how vividly the shadow information renders the folds of Robert Mitchum's trenchcoat in the shot from *Out of the Past.* Light organizes and defines space. The distribution of light and shadow conveys physical properties of depth, distance, and surface texture, expressed by the ways light falls across objects in a room or scene. Motion picture images easily copy this source of everyday perceptual information, and filmmakers use this information in light to create a convincing impression of three-dimensional space on a flat screen.

In contrast with hard light, soft light is highly diffused or scattered. It is produced by using a filter in front of the light source or by bouncing light off a reflective surface (cinematographers use "bounce cards" to accomplish the latter goal). Once light is scattered in this fashion, it will move in all directions to wrap around and envelop the actors and set. For this reason, soft light is much less directional than hard light, which can be precisely controlled to spotlight small details or areas of a set or an actor's

Out of the Past
(RKO, 1947)
Low-key lighting in a sophisticated, complex design typical of 1940s film noir. Small portions of the frame are selectively exposed using hard light, leaving other areas to fall quickly into shadow. The effect is moody and ominous. Frame enlargement.

face. In *The Others,* Grace Stewart (Nicole Kidman) reads by lamplight, and Javier Aguirresarobe's cinematography creates a strong, single-source effect. The soft light creates a gradual transition between light and shadow, and the design is realistic. It looks as if the oil lamp is casting all of the visible light within the frame. By contrast, Roger Deakins's lighting in *The Man Who Wasn't There* uses hard light to sculpt and model Billy Bob Thornton in a striking way. The hard light is precisely controlled to create such sharp fall-off. The light does not wrap around the actor. The portrait employing the hard lighting design appears more three-dimensional because the distribution of light more effectively conveys the physical characteristics of the object before the camera.

Hard and soft lighting can very effectively establish time of day in a scene by mimicking the way sunlight changes during the course of a day. At noon sunlight tends to be very hard and shadows tend to be short. During the morning and dusk, sunlight is more highly diffused and produces longer shadows. Bright exterior lights visible through windows of an indoor set and diffused light on the interior of the set will establish daytime, whereas night is indicated by using dark or dim exteriors and

The Others
(Miramax, 2001);
The Man Who Wasn't There
(USA Films, 2001)
Soft lighting envelops Nicole Kidman in a realistic design that suggests that the oil lamp is casting the visible illumination. Note how the light wraps around her and falls off gently into shadow. By contrast, the hard light on Billy Bob Thornton creates higher contrast and more sharply defined shadows. Roger Deakins lighting designs imitate the look of classic film noirs like *Out of the Past* (see page 67). Deakins points out that "Lighting is not only about lighting; it's also about *not* lighting, and cutting light off of objects as much as shining light on them." Frame enlargements.

hard, contrasting illumination on the interior. In Peter Weir's *Fearless* (1993), cinematographer Allen Daviau used hard light to establish the late-morning hour during which a critical airline flight occurs. He positioned lights at a high angle to cast short shadows through the windows of the airplane set. The lighting arrangement realistically replicated qualities of light at this time of day.

High- and Low-Key Set-Ups

Hard and soft lighting designs can be achieved by using **high-key** and **low-key** lighting set-ups. The **key light,** in the traditional three-point lighting employed in Hollywood films, is the main source of illumination usually directed on the face of the performer. The other two light sources are the **fill light** and the **back light.** The back light illuminates the rear portion of the set and/or the performer to establish a degree of separation between the actor and the rear of the set. The fill light fills in undesirable areas of shadow that are created by the positioning of the key light and the back light.

Low-key lighting features a relatively bright key light in comparison to a small use of fill light. This produces abundant shadows. In low-key lighting, most of the frame is underlit while other, usually small, portions are adequately exposed. Typically, low-key lighting employs hard light in a high-contrast, fast fall-off image. This style was very popular in crime films throughout the 1940s and early 1950s. Many of these were called *film noir,* meaning "black film," a term designating the low-key lighting set-ups they employed as well as the moral darkness of their stories and characters. The shot from *Out of the Past* (page 67) is low-key.

High-key lighting is the opposite of low-key. High-key employs similar, bright intensities of key and fill, producing an even level of illumination throughout the scene with low contrast and few shadow areas. While low-key set-ups are suited to the gloomy, sinister films noir, high-key styles brightened the tone of Hollywood's popular musicals. High-key styles assertively displayed the cheerful sets, colors, costumes, and dancing in such films as *Singin' in the Rain, An American in Paris,* and *The Band Wagon.*

Figure 2.5: Three-point lighting.

An American in Paris
(MGM, 1951)
High-key lighting balances key, fill, and backlights to create an even level of illumination throughout the frame. Notice how minimal is the shadow information in this shot of Gene Kelly. The brightness of high-key lighting was suited to the optimism of the Hollywood musicals. Frame enlargement.

The MGM studio, in particular, favored high-key styles to showcase the sumptuous sets and costumes in their productions, musical and nonmusical alike.

Lighting Continuity

Continuity of Lighting across Shots   Viewers watching a narrative motion picture generally want to believe in the plausibility and integrity of the world represented on screen. In other words, it should behave much as the viewer's own world does, obey the same kinds of physical laws of time and space, unless, as in adventure, fantasy, or science fiction, there is a clearly established reason for not doing so. Filmmakers manipulate cinematic style to represent *and* transform the viewer's sense of reality. Viewers, in turn, expect films to reference, and correspond in key ways with, their experience of the world while granting filmmakers a great deal of freedom in the ways they do this. Stylistic manipulations operate within limits. These are partly dictated by the logical demands of the style itself. Sylvester Stallone's character Rambo can have superhuman abilities, but if these are too excessive, his adventures will lose all sense of danger and peril, and the films will lack suspense.

Stylistic manipulations are also limited by the viewer's demands for reference and correspondence in the represented screen world. In this respect, continuity principles impose fundamental limitations on style in the interest of achieving reference and correspondence. In the areas of image editing and sound editing, principles of continuity are fundamental to narrative filmmaking. The same is true for lighting, irrespective of whether a filmmaker employs a realistic or pictorial design.

Cinematographers follow principles of continuity in their lighting designs. They are not free to drastically change light values from shot to shot. Changes of camera perspective from shot to shot should not produce major changes in the light values that have been established for the scene. A cinematographer, therefore, must take adequate measurements of the amount of light available within a scene and understand how to make small adjustments in that light depending on the camera's position. Close-ups, for example, are generally lit a bit brighter than long or medium shots, but viewers do not notice these small variations.

Filming on location can introduce complications into the way cinematographers plan for lighting continuity. When shooting out-of-doors, filmmakers must often supplement naturally available sunlight with artificial lights. The position of the sun in the sky overhead changes during the course of the day and so does the apparent hardness of the light. Light is hardest at noon. While filming *The Last of the Mohicans* (1993), cinematographer Dante Spinotti found that artificial electrical lights offered several advantages during location shooting in the forest where much of the film's action is set.

In designing a visual look for the film, Spinotti wanted to be faithful to the story's eighteenth-century period. At that time, there were no electric lights, so illumination in the forests would have been produced by sunlight during the day and by moonlight and firelight at night. To simulate the effect of powerful shafts of sunlight pouring into the forest, Spinotti used a few very large, very powerful electric lights. These cast narrow beams of light to effectively simulate rays of sunshine penetrating the dark forest.

This use of artificial light accomplished two things. It established lighting continuity across shots regardless of the different times of day or dusk when filming occurred. Using electrical lights that could be positioned at appropriate angles enabled filmmakers to compensate for changes in the sun's position. Using these lights also extended principal hours of cinematography beyond the noon hour when light was at its hardest and least diffused. Supplementing sunlight with the electrical lights permitted shooting to occur well past the noon hour, even at dusk.

Continuity of Lighting within Shots   A cinematographer must plan for lighting continuity within shots as well as across shots. Many shots involve camera movement and most involve actors who change positions in the frame. Lights that provide adequate exposure and atmosphere for a camera in one position will not do so if the camera moves to another portion of the set. The cinematographer must plan for a lighting design that can accommodate the entire range of the camera's movement. This may require adjusting the light level, and the exposure level in the camera, during the shot itself. Cinematographer Vittorio Storaro (*Bulworth,* 1998) regularly uses an elaborate dimmer board that enables him to raise and lower light levels during filming and while the camera and actors are in motion.

Filming Robert Altman's *Short Cuts* (1993), cinematographer Walt Lloyd confronted a scene in which a chauffeur drives a limousine in bright, hard sunlight, parks it by a trailer, and goes into the trailer's dim interior. In one shot, the camera follows the chauffeur as he gets out of the car in the hard sunlight and walks over to the trailer, opens the screen door, and goes inside. To accommodate this drastic change in light levels from exterior to interior within the moving camera shot, Lloyd executed a wide range of "stop pulls," changes in the lens aperture setting that determines how much light the lens is letting into the camera. The stop pulls helped maintain light continuity as the action of the shot moved from the bright exterior to the dim interior.

These examples indicate one of the key requirements of a cinematographer's job: the ability to quickly and creatively solve artistic and practical challenges.

Cinematographers must strategically fit the demands of a location shoot or a director's preferred visual design with available camera resources and the imperative for lighting continuity. This may entail supplementing natural light with artificial light, executing elaborate on-set lighting adjustments during the course of a shot, or readjusting exposure levels in the camera to compensate for changes in light level.

Lighting for Color

Black-and-white film registers only brightness levels, not colors. Brightness values range from white through gray to black. When shooting black and white, the cinematographer must be careful to avoid using colors in a scene, such as red and green, that have the same degree of brightness and will be indistinguishable on film.

By contrast, the cinematographer who works in color can use it to add to the tone and atmosphere of the scene. By appropriately choosing film stocks with an understanding of their sensitivity to color, by employing color gelatins over the lights to intensify a dominant color motif within a scene, and by working closely with the production designer to establish the range of colors to be employed in sets and costumes, the cinematographer helps organize the color design of a given film.

Functions of Color Cinematography   Color design performs three basic functions in film. It establishes symbolic meaning, narrative organization, and psychological mood and tone.

Conveying symbolic meaning   Filmmakers often use color to establish a symbolic association or idea in the mind of the viewer. In *Pleasantville*, a teenage brother and sister find themselves trapped within a 1950s-era television sitcom whose characters lead humdrum and predictable lives. The siblings disrupt the scripted equilibrium of the show, causing some of its characters to reflect on and examine their personalities and identity. Color emblemizes this dawning self-awareness. The sitcom world is initially a black-and-white world, corresponding to the simplified morality of the show. But as the characters awaken into complex selves, color begins to appear, at first in selective parts of the black-and-white image and eventually into the entire image. The shift from black and white to color suggests the transition by the sitcom characters to a fuller, more emotionally rounded life.

Cinematographer Vittorio Storaro (*Apocalypse Now, Bulworth*) believes that colors have an inherent symbolism, based in their wavelength, to which viewers respond physiologically. Of all contemporary cinematographers, Storaro has the most elaborate theory of color expression in cinema, and he typically uses colors for highly specific purposes. In *Bulworth,* he used an elaborate color pallette to suggest the spiritual crisis and regeneration of the title character, played by Warren Beatty. A senator, Bulworth is in despair as the film begins, and, during the course of its narrative, he rediscovers a purpose in life and a mission for his political career. To express these changes, Storaro designed a color plot for the film. To suggest Bulworth's initial despair, the film opens in darkness, with no color, and then its scenes move through the hues of red, orange, yellow-cyan-magenta, blue, indigo, and white. Storaro's color design bookends the film with the absence of color (black) and, at the end, the unity of all colors (white). For Storaro, the aesthetic structure of *Bulworth* is determined by this color plot and the symbolic ideas associated with its progression of hues.

Establishing narrative organization   Many contemporary films use color design in an overt way to establish narrative organization. The complex narrative of Steven Soderbergh's *Traffic* takes place in three locations, two of which are color-coded (see Color Plates 6 and 7). The Washington, DC sequences were shot unfiltered to achieve a cold, blue look. Scenes in Mexico were overexposed and shot with a tobacco filter to give them a hot, brown look. As the story switches between the locations, the color change is quite striking. In *Blow,* the story spans the 1950s–1990s, and each decade gets a distinctive color characterization. Steven Spielberg's *Schindler's List* and *Saving Private Ryan* bracket their narratives with a prologue and epilogue and use color to differentiate these sections from the narrative body of the films. In both films, prologue and epilogue are shot in naturalistic color, while the narrative body of *Schindler's List* is filmed in black and white and that of *Saving Private Ryan* is filmed in desaturated color. These color differences create a counterpoint within the structure of each film that invites the viewer to reflect on what each section of the films is expressing.

The narrative of Spike Lee's *Malcolm X* (1993), about the life of the charismatic black leader, is divided into three sections. The first section of the film, dealing with Malcolm's life as a young man, is the most colorful, the most visually romantic, and the section that features the warmest colors. The sections dealing with Malcolm's time in prison contrast with the warmth of the earlier episodes by utilizing a color scheme that stresses grays, blacks, and bluish grays. The lighting scheme is very cool and hard, eliminating all diffusion.

The third section of the narrative, dealing with Malcolm's career as a civil rights leader and relationship with the Nation of Islam, features browns, greens, and very natural tones. Dickerson wanted each of these schemes to work on the viewer subliminally and to provide a way of visually characterizing the content of Malcolm's life during these periods.

Conveying mood and tone   The most common use of color design in film is probably to augment and intensify the emotional mood and tone of a scene. The filmmakers constructed a color plot for *The Lord of the Rings: The Fellowship of the Ring,* using color to convey emotional tones for the diverse locations (see Color Plates 8, 9, and 10). Bags End, the Hobbits' village, has a cozy, comfortable feel, with a warm, yellow-orange fire in the fireplace. In the sinister village of Bree, in contrast, the fireplace has a dirty greenish-yellow glow. Autumnal colors help give Rivendell, the decaying empire of the Elves, a melancholy quality. Green light, draining color from the actors' faces, gives the Moria Mines a tomblike atmosphere. In *L.A. Confidential* (Color Plate 13), Kim Basinger plays Lynn Bracken, a Hollywood hooker who lives in a palatial Los Angeles house where she has two bedrooms, one the working bedroom, the other her own. Cinematographer Dante Spinotti used color to contrast the emotional tone of these two rooms. He shot the working room with cool blue light to give it a slightly harsh and emotionally distant aura. By contrast, when Lynn takes a man she loves to her real bedroom, Spinotti used a romantic amber lighting to create a sense of warmth and emotional security.

In James Cameron's *The Terminator* (1984) (Color Plate 11), a science fiction fantasy set in Los Angeles during two time periods, 1984 and 2029 A.D., cinematographer Adam Greenberg used hard, strong, blue light to photograph the terminator (played by Arnold Schwarzenegger). Greenberg found that hitting Schwarzenegger with this light from a high angle made the character seem less human and more savage. When he lit Schwarzenegger with strong light, the actor looked like a piece of sculpture. The high angle of the light increased the shadows on Schwarzenegger's physique and created a harder look, and the blue cast of the light accentuated his coldness.

Much has been written about the psychological and emotional effects of color schemes, and many cinematographers have very intense preferences for and against certain colors and a belief that specific colors can have precise effects on the emotional responses of viewers. In general, however, the emotional effects of color are strongly context-dependent. Color can augment, intensify, sometimes contrast and cut against the dominant emotional tone and mood of a scene, but an individual color in itself can rarely supply emotional and psychological content that is otherwise missing in a scene. In the case of the contrasting color schemes of the two bedrooms in *L.A. Confidential,* the action of the scenes in those locations works with the lighting to help set a unified emotional tone in each locale. Rather than imposing extraneous meaning on a scene or film, color design extends, sharpens, heightens, or, conversely, minimizes, mitigates, or contrasts with the existing narrative, dramatic, or psychological material of a given scene.

◻ CINEMATOGRAPHY AND THE DIGITAL DOMAIN

Digital imaging is now a standard part of contemporary film, and the cinematographer's job intersects with the work of computer-effects artists. Light, color, camera perspective, and movement can be created either digitally or through traditional cinematography.

The Anniversary Party (Fine Line, 2001)
Cinematographer Roger Deakins, who frequently works (on film) with directors Joel and Ethan Coen (*The Big Lebowsky, O Brother Where Art Thou, Fargo*), shot this feature on digital video. Changing his shooting methods, he worked carefully to control highlights and minimize digital video's inherent deep focus. In a clear sign of the future, digital video increasingly is becoming an acceptable and inexpensive alternative to film. Frame enlargement.

Cinema is no longer exclusively a film medium. An increasing number of films today are being shot on **digital video** or on **high-definition video,** with *Star Wars Episode II: Attack of the Clones* being the most famous. Others include *The Anniversary Party* (2001), *Session 9* (2001), and *Our Lady of the Assassins* (2001). Although most of it was shot on film, *Ali* (2001) used high-definition video for a few scenes.

Digital video (dv) looks quite different from film. It is cleaner and crisper because it lacks grain (many dv cinematographers will add grain to simulate a film look). Everything in the frame from near to far tends to be in focus, creating a consistent wide-angle look. Highlights—bright areas—are harder to control and tend to blow out. Currently, all of these factors tend to create a shot-on-video look.

Whether productions are shot on video or film, *digital timing* (or **digital grading**) is increasingly used to adjust and balance color and tweak other image elements. Traditional laboratory methods in earlier periods (a process known as lab timing) enabled cinematographers to make color adjustments in the entire image overall, whereas today they can selectively remove or alter individual colors or sections of the image, as cinematographer Andrew Lesnie did on *The Lord of the Rings: Fellowship of the Ring*. Whereas traditional lab timing only makes gross adjustments in the three primary colors of red, blue and green, digital timing enabled Lesnie to work directly with delicate blends, such as lavenders and salmons, and in small, precisely defined areas of the image (skin tones, for example). *O Brother, Where Art Thou?* was the first feature film to be entirely digitized and color corrected using this method. Because of the image control that digital timing affords, cinematographers are becoming increasingly involved in this area of postproduction, whereas in previous decades their work was largely finished with the completion of principal photography.

In the area of special effects, the province of cinematography overlaps with the contributions of the **visual effects supervisor** and his or her digital artists. The challenge that cinematographers and effects artists face is to convincingly blend the **live action** and **digital effects** components of shots and scenes. Live action elements are the actors and sets that are photographed before the camera. Digital effects, by contrast, are built inside a computer using sophisticated software to render objects with convincing three-dimensional features: textures, movements, color and lighting cues. To build a digital effects shot, live action elements are **composited** (joined) with the digitally created elements, and, for the illusion to work, the compositing must be seamless, that is, the information about light, color, and movement must match for both domains.

Motion control cinematography helps achieve this match. A motion-control camera is computer-guided and programmed to make a "pass," a prespecified movement, through a set and around its actors. By replicating the coordinates of the movement inside the computer, a moving camera shot can be simulated inside computer space, which is necessary to conjoin, for example, the starship troopers and their bug enemies in a single shot as seen by a moving camera. To facilitate the insertion of actors into the digital effects shot, they are often photographed against a blank screen—a process known as **greenscreening**—from which they can be extracted and composited into a digitally animated environment. In the *Jurassic Park* films—or any digital effects creature film—the actors and the creatures never coexist in front of the camera. The creatures exist only in the computer as digital creations.

Starship Troopers
(TriStar, 1997)
The troopers battle giant bugs on the planet Tango Urilla. The live actors were filmed using motion-control camerawork and were subsequently composited with the computer-animated bugs. Thus, the actors never saw the enemy they were supposed to be fighting, except, of course, by watching the movie when it was finished. Frame enlargement.

Often, a digital shot will require several motion-control passes, as did the most elaborate effects shot in *Saving Private Ryan,* a boom shot showing the Allied fleet anchored off the Normandy shore, replete with scores of ships, barrage balloons, and a horde of soldiers on the beach. Because only 400 extras were available to simulate thousands of troops, the film's visual effects supervisor made several passes, each time repositioning the extras at different places on the beach. When composited, the information from the different passes created a beach full of soldiers. The other elements—the ships and balloons—were never photographed; they were **computer-generated images** (CGI), built from scratch as a computer effect.

At present, two modes of computer imaging exist in contemporary film. One mode is the subtle use of digital effects to heighten the dramatic impact of generally realistic narratives. *Saving Private Ryan* is an example of this mode. During the chaos of the D-Day invasion, as Allied soldiers are cut down in the water by German fire, Spielberg shows some underwater views of bullet strikes slicing below the surface and striking hapless victims. These underwater bullet strikes were computer-generated effects. While they are extremely vivid, they do not call attention to themselves as a digital effect. Similarly, the digital cloning of thousands of passengers on the decks of *Titanic* was an effect that did not advertise its origins. Many of the industry's visual effects artists feel that these are the best examples of the technology because they are the ones that viewers never notice. Actor Oliver Reed died during the filming of *Gladiator* (2000) with one of his scenes yet to be shot. He was inserted into the new scene as a digital creation. The actor completed the scene with an appearance after his death.

The other mode of digital effects tends to advertise them, to call explicit attention to the effect as an effect. The armies of warriors and demon gods in *The Scorpion King* (2002) and the aliens in *Star Wars Episode II: Attack of the Clones* are obvious special effects. They are delightfully imaginative, but they are not photographically real. They did not exist before the camera as we see them.

Taken to the extremes of *The Scorpion King* or *The Mummy 2* (2001), digital effects can seem like a cartoon, like animated footage, which, of course, is precisely what they are. For this reason, some filmmakers prefer to minimize their use. Mick Jackson, for example, the director of *Lord of the Rings: Fellowship of the Ring,* built his locations using real sets and models so that the locales in the story would feel real. He didn't want the film to feel like a CGI cartoon.

The use of digital effects in contemporary film, then, has expanded the traditional domain of cinematography. The customary tools of the cinematographer are also the tools of digital effects artists, which entails that these filmmakers have a shared vision towards which they are working in common.

VISUAL STYLE AND DESIGN QUOTATIONS

The discussion thus far has tended to emphasize how cinematography functions within individual films, with a stylistic design suited to expressing the needs of a given production. But one can also understand cinematography in terms of visual styles across groups of films. The cinema is now a century-old medium, and cinematography has established some important visual traditions. Certain lighting and color designs, used extensively across many films, have emerged as enduring features of style. Filmmakers can quote from these in their own work, and what is "real" for an audience is sometimes a function of how films in the past have represented the world.

During the decade of the 1940s, hard, low-key lighting was an established visual convention pervasive in Hollywood cinema. (**A convention** is an agreement shared by filmmaker and audience about what will be valid and acceptable in a film.) Dark, moody, shadowy compositions were firmly established in crime and detective films, especially film noir. The low-key shot from *Out of the Past* is such an example.

Contemporary cinematographers photographing crime films whose narratives are set during the 1940s consciously try to evoke this lighting style. In *Bugsy* (1991), dealing with real-life gangster Ben Siegel's experiences in Hollywood in the 1940s, cinematographer Allen Daviau used abundant hard lighting because this was one of the staples of 1940s crime film cinematography. Barry Levinson, the director of *Bugsy*, wanted the dark areas of the compositions to be extremely dark, and to comply Daviau worked small pieces of highly directional hard light.

What is striking about this aesthetic choice, from the standpoint of visual conventions, is that to evoke a period style and setting for *Bugsy* the filmmakers chose to imitate the lighting style of 1940s Hollywood pictures. In this regard, the lighting style has established its own reality and its own validity. To visually represent the world of 1940s crime on film means to evoke the lighting style that Hollywood employed in its films during those years. Roger Deakins's black-and-white, low-key cinematography for *The Man Who Wasn't There* reproduces the look of Hollywood film during this period, appropriately because the story is set in the 1940s.

Hollywood is a very small community whose artists know each other and study one another's work. This accentuates the speed at which influences can operate. The striking visual designs created by one cinematographer can shape the work of other artists and their films. In *JFK* (1991), cinematographer Robert Richardson created a distinctive halo-style lighting that made the characters glow under hot lights. Shooting Spike Lee's *Clockers,* cinematographer Malik Sayeed emulated this look during a police interrogation scene. Using floor and ceiling lights and a reflective table surface,

Sayeed replicated "the Richardson aura." The frame enlargements from these films demonstrate the influence of the lighting design.

Among their many visual innovations in *Saving Private Ryan,* Steven Spielberg and Janusz Kaminski used an oddly configured shutter inside the camera, which created a streaking effect on the image. In reviewing the footage shot by combat cameramen in World War II, they noticed these streaking effects (which occurred when the cameras lost their loops), and they wanted to reproduce that look.

It became one of the memorable visual effects in *Saving Private Ryan,* and it has impressed other filmmakers, who have incorporated it into their own work. Michael Bay used it in *Pearl Harbor* (2000) during the bombing attack. In *The Limey* (2000), Steven Soderbergh removed it from the combat context of these films and used it for a flashback scene in which a character accidentally kills his girlfriend. The streaking effect helps to stylize the flashback and to visually suggest the tension and stress of the moment.

In *Vertigo* (1958), Alfred Hitchcock and cinematographer Robert Burks created a highly influential shot—the combination zoom and track in opposite directions—used to simulate the main character's fear of heights. In the years since, the combination

JFK (Warner Bros., 1991); **Clockers** (Universal, 1995) In *JFK*, cinematographer Robert Richardson's lighting created a glowing, halo effect, which inspired Malik Sayeed to emulate it for the police interrogation scenes in Spike Lee's *Clockers.* Cinematographers study and are influenced by the work of their peers. Frame enlargements.

Saving Private Ryan
(Paramount/DreamWorks,
1998); **The Limey** (Artisan,
1999)
Filming with the shutter inside
the camera out of synch produces these streaks of light in
the image. Steven Spielberg and
cinematographer Janusz Kaminski were emulating the look of
World War II combat footage,
which frequently had this flaw.
The look they achieved was so
striking that other filmmakers
have incorporated it into their
own work, often with greater
exaggeration, as director Steven
Soderbergh did in *The Limey*.
Frame enlargements.

zoom-track has been used by a great number of filmmakers to express unease, disturbance, or anxiety. Steven Spielberg used it in *Jaws* (1975) to capture the fears of police chief Brody (Roy Scheider) as he nervously watches bathers frolicking offshore.
Martin Scorsese used it in *Goodfellas* (1990) to capture the disorientation of a gangster who realizes a trusted friend might be planning his execution. Spike Lee employed
it in *Clockers* to show a mother's reaction to the spectacle of her son's being beaten by
a policeman. In *The Ghost and the Darkness* (1996), the zoom-track visualizes the rush
of fear in a hunter, facing a killer lion, when his gun misfires. Hitchcock and Burks did
more than create an effective visual metaphor for their main character's psychological
affliction. They fashioned an enduring visual symbol for emotional disorientation, a
template for other filmmakers interested in evoking this quality of mind, a convention
that has passed into the general vocabulary of contemporary filmmaking.

The repetition of visual conventions establishes compelling artistic realities,
not only for audiences, but also for the artists who make films and who borrow from
and are influenced by the designs of their peers. Memorable cinematographic designs establish powerful artistic traditions and influences on the work of subsequent filmmakers.

SUMMARY

The cinematographer helps the director achieve a desired visual design by using the camera to capture images that reflect the director's visual goals for the film. To do this, the cinematographer chooses a film stock and aspect ratio, controls and designs the use of light and color in film, and the planning and placement of camera set-ups. Cinematographers employ realistic and pictorial lighting designs. In the first, they simulate the effects of a real light source on screen, whereas, in the second approach, they aim for more purely pictorial effects.

Either approach to lighting design will employ varying proportions of hard (high-contrast) and soft (low-contrast) light. Specific lighting set-ups tend to create a hard or soft look. Low-key lighting is hard. High-key lighting is often soft. Like image and sound editing, lighting designs follow continuity principles. Light levels and angles must match across shots and even within shots when the moving camera is employed.

With respect to color design, a cinematographer lights objects on the set or uses colored gels over white lights to manipulate color hue, saturation, and intensity. Color can be used to separate and define objects in a composition, but when shooting black and white, a cinematographer has to use gray-scale values when organizing a composition. Color cinematography establishes symbolic meanings, narrative organization, and psychological moods and emotional tones. In each of these functions, color is integrated into the overall dramatic context and design concept of a scene or film.

The cinematographer's tools are shared by digital effects artists, and the scope of cinematography, as traditionally defined, has expanded to include the collaboration necessary for creating convincing digital effects.

Light and color designs, once established, can become enduring features of style, repeated across many films. When this happens, those designs take on a high level of representational reality. Filmmakers are sensitive to this, and if they need to express a particular social milieu, such as urban crime, or a time period, such as the 1940s, they may deliberately imitate famous lighting designs from older movies picturing those settings or periods. Filmmakers may also replicate the striking visual designs of fellow filmmakers, deliberately borrowing design elements in a way that "quotes" from other films.

SUGGESTED READINGS

Dan Ablan, *Digital Cinematography and Directing* (Indianapolis, IN: New Riders, 2002).

John Alton, *Painting with Light* (Berkeley: University of California Press, 1995).

American Cinematographer, monthly journal of film and electronic production techniques published by ASC Holding Corp., Hollywood, CA.

Kris Malkiewicz, *Cinematography: A Guide for Film Makers and Film Teachers* (New York: Simon and Schuster, 1992).

Kris Malkiewicz, *Film Lighting: Talks with Hollywood's Cinematographers and Gaffers* (New York: Simon and Schuster 1992).

Pauline B. Rogers, *The Art of Visual Effects: Interviews on the Tools of the Trade* (Boston, MA: Focal Press, 1999).

Pauline B. Rogers, *Contemporary Cinematographers on Their Art* (Boston, MA: Focal Press, 1998).

Dennis Schaeffer and Larry Salvato, *Masters of Light: Conversations with Contemporary Cinematographers* (Berkeley and Los Angeles: University of California Press, 1986).

Color Plate 1. *Ali* (Columbia, 2001). Color cinematography does not typically aim to reproduce color naturalistically or to capture all the colors in nature. Most cinematographers prefer to stylize their color design. A simplified color palette can be very powerful, as here in the melding of midnight blue and green. When Muhammad Ali (Will Smith) dances with Sonji (Jada Pinkett Smith), the color design adds to the drama. Frame enlargement.

Color Plate 2. *Monsters Ball* (Lion's Gate, 2001). Color effects can be completely unmotivated by a source within the scene and yet can be emotionally true. When Hank (Billy Bob Thornton) makes a phone call from a nearly-empty café in the early morning hours, a sickly green-yellow light bathes his face. The color conveys his psychological distress and the essential loneliness and unpleasantness of the café. Frame enlargement.

Color Plate 3. *Moulin Rouge* (20th Century Fox, 2001). Going for artificially "heightened reality," the cinematographer used blue daylight filters for the night scenes in order to produce an effect of intensely blue moonlight. The effect is highly stylized and not subtle. Note the color contrast between Ewan McGregor's face, bathed in the fake moonlight, and the wall behind him. Frame enlargement.

Color Plate 4. *Planet of the Apes* (20th Century Fox, 2001). Director Tim Burton did not want any blue skies on his desert location, believing them to be a cliché of desert scenes. Cinematographer Philippe Rousselot used a Varicolor polarizing filter, which can be rotated over the camera lens to produce unique color effects, as in this shot where astronaut Mark Wahlberg appears beneath a green sky. Frame enlargement.

Color Plate 5. *O Brother, Where Art Thou?* (Universal/Touchstone, 2000). This was the first feature film to be entirely color corrected using digital means. To create a dry, brown, dustbowl look, appropriate for a story set in Texas during the Great Depression, cinematographer Roger Deakins had the film scanned to digital video, and then reprocessed all of the colors, making them dryer, less vibrant, browner. None of the film's colors, as seen by viewers, correspond to what the camera negative recorded. Digital grading is now a widespread part of contemporary film production. Frame enlargement.

Color Plates 6 and 7. *Traffic* (USA Films, 2001). The color coding of different locations in this film helps give structure and organization to its complex story. Blue filters and hard light give a cold, steely tone to the Washington, DC locations, while tobacco filters and digital grading make the Mexico locations look hot and brown. In each case, the filtration effect creates a monochromatic look. The color design is very stylized. Frame enlargements.

Color Plates 8, 9, and 10. *Lord of the Rings: The Fellowship of the Ring* (Warner Bros., 2002). The story's diverse locations and landscapes were color coded in order to distinguish them and to symbolize their respective qualities. Highly saturated golds and greens convey the lush natural settings of The Shire, the pastoral landscape that surrounds Bags End (Plate 8). Autumnal colors and falling leaves suggest the end of the Elvish empire at Rivendell (Plate 9). Lavender and other cool-toned colors suggest the ethereal, delicate, otherworldly character of Lothlorien, the realm of the High Elves (Plate 10). Frame enlargements.

Color Plate 11. *The Terminator* (Orion, 1984). Cinematographer Adam Greenberg uses hard, blue lighting to bring out the violence and savagery of the title character. Color and lighting design intensify the dramatic and emotional impact of the film's violent narrative. Frame enlargement.

Color Plate 12. *Clockers* (Universal, 1995). Film stock can be a determinant of color rendition. For *Clockers,* the cinematographer used an industrial grade film stock never before used in a professional motion picture. The stock created very grainy, high contrast images (as evident here), and it was exceptionally sensitive to primary colors. Note how the actor's red shirt glows and leaps out of the frame. Frame enlargement.

Color Plate 13. *L.A. Confidential* (Warner Bros., 1997). Soft light and warm color give this scene its romantic aura. This is Lynn Bracken's (Kim Basinger) real bedroom, to which she has brought the man she loves. Her working bedroom (as a Hollywood call girl) is downstairs and is lit in hard, blue light. Frame enlargement.

Color Plate 14. *West Side Story* (United Artists, 1961). This popular musical version of Shakespeare's *Romeo and Juliet* updates the story to a modern New York City setting and a conflict between rival youth gangs. Tony and Maria, the lovers from opposing gangs, console one another, but the color design—with different primaries as background for the characters—suggests the conflicts they face and that will bring tragedy to their lives. Frame enlargement.

Color Plate 15. *Vertigo* (Paramount, 1958). While black and white film registers only shades of gray, color provides more abundant information about objects and environments. Because of their different hues, these red, yellow, purple, orange, and pink flowers separate naturally from one another. Their colors provide a striking backdrop for the action in this scene from *Vertigo* (1958). Frame enlargement.

Color Plate 16. *Do the Right Thing* (Universal, 1989). The production designer added a flaming red wall behind these characters. The color design helped visualize the film's theme about the oppressive heat and racial tensions of a summer in New York City. Frame enlargement.

Color Plate 1

Ali (Columbia, 2001).

Color Plate 2

Monster's Ball (Lion's Gate, 2001).

Color Plate 3

Moulin Rouge
(20th Century Fox, 2001).

Color Plate 4

Planet of the Apes
(20th Century Fox, 2001).

Color Plate 5

O Brother, Where Art Thou?
(Universal/Touchstone, 2000).

Color Plate 6

Traffic (USA Films, 2001).

Color Plate 7

Traffic (USA Films, 2001).

Color Plate 8

*Lord of the Rings: The
Fellowship of the Ring*
(Warner Bros., 2002).

Color Plate 9

Lord of the Rings: The Fellowship of the Ring (Warner Bros., 2002).

Color Plate 10

Lord of the Rings: The Fellowship of the Ring (Warner Bros., 2002).

Color Plate 11

The Terminator (Orion, 1984).

Color Plate 12

Clockers (Universal, 1995).

Color Plate 13

L.A. Confidential (Warner Bros., 1997).

Color Plate 14

West Side Story
(United Artists, 1961).

Color Plate 15

Vertigo (Paramount, 1958).

Color Plate 16

Do the Right Thing (Universal, 1989).

Chapter 3

Production Design
and Performance Style

Chapter Objectives

After reading this chapter, you should be able to:

- explain the work of production design
- describe costumes, sets, mattes, and miniatures, the basic tools of production design
- explain how production creatively transforms existing locations
- explain how production design can fabricate locales that are made to seem real
- describe how a design concept organizes a film's production design
- explain changing production designs in contemporary science fiction films

- describe how production design in fantasy films utilizes realistic perceptual information
- explain the special challenges of film acting that differentiate it from performance in theater
- list the basic types of film performers
- differentiate between method and technical approaches to performing
- describe four ways in which performance becomes an element of visual design
- explain how performance elicits interpretive and emotional responses from viewers

Key Terms and Concepts

design concept
production design
unit art director
supervising art director
costume
set
matte
miniature

pixel
translite
Stanislavsky
master shot
coverage
star
supporting player

extra
star persona
method acting
technical acting
homage
typage
expressionist

In addition to cinematography, filmmakers use sets, props, costumes, and actors to achieve a film's total visual "look." This chapter examines the contributions of production design and performance style.

☐ WHAT THE PRODUCTION DESIGNER DOES

The production designer is the individual who supervises the design of a film's visual environments. The production designer oversees the work of set decorators and designers, costume designers, and the prop crew. This array of artists and technicians cre-

Malcolm X
(Warner Bros., 1993)
Skillful production design
vividly re-creates historical eras.
Malcolm X (Denzel Washington) speaks next door to the
Apollo Theater in Harlem in the
early 1960s. Note the period
musicians featured on the
marquee, the clothing styles,
the antiquated microphone,
and the storefront signs.

ates costumes and sets using colors and concepts supplied by the production designer,
who arrives at an overall visual organization through close consultation and collaboration with the director and cinematographer. As a result of these conferences, the production designer prepares a series of sketches that illustrate the basic **design concept**
and organization of the film. Set and costume designers then work to produce settings
and costumes that embody the concepts outlined in the production designer's sketches.
During preproduction, the sketches are turned into storyboards and into miniature
models that are used to plan camera and lighting positions.

As in other areas of contemporary filmmaking, digital tools have become important aids to **production design.** Digital previsualization enables filmmakers to build
three-dimensional computer models of sets and locations. By rotating and reformatting
these models, filmmakers can simulate views of the set from different camera positions
and with lenses of differing focal lengths. The process enables filmmakers to see in advance how the set will look under a variety of filming conditions. Based on this information, filmmakers can plan camera set-ups or, if necessary, revise the design of a set.

The production designer thinks about the visual statements made by the layout
of sets, architectural styles and building materials, coloring and texture of buildings
and costumes, and the interplay of all design elements in the frame. The goal is to
use these elements to make a unified and coherent design statement or series of such
statements. *Chinatown* (1974) was one of the best designed films of the 1970s, and
it is instructive to hear how its production designer, Richard Sylbert, conceptualized
the different details that went into that film's highly distinctive mise-en-scène. The
film takes place in 1937 in a drought-stricken Los Angeles and follows Jake Gittes
(Jack Nicholson), a private eye investigating the death of Hollis Mulwray.

> There will be no clouds in the sky, because if there are clouds in the sky, it could rain.
> It's in L.A., every building will be Spanish and white. The reason they're white is be-
> cause it's hotter that way. Every building that Gittes visits will be above eye level, be-
> cause it's harder to go uphill than down. Every color will be related, from the white
> to the color of burnt grass to the color of a shadow on the deepest end. Every door
> in certain official buildings will be opaque glass, because it looks like frozen water

Chinatown
(Paramount, 1974)
Detective J. J. Gittes (Jack
Nicholson) and the mysterious
Evelyn Mulwray (Faye Dun-
away) grapple with murder and
deceit in 1930s Los Angeles.
The film's unified production
design evokes the period setting
with exceptional concentration
and metaphoric suggestiveness.

and you can't quite tell what's behind it; it's mysterious . . . Except for the first time
you see him, the man who dies is looking down; he's doomed. You don't see any green
unless you know it's a statement. So the lawn in the Mulwray house is the greenest
thing in the picture.

As Sylbert's description indicates, each element in a well-designed film has a reason for being there, some contribution that it is making to the story, theme, or style
of the production. Throughout cinema history, films have been designed in this fashion, even though the title "production designer" is of relatively recent vintage. While
the title is commonly employed in contemporary productions, during the studio era
of the Hollywood period the title barely existed. During the 1930s and 1940s, each
studio had an art department that employed illustrators, model builders, set decorators, prop men and prop women, and costume designers, all of whom worked under
a given production's **unit art director.** The head of the art department who oversaw
all the films in production was the **supervising art director.** At MGM, this individual was Cedric Gibbons. At 20th Century Fox, the equivalent figure was Lyle Wheeler.

Producer David O. Selznick first employed the term "production designer" on
Gone With the Wind (1939) as a tribute to the importance of William Cameron Menzies's design sketches. These sketches and storyboards provided the unifying visual
structure that helped give *Gone With the Wind* its stylistic coherence. This contribution was especially important in light of the fact that several different directors worked
on *Gone With the Wind*. The man who gets screen credit as director is Victor Flem-
ing, but during production Selznick changed directors several times, and it was Men-

Gone With the Wind
(MGM, 1939)
William Cameron Menzies's design sketches helped provide a unifying visual structure for a production that frequently changed directors. Menzies's architectural visions brought the novel's settings memorably to life. This grand, curving staircase at Ashley Wilkes's Twelve Oaks plantation is the stage for several critical scenes in the film's first act. The sumptuous set provides a vivid backdrop for the drama, and the filmmakers take care to display their set in a luxuriant fashion. Frame enlargement.

zies's design concept that furnished a unifying visual structure. Menzies was a brilliant visual artist whose work has inspired generations of production designers. For this reason, he is sometimes referred to as the father of production design, although, as we shall see, imaginative set design extends well back into silent cinema. As a director, he made one of the classic early science fiction films, *Things to Come* (1933), notable for its flamboyant and imaginative futuristic sets.

☐ BASIC TOOLS OF PRODUCTION DESIGN

Filmmakers design the visual environments of a film by using a set of tools that have remained essentially the same over many decades of filmmaking, although today they are augmented by digital effects. These tools are **costumes, sets, mattes,** and **miniatures. Costumes,** of course, are worn by performers on the set in front of the camera. Period films use historical costuming whose style and fashions designate a particular time period. The sumptuousness of James Cameron's *Titanic* (1997) is evident in the lavishly detailed costumes (and sets) that evoke the early modern world of 1912.

    Sets are the physical locations on which the action occurs. These locations can be outdoors or indoors in the studio. At times, an indoor location may masquerade as an outdoor location. In Steven Spielberg's *Amistad* (1998), scenes that were supposed to be taking place outdoors in the courtyard of a New England prison holding African slaves were actually filmed on an indoor set. The filmmakers hung a giant silk shroud from the ceiling of the stage and lit it brightly from behind so that it would "burn out" on film. To the camera—and the viewer—it looked like a bright, cloudy sky.

Mattes are special paintings that are printed into the shot in the laboratory, or, more often today, are digitally composited, as a part of the background of a setting. Mattes very effectively extend the scale and depth of the represented scene. Matte work can be exceptionally sophisticated and subtle, and, when done well, is virtually impossible for the casual viewer to spot. Digital mattes, created on the computer, are employed in many contemporary films.

Miniatures are small models that stand in for a portion of the set. Filmmakers often need miniatures when a very large set, such as a castle, or, in the case of the *Batman* films, the entire city of Gotham, is required for a scene but cannot be built on its true scale. In the opening, precredit sequence of *Goldeneye* (1995), James Bond blows up a poison gas factory. While the effect is spectacular, it was executed using a small-scale model surrounded by a replica of the Swiss Alps. Let us now examine each of these tools in more detail.

Costumes

Costume design performs several functions. It furnishes details of period or setting appropriate to the story. Second, it provides opportunities for color and spectacle. Third, it provides a commentary on the characters, suggesting or revealing essential aspects of their personality or function in the story. Let's consider some examples of these functions.

Costume designers typically research the clothing styles associated with a film's period or locale because these styles can vividly evoke the period. On the Civil War film, *Glory* (1989), the filmmakers wanted to be as authentic as possible and used Matthew Brady's documentary photographs as guides and relied on a large community of Civil War reenactors, buffs who had designed their own uniforms with exacting historical precision, down to the salt stains on their jackets and the scuffs on their boots.

In contrast to the historical realism of *Glory,* the costume designs Cecil Beaton furnished for the classic musical *My Fair Lady* (1964) are considerably more flamboyant. They demonstrate the way that costuming creates opportunities for spectacle. Audrey Hepburn plays an uneducated, working-class woman who, by learning to speak proper English, is transformed into a beautiful and poised epitome of high fashion. Note the extraordinary hat that Beaton has furnished her with. As an article of clothing, it is impractical and dysfunctional. But as a visual design, it is sumptuous and magnificent, commanding the viewer's attention and suggesting the gorgeous butterfly into which the drab character has changed.

The costuming in *Planet of the Apes* (2001) provides one of the film's main attractions, and makeup designer Rick Baker improved on the ape designs used in the 1968 version of the film. In the earlier film, the actors in ape makeup could not move their lips and teeth independently because the teeth were glued onto the prosthetic lips. Moreover, their masks were relatively inflexible so they couldn't show much facial expression. Baker designed masks that were much more flexible and made the teeth and lips as separate rigs. This enabled the actors to move their lips over their teeth and to convincingly simulate ape speech.

My Fair Lady (Warner Bros., 1964)
When Eliza Doolittle (Audrey Hepburn) makes her high society debut, her effect is electric, due in no small part to the eye-catching attire costume designer Cecil Beaton provided. Her hat is beyond words. Frame enlargement.

Costuming also provides a way of revealing character, creating subliminal messages about the person wearing the costume. In *The Graduate* (1967), an older woman, Mrs. Robinson (Ann Bancroft), makes a habit of seducing young men, and when she sets her sights on the film's hero (Dustin Hoffman), a recent college graduate, she wears a predatory costume, a leopard-print coat. The costumes worn by Satine (Nicole Kidman) in *Moulin Rouge* (2001)—red dress, black top hat, garters and stockings—link her to

Planet of the Apes (20th Century Fox, 2001)
Actor Tim Roth, as ape General Thade, demonstrates the benefits of Tim Baker's makeup designs, which enabled the actors to portray a greater range of facial expression and speech than could their counterparts in the 1968 version of the film. Frame enlargement.

The Graduate (Embassy Pictures, 1967)
When Mrs. Robinson (Ann Bancroft) seduces Benjamin (Dustin Hoffman), she wears a leopard-print coat, providing a visual commentary on her predatory behavior. Frame enlargement.

Star Wars Episode I: The Phantom Menace
(20th Century Fox, 1999)
Queen Amidala's (Natalie Portman) costumes create an exaggerated futuristic spectacle. They blend a variety of ethnic and regional elements into a series of outlandish designs. From scene to scene, the viewer never knows in what flamboyant manner she will appear. Frame enlargements.

the famous movie temptresses, and the actresses who played them, on whom she is modeled. In *Titus* (1999), director Julie Taymor shows the growing weakness and vulnerability of Rome's General Titus (Anthony Hopkins) using costume changes, taking him from dark colors, armor, and hard fabrics early in the film to light colors and soft, revealing fabrics later on. In *Bram Stoker's Dracula* (1992), costume designer Eiko Ishioka reserved the color red for Dracula. He is the only character in the film to wear this color, except when the plot foreshadows his next victim, who then also appears in red.

Sets, Mattes, and Miniatures

Using sets, mattes, and miniatures, production designers have an opportunity to create extraordinary visual statements that become an essential part of a film's mise-en-scène. Viewers remember not only what happened in a movie but how a given film *looked*. Memorable screen environments, achieved through set design, can be an indelible part of the film experience.

Inspired by William Cameron Menzies's work, Ken Adam has been one of cinema's most imaginative production designers, designing two films for Stanley Kubrick (*Dr. Strangelove* and *Barry Lyndon*) and seven of the James Bond films, an enormously popular and influential series. Adam's work on the first Bond production, *Dr. No* (1962), established an essential feature of the series: The villain's huge, futuristic headquarters, the designs for which blended serious and comic elements and have influenced many films in the action–thriller genre. Built to colossal proportions, these sets were often constructed on the huge soundstage at Pinewood Studios in England. So essential has Adam's design become for the series that even productions like *Goldeneye*, on which he did not work, utilize Ken Adam-like sets for the villain's lair. Trained like many production designers as an architect, Adam was skilled at using space to create a visual statement. His brilliant set for the war room in *Dr. Strangelove*—where the president and military generals gather to plan for nuclear war—utilized a giant round table suspended beneath a hanging circular

Bram Stoker's Dracula
(Columbia Pictures, 1992)
The imaginative design of
Dracula's suit of armor evokes
a body flayed of its skin. The
helmet is batlike, with horned
ears and menacing slits for eyes.
It is both angel and devil and is
rust-colored, a variation of red.

Dr. Strangelove
(Columbia, 1964)
Global nuclear war as a high-stakes poker game. Ken Adam visualized the Pentagon war room in these memorably metaphoric terms for director Stanley Kubrick. Illuminated maps against the back wall track the flights of bomb-laden planes. The hanging circular light panel supplied the source lighting in the scene. Frame enlargement.

light panel. The design was eye-catching and explicitly metaphoric, a giant poker table around which the president and military had gathered to gamble on the fate of the world.

The tradition of building huge sets to serve as film locations has very deep roots in cinema, going well back to the silent period. One of the most famous examples in early cinema is the mammoth set D. W. Griffith erected to serve as a Babylonian palace in *Intolerance* (1916). The set was so huge it could accommodate scores of extras, and its most famous feature was six fabulous white elephants, statuary atop glistening marble pillars. Griffith introduced the set to viewers with a dramatic crane shot, with the camera slowly descending through the vast open space of the set. For many years after the film's production, the set remained standing, a reminder of this opulent chapter in the history of production design.

In the 1920s, the German expressionist filmmakers preferred to work on sets because they could design them to perfectly embody a film's style and theme. Fritz Lang's *Metropolis* (1926) used imaginatively designed, large-scale sets to evoke a city of the future, and, together with Menzies's *Things to Come*, established the tradition in cinema of using set design to visualize ultramodern cityscapes, a tradition that includes the *Batman* movies, *Dick Tracy* (1990), *Blade Runner* (1982), *Robocop* (1987), *Dark City* (1988), *The Fifth Element* (1997), and other films.

Large-scale set design in contemporary film includes the climax of *Saving Private Ryan*, a fierce battle between the Allies and the Germans in the fictitious French town of Ramelle. The Ramelle set, built from scratch, was three blocks long, with multi-story buildings and a bridge over a canal, with massive buildings constructed in various states of rubble to simulate the effects of years of war. Because the set enabled the lighting crew to bury its electrical cables beneath the rubble and to hang fixtures inside its buildings, it facilitated many elaborate and complex lighting set-ups.

Using Real Locations

Filmmakers frequently "dress up" real locations to make them part of a film's unified style. Spike Lee's *Do the Right Thing* (1989) explores racial tensions that explode into violence on a hot summer's day in a New York City neighborhood. Translating the ideas of heat and tension into a visual design for the film, production designer Wynn Thomas transformed a real location in ways suitable for the film's themes and visual concepts.

While scouting locations, Thomas wanted to find a block with few trees to suggest the absence of shade and the inescapability of the summer heat. When he found the location, the filmmakers had to refurbish the buildings because the brownstone exteriors were decayed. Their fronts were cleaned and repainted in warm browns to evoke the summer climate. Because the action was largely confined to this block, however, Thomas wanted to add additional colors to the setting, and he began to see his own function on the film in terms of finding opportunities to add color to existing scenes. A recurring set of characters are the three men who sit on the street corner under an umbrella and gossip about their neighborhood. The action in these scenes was static; the men sit in their chairs in front of a concrete wall. To add energy to the scene, Thomas wanted to paint the wall red. When he suggested this to director Spike Lee, Lee visualized it as fire-engine red, and that is how it exists in the film (see Color Plate 16). The wall's fiery coloring intensifies the film's mise-en-scène and its underlying concepts of heat, fire, and explosion. By skillfully applying color to the setting, the production designer made the locale an embodiment of the film's themes.

In many films, locations that may seem real and authentic are actually the work of clever production design. The conclusion of *Terminator 2* (1991) is set in a steelworks factory where the evil Terminator hunts his victims and eventually perishes in a vat of molten steel. The location was a real steel mill, but it had been shut down since the mid-1980s and was about to be dismantled. It was totally inoperative, but in the film it

---

City of Angels (Warner Bros., 1998)
A real location—the San Francisco Public Library—represents heaven on earth, where the angels congregate. The production designer found the library's white lights, white walls, and simple color palette to be uplifting, pulling one's gaze heavenward. Frame enlargement.

Terminator 2 (Tri-Star Pictures, 1991)
Through some basic manipulations of light and color, an abandoned steel mill comes to fiery life in *Terminator 2*. Frame enlargement.

had to appear active, with fiery, sparking furnaces. To create the illusion—to make the factory spit fire and glow with molten heat—the filmmakers used lights and colored gels.

To create the the vats of molten steel in which the evil Terminator perishes, the filmmakers placed powerful lights inside the vats and used orange gels over the lights to give a fiery glow. They then covered these with sheets of plastic, on which they placed a mixture of water, mineral oil, and white powder. This created the impression of molten steel moving in the vat. To simulate flame, they manipulated the lights to create a flickering effect, which they augmented with the use of heaters near the camera to create ripples in the atmosphere, heat waves from the molten steel. In the background, artificially produced sparks added atmosphere and a sense of realism to the scene. With these techniques, the dead factory came alive. The molten steel on screen had a terrifying reality, but the illusion rested on some very basic manipulations of light and color.

On many films, real locations in one region or country may double for those in another, primarily to save money. It's often cheaper to shoot somewhere other than where the story dictates. *From Hell* (2001), about Jack the Ripper, was shot in Prague, Hungary, with East European castles and museums doubling for nineteenth-century London, the period and locale of the story. In Oliver Stone's *Born on the Fourth of July* (1989), scenes set in Vietnam and Mexico were filmed in the Philippines and those set in Massapequa, Long Island were filmed in Texas.

Mattes

To extend the the size and scope of their sets, filmmakers use matte paintings, which are usually placed behind a set or miniature model and may show a distant horizon or landscape. When these are used effectively, viewers do not notice the shift from a three-dimensional set or model to a two-dimensional matte painting.

Today, filmmakers often create digital matte paintings in the computer. Light and color effects on a simulated landscape are easily achieved by coloring **pixels** in

Moulin Rouge (20th Century Fox, 2001) A digital matte with twinkling stars provides the backdrop for this musical number. Actors Nicole Kidman and Ewan McGregor were composited into the shot. The moonface is a reference to Georges Melies's *A Trip to the Moon* (1902, see page 283).

the computer image. Once the digital matte has been painted by computer, it is composited with the live-action components of a shot. The spectacular long shot in *True Lies* (1994) of a Swiss chateau nestled by a lake and the Alps was a digitally composited image employing a computer matte painting of the Alps. In working with digital mattes, filmmakers sometimes face an interesting problem. Light and color in a digital painting can be optimized for style and beauty, while live-action imagery cannot. In Martin Scorsese's *Kundun* (1997), for a scene where the Dalai Lama leaves the Tibetan capital in a small boat, digital artists added mountains and a star-filled sky to the background of the shot. The soft, beautiful moonlight in the matte, however, was better looking than what the cinematographer could achieve with the live action elements. The digital artists had to redo their lighting, making the light harder and more directional so that it would match the cinematography.

Fight Club (20th Century Fox, 1999)
The dramatic skyline in this scene at the climax is a translite, an enormous photographic image mounted on a translucent screen. A thin netting hung in front of the translite, and as it moved in the air currents on the set, the distant lights of the city seemed to twinkle. Frame enlargement.

Similar to a matte painting, a **translite** is another common way of creating a distant background for a scene or set. A translite is a photograph, blown up to huge proportions, mounted on a translucent screen, and then lit from behind. A translite provides the dramatic skyline in the background of the set at the climax of *Fight Club* (1999). The translite was composed of several 8" × 10" photographs, combined and blown up to a size measuring 130' wide by 36' tall. This is a very common method for creating landscapes or city views glimpsed outside the windows of indoor sets. The views of the city outside the windows of the Nakatoni Hotel in *Die Hard* (1989) are translites, as are the views of rural countryside surrounding the home in the first section of *A.I.: Artificial Intelligence* (2001).

☐ THE DESIGN CONCEPT

Production designers tpyically work from a detailed visual concept that organizes the way that sets and costumes are built, dressed, and photographed. Let's examine two examples of this.

Case Study: *Lord of the Rings: The Fellowship of the Ring*

Director Peter Jackson and his team of filmmakers used set and costume design with great care and intelligence to convey the illusion that the fanciful locations in the story were real and authentic. To accomplish this, although the film involved a considerable amount of digital effects, the filmmakers relied on traditional tools of production design: hand-built sets, miniatures, props, and costumes. They believed that these hand-built sets and costumes would establish the reality of the film's fictional worlds and

---

Lord of the Rings: The Fellowship of the Ring (Warner Bros., 2002)
A variety of illusions help convey the small size of the Hobbits at Bag End, including scale sets and scale doubles. In this over-the-shoulder shot, a seven foot tall stand-in, doubling for Ian McKellen, the actor playing Gandalf, looms above Bilbo Baggins, providing the perspective information that makes Bilbo and his house look tiny. Frame enlargement.

Lord of the Rings: The Fellowship of the Ring (Warner Bros., 2002)
The interiors at Bilbo's house were created using double sets, with one group of sets scaled 40 percent smaller than the other in order to convey the size difference between Gandalf and Bilbo. Short and tall characters were filmed in the separate sets. In this scene where Bilbo fixes Gandalf some tea, Bilbo and his portion of the set are actually thirty feet behind Gandalf, which creates the illusion that the characters are different sizes. Frame enlargement.

help anchor the digital effects. As a result, the film achieves a careful and successful balance of digital and traditional design methods. This helps to avoid the cartoonish quality that sometimes results when a film goes overboard on digital effects.

The size of the film (actually, it was three films because the entire trilogy was shot at once—principal photography lasted over fifteen months and total production time four years) was unusually large. Three hundred fifty sets were constructed, plus sixty-eight miniatures, and each of the Middle-Earth civilizations visited by the characters required an average of 150 costumes. Forty-two tailors, cobblers, jewelers, and embroiderers worked on these. Different styles of production design distinguish the various civilizations visited by the main characters.

Bags End. The village of the Hobbits—a race of beings three and a half feet tall—was constructed in New Zealand on a huge piece of farmland. The filmmakers (assisted by the New Zealand army) built a lake, moved 3,000 miles of earth to create rolling hills, and planted hedges, flowers, vegetables, grass, and an orchard. The vegetation was planted a full year before the set was used for filming so that it would be fully established and would look real and abundant when it appeared on camera. As a result, Bags End, and the Shire that surrounds it, conveys an aura of peace, beauty, and luxuriant nature.

The interiors of the Hobbit houses were shrewdly designed to create the illusion of tiny people interacting with the wizard Gandalf, who is normal sized. The sets were built twice, once at normal scale (for the Hobbits) and once at a scale 40 percent smaller (for Gandalf, so that the actor playing him—Ian McKellen—would have to stoop over in order to avoid bumping his head on the ceiling). To suggest the smaller dimensions of the sets in which Gandalf appears, the oak paneling used in the normal-sized sets had to be precisely duplicated but with finer grain.

Motion-control cinematography integrates these traditional sets with digital effects work to create convincing interactions of Bilbo (a Hobbit) and Gandalf. Sometimes the actors were shot on bluescreen and composited into the sets. A more ingenious technique involved moving the entire set with the Hobbit, on a sliding platform slaved to the camera's moves, to create convincing perspective changes in relation to Gandalf. The illusion of differently sized characters interacting is achieved with near perfection using real actors, not computer creations.

Isengard. The evil Saruman creates his army of Orcs in this forge. To make the armor look authentic, real smithing methods were employed. The body armor worn by the Orcs was hand-detailed by 200 artisans and was beaten out of plate steel by two armor-smiths. Silicon molds then were used to duplicate the original designs from this metal armor and mass-produce it as 48,000 separate pieces of polyurethane. Although the vast bulk of the Orc army wears fake armor, the designs started as real forged metal. This provides a good example of how digital effects—much of the Orc army is computer-created—can be anchored in designs that are hand-built using methods that emulate the story's primitive time setting.

Rivendell. The Elves live in harmony with nature, and the sets here integrate living quarters with forest and stream. Rivendell buildings have no glass windows separating characters from nature. They open directly onto the forest, without walls, so characters can move easily from indoors to outdoors, and the woodwork is hand-carved and includes many floral and leaf designs. The coloration is autumnal and faded, to suggest that the Elven empire is coming to its end. (See Color Plate 9.)

The Mines of Moria. The film's biggest action scenes occur here, as the Fellowship of adventurers battle Orcs and Trolls in these vast underground spaces. To suggest a world without sunlight, the colors in the sets and costumes were desaturated using digital grading. The sets were created in miniature and full-size, but the biggest ones—such as the huge cavern surrounding the footbridge on which Gandalf battles a huge Balrog—were digital.

The majority of the creatures in the mines were also digital effects, but they had been first created as scale models, which were then digitized and animated. These included the fiery Balrog and the huge Cave Troll. As in the sequences at Hobbiton, the Mines of Moria seamlessly integrate digital and traditional methods of production design.

Director Peter Jackson said that, "We wanted to create a feeling that we'd gone to Middle Earth and were able to shoot on authentic locations. . . . The mantra of our design work became 'Make it Real.'" He knew that digital effects alone could not achieve this. Thus, traditional methods of production design became key ingredients in this strategy of visiting Middle Earth "for real."

Jackson continued this strategy on the sequel, *The Two Towers* (2002). That film's climactic battle at Helm's Deep fortress, for example, incorporated full-scale sets of the Hornburg Castle (façade only) and the 24-foot high defensive wall that surrounds it. The sets were built in a quarry and made use of its natural rock formations. With their bias toward getting a realistic look, the filmmakers wanted to do a real camera move (not a digital one) over this wall, and its huge size required the use of an 80-foot crane, specially constructed for the film, to execute the move.

Case Study: The Evolution of Design
in Contemporary Science Fiction Films

Stanley Kubrick's *2001: A Space Odyssey* (1968) had special effects far more sophisticated than any film of its time, and even today they remain impressive. Kubrick's model space-ships were remarkably detailed and three-dimensional, and he used mattes to insert moving images of people into their interiors, glimpsed behind windows. Inside the spacecraft, the production design emphasized blank, white, controlled, and regulated environments that suggested an antiseptic future, in which human behavior was rational and orderly, rather than unpredictable and impulsive. The designs spoke to control and authority, rather than decay and chaos. Doing so, they embodied the central irony of the film, namely, the way in which people had ceded control over their lives to the mechanical systems and synthetic environments they created. The pessimism inherent in this view would inspire the next generation of science fiction film and give rise to an alternative way of visualizing the future. *Alien* (1979) initiated this alternative visual design.

Ridley Scott, director of *Alien* and *Blade Runner*, has acknowledged the importance and influence of Kubrick's film. *Alien* replicated the antiseptic Kubrick design in selected sets of the spaceship, Nostromo, but in other ways it established a new design template for the next decade and a half of science fiction filmmaking. The Nostromo has two faces. The control rooms and science bays upstairs are gleaming and antiseptic. By contrast, sets in the bowels of the ship—its engine rooms and storage areas—were grimy, dark, and dank. These established a mise-en-scène that became the norm not just for the *Alien* series but for subsequent science fiction film in general, including such pictures as *Blade Runner*, *Escape from New York* (1981), *Robocop*, and *Dark City*. Locales are dirty and dimly illuminated, with rain and smoke-filled air. This

---

2001: A Space Odyssey (MGM, 1968)

Human figures against a sterile, white environment. The production design evokes an antiseptic, sterile future in which human beings have ceded authority to the technological systems they have created. Frame enlargement.

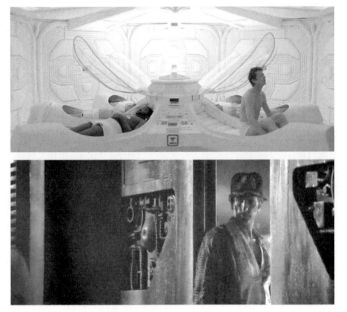

Alien (20th Century Fox, 1979)
Production design of the spacecraft
Nostromo evoked two sharply contrasting environments. The sterile,
antiseptic science bays and computer
rooms showed the influence of Kubrick's
2001. But it was the dark, grimy interior
of the Nostromo, and its low-key lighting, that helped establish "future noir"
in science fiction films for years to come.
Frame enlargements.

mise-en-scène might be termed *future noir* because of its similarity to the gloomy and
oppressive look of classic film noir. It has another root in Fritz Lang's *Metropolis*, specifically that film's underground city where the workers reside and labor, a place of enormous machinery, darkness, and congestion.

    Alien's future noir transitioned film away from the antiseptic *2001* look, and *Blade
Runner*'s landmark production design reinforced this shift with its dark vision of a future city. Production designer Lawrence G. Paull based his design concept on the so-

Blade Runner (The Ladd
Company, 1982)
Blade Runner's influential
design concept followed the
social realities depicted in script
and novel. The visual clutter
evokes a ghettoized urban future
marked by social breakdown.
The film's production design
brilliantly embodies the novel's
themes of entropy and decay.

cial realities evoked in the film's script and the novel from which it derived. The film is set in a futuristic society where the middle class has relocated to pleasurable off-world colonies, leaving the cities to choke in urban decay, architectural collapse, and over-population. The visual design of the film creates a world of clutter, a ghettoized alley environment in which transient, jobless, urban poor jostle together in a mix of nation-alities and languages while, far overhead, video monitors and electronic billboards carry corporate advertisements and media messages. High-rise buildings of high-tech opu-lence coexist with the crumbling alley environment, creating a striking mix of contrast-ing architectural and social styles and realities. Paull's production design is a stunning translation of the social realities of the story into extremely powerful visual environments.

The noirish, pessimistic mise-en-scène established by *Alien* and *Blade Runner* pre-dominated in science fiction films for the next fifteen years. Even fantasies like the *Bat-man* series visualize a noir environment. So prevalent had it become that, when director Luc Besson and designer Dan Weil were planning *The Fifth Element* (1997), they felt it imperative to break with this style and define an alternative. Accordingly, *The Fifth El-ement*'s city is seen mostly by day, has a recognizable Manhattan skyline, and, in place of the tangled and shadowy architectural styles in sci-fi noir, it was built on a grid pat-tern, like Manhattan, with vanishing single-point perspective. This design connects this futuristic cityscape with the recognizable metropolis of today. Innovative and startling in its time, the future noir look had become conventional, a mise-en-scène to avoid for *The Fifth Element*'s filmmakers, interested in creating new imagery. Like cinematogra-phers, production designers study and borrow from the work of their peers, and really successful design concepts in time can become obstacles to fresh creation.

☐ PRODUCTION DESIGN AND SPECIAL EFFECTS

As with cinematography, production design in contemporary filmmaking overlaps with the creation of digital effects. Many special effects sequences in film blend miniature models with digital mattes or digital animation. In *The Truman Show*, the tall build-ings on the main street set of Seahaven, Truman's home town, were only partially con-structed as ground-level facades. The upper floors were digital creations, giving the sets greater mass and height than they actually possessed. The same strategy was used to create the huge Coliseum in *Gladiator* (1999). Audiences delight in these manip-ulations of place and setting and embrace the movie magic that makes them possible.

Viewers look to the cinema to provide images, narratives, and spectacles that trans-form their sense of life and the world, but they also demand reference to life and cor-respondence with experience from motion pictures. These provide a grounding and a base for the sometimes elaborate transformations wrought by style. Even at its most fantastical, production design can take the unreal and make it look real or, at least, credible and convincing to viewers. One powerful way of doing this is by building cor-respondences to real perceptual experience into unreal and stylized images.

Steven Spielberg's dinosaurs in *Jurassic Park* and *The Lost World* were created as computer animation, then composited with the live-action footage containing the real actors. When the dinosaurs stalk the children through the kitchens of the park, they seem real because they interact in perceptually valid ways with the live-action environment. Their reflections are mirrored in the steel surfaces of the tables behind which the children hide, and their shadows fall across the actors' faces. This reflective and shadow information connects the dinosaurs to the live action set, and it is realistic perceptual information. When such information is lacking, special effects sequences often fail to grip the viewer, look flat, or seem ridiculously unpersuasive. Digital tools have added new levels of credibility to special effects because they give artists much greater control over image properties of texture, movement, light, and color, elements of realistic perceptual information, used to "sell" the credibility of the special effect or design.

☐ ACTING

The actor is the human element in film. Many components of cinema involve machinery—lights, camera, computers for editing and special effects—but performance puts the reality of human emotion directly onto screen. Carl Dreyer, one of cinema's greatest directors, felt that the human face was the most important element of cinema, and many filmmakers agree with him. Dreyer's most emotionally intense film, *The Passion of Joan of Arc* (1928), is composed almost entirely of close-ups of faces.

Nearly all film acting derives from the tradition of naturalism established by **Stanislavsky (1863–1938)**, a Russian teacher, actor, and director who emphasized that performance should be anchored in the emotional reality of the script and story, the characters, and their situation. Good film actors aim to these find moments of emotional truth in a scene and to play these as honestly as they can using the tools of their craft—their face, voice, and body. Many of cinema's greatest actors—Barbara Stanwyck, Jean Arthur, James Stewart, Spencer Tracy, Tom Hanks—are so honest that they don't seem to be acting at all. Their performances become totally transparent, revealing the characters with exceptional clarity.

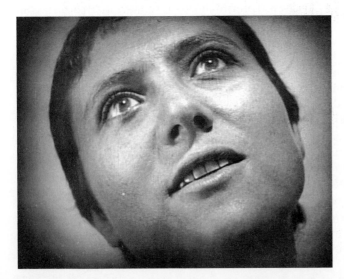

The Passion of Joan of Arc (1928) Director Carl Dreyer felt that the human face was the most cinematic element of all, and he composed this film, about the trial and execution of Joan of Arc, almost entirely as a series of facial close-ups. Most films are not as stylistically radical as this, but Dreyer was right about the special emotional truth that the actor's presence before the camera uniquely conveys. Frame enlargement.

Actors have different methods of preparation, but the good ones all try to find the emotional arc in the story and to play that. They search for correspondences between their inner emotional life and the situation of the characters they are playing. A good actor is always "in the moment," speaking and moving in ways that honestly embody the drama at each moment in a scene.

Good film acting has an element of unpredictability, and that is why many directors are uncomfortable with actors. Directors have to turn actors loose in front of a camera, and, to get good results, they can't control actors with the mechanical precision that they can exercise over lighting or editing.

But this lack of control is where the artistry of acting resides, where the actor's interpretation of the material arises. During a tender scene between actors Marlon Brando and Eva Marie Saint in *On the Waterfront* (he plays a tough dockworker and ex-boxer, she's a proper young lady), Saint accidentally dropped her white glove on the ground. Brando picked it up, but instead of handing it back to her, he put it on and wore it for the remainder of the scene. Watching the scene, you can see that Saint expects him to give her back the glove. She reaches for it, but Brando holds onto it, plays with it as they talk, and then wears it. It was a spontaneous, unscripted moment that is wonderful because it's true to the scene. It conveys the tenderness in Brando's tough character and the unspoken attraction he feels for her.

On the Waterfront (Columbia Pictures, 1954)
Good acting conveys the emotion of a scene with truth and honesty. Good actors can be so "in the moment" that they create new, unscripted material in their performance that adds to and improves the scene. Brando's brilliant gesture with the glove re-frames all of the scene's dialogue with this spontaneous expression of his character's attraction to Edy (Eva Marie Saint). In this frame enlargement, Saint clearly expects Brando to give back her glove.

Acting in Film and Theater

What are the basic characteristics of acting in the cinema, and how does performance style become an element of a film's visual design? Acting in the cinema is a uniquely difficult challenge. While screen acting would seem to bear some similarity with performance in the theater, the differences between acting in the two mediums are more significant. Five characteristics of the motion picture medium make the actor's task quite difficult: lack of rehearsal, out-of-continuity shooting, the amplification of gesture and expression by the camera and sound recording equipment, the effects of lighting, lenses, and greenscreening, and the absence of an audience.

Lack of Rehearsal

In theater, rehearsal is an essential part of the production process. Actors do not go before a live audience until the play and their performance in it have been thoroughly rehearsed. This enables actors to achieve the right nuances and timing in their performance and to work on, and hopefully resolve, problem areas in the production.

By contrast, in cinema rehearsal is a relative rarity. For a film production to accord its actors a two-week rehearsal period is a luxury. With hundreds of thousands of dollars consumed by each day of a shoot, the great expense of film production works against a lengthy rehearsal period. Moreover, the sad fact is that many film directors dislike working with actors and mistrust the actor's contribution to a scene or shot and feel relatively insecure about collaborating with performers to secure the right nuance in a scene. Other directors who are skilled at working with actors, like Sydney Pollack (*Out of Africa*, 1985), prefer to avoid rehearsing because the time that is available is simply too short. Because of these factors, actors in film lack the elaborate prep time to develop a role and a performance that is standard in theater. Film actors have to hit the ground running, learn their lines, arrive on the set, and play their character for the camera. This is an extraordinary demand, but it is compensated by the fact that, in most cases, the performer is one element among many in the frame, and the filmmaker can use lighting, camerawork, editing, and sound to modulate and strengthen the actor's performance.

Shooting Out-of-Continuity

Motion pictures are filmed out-of-continuity. The order in which scenes are filmed is very different from the order in which they appear in the finished film. The sequencing of scenes as they appear in the final finished film is achieved during the process of editing and does not occur during shooting. Economies of time and cost determine the order in which scenes are filmed, the goal being to do it in the most cost-efficient way possible. To save time and money, all scenes occurring in a given location or on a particular set may be filmed at one time, regardless of how they are distributed throughout the narrative. When the filming of all scenes occurring in a given location or set has been completed, the production company moves on to the next set or location to film the scenes that occur there.

The filming of each scene also fails to observe proper continuity. Typically, the **master shot** is filmed first, and the performers run through the entire action of the scene from the master shot camera position. This is generally a framing of the action in medium long shot that shows an overall view of the set and the actors in it. Then the actors recreate bits of the action for inserts and close-ups. These supply what is known as **coverage,** which the editor will intercut with the master shot to create the edited scene.

When filming coverage, an actor typically will deliver all of his or her dialogue that is recorded from a given camera position, regardless of when it may appear in the scene.

One of the most famous acting scenes in U.S. films, the so-called Brother Charlie scene from *On the Waterfront* (1954), dramatically illustrates these challenges. Terry Malloy (Marlon Brando) and his brother Charlie (Rod Steiger) are part of the mob that controls the longshoremen's union on the New York dockyards. Sickened by its corruption, Terry wants to leave the mob, but his brother tries to persuade him to stay because he knows if Terry leaves and turns informant, as the State prosecutor wishes him to do, a mob contract will be issued on his life.

In the scene, a master shot of the two actors alternates with close-ups of each. In the close-ups, actor Rod Steiger had to deliver all his dialogue in the scene that was

On the Waterfront (Columbia Pictures, 1954)
Rod Steiger and Marlon Brando in two camera set-ups from *On the Waterfront*. In the two-shot, both actors are present, and each can build a performance by playing off the other. In the close-up, however, Rod Steiger (pictured) had to deliver his lines while Brando was absent from the set. The angle of Steiger's eyes makes it seem as if he is looking at Brando, but he had to create his character in the scene under highly artificial conditions. Frame enlargements.

to be recorded from this camera position, regardless of when the dialogue occurred. Complicating this task, as Steiger later reported, was the fact that Brando left the set on the days Steiger had to deliver these lines. Steiger played his scene and projected his emotions to an actor who was not there.

These conditions of filming require that actors be able to recreate their character at any moment in the drama as required by the shooting schedule. By contrast, the performer in the theater has it a bit easier. He or she creates a character sequentially and chronologically in real time, from act one to the last act of the play.

Amplification of Gesture and Expression

On stage, the actor plays to an audience that is sitting some distance away in the auditorium. The actor's gestures and vocal inflections must be large and loud enough to reach the most distant point in the auditorium. By contrast, the film camera and sound equipment act as magnifying instruments, amplifying even the tiniest of gestures and the smallest of vocal inflections. The film actor has to understand when a little is too much, has to know how to precisely calibrate the smallest degree of facial and vocal reaction with the knowledge of how that will play when magnified on the giant motion picture screen.

The acting styles of many famous motion picture stars would be totally inappropriate and ineffective on stage. The quavering, tremulous undertone in Judy Garland's voice is a subtlety of performance that precisely and powerfully conveys the vulnerability of her characters in movies like *The Wizard of Oz* (1939) and *A Star Is Born* (1954). It is a characteristic captured by the motion picture medium in its ability to amplify voice and gesture. Humphrey Bogart's nervous facial tics and James Cagney's trademark shrug of the shoulders, repeated from film to film, helped establish the star presence of these performers. These tiny gestures would be lost if played in a theater auditorium.

Lighting, Lenses, and Effects Work

The film actor has to know not just the emotional arc of the character in the story and how to play this arc but also how to play for the camera's view of the scene. In other words, the actor has to know precisely how the camera is viewing the area within its frame. What is the depth of field? Where is the focal plane of the shot—the area in focus—and where are its borders? Where does the light fall off into shadow *as the camera reads it*, not as it appears to the eye? These considerations greatly complicate how an actor must move on screen.

Performing with these considerations in mind is called *hitting the mark*. Actors hit their mark when they move in precise accord with the constraints imposed by lighting and depth of field. In a complex and highly specific lighting set-up, if an actor misses her mark by taking one extra step crossing the set, she may deliver her line from an unexposed or out-of-focus area of the frame. Hitting the mark, without letting the audience see this dimension of performance, requires tremendous skill from a performer.

Special effects scenes in film impose an additional set of demands on performers. Actors play these scenes in nonexistent sets and often to nonexistent characters, if those characters are effects creations like Godzilla or the bugs in *Starship Troopers*. The actor performs in front of a greenscreen, a blank colored wall that will be digitally subtracted from the shot, leaving the performer as an element that can be composited with other digital elements in a special effects shot. Much of Keanu Reeves's performance in *The Matrix* (1999) and Liam Neeson's in *The Phantom Menace* (1999) were greenscreened.

For the performer, this is as artificial as acting can get. The actor performs in a void, without the emotional gratifications that performing with a cast on a set typically provides. Performance is almost never the point of such shots. Instead, the point is the visual effect, which is created not in front of the camera but in digital postproduction.

Indeed, the continuing widespread use of digital effects in cinema will tend to undermine the importance of the actor's performance in film. Actors are needed in many films today only because there is no digital substitute, but things are moving in that direction. In *Star Wars Episode Two: Attack of the Clones,* George Lucas continued to "direct" his actors long after they'd gone home. Converting them to digital video enabled him to alter facial expressions and dialogue readings in the computer rather than "in the flesh," using the real actors. Acting in that film became a digital effect. In another context, actor Oliver Reed died during production of *Gladiator,* but he finished his scenes as a computerized creation.

Actors make a vital contribution to film art, but their domain is being encroached on by digital technologies.

Lack of a Live Audience

Greenscreening points toward another major distinction between acting for film and theater. On stage, performers play to a live audience, and they typically modify their performance based on the immediate feedback they get from the audience. The film performer does not have this luxury. To shape a performance, the actor has to depend on the guidance of the director, and those who have the reputation of handling actors well—Robert Altman, Woody Allen, Sydney Pollack, Oliver Stone—consistently attract the industry's finest performers to their films.

Some film actors periodically do stage work precisely because they value the immediate feedback of a live audience and consider this to be essential to developing their

---

Gladiator (DreamWorks, 2000)
Oliver Reed played Proximo, who runs a gladiator training school and helps prepare Maximus (Russell Crowe) for the arena. Reed died before his scenes were finished, but he "completed" them as a digital creation. Digital effects today are increasingly used to simulate aspects of performance. This development tends to undermine the actor's role in cinema and the need for perfecting and capturing a live performance on film. Frame enlargement.

skills as an actor. By contrast, other performers have found film acting more congenial precisely because the audience is absent. Perhaps the most famous example of this is Charlie Chaplin, who had a fear of playing to live audiences and felt more comfortable perfecting his performances in the relative seclusion of the motion picture studio.

Categories of Film Performers

Motion picture actors tend to fall into three categories. There are **stars, supporting players,** and **extras.** The star is an indelible feature of motion pictures. Audiences go to the movies in large part because of the stars who appear in them, and this has been the case for decades. This is true not just for the U.S. film industry, but for virtually every film industry in the world.

Stars are distinct from **supporting players** in that the star commands the largest salary, usually gets top billing, and is foremost in the minds of viewers. Supporting players, as their name implies, have secondary and supporting, rather than starring, roles in a production. By contrast, **extras** occupy the smallest amount of screen time. Extras are performers who appear incidentally and briefly—pedestrians crossing a street, the crowd watching a baseball game.

Although stars typically get the most attention from viewers, many supporting players have established careers with considerable distinction and have created recognizable screen personalities. Supporting players like Walter Brennan, for example, developed very distinct screen personalities in films like *Mr. Deeds Goes to Town* (1936), *Red River* (1948), and *Rio Bravo* (1959). Brennan frequently portrayed cantankerous old coots who came close to stealing the film from the established stars. Other supporting players, such as Danny Aiello and Robert Duvall in more recent years, have approximated star status. Duvall began his career with memorable supporting work in pictures like *To Kill a Mockingbird* (1962) and *The Godfather* (1972) and, by virtue of his star turn in *Lonesome Dove* (1989), graduated to leading player status. *The Apostle* (1997), which he wrote, directed, and starred in, showcases his charismatic personality and subtle, nuanced playing style. It is very much an actor-centered film, emphasizing the human emotional drama for which performance, not effects, is essential.

The Star Persona

The **star persona** is the collective screen personality that emerges over the course of a star's career from the motion pictures in which he or she appears. The star persona or on-screen personality is a collective creation generated by many films and is greater than any single performance in an individual film. One of the easiest ways of gauging whether a performer has become a star is to evaluate whether a star persona exists. Names like John Wayne, Charlie Chaplin, Bette Davis, and Katharine Hepburn instantly call to mind a very fixed, distinct screen personality that exists beyond their individual film appearances and that unifies these.

Stars with long careers evidence interesting changes in their star personas. If one looks at the screen appearances of a performer before they became a star, one often sees a different persona, resulting from atypical roles that the performer, once a star, thereafter avoided. Before he became a star, Humphrey Bogart spent many years as a supporting player in Warner Bros. crime films. In such pictures as *Angels with Dirty Faces* (1938) and *The Roaring Twenties* (1939), Bogart portrayed a series of unsym-

Casablanca (Warner Bros., 1942); **The African Queen** (United Artists, 1951)
Evolution of a star performer. Two phases of Humphrey Bogart's career: the romantic leading man (with Ingrid Bergman) in *Casablanca* and the player of grizzled, quirky, neurotic characters, as with Katharine Hepburn in *The African Queen*.

Erin Brockovich (Columbia TriStar, 2000)
As a star vehicle, this film provides a showcase for Julia Roberts' screen personality and charisma. She commands the camera's attention with her beauty and force of personality. Frame enlargement.

The Searchers (Warner Bros., 1956)
After years of struggling in low-budget B Westerns, John Wayne achieved
stardom in *Stagecoach* (1939) and during the next four decades projected
a powerful masculine image characterized by physical strength, moral
dignity, fair play, and stubborn independence. Directors John Ford and
Howard Hawks appreciated Wayne's physical power on screen and considered it essential to the making of a good Western. Wayne's physical
presence easily dominates the frame.

pathetic, if interesting, villains. These roles did not showcase the essential feature of
his star persona, namely, Bogart's world-weary romanticism, his cynicism with a heart.

It was not until *High Sierra* in 1941 that Bogart, still playing a gangster in a
Warner Bros. picture, became a star in a role that allowed him to embody the kind
of bruised romantic idealism that he would go on to perfect in such enduring pictures as *The Maltese Falcon* (1941), *Casablanca* (1942), *To Have and Have Not* (1944),
and *Key Largo* (1948). In Bogart's later career, his star persona underwent another
change. In the late 1940s and early 1950s, he stopped playing romantic leading men
and turned toward interesting character types in such pictures as *The Treasure of the
Sierra Madre* (1948), *The African Queen* (1951), and *The Caine Mutiny* (1954). Gone
from these pictures were his romantic star qualities. In their place was a series of
neurotic, quirky, and eccentric characterizations.

The greatest stars give their pictures an electricity and charisma that ordinary performers can't provide. Consider Julia Roberts and the excitement of her star-making
performance in *Pretty Woman* (1990). When she is on-screen, she dominates the scene.
Her star performance carries *Erin Brockovich* (2000), a picture for which she won an
acting Oscar. In *Ocean's Eleven* (2001), her character doesn't appear until halfway
through the film, and director Steven Soderbergh was counting on her to make a strong
impression on the viewer very quickly, and she did. There is an indefinable quality of
charisma that stars provide, and each of these pictures is a vehicle for the star.

Some stars have a greater acting range than others. John Wayne tended to play
the same type of characters from film to film. His acting range is quite small compared to Robert De Niro's, but this is not to say that he was a poor actor. His per-

Training Day (Warner Bros., 2002)
Playing against type can be very effective but also risky. Sometimes audiences don't want to
see their stars in a different kind of role. Denzel Washington has tended to play very coura-
geous and moral characters. Here, though, he plays an evil, corrupt cop with savage intensity.
Washington's daring switch of character, and the brilliance of his performance, had a sensational effect on the film's critical and box-office performance. For the role, he earned an
Oscar for Best Actor. Frame enlargement.

---

formances in *Red River* (1948), *The Quiet Man* (1952), *The Searchers* (1956), *The
Cowboys* (1972), and many other films are carefully crafted, and his power and charisma
are essential components of those films.

Other stars, such as Meryl Streep, have an extraordinary range. She has played
an actress and country-western singer in *Postcards from the Edge* (1990), a distraught

---

The River Wild (Universal, 1994)
As a performer, Meryl Streep has no limits. She is equally adept at comedy and drama, and
there seems to be no role she cannot play. She delivers an extremely physical performance in
this rugged action film. Frame enlargement.

Australian mother accused of murdering her baby in *A Cry in the Dark* (1988), a Polish woman who has survived internment in the Nazi concentration camps in *Sophie's Choice* (1982), a Danish author who establishes a life in Nairobi in *Out of Africa* (1985), a whitewater adventurer in *The River Wild* (1994), and an Italian-American housewife living in the midwestern farm belt in The *Bridges of Madison County* (1995).

Even stars who can play a range of characters often project a relatively consistent personality from role to role. Robert De Niro, for example, is known for his psychopaths in films like *Taxi Driver* and *GoodFellas,* while Dustin Hoffman tends to play more introverted, withdrawn characters who have trouble expressing themselves, in films like *The Graduate* (1967), *Midnight Cowboy* (1969), *Hero* (1992), and *Rain Man* (1988).

What finally counts in cinema is not acting range, but the magnetism of the actor's personality before the camera. John Wayne is a great film actor, as are Streep, De Niro, and Hoffman, despite the differences in their range.

Method and Technical Approaches to Performing

In creating a character, film actors today tend to use a blend of **method** and **technical** approaches. For the sake of clarity, these approaches will be discussed in distinction to one another, though in practice most actors use some elements of both. **Method acting** grew out of acting teacher Lee Strasberg's workshops and exerted a powerful influence over a generation of actors in U.S. motion pictures beginning in the 1950s. This generation included Marlon Brando (*A Streetcar Named Desire,* 1951; *On the Waterfront,* 1954); James Dean (*Rebel without a Cause,* 1955); Paul Newman (*The Left-Handed Gun,* 1958; *Cat on a Hot Tin Roof,* 1958), and others. They brought to their roles a more reflective psychological dimension than had existed in preceding decades of screen acting. In a performance by Brando or Newman, one senses a reservoir of thought and feeling within the character, a rich inner life, that is only partly disclosed through dialogue and gesture. Their playing style was emotionally rich and projected volatile and at times contradictory psychological dynamics.

The method involved utilizing emotional recall to play a role. Called on to portray fear, anxiety, sadness, or other emotions, the method actor searches his or her personal experience for moments when these emotions were experienced and tries to reimagine the situations that led to those feelings and internally re-create them. Reexperiencing the emotion, or one similar, becomes the basis for its performance. The method actor searches for the relevant personal experiences that will enable him or her to feel the character.

Marlon Brando is one of the supreme exemplars of this approach. One of his greatest performances is in Bernardo Bertolucci's *Last Tango in Paris* (1972). During a lengthy scene in the middle of the film, shot largely in a single take to accentuate the continuity of Brando's performance, his character reminisces about his youth and his parents. Brando improvised the scene on camera and largely drew on his own life to flesh out the memories of the character he was playing, as he did in other scenes of the picture. The result is a performance of authentic emotion that shocks and disturbs the viewer with its candor.

An alternative to the method is a more technical approach. Here, instead of basing a character on personal emotional memories, the actor thinks through the role and creates from a more detached intellectual perspective, doing what seems right

Last Tango in Paris
(United Artists, 1972)
In this single, lengthy shot,
Marlon Brando used details
from his own childhood to create his character in *Last Tango
in Paris*. The raw emotional
candor of this performance
remains unsurpassed in his
career. Frame enlargement.

and seems appropriate given the scene. The classic Hollywood actors of the 1930s
and 1940s represent this approach, perhaps none better than James Cagney. Cagney
was one of the industry's finest actors and possessed an impressive range, excelling
in gangster movies (*The Public Enemy*, 1931; *The Roaring Twenties*, 1939), light
comedy (*The Strawberry Blonde*, 1941), and the musical (*Yankee Doodle Dandy*,
1942).

In his autobiography, he discussed one of his most famous scenes in *White Heat*
(1948), where, as gangster Cody Jarrett, he goes berserk in a prison cafeteria on learning of his mother's death. Cagney wrote his autobiography after the method performers had arrived in the 1950s, and his discussion contains an implied criticism of
that approach. He recalled being asked by reporters whether he prepared himself in
some special way for the extraordinary emotional and physical outburst he displays

White Heat
(Warner Bros., 1948)
Exemplifying a technical
approach to acting, James
Cagney, as gangster Cody
Jarrett, goes berserk upon learning of his mother's death. The
scene is a classic in the history
of American screen performance. Frame enlargement.

in the scene. He said that he didn't psych himself up in any special way and (here was the implied criticism) that he didn't understand actors who felt the need to emotionally pump themselves up in order to do a scene. Cagney said that he remembered seeing some lunatics in an asylum when he was a boy and tried in the scene to imitate the way they looked and sounded. While Cagney admitted drawing on personal experience to play the scene, it is significant that he did not phrase it in emotional terms. He did not try to recall the emotions he felt as a boy viewing people in the asylum, or to imagine what those so confined must have felt. He merely tried to imitate some of the inmates' gestures and behavior patterns. He created the role from the outside in rather than from the inside out. Cagney took pride in maintaining that the pro knows how to do a scene without extensive "psyching up" and just goes and does it.

Prior to the arrival of the method performers, most Hollywood acting tended to be of this sort, extremely accomplished but without much psychologizing about a character's motivations and personality. It was in this context that the more introspective approach of Brando, Newman, and their generation of actors seemed so revolutionary. While today it may seem less so, that is because the playing styles of so many contemporary actors—Johnny Depp, Brad Pitt, Sean Penn—owe much to the 1950s method actors.

The Performer as an Element of Visual Design

Now that the fundamentals of motion picture acting are clear, it is time to examine how performance style becomes an element of mise-en-scène. Filmmakers can treat actors as design elements in several ways: by emphasizing a performer's unique body language, by choreographing performance and regulating its intensity, by transforming the performer into a visual "type," and, finally, by relating the performer to additional structural elements of design.

Unique Body Language

Many stars have distinctive, highly identifiable ways of moving. Denzel Washington, for example, has a centered, rolling gait that projects calmness and power. Filmmakers often capitalize on the body language of an established star so that it becomes part of the visual design of a film. John Wayne had a peculiar manner of walking that, in time, became famous. A large and very graceful man, his feet were quite small in relation to his bulk, and he developed an easy, fluid gait that riveted attention—such a large man moving so easily on small feet. Actress Katharine Hepburn (with whom he worked in *Rooster Cogburn*, 1975) was impressed with "the light dancer's steps he took with them." Wayne's graceful, catlike movements became a justly famous part of his screen persona, evident in scores of films over many decades. In *Red River*, Wayne walks through a herd of cattle, and they scatter to get out of his way. It's an impressive thing to see.

In 1976, at the end of his career, Wayne appeared in *The Shootist*, a film with strong biographical elements in which he played an aging gunfighter dying of cancer, much as Wayne, the actor, would soon do. At the climax of the film, Wayne's character, J. B. Books, agrees to meet three gunfighters for a shoot-out in the town saloon. Wayne enters the saloon, and the film's director, Don Siegel, privileges his walk by letting

The Shootist (Paramount Pictures, 1976)
John Wayne's unique body language became an essential element in the visual style of his films. When he enters the saloon in the climax of *The Shootist*, Wayne's famous walk commands the camera's attention.

Wayne traverse the length of the saloon from the front door in the background to the bar in the foreground. Siegel lets the moment play without cutting, enabling the viewer to observe and enjoy the walk one final time in what was to be his last film.

By emphasizing the unique body language of its star, the visual design of *The Shootist* tailors its mise-en-scène to blend Wayne's screen persona and the character of J. B. Books into a seamless whole. It does so most explicitly during the opening credit sequence, when Books is introduced through clips from earlier John Wayne Westerns. In each clip, Wayne gracefully performs some physical action—galloping a horse across a river, diving off a wagon under gunfire, snatching a thrown rifle from midair. The clips span twenty years of filmmaking, their images encoding a history of John Wayne's physical performances, a history that in *The Shootist* becomes the identity of the character he plays.

Charlie Chaplin is another performer whose films center on his unique and expressive body language. Chaplin's famous exit at the conclusion of his pictures showed him walking away from the camera with his back to it, waddling in his famous splay-footed fashion and twirling his cane. Chaplin's camerawork was extremely simple and functional. He avoided extravagant camera movements and fancy angles, preferring, instead, to use the camera as a passive observer of his pantomime performance, believing, correctly, that what he did in front of the camera was more important than how the camera itself might move to comment on the action of a scene. The mise-en-scène of his films centers on his body language and costume.

Choreographing Expression

Filmmakers regulate acting style in keeping with their design objectives for a film. This often entails a deliberate placement of the performers in relation to the camera. Alfred Hitchcock, for example, precisely choreographed his performers, and they had very limited freedom to bring material of their own devising that affected the content and design of Hitchcock's shots. During a love scene in *Notorious* (1946), in one extended shot Cary Grant and Ingrid Bergman walk from a balcony to the interior of a hotel room, and Grant picks up a telephone and converses with his boss. Hitchcock insisted that Grant and Bergman maintain an embrace, kiss, and nuzzle during the length of the shot as they walked across the set, and they were filmed by a moving camera. The maneuver was extremely difficult to execute. It required that the actors maintain a very unnatural posture, but Hitchcock wanted the visual effect of the sustained embrace and the camera's intimate involvement with the lovers.

A filmmaker can also regulate performance by controlling its degree of emotional expression. At one extreme, severe restraint can work to orient the viewer to surface rather than depth. *Citizen Kane* (1941) revolves around the mystery of how Charles Foster Kane came to be the man he was. In a crucial scene from childhood, where he is taken from his parents to be raised by a rich guardian, director Orson Welles has actress Agnes Moorehead play Kane's mother in an opaque and impenetrable way. Her facial expressions and voice are flat and unmodulated, even when the character appears in close-up framings. As a result, the viewer can only attend to the surfaces of this character—her face, her posture—as Moorehead's performance establishes these. It is very difficult to "read" beyond them, to see into the character, to infer her motives and feelings in abandoning her child and to understand the nature of Kane's relationship with his parents. This difficulty helps state the film's overall theme and design, which stress that Charles Foster Kane is, in fundamental ways, unknowable. The impenetrability of the mother deepens the mystery of Kane. The acting style expresses the theme that is evoked elsewhere in the film by low-key lighting, camera movement, and editing.

French director Robert Bresson generally preferred that his performers be empty vessels. He avoided using actors whose facial expressions and gestural styles projected specific emotions. He wanted his actors be recessive, passive, and neutral in their playing style.

Bresson's preference for relatively emotionless acting is very different from the norms of U.S. filmmaking, which tend to emphasize acting that communicates a great deal of emotional information. Bresson's style, however, has influenced U.S. filmmakers. The end of Bresson's *Pickpocket* (1959) shows the titular thief, now in jail, finally acknowledging the grace a woman's love has brought into his life. By acknowledging this, he achieves a kind of spiritual redemption. Director Paul Schrader was so impressed with this ending and its emotional restraint that he recreated it as an **homage** in two of his own films, *American Gigolo* (1980) and *Light Sleeper* (1992). (An *homage* is a reference in a film to another film or filmmaker.)

Compare the thief's relative lack of expression in the still from *Pickpocket* with the expression on Chaplin's face in the concluding close-up of *City Lights* in Chapter 1. Chaplin conveys a great deal of emotional information about his character, and, consequently, his expression is richer. In each case, though, the playing style results from specific decisions made by the filmmakers. These differences are tied to the respective mise-en-scènes of the films and the creative approach of their directors. In each case, the actor's level of expression becomes a crucial element in the design of the film.

Many films feature more extroverted playing styles. Much comic acting depends on exaggerating a character's responses and emotions. Jim Carrey or Mike Myers (*Austin Powers*, 1997) are funny because their reactions are disproportional to the situation in

Pickpocket (1959)
The blank expressions and emotionless playing style of performers in Robert Bresson's films help establish an extremely restrained visual style in which all elements of expression are carefully reduced and stripped to a minimum. Whereas most filmmakers work by piling on expressive details, Bresson works by cutting these back.

which the character finds himself. But outside of comedy there are important examples of this playing style. Akira Kurosawa's *Rashomon* (1950) is set in twelfth-century Japan and deals with a rape and murder, the circumstances of which are told differently by all of the witnesses who recall it. As they recall the crime, they assume extremely exaggerated and flamboyant acting styles. Actors in the film gesture wildly, laugh hysterically, and contort their faces into extreme emotional expressions.

Many viewers are struck by what seems to be a flamboyantly melodramatic and excessive acting style. In part, this was precisely Kurosawa's intention. In *Rashomon* he wanted to recover some of the visual aesthetics and performance styles of the silent cinema. Acting in early silent films was coded in uniquely different terms than those that would become established during the sound period.

Rashomon (1950)
Exaggerated performance styles may deliberately break with traditions of naturalism and realism. Toshiro Mifune and Machiko Kyo's mannered acting enables director Kurosawa to recover the visual aesthetics of silent cinema.

One scholar has termed early silent performance style "histrionic" because it was based on a series of precise and exaggerated gestures. The histrionic gesture for fear was to extend the arm palm out, and clutch the throat with the other hand, whereas shame was indicated by covering the face with one's hands or arms. The histrionic style of silent film melodrama was replaced in sound films by a more naturalistic style, incorporating a more subtle and wider range of gestures based on concepts of realism and naturalism. But Kurosawa had his performers overplay their roles as if they were in a silent film.

Filmmakers regulate expression to integrate the actor into the design structure of a shot. Acceptable modulations range from the extremely minimal, as in the films of Bresson or the acting of Clint Eastwood, to the histrionically exaggerated as in the films of Kurosawa, early silent cinema, or popular comic performers.

Typage

A third way in which performance style becomes an element of mise-en-scène is through the employment of **typage.** Here, actors and their performances are visually stylized, often in extreme terms, to suggest that the character embodies a particular social or psychological type or category. This visual encoding of social or psychological information often predominates in a film's mise-en-scène.

Social Typage   Social typage was a major feature of classic Soviet filmmaking in the 1920s. Directors like Sergei Eisenstein cast performers whose physical appearance could be made to suggest the more abstract characteristics of social class. In Eisenstein's *Battleship Potemkin* (1925), the sailors on board the battleship who mutiny against their oppressive officers are embodiments of working-class virtue. The actors portraying

---

Battleship Potemkin (1925); **Alexander Nevsky** (1936)
Social typage in the films of Eisenstein. In *Battleship Potemkin* a snarling naval officer personifies the evil of the old regime. He commands a firing squad about to execute the film's noble heroes. In *Alexander Nevsky,* helmets give the evil Teutonic Knights a sinister and dehumanized appearance. Frame enlargements.

these sailors are beefy, muscular, and handsome. The actors portraying the ship's officers have unappealing physiques, alternately thin and wizened or obese. A master of visual caricature, Eisenstein correlated the appearance of actors, their faces and bodies, with more general ideas about social identity.

A recent instance of this kind of visual caricature is evident in *Starship Troopers,* in which the military officers wear Nazi-like uniforms and insignias and are filmed in stark, geometric patterns to express the film's underlying theme that war makes fascists of everyone. Like many of the combat veterans in the film, Rasczak (Michael Ironside) is an amputee with a mechanical appendage, making the character an emblem of the State's war machine.

In Sergio Leone's epic Western *Once upon a Time in the West* (1969), the spread of corrupt business practices into the undeveloped American West is symbolized in the bone cancer that has twisted and crippled the body of the wealthy railroad baron, J. P. Morton (Gabriel Ferzetti). Morton's twisted body is given significant visual attention in the scenes where he appears. In Sylvester Stallone's *Rocky IV* (1985), a political belief that Soviet communist society dehumanizes its citizens is expressed through the social typage of Rocky's Soviet opponent, Drago (Dolph Lundgren), who has a robotlike appearance and behaves as a merciless fighting machine.

Psychological Typage   Psychological typage can be seen in the **expressionist** style of filmmaking that has its origin in 1920s German cinema. Expressionist films like *The Cabinet of Dr. Caligari* (1919) and *Nosferatu* (1922) present grotesque characters, pathological emotional states, and fantastic settings in which the visual distortions were indicators of twisted minds or spirits. The expressionist style entered U.S. cinema in the 1930s in the cycle of horror films made at Universal Pictures. The physical deformities in characters like Frankenstein's monster externalize their warped inner humanity.

The Night of the Hunter (1955), a psychological thriller about good and evil focusing on a maniacal preacher's pursuit of two young children who know the whereabouts of a fortune, utilized expressionist pictorial and performance styles. Actor Robert Mitchum's contorted face intentionally recalls the expressionism of early

Starship Troopers
(Columbia Tri-Star, 1997)
The war veterans of the Federation Empire have mechanical appendages that replace their missing limbs. They thus embody the war machine that sustains the Empire as well as its human cost. Frame enlargement.

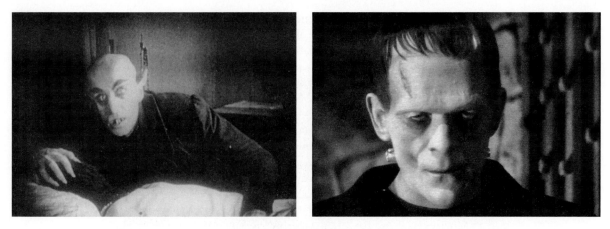

Nosferatu (1922); **Frankenstein** (Universal Studios, 1931)
Contorted bodies, twisted psyches in the German expressionist style. In Germany, the vampire killer in F. W. Murnau's version of *Dracula*. In Hollywood, the expressionist style used in the horror classic, *Frankenstein*. Frame enlargements.

German cinema. Conceived in homage to this tradition is the villain Max Schreck (Christopher Walken) in *Batman Returns* (1992). The character is named for the German actor who played the vampire in *Nosferatu*, and he sports a hairpiece that makes him look like Rotwang, the mad inventor in *Metropolis*.

Performance style, then, can be manipulated to evoke ideas of social category or psychological condition. Soviet political typage evokes the idea of the virtue of the proletariat while the visual typage operative in expressionist styles elicits the anxieties associated with the supernatural, madness, or psychological disturbance. Warren Beatty's production, *Dick Tracy* (1990), illustrates a combination of psychological and social typage. The visual style of the film is borrowed from comic strips, and the grotesquely exaggerated features of the gangsters, in comparison to Dick Tracy's clean-cut good looks and the virtuous appearance of his lover, Tess Trueheart, are a powerful shorthand way of visually expressing the social Darwinian view that criminals are mentally deformed and sick and that the law-abiding are virtuous and emotionally sound.

Visual Mediation of Performance

Filmmakers use elements of visual design in ways that affect how a viewer understands a character at given moments in the story. In such ways, the performer is integrated as one component in the visual design of shots and scenes. In the expressionist style of early German films, low-key lighting enclosed grotesque characters in a surrounding sea of darkness. The lighting adds to the performance styles used in those films, accentuating the creepiness of the characters and situations. In a somewhat different fashion, the lighting in *The Silence of the Lambs* makes serial killer Hannibal Lecter look especially creepy. Placing a light below his face reverses the normative distribution of shadows. Actors are virtually always lit from an elevated angle, and reversing this practice gives the character an unnatural appearance.

The Silence of the Lambs (Orion Pictures, 1991)
The lighting of Hannibal Lecter (Anthony Hopkins) reverses the normative distribution of shadows on the human face to give him an eerie and
unnatural appearance. Hopkins's performance accentuates Lecter's disturbing qualities, but the lighting and composition (he looks directly into
the camera) enhance and intensify the performance, integrating the actor
into the shot's visual design. Frame enlargement.

A love scene (Color Plate 13) in *L.A. Confidential* between Lynn Bracken (Kim
Basinger) and Bud White (Russell Crowe) was filmed with warm amber light. A subsequent argument between the characters was shot in harder, bluish light. The color design visualizes a tone that extends the emotions of the characters as conveyed by the actors.
The two are not separable. The viewer's emotional impression of the scenes is a product
of both the performances and the color design. By being compatible with the psychological mood of the scenes, the color design externalizes the emotional quality of the
performances and the shift from passion to psychological distance in the characters.

Consider another example. In *Citizen Kane,* the title character, newspaper owner
Charles Foster Kane, announces to his employees that his newspaper will be guided
by a series of principles. Among these are truthfulness in reporting and a commitment to look out for the interests of the poor. Kane announces these by leaning over
his desk. As he does so, his face goes into the shadows. (The scene occurs at night
and is lit using low-key set-ups.)

Because of the lighting, the viewer has an ambivalent response to Kane's declaration of principles. The viewer suspects that he doesn't really mean them. On the
one hand, this conviction is based on the understanding of Kane that has been developing through the narrative and from the performance of Orson Welles, who masterfully suggests Kane's mercurial, opportunistic, and ever-changing personality. On
the other hand, the viewer's ambivalence arises from the lighting design. The shad-
owing of Kane's face as he reads the principles extends and comments on his opportunism and lack of sincerity. Performance style and visual design become part of a
unifying whole called mise-en-scène.

Citizen Kane (RKO, 1941) Lighting and composition add information to an actor's performance to make it part of a film's visual design. Charles Foster Kane reads his declaration of principles but steps into the shadows as he does so, enhancing the viewer's suspicion that he is insincere. Frame enlargement.

Performance, Emotion, and the Viewer's Response

As with other areas of film structure, the performance component includes stylistic transformations of human behavior and feeling but also establishes clear references and correspondences with that behavior. Viewers evaluate performances and characters by drawing comparisons with their knowledge of human behavior and what seems to be a plausible, likely, or consistent response by a character in a scene's dramatic or comedic situation. These judgments are based on standards derived from real-life experience, as well as expectations based on genre or other storytelling conventions.

Experimental evidence indicates that people are extremely skilled at evaluating and identifying the emotions that can be conveyed through gesture and facial expression. Many of these emotions are context-dependent. Certain expressions have particular meanings in given cultures. Other kinds of expressions, though, seem to cross cultures and function as universal signs of human emotion (in particular, expressions associated with the emotions of fear, anger, happiness, sadness, surprise, and disgust). A viewer can watch a movie from another country or culture and easily identify from the actors' expressions many of the emotions being conveyed in the scene. This universal aspect of facial expression, and the camera's ability to emphasize it, is a major reason for the cinema's appeal throughout the world and across cultures.

Interpretive and Emotional Responses by Viewers

Because the facial and gestural components of performance invite comparisons with real-life emotions, situations, and circumstances, they elicit both interpretive and emotional responses from viewers. Interpreting the performance, a viewer asks whether the character's response is plausible, likely, convincing, and/or proportional to the situation. These are cognitive judgments that influence emotional responses. In many older movies, characters behave quite differently than in contemporary cinema. In Hitchcock's *Shadow of a Doubt* (1943), for example, a young woman and a police detective, who have just met only a few days ago, declare their love for one another and talk of marriage. Despite the evident sincerity of the actors' performances, many contemporary viewers find this turn of events implausible. It doesn't square with their understanding of how people under those circumstances would behave. This judgment, in turn, underlies such viewers' decision not to invest their emotions in the scene.

On the other hand, if viewers decide that a character's behavior and an actor's performance is appropriate and convincing, given the narrative circumstances, they may go on to share in the character's emotions by way of empathy. Empathy is a willingness to understand a character's feelings and even, under the right circumstances, to feel similar emotions. It is based on complex allegiances with characters, as viewers evaluate the moral and emotional acceptability of a character's screen behavior. This, in turn, influences their readiness to empathize with the characters and situations.

In *The Silence of the Lambs* (1991), most viewers are probably scared of the insane serial killer Hannibal Lecter, although they may find him a compelling and

The Silence of the Lambs
(Orion Pictures, 1991)
Watching *The Silence of the Lambs,* viewers react to Clarice Starling (Jodie Foster) and serial killer Hannibal Lecter (Anthony Hopkins) by forming complex cognitive, emotional, and moral judgments about the characters. The elements of structural design guide viewers in forming these judgments. Frame enlargements.

fascinating figure. By contrast, the film's heroine, Clarice Starling, behaves in a way that most viewers probably deem exceptionally heroic, displaying extreme honesty and courage in her dealings with both Lecter and her male superiors at the FBI. As a result of the cognitive, emotional, and moral judgments they make about these characters, viewers have differing emotional responses toward them. They are frightened *of* Hannibal Lecter but are frightened *for* Clarice Starling when she is in a situation of danger. Of the two serial killers in the film—Lecter and Buffalo Bill—viewers respond with loathing and disgust toward Bill because he has no redeeming qualities. Lecter, by contrast, is funny, witty, cultivated, and shows real tenderness toward Clarice, qualities that Anthony Hopkins emphasizes in his performance. Thus, while viewers morally condemn both killers, their response to Lecter is far more ambivalent.

A viewer's reaction to a character and the actor's performance is a complex process. It involves an intricate series of inferences and evaluations, judgments, and appraisals at cognitive and emotional levels. In films displaying high levels of craft and artistry, performance style becomes part of a unified mise-en-scène in evoking these reactions. Camera placement, color, composition, and other aspects of mise-en-scène work to emphasize the emotional displays by performers. A director can cut to a closer camera position—the better to highlight a character's response and the actor's facial display at a crucial moment in the narrative—or a cinematographer and production designer can employ a palette of colors expressly designed to heighten the psychological mood or atmosphere of the scene. The design of a coherent mise-en-scène gives the filmmaker a uniquely powerful way of guiding the viewer toward a desired set of intellectual and emotional responses.

SUMMARY

The term *mise-en-scène* refers to the design and manipulation of all the objects placed in the frame in front of the camera. These typically include sets, costumes, light and color, and the actor's performance. The three chief members of the filmmaking team who are responsible for mise-en-scène are the director, cinematographer, and the production designer. They form a close three-way partnership to arrive at the visual concepts that will underlie and guide the visual design of the film.

Both cinematographer and production designer have the responsibility of helping the director to realize his or her vision for the film. The cinematographer does this by planning lighting and camera set-ups and assisting in the coordination of color as it will appear in the scene, often by placing colored gelatins in front of the lights. The production designer assists the director, organizing a visual design for the environments of the film. Components of these environments include sets, costumes, mattes, and miniatures. The production designer, in conference with the cinematographer, helps organize the film's color design through the choices that are made about sets and costumes.

The importance of an organizing visual design for a film, agreed on by the director, cinematographer, and production designer, is to facilitate a unified mise-en-scène in which all of the elements—costumes, sets, lights, color, and performance—work together to advance the narrative and to represent mood and atmosphere on screen and to evoke appropriate interpretive and emotional responses by the viewer.

The creation of mise-en-scène illustrates how richly collaborative the process of filmmaking is, the final result being the work of collective judgments made by a variety of production team members about how to achieve a given effect. An exceptional film requires a good script, strategic camera positioning, and sensitive image and sound editing, and it also requires a sophisticated use of light, color, and architectural design. There are so many crucial creative responsibilities on a film production, so many collaborators in the process, and so many key points where design and concept can break down that it is easy to see why it is so difficult to make a good movie.

SUGGESTED READINGS

Charles and Mirella Jona Affron, *Sets in Motion: Art Direction and Film Narrative* (NJ: Rutgers University Press, 1995).

Michael Caine, *Acting in Film: An Actor's Take on Movie Making* (NY: Applause, 1997).

Steve Carlson, *Hitting Your Mark: What Every Actor Really Needs to Know on a Hollywood Set* (Studio City, CA: Michael Wiese Production, 1999).

Sybil DelGaudio, *Dressing the Part: Sternberg, Dietrich, and Costume* (Madison, NJ: Fairleigh Dickinson University Press, 1992).

Jane M. Gaines and Charlotte Herzog, eds., *Fabrications: Costume and the Female Body* (New York: Routledge, 1990).

Beverly Heisner, *Hollywood Art: Art Direction in the Days of the Great Studios* (Jefferson, NC: McFarland, 1990).

Vincent LoBrutto, *By Design: Interviews with Film Production Designers* (Westport, CT: Praeger, 1992).

James Naremore, *Acting in the Cinema* (Berkeley and Los Angeles: University of California Press, 1990).

Roberta Pearson, *Eloquent Gestures: The Transformation of Performance Style in the Griffith Biograph Films* (Berkeley and Los Angeles: University of California Press, 1992).

Carole Zucker, *Figures of Light: Actors and Directors Illuminate the Art of Film Acting* (NY: Plenum, 1995).

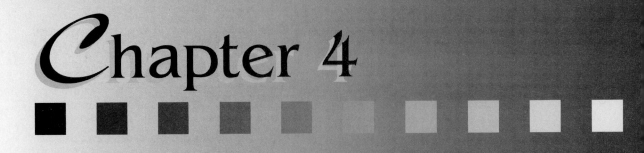

Chapter 4

Editing: Making the Cut

Chapter Objectives

After reading this chapter, you should be able to:

- define the role of editing in the production process
- describe the difference between linear and nonlinear editing systems
- explain the basic methods of joining shots
- explain how editing helps create continuity, dramatic focus, tempo, and narration and point of view
- explain how editing establishes parallel action
- describe the basic rules of continuity editing and the ways in which they establish continuity of action from shot to shot

- explain how continuity editing establishes a coherent and orderly physical world on screen
- explain how editing approaches that emphasize jump cuts, spatial fragmentation, and thematic montage work as alternatives to continuity editing
- describe how editing cues viewers to draw connections and interpretations across shots
- explain how editing establishes perceptual constancies across shot and scene transitions

Key Terms and Concepts

editing
rough cut
final cut
nonlinear editing system
linear system
montage
cut
dissolve
fade

iris
wipe
voice-over
schema
parallel action
cross-cutting
continuity editing
master shot
matched cut

eyeline match
shot-reverse-shot series
180-degree rule
errors of continuity
jump cut
thematic montage
long take
sequence shot

Many filmmakers regard editing as the single most important creative step in determining the look and shape of the finished film. A good editor can save a film that has been directed in a mediocre fashion, and poor editing can damage the work of even the finest director. This chapter looks closely at the role of editing in the production process, continuity editing codes (these are the rules of editing that are found in most commercial feature films), and alternatives to continuity editing.

☐ WHAT IS EDITING?

Editing is the work of joining shots to assemble the finished film. The **editor** selects the best shots from the large amount of footage the director and cinematographer have provided, assembles these in order, and connects them using a variety of optical transitions. In theory, the process of editing begins with the completion of filming or cinematography. In practice, however, the editor may begin consultations with the producer and director and may even begin cutting the film while principal filming is being completed. Most editors, however, will not watch the process of filming or view the locations where the film is shot. This allows them to view the footage unhampered by knowledge about the actual conditions that existed in front of the camera and to visualize with greater freedom various ways of combining the shots.

The amount of authority that the editor has may vary from production to production and, consequently, so may the editor's relationship with the director and producer. These factors determine when the editor may begin work and in what capacity on any given production.

Despite these variations, the basics of editing have remained relatively constant. The first task is to assemble a **rough cut,** which is done by eliminating all of the unusable footage containing technical or performance errors. These may include out-of-focus shots or shots containing unstable camera movement, flubbed lines by an actor, inaudible sound recording, or lighting problems. Once all of this footage has been removed, the editor then assembles the remaining footage in scene and sequence order. This rough assembly will be pruned, refined, and polished to yield the **final cut.** The final cut is the completed product of an editor's work. It includes the complete assembly and timings of all shots in the film's finished form. It is in going from the rough cut to the final cut that the real art and magic in editing lies.

Linear and Nonlinear Systems

Editors today use a **nonlinear editing system** to accomplish their work. A nonlinear system, such as the Avid, is computer-based. Film footage is converted to videotape, which is then digitized and stored on computer disk, giving an editor instantaneous access to any frame, shot, or edited sequence distributed anywhere in the existing footage. The editor decides which footage to work on by using notes that describe the characteristics, strengths, and flaws of particular shots. Prior to the 1990s, when the film industry adopted digital editing systems, editors worked directly on celluloid film and had to search manually through all of the footage to find a desired shot or segment. This older approach was a **linear system** because the editor could only search for one shot at a time and had to do so by viewing footage sequentially, from beginning to end.

Digital systems have made editing a much faster process, and the complex and instantaneous control they give an editor over the digitized footage helps explain why so many films—*Mission Impossible 2* (2000), *An Enemy of the State* (1999), *Armageddon* (1998)—have such fast and aggressive editing.

Films today have many, many more cuts and shot transitions than in earlier decades. Many shots are only a few frames long, less than a second of screen time. Nonlinear systems facilitate this more intensive editing style. To create the hyperfast shot transitions

Moulin Rouge (20th Century Fox, 2001)
Like many films today, *Moulin Rouge* has an especially fast cutting rate, with shot transitions occurring at a rate of more than one per second. This shot of a Cancan dancer, pirouetting past the camera, is only 4 frames long or 1/6 of a second in duration. The viewer barely sees it as a single shot. Nonlinear editing systems have accelerated the editing rate of contemporary films, giving editors new levels of control over huge amounts of footage, enabling them to create the complex montages that have become typical of modern film. Frame enlargement.

of *Moulin Rouge* (2001), editor Jill Bilcock worked with a massive amount of digitized footage. Scenes in the film were covered with a huge number of camera angles and set-ups. She then created files of shots labeled "men in top hats and tails" or "glamour shots of Nicole [Kidman]" and had instant, electronic access to this material to use in building the film's montage sequences. (A **montage** is a scene composed of a rapid series of shots.) Nonlinear systems enable editors to organize and manipulate such vast amounts of footage. A film like *Moulin Rouge* could not exist without computerized editing.

While digital systems have given editors greater control over their footage and increased their abilities to manipulate it in ever more elaborate ways, these systems have disadvantages. Unlike linear systems, the editor does not view a film image but rather an electronic image on a small monitor, which is degraded in quality, with poor resolution. This can bias editors toward close-ups because they will look better on the monitor than long shots. Furthermore, because the monitor's image is a poor guide to the visual qualities of the actual film images, it forces an editor to rely more heavily on his or her notes about the footage. It is arguable that editors using linear systems get to know their footage better because they must manually search through all of it to find what they need. The editor working on a digital system will not access footage that the notes have excluded.

Types of Visual Transitions

In joining the shots together into a rough and then a final cut, the film editor typically employs three basic types of visual transition. The most commonly used transition is the straight **cut,** which is visible on screen as a complete and instantaneous change of one image or shot to another. The cut is typically used to join shots where there is no change of narrative time or place involved. A cut from a shot of Mel Gibson looking off-frame right to a shot of Danny Glover looking off-frame left tells the viewer that Gibson and Glover are looking at each other and that no changes in time or place have occurred in the story between the shots.

When changes of time or place do need to be specified, the editor has several techniques available. One is the **dissolve.** One shot begins to fade out to black, but, before it is gone completely, the next shot begins to appear on top of it so that there is a moment of superimposition in which the two shots are visible together. If an editor dissolved from a shot of Mel Gibson to a shot of Danny Glover, the viewer would know that some change in time or place in the story had occurred. The shot after the dissolve might be taking place several hours after the shot preceding the dissolve or it may be occurring in a new location.

A substantial change of time or place is often indicated by the use of a **fade.** In this case, the first shot fades completely to black. The darkness lasts on screen for a few moments and then the next shot begins to fade in. In a fade, there is no moment of superimposition. If the editor faded from a shot of Gibson to Glover, the shot after the fade could be taking place several days or even weeks after the first.

By using these basic transitions, editors can establish important relations of time and place in the story. These visual codes developed early in the history of film to enable filmmakers to organize their story material and construct complex narratives by, for example, using a fade to establish that one set of events is occurring at a later time than a previous scene. But filmmakers also use these optical transitions for their poetic and expressive visual effects. Editors examine the footage closely and when they join shots together, they often do so because of the suggestive effects and ideas these combinations can create. An editor may use a cut to join shots with similar graphic properties. The instantaneous change of images produced by the cut calls attention to the graphic similarities, as the frame enlargements from *Lawrence of Arabia* demonstrate. In *Apollo 13*, the cut was used poetically to show astronaut Jim Lovell (Tom Hanks), stranded in a crippled spacecraft thousands of miles from Earth, and his anxious wife "looking" at one another (across the cut and the thousands of miles that separate them).

Because it overlaps images, a dissolve can create many poetic effects. For a scene in *Blow,* when drug kingpin George Jung (Johnny Depp), in prison for the remainder of his life, writes a tender letter to his father (Ray Liotta), whom he will never see again, the editor joined shots of the characters, seen in separate locations, with dissolves. One series of shots shows George taping a letter in prison, and the other shows his father listening to the letter at a later date. The edited scene goes back and forth between shots in each series. Each pair of shots is linked with a dissolve, which connects the images of each character and suggests that the emotional bond between them persists despite their physical separation.

In *The English Patient,* editor Walter Murch used a dissolve as the transition out of a flashback to show the youthful Count Almashy (Ralph Fiennes) touching the face of his older self (by overlapping these images at the midpoint of the dissolve) as he lay dying at a point many years later in the story.

Blow (New Line, 2001)
Because the dissolve overlaps two images, editors frequently use this transition to create
poetic effects. The dissolve that connects George (Johnny Depp) with his father (Ray Liotta)
suggests their enduring bond, despite the fact that these characters will never see one
another again. In this scene, the dissolve overlaps images from two different time frames and
locations. Frame enlargements.

Other Optical Transitions

Editors can use other optical transitions to sequence story information and create
visual effects. In this regard, however, contemporary film is relatively impoverished.
A viewer who looks at films from the silent period, for example, may notice devices
like the **iris.** Irises were used much like fades to signal the end of an important chapter in the story or to conclude a scene or film. In an iris-out, a circular pattern appeared

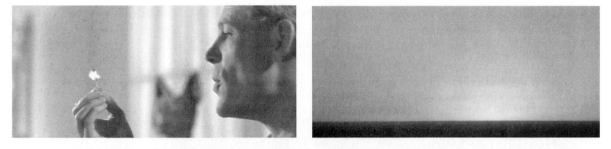

Lawrence of Arabia (Columbia Pictures, 1962)
Editors pay very close attention to the visual properties of the shots they join together. They carefully choose the edit points, where they place cuts and other optical transitions. This famous cut in *Lawrence of Arabia*—from a close-up of Lawrence (Peter O'Toole) blowing out a match to a long shot of the Arabian desert with the sun just below the horizon—startles the viewer with its radical change of scale and with the poetic association that motivates the cut, one that links the burning match with the fiery desert. Frame enlargements.

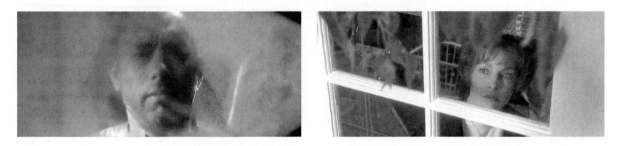

Apollo 13 (Universal, 1995)
Separated by thousands of miles, Jim Lovell (Tom Hanks) and his wife (Kathleen Quinlan) "see" each other across the cut. Their matching eyelines and the camera angles imply that they are looking at one another, despite the literal impossibility at this point in the story for them to do so. The film's editor has created a moment of visual poetry. Frame enlargements.

on screen and gradually closed over the image. To open a scene, an iris-in might be employed, in which case the image appeared inside a small circular opening that gradually expanded on the screen.

In the 1930s and 1940s, Hollywood's editors used **wipes** quite frequently. The wipe is visible as a solid line travelling across the screen, sometimes vertically, sometimes horizontally. As it moves, it pushes one shot off the screen to reveal another. Unlike fades and dissolves, which tend to be more gradual and more subtle transitional devices, the wipe is a very aggressive, highly visible, and noticeable device. Perhaps for this reason, Hollywood eventually stopped using it.

However, when contemporary filmmakers want to evoke early film style, they may choose to use these archaic editing devices. Joel and Ethan Coen use irises in *O Brother*

Where Art Thou! (2000), a film whose story is set during the Great Depression, and George Lucas uses wipes throughout his *Star Wars* films, emulating the early movie serials that were an inspiration for the series.

The Circus
(United Artists, 1928)
Contemporary films seldom use the iris, which is a shame because it offers filmmakers a uniquely expressive visual effect. It directs the viewer's attention to a selected portion of the frame, providing visual emphasis. When used to conclude a scene or film, it does so with great finality. At the end of *The Circus,* Chaplin's melancholy tramp walks away from the camera as an iris slowly closes down around his figure. Visually poetic, it makes for a splendid exit and conclusion to the film. Frame enlargement.

Seven Samurai
(Toho, 1954)
Japanese director Akira Kurosawa frequently used the wipe. He liked the aggressive, decisive way that it replaced one shot with the next. In *Seven Samurai,* a wipe traveling from screen right to screen left erases the shot of an old farmer and reveals a crowded town square. The wipe is visible as the hard bar or line bisecting the frame and dividing the two shots. Frame enlargement.

☐ FUNCTIONS OF EDITING

In close consultation with a film's director, an editor combines shots to create narrative and expressive effects. Let us now examine the editor's work in more specific terms. In turning a rough cut into a fine cut, the editor works to create: (1) continuity, (2) dramatic focus, (3) tempo, rhythm, mood, and (4) narration and point of view.

Continuity

Continuity is a fundamental principle of narrative filmmaking. The story, and the images used to tell it, must move along in an orderly and organized fashion. Editors join shots in ways that emphasize relationships of continuity—of orderliness—between them. If, during the course of a story, a character grows a beard, then shots must be carefully selected to establish the proper continuity of growth. In an early scene, the beard should not be longer or fuller than it appears in a later one.

Proper continuity may also apply to movement. During a chase scene, if camera positions establish that the escaping prisoner is running from screen right to left, followed by a posse hot on his trail, it will not do to change direction by editing subsequent shots with the escaping prisoner running from left to right while the posse moves from right to left. If this were to happen, it would seem as if both the prisoner

a

b

Titus (Fox Searchlight, 1999) This conversation scene composed of reverse angle shots was photographed in two different locations and a month apart. One set-up (A), showing Tamora (Jessica Lange) and Saturninus (Alan Cuming) on the stairs, was shot at Mussolini's government building in Rome. The other set-up (B), showing them with Titus (Anthony Hopkins, center background), was shot a month later at the Villa Adriana, a historical site outside of Rome. The editing joins the locations as if they were one. The continuity that editing creates may be very different from the reality of what the camera has actually photographed. Frame enlargements.

and the posse were running towards each other. These principles of continuity are a little complicated, but they are extremely important and we will cover them fully later in the chapter.

The continuity that editing creates often exists only on screen and not in the material *as it was filmed*. A dialogue scene in Julie Taymor's *Titus* (2000), for example, is composed of reverse-angle shots of two groups of characters. In the film's story, they are conversing in one location. In reality, as the scene was filmed, each reverse angle set-up was filmed in a different location, miles away from one another, and were shot a month apart. The editing joined the locations together and made them seem connected as one. Many films are made this way.

Dramatic Focus

The editor cuts the footage to find or emphasize the dramatic focus of a scene. In this respect, the editor can actually improve an actor's performance by deleting footage in which the actor may give an improper line reading or by tightening up the reaction time between shots to make the actor appear to have swifter psychological reflexes. In extreme cases, the editor may entirely reshape the film so that a secondary character becomes a major character. This happened in Woody Allen's Academy Award-winning *Annie Hall* (1977).

In Allen's initial conception and all through shooting, the character of Annie Hall was a subsidiary one. The focus was on Alvy Singer, the character played by Woody Allen, and, rather than telling a story about a relationship, the film was conceived as a loosely connected series of skits emphasizing Alvy's personality and psychological hang-ups. But the editing changed the nature and structure of the film, making Annie a major character and the movie a story of the affair between Alvy and Annie. During editing, it became apparent that the original conception for the film was not working. With Allen's approval, Rosenblum began to cut to emphasize the

Annie Hall
(United Artists, 1977)
Intensive collaboration between director Woody Allen and editor Ralph Rosenblum drastically rearranged the design of *Annie Hall*. Most significantly, Annie (Diane Keaton) became a major character and a stronger narrative emerged. Frame enlargement.

Alvy–Annie relationship. The resulting film won Academy Awards for Best Picture and Best Direction.

In finding the dramatic focus of the scene, the editor may, on occasion, create scenes that did not exist in the script or the filming but result purely from editing. *Annie Hall* furnishes another example. At the end of the film, after Alvy and Annie have broken up, the story concludes with Alvy in a reflective mood thinking back on their relationship. Editor Rosenblum put together a memory sequence in which Alvy speaks in **voice-over** about his attitudes towards relationships while the images show a series of highlights from previous episodes in Alvy and Annie's affair. The sequence was cut to music, a reprise of Annie singing "Seems Like Old Times" from an earlier scene. This concluding montage enabled the film to end in a visually creative way and one which was emotionally complex and evocative. But the montage had not been scripted; it resulted purely from the editing process.

A similar experience occurred during the editing of Francis Ford Coppola's *The Godfather* (1972). At the end of production, Coppola had to go to Sicily to film some sequences there, the last he needed to complete even though they dealt with material much earlier in the story. The script called for the film to conclude with the baptism of Michael Corleone's son followed by the assassination of Michael's enemies. While Coppola was in Sicily, editor Peter Zinner, believing the original conception to be somewhat flat, decided to create a montage in which the baptism was intercut with the assassination scenes. This sequence, conjoining the baptism with the bloody executions, is one of the most memorable and powerful montages in modern cinema, concluding the film on an exceptionally strong note.

Tempo and Mood

By varying the lengths of shots, the editor establishes rhythm, tempo, and pacing. Brief shots will produce a faster pace, while shots of longer duration typically produce a fuller, more measured pacing. The length of the shots never remains constant throughout a film. By varying their length, the editor modulates the pacing of a film. Action films today are cut at an extremely fast pace, while a historical epic like *Dances with Wolves* (1990) establishes a measured tempo with shots of longer duration.

The editor may also cut to establish appropriate moods. In a horror film, for example, the cutting can help create suspense and shock. If a character goes into a dark room where viewers know a monster is lurking, the editing might emphasize tight close-ups of the character's face. Typically, the director and cinematographer would have filmed these with the express purpose of facilitating this approach to the scene's editing. The tight close-ups prevent viewers from seeing the room and what may be lurking there. If the monster suddenly lurches into the frame, or if the editor abruptly cuts to a longer shot showing the monster just behind the character, viewers will jump with fright.

In *The Bridges of Madison County* (1995), director Clint Eastwood and editor Joel Cox purposely created a slow pace, letting shots linger on screen, in order to give the screen romance room to develop in a convincing manner and to let the lovers have ample time with one another and the viewer with these characters. The lush, full-bodied romantic tone of the film is very much a function of its editing.

Narration and Point of View

Editing permits filmmakers to control the flow of story information and point of view as it is established through changing camera positions. Editing determines the way in which a scene's story information is conveyed.

Case Study: *Rear Window*

A sequence from Alfred Hitchcock's *Rear Window,* edited by George Tomasini, demonstrates this relationship between editing, storytelling, and the control of point of view. Hitchcock designed *Rear Window* as an experiment. He wanted to restrict the physical scene and setting of the action, while maintaining dramatic interest. Most of the camera's positions are restricted to what the main character—a professional photographer with a broken leg who is confined to a wheelchair—can see from his apartment window. The photographer, Jeffries (James Stewart), begins to eavesdrop on his neighbors; from his window, he can see into the windows of their apartments across the courtyard. Jeffries comes to believe that a murder has been commited by one of his neighbors, a salesman named Thorwald (Raymond Burr). In the sequence to be examined here, Jeffries hears a mysterious scream during the night and then sees Thorwald mysteriously going in and out of his apartment carrying a large suitcase. Because this is a Hitchcock film, viewers are not surprised to learn that the contents of the suitcase turn out to be quite ghoulish. They are the dismembered pieces of Thorwald's wife.

Implying Associations between Shots.

Throughout this sequence, the editing implies associations between the shots. This is an important principle of narrative filmmaking. Each shot means what it does by virtue of its surrounding context. Hitchcock and Tomasini cut back and forth between Jeffries's face and shots of what he is meant to be seeing across the courtyard. These latter are his point-of-view shots; they simulate what he can see out his window. Hitchcock and Tomasini want viewers to interpret Jeffries's facial expressions and reactions as responses to what has occurred in the point-of-view shots. Notice, however, that Jeffries and what he sees and reacts to are never shown within the same shot. It is the editing that creates the association.

The scene opens with a pan of the courtyard from Jeffries's point of view (**a**). A scream is heard on the soundtrack but its source is not visible. The film cuts immediately to a medium shot of Jeffries's face (**b**) as he looks off-frame left, listening. Then the image fades out. The fade serves to bracket the action and to provide a punctuation point following the scream. This emphasizes the importance of the scream both for the film's plot and for Jeffries's developing fascination with Thorwald.

Shot 3 (**c**) fades in, a medium shot of Jeffries sleeping in his chair. Thunder rumbles on the soundtrack, and he wakes. Shot 4 (**d**) is a long shot of the courtyard and Thorwald's apartment. Notice the special subtlety with which Hitchcock and Tomasini are working. Nothing in the film has yet established that Thorwald is any kind of murderer or criminal. Viewers do not know who the scream belonged to or what caused it, but, on Jeffries's waking, the first image shown is a long shot of Thorwald's apartment. The editing thus focuses narrative interest on the Thorwald apartment.

a

b

c

d

The next seven shots (**e–k**) show Jeffries watching a married couple sleeping on their balcony and laughing at them when they are caught in the rain. Here, as elsewhere, the cutting alternates between the point-of-view shots and Jeffries's implied reactions. Shot 10 (**j**), for example, shows the fellow on the balcony tumbling head first into his apartment. Shot 11 (**k**) shows Jeffries laughing. Viewers make the narrative connections implied by the editing. By encouraging viewers to draw inferences across shots, the editing suggests the actor's performance. Viewers react as if James Stewart, as Jeffries, were laughing at his neighbor, even though this is not actually shown. (Nor did it exist at the time of filming. Stewart was not seeing any of the action across the courtyard. Hitchcock merely had him look off-camera and model different expressions.) This is one of the most powerful narrative effects that editing can cre-

ate. It stimulates viewers to make associations and draw interpretations and connections from material presented in separate shots.

Establishing Geographic Consistency   From shot to shot, the physical layout of the apartment complex where Jeffries lives is geographically consistent. The editing of the sequence carefully establishes this consistency.

As shot 12 (**l**) continues, Jeffries looks down, and his laughter and smile freeze. Shot 13 (**m**) shows Thorwald leaving his apartment carrying a suitcase, and then, in shot 14 (**n**), Jeffries looks off frame right at a more extreme angle than in shot 11. Shot 15 (**o**) is a long shot of the alley and the street beyond. After a beat, Thorwald appears and crosses the street. Notice how the more extreme angle at which Jeffries looks, in

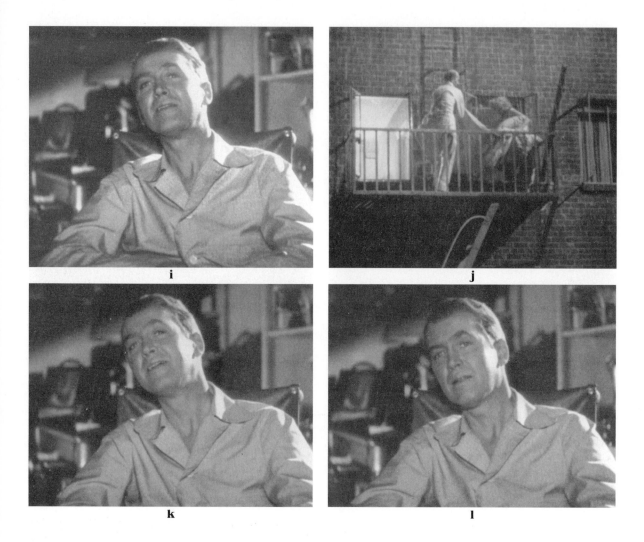

shot 14 (**n**), compared with shot 11 (**k**), serves to establish a different geographic location as seen by Jeffries—the alley and the street beyond it. These are positioned beside the edge of the building containing Thorwald's apartment.

In keeping with the principle just discussed—the way that editing cues the viewer to make associations and draw interpretations across the cut—the extreme angle change of Jeffries's glance in shot 14 (**n**) provides a cue for the viewer to assemble the geographic layout of the apartment's courtyard, Thorwald's building, and the street in relation to one another. In each of Jeffries's reaction shots, Hitchcock has carefully coordinated the angles at which he glances, relative to the camera, with the implied positioning of objects and characters across the courtyard. The relationship between the angles of Jeffries's glances and the physical positions of objects across the courtyard is so carefully and systematically worked out that the powerful illusion emerges in *Rear Window* that Jeffries is a spectator in front of his apartment window

watching a coherent and stable world outside that window. Using the angles of Jeffries's glances, viewers can anticipate the objects or characters at which it is implied he is looking.

As the sequence continues, from shots 16–32 (**p–ff**), Jeffries continues to watch Thorwald come and go, carrying his suitcase, and the activities of his other neighbors. The coordination of Jeffries's angled glances with the views outside his window, and the repetition of previously established compositions and locales (shot pairs 14 and 31 [**n** and **ee**], 15 and 32 [**o** and **ff**], for example) reinforces the viewer's impression that the partial views of the apartment complex are part of a coherent and extended physical landscape. Viewers construct a general impression of the entire landscape—the courtyard and its apartment buildings—from the fragmentary close-ups that the editing presents. Viewers thus go beyond the information in the individual shots to build a larger mental image of the courtyard into which the locale shown in each individual shot can be integrated.

w

x

y

z

aa

bb

cc

dd

ee

ff

Schemas   Perceptual psychologists refer to such a comprehensive mental image as a **schema,** a framework that helps organize new information by specifying where that information is likely to fit within an established structure or pattern. The structure here is the physical layout of Jeffries's apartment complex, about which viewers have formed a composite mental image based on the projective geometry—the matching of Jeffries's angled glances with particular views of the courtyard—established by individual shots. By facilitating the viewer's creation of schemas pertaining to the layout of settings and locales, editing performs a powerful narrative function. It enables the viewer to form the impression of a coherent and stable physical world on-screen, independent of changes in the camera's angle of view from shot to shot. This is a very important point. By facilitating the viewer's ability to link shots together into meaningful patterns, and to infer larger relationships from the content of individual shots, editing helps the viewer connect and relate story information in ways that are essential for narrative comprehension.

Altering the Pattern of Narrative Disclosure   The next shots in the sequence maintain the pattern of narrative disclosure established thus far by the editing. Jeffries continues to watch Thorwald, Thorwald's apartment, and other neighbors, as the editing alternates, very precisely, between shots of Jeffries looking off-frame and shots that represent what he sees across the courtyard. No shot includes both Jeffries and what he sees across the courtyard. At the end of the sequence, however, Hitchcock and Tomasini change their pattern of narrative disclosure. The final shot of the sequence fades in, a close-up of Jeffries asleep in his chair. It is dawn, and the camera pans away from Jeffries, out his window, and across the courtyard to Thorwald's apartment where the viewer sees Thorwald leaving with a woman. The camera then pans left, back across the courtyard to Jeffries, who the viewer realizes is still asleep. The image fades out, and the sequence ends.

Hitchcock established a specific point-of-view structure—alternating in separate shots between Jeffries's implied views across the courtyard and his reactions—only to change this structure at the conclusion of the sequence by showing, in a single shot, a view of Jeffries and the events across the courtyard. In this last shot, viewers are given information that Jeffries does not have, the only time in the film that this happens. Viewers see Thorwald leaving the apartment with a woman. It could be his wife, and Jeffries could be wrong about a murder. This information undermines the viewer's desire to trust Jeffries's judgments and emphasizes the moral problem of Jeffries's rear window, peeping Tom behavior. Jeffries becomes increasingly convinced that Thorwald has killed his wife, but viewers cannot be so sure. Hitchcock emphasizes this information and the doubts it generates by bracketing the last part of the sequence with a fade and by changing the visual design. By using the panning camera movement—showing Jeffries asleep at the beginning and at the end of the shot—Hitchcock clearly establishes that Jeffries does not see what viewers have just seen.

The editing carefully regulates the flow of story information and point of view. The mood, tempo, dramatic focus, and continuity of the sequence are exceptionally strong. The sequence has no dialogue, and Hitchcock was especially proud of its purely visual design. He relied on the viewer's tendency to infer associated meanings between adjacent shots. He also relied on the viewer's ability to infer a comprehensive landscape from isolated details. He relied, in other words, on two essential narrative functions that editing performs.

Parallel Action

To tell sophisticated stories, filmmakers need a way of suggesting (simultaneous) parallel action, that is, that two or more things are happening at the same time. This enables them to weave together several lines of action in the telling of their story. **Parallel action** is achieved through editing. The sequence just examined from *Rear Window* manipulates multiple lines of action: Thorwald's trips to and from his apartment, the arrival home of the composer, the return home of Miss Torso, the comical response of the couple sleeping on their balcony in the rain, and Jeffries's surveillance of all this and his reactions to it. The editing references each of these lines of action to the others by establishing relationships of time and location. Without the use of parallel

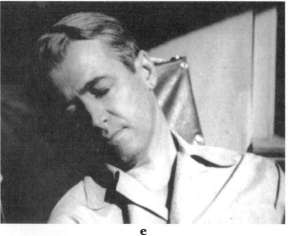

In this extended panning shot, Hitchcock shows viewers that Jeffries cannot possibly see Thorwald leaving with a woman who may be his wife (**c**). Frame enlargements.

editing, that is, editing that interrelates multiple lines of action, filmmakers could not create complex narratives involving the actions of numerous characters, story lines, and subplots.

One especially important form of parallel action is **cross-cutting.** In cross-cutting, the editor goes back and forth, typically with increasing speed, between two or more lines of action. *The Fugitive* (1993) opens with a spectacular train wreck during which the fugitive (Harrison Ford) escapes from his jailers. The cross-cutting goes back and forth with increasing speed between shots of the oncoming train and the frenzied, panicked reactions of prisoners trapped inside a bus that has fallen across the tracks. By cross-cutting shots of increasingly shorter duration, the editor creates an accelerating tempo and speed and an increasing amount of tension.

Among the inferences viewers routinely draw across cuts are inferences of simultaneous action. The cross-cut shots of the train and the frantic prisoners prompt the viewer to make an unambiguous interpretation: The train is about to smash the bus. Filmmakers guide viewers in drawing these inferences by composing and editing shots to create a strong flow of action across the cuts. How is this accomplished?

THE PRINCIPLES OF CONTINUITY EDITING

As its name implies, **continuity editing** is a style of cutting that emphasizes smooth and continuously flowing action from shot to shot. Instead of noticing the abruptness of a cut in a popular movie, the viewer pays attention to story information and character relationships. Shots are joined so that the action flows smoothly over the cut. The remarkable achievements of the continuity editing system are sometimes disparaged in discussions that describe the style as "transparent" or "invisible." In reality, continuity editing is a highly constructed and accomplished style that creates an impression of realism and naturalism from carefully applied editing rules.

A Continuous Flow of Action

The goal of continuity editing is to emphasize the apparent realism and naturalness of the story and to minimize the viewer's awareness of film technique and the presence of the camera. The remarkable achievement of continuity cutting lies in successfully meeting this goal. When viewers see a popular commercial film in the theater, they rarely notice details of camera position and movement. Instead, they are swept up by the story and the characters. There is a major paradox here. As viewers watch a movie, they see a rapid succession of individual shots on screen accompanied by an ever-changing series of camera positions and angles. What they *see*, therefore, is fragmentary and discontinuous. A film is assembled from hundreds of individual shots. Its structure is inherently fragmentary. What viewers *experience,* however, is the impression of a smoothly flowing, unbroken stream of imagery in which the story and the characters come convincingly to life. How is this apparent contradiction between the reality of what viewers see and the impression of what they experience explained?

The answer is that filmmakers have discovered methods of connecting their shots that minimize the disruption of shot changes. In other words, continuity editing makes possible the impression of narrative wholeness and completeness. Continuity editing has also helped make cinema very popular because it can be so easily understood. Films edited according to these principles do not pose difficult perceptual or interpretive challenges. Films can be edited so they will be easy to understand and will therefore appeal to wide segments of the market.

Here lie the true achievements of the continuity system. The system emphasizes visual coherence and ease of comprehension. These are things that must be created in film. Because of the camera's ever-changing angle of view, the potential in film for incoherence and discontinuity is always much greater, and filmmakers accordingly have to strive very hard to achieve the opposite.

Case Study: *Casablanca*

The Hollywood classic *Casablanca* (1942) provides some representative sequences that display continuity editing codes in action. Among the most important codes of the continuity system are the following: The use of a master shot to organize the subsequent cutting within a scene, matching shots to the master, the shot-reverse-shot series with the eyeline match, and the 180-degree rule.

Casablanca is a wartime adventure film about heroic resistance against the Nazis, and it is also a lush romantic melodrama. Rick (Humphrey Bogart), a nightclub owner, has come to Casablanca to get over a disastrous love affair with Ilsa Lund (Ingrid Bergman). Ilsa turns up unexpectedly one night in Rick's cafe and sets in motion the romantic fireworks that move the plot along to its exciting conclusion.

Matching to the Master Shot   In the first scene illustrated here, one of the attendants in Rick's nightclub awaits Rick's approval before admitting some customers into the room where roulette and gambling occur. Rick is filmed from behind, in the foreground, and the door to his casino is visible in the background of the shot (**a**). This shot functions as the master shot position for this scene. The **master shot** shows the spatial layout of a scene, all of the characters' positions in relation to each other and to the set. The master shot is typically filmed first, with all of the action in a scene from beginning

a

b

c

d

e

f

to end photographed from this position. Then directors typically go back to film inserts, close-ups, and medium shots that will be cut with the master shot to create the final edited scene and whose compositional elements will match with the master.

Rick sees the doorman pausing in the entrance with several guests, awaiting his approval to enter the casino. Shot 2 (**b**) is an example of a **matched cut.** The two compositions—the master shot and the medium close-up of the doorman and guests— match. The camera's angle of view is similar in each shot. The only difference is that the camera is closer to the characters in shot 2 (**b**). A second matching element is the positioning of the doorman and guests. They are oriented toward screen left, a sim- ilar position in both shots. The match here is so strong that a casual viewer does not notice the cut.

The Eyeline Match   The doorman glances off-frame left (**c**) (implying that he is look- ing at Rick, who is off-screen), and the film cuts to Rick, in shot 4 (**d**), looking off- frame right. Each looks in an opposing direction, one to the right, the other to the

g

h

i

left, creating the impression that they are looking at each other. This match is known as the **eyeline match,** and it is an important code used to link the spaces in separate shots. The eyeline match establishes that two characters are indeed looking at each other and that the spaces they inhabit, though seen in different shots, are connected. Often in a scene, characters are interacting with each other but are presented in separate shots. The eyeline match helps create continuity between the separate images.

In organizing the cut to shot 4, the master shot remains important. What else, besides the eyeline match, establishes that these characters are looking at each other? It is the information viewers remember from the master shot about the spatial layout of the room. From the master shot, viewers know there is a direct line of sight from Rick's table to the door and that Rick and the doorman have an unobstructed view of each other. The angles of their glances in shots 3 and 4 (**c, d**) match the information viewers were given in the master shot.

The Master Shot and Viewer Perception   As viewers watch a movie, they are responding to more than the information that is on-screen at any one moment. Viewers interpret shots by relating them to the larger context of an edited scene. In this regard, the master shot furnishes viewers with a map or visual schema of the set or locale (a room in this scene from *Casablanca*). Using this schema, viewers integrate fragmentary details, like the composition of shot (**b**), with their recollected sense of the layout of the room. Using master shots facilitates a viewer's understanding of the action of a scene.

The Shot-Reverse-Shot Series   In shot 5, a Nazi supporter tries to enter Rick's casino (**e**). In shot 6 (**f**), the doorman and the German talk outside the room, where Rick shortly joins them in shot 7 (**g**). The cutting now goes into a brief **shot-reverse-shot series** (**g, h, i**) as Rick and the German exchange words. The camera is positioned over the shoulder of one character and then, in the reverse shot position, over the shoulder of the other character. This series of alternating compositions is a standard method for filming dialogue scenes. It creates something of a ping-pong effect as the composition continually shifts into reverse shot positions. The cutting is typically coordinated with the flow of dialogue so that, as speakers change, so does the camera position. Should the camera shift into an extreme close-up isolating each character in a single shot, the eyeline match would be employed. In shot-reverse-shot cutting, editing follows the flow of dialogue, and the shifting camera positions mark the changes of speakers in the conversation. This emphasizes the dialogue and facilitates the viewer's pickup of story information.

The 180-Degree Rule   The **180-degree rule** is one of the most important codes of the continuity system. This rule is the foundation for establishing continuity of screen direction. The right–left coordinates of screen action remain consistent as long as all

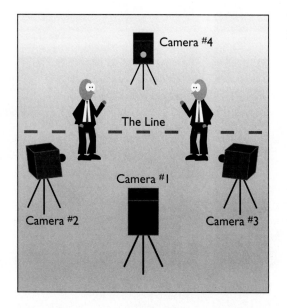

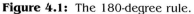

Figure 4.1: The 180-degree rule.

camera positions stay on the same side of the line of action. Crossing the line entails a change of screen direction.

Because filmmakers change camera positions and angles from shot to shot, screen direction is something that must be carefully established and maintained. Right and left must remain constant across shot changes, but the potential for creating inconsistent right and left orientations from shot to shot is very great. The 180-degree rule specifies how this may be prevented.

Within any given scene, a line of interest or action can be drawn between the major characters. The 180-degree rule councils filmmakers to keep their cameras on one side of this line from shot to shot within a scene. If a filmmaker were to cross the line by cutting to a camera position taken on the other side of the line, the right–left coordinates on screen would be reversed. Characters who were on screen right in one shot would appear on screen left in the next.

j   k

l   m

The 180-degree rule operates in the next scene in the film (**j–m**). Ugarte (Peter Lorre) comes into the casino to tell Rick that he has some "letters of transit" that guarantee their bearer safe passage from Casablanca, and he asks Rick to keep them for him. As Ugarte talks to Rick, they are seated at the table. The line of interest extends between them. Notice that the camera stays on the same side of the line in all of the subsequent shots (**k–m**). When both characters are in the shot, Ugarte is always on screen right and Rick is always on screen left despite the changing camera positions. When a close-up isolates Rick, he is facing screen right, consistent with his position in the two-shot.

Notice also that the line of interest is consistent with the line of interest established in the previous scene with the doorman and guests. Rick sits at his table in both scenes, and the camera positioning has kept Rick on screen left. In this sense, visual continuity has been maintained from scene to scene because a consistent line of interest is used as the basis of the 180-degree rule.

Scenes are dynamic, however, and filmmakers frequently need to define new lines of action to follow changes of character positioning as the drama unfolds. How does a filmmaker define a new line of action by crossing the existing one? There are several possible ways. A filmmaker may cut first to a series of camera positions on or near the line before crossing it. A filmmaker may use a moving camera to cross the line within a shot. Whatever strategy is employed, the problems associated with maintaining or crossing the line raise issues about the relationship between visual change and perceptual constancy in the represented action on screen.

Camera Position and Perceptual Constancies   Filmmakers typically provide viewers with continuously changing visual perspectives on the action. They build a scene by cutting among different camera set-ups. The problem is how to create this variety without confusing and disorienting the viewer, particularly when it is important to establish a coherent sense of a fixed visual landscape. The viewer must understand that, though the camera's angle of view may change, the layout of the physical world on-screen remains constant. In other words, if a character is shown standing at the bottom of a hill, the character must seem to remain there, unless shown moving elsewhere, regardless of whether a high-angle or a low-angle shot is employed, regardless of whether the camera photographs that character from the left or right side. The camera's relative positions, which change as the action unfolds on screen, are distinct from the perceptual constancies (e.g., up, down, left, right) that must prevail, that must not change, in the represented action. The sheriff pursuing the prisoner must always be understood to be chasing his quarry regardless of the directions in which pursuer and pursued are shown moving on screen.

This relationship between the editing codes pertaining to screen direction and the constancies of the physical world that is represented on screen can be demonstrated with an example from *Out of Africa* (1985). Karen Blixen (Meryl Streep) arrives in Kenya and rides by coach from the train station to meet her new husband. During the shots that show her riding in the coach, screen direction is reversed. The reversal, though, occurs in a way that is consistent with principles of continuity.

The first shot (**a**) showing Blixen travelling by coach is a telephoto long shot in which she appears, through crowds of pedestrians, riding toward screen left. The

Out of Africa (Universal, 1985)

In *Out of Africa*, continuity of movement is maintained despite a change in its right–left orientation. The shot (**b**) of Karen Blixen (Meryl Streep) riding toward the camera erases the right–left coordinates established in (**a**) and provides the transition necessary for maintaining continuity across the change (**a** and **c**) in screen direction. Note also the motion blur produced by the panning camera in the first and last shots of the series. Because the camera is panning with the coach's movement, stationary pedestrians and buildings are subject to motion blur. Frame enlargements.

filmmakers then cut to a new camera position framing her as she rides directly toward the camera. Consequently, this new framing (**b**), which is on the line of action (motion) established in the previous shot, erases the right–left coordinates. In this shot, movement occurs toward the camera, not to the right or left.

The next shot (**c**) shows Blixen riding toward screen right and represents a reversal of screen direction relative to the first shot (**a**). The editing, however, softens the abruptness of the reversal by using the intervening shot in which she rides directly toward the camera. By establishing a dominant line of action and then cutting to a camera position on the line, filmmakers can subsequently cross it and define a new line.

This method preserves screen continuity perfectly. Directional change occurs gradually, and the viewer understands that the layout of the physical world on-screen has remained constant, despite changes in the camera's angle of view and the direction of motion on-screen.

Errors of Continuity

Filmmakers never achieve perfect continuity, and viewers with sharp eyes can often spot errors. **Errors of continuity** are mismatched details in a series of shots. The vanishing water jug in the shots from *The Waterboy* (1998) is an especially flagrant example.

Continuity errors arise because moviemaking proceeds on a shot-by-shot basis, with everything, from character positions and costumes to lights and props, re-created for each new shot. The possibilities of flubbing these re-creations, of mismatching their details, are enormous. The conditions of film production make it difficult for filmmakers to avoid such errors. Take, for example, Kevin Costner's *Robin Hood: Prince of Thieves* (1991). When Robin (Costner) and Azeem (Morgan Freeman) land on the shores of England, Azeem helps Robin up from the beach. In medium close-up, Robin holds out his right arm for assistance, and in the following shot viewers see Azeem helping Robin up by grasping his left arm.

The error arose because the action had to be created separately for each shot and was done so without the proper matching continuity. In such cases, the editor's best hope is that the viewer will not notice the discrepancy, and, indeed, if the gaff is not glaring, viewers often fail to notice because they are busy following the story.

Continuity errors can develop when portions of a scene are shot at widely spaced intervals. For example, in *Cocktail* (1988), Tom Cruise passes a New York theater whose marquee advertises the film *Barfly* and then, a few minutes later, when he passes that theater again, the marquee advertises *Casablanca*. As many readers know, some films have abundant continuity problems. In *Pretty Woman* (1990), continuity errors ranged from scenes in which Richard Gere's tie appears and disappears from shot to shot to other scenes in which his shoes and socks do the same thing, and still others in which Julia Roberts takes a bite at breakfast from what is alternately a pancake and a croissant.

The Waterboy (Touchstone, 1998)
The disappearing water jug—now you see it, now you don't. A brief cutaway to the face of another character separates these two shots of Adam Sandler. In the second shot, the water jug is conspicuously missing. This is a relatively glaring continuity error. Frame enlargements.

Facilitating the Viewer's Response

The editing codes just reviewed—cutting to match the master shot, the use of the 180-degree rule, the shot-reverse-shot series, and the eyeline match—are cornerstones of the continuity system. The system emphasizes naturalism and realism to the extent that it minimizes the amount of perceptual work that the viewer needs to do. This work is minimized because the positioning of characters, the direction of their movement, and the camera's angles of view are related across shots in an orderly way. This enables the perspective of each shot to link up with the perspectives in other shots, establishing for the viewer the sense of a unified landscape stretching across all of the shots, of which each offers only a partial view.

Think of film viewing as a an activity like a picture puzzle in which the overall picture—Rick's casino or Jeffries's apartment complex—emerges when all the little pieces have been fit together. Each piece is a shot, and, if they fit properly, the viewer sees the overall picture and not the pieces, just as with a puzzle. In this way, continuity editing helps make the visual perspectives of each shot easy to interpret and movies themselves very easy to understand.

Continuity editing codes are so successful at simplifying the viewer's perceptual task that they can actually facilitate the comprehension of story information. Ample experimental evidence indicates that viewers understand story information more easily when continuity editing is used than when it is not. Rather than interfering with normal perception, continuity editing facilitates it. As a result, it makes films more accessible and attractive for diverse audiences whose educational and cultural backgrounds vary. To the extent that continuity editing poses few interpretational problems for viewers, it has helped establish the enormous popular acceptance and emotional appeal of motion pictures.

Subverting Continuity Editing

Case Study: *The Silence of the Lambs*

Because audiences are so familiar with continuity editing, clever filmmakers can fool viewers by applying its rules in a misleading way. An especially brilliant example of this occurs in *The Silence of the Lambs* (1991). FBI agents encircle a house in Calumet City, believing it to be the lair of serial killer Buffalo Bill. This action is intercut with shots of Bill in his basement tormenting one of his victims. Outside, an agent is sent to ring the doorbell. Other agents crouch nearby, hidden in the bushes. When Bill opens his door, however, viewers are startled and frightened to find not an FBI swat team but lone agent Clarice Starling (Jodie Foster), unaware that she is face-to-face with Buffalo Bill. Meanwhile, the swat team breaks into an empty house. It turns out that the viewer is seeing two different locations. How did the filmmakers trick viewers and spring this surprise on them?

The sequence opens with an establishing shot of the Calumet City house (**a**). FBI agents swarm the property and hide. Extensive intercutting joins this action with shots of Bill in his basement. Outside, one agent, disguised as a man delivering flowers, approaches the front door and rings the bell (**b**). The next shot shows a bell ringing in Bill's basement (**c**) and Buffalo Bill listening with annoyance (**d**). When the bell

stops ringing, the next shot (**e**) shows the FBI agent taking his finger off the doorbell outside. The shot series implies continuity of action and place, and the viewer concludes that the Calumet City house is, indeed, Bill's lair.

The agent rings the bell again, followed by shots of Bill listening. Bill goes upstairs to answer his door, and the action cuts to an exterior view of the Calumet City house as the agents decide they will have to break in. In the next moment, Bill opens his door to reveal Clarice (**f**), alone and unsuspecting. In shock, viewers realize that they have been misled, that the Calumet City house is not occupied by Bill. The sequence ends with an establishing shot of the real house where Bill lives.

The cross-cutting of the FBI's maneuvers with Bill's activities in his basement prompts the viewer to make a correct assumption of *temporal continuity* (the sequence of events is properly chronological, with no distortions of time) but a false assumption of *spatial contiguity* (that the locales shown in the cross-cut shots are connected). The deception depends on the viewer's familiarity with parallel editing, conventionally used to establish linkages of time and/or place among several lines of action. It depends also on using matching sound and visual elements to make the viewer infer continuity of action. The agent rings the bell, the viewer sees it ring and Bill react. The viewer cannot know from the editing that these are two separate bells and different locations.

When Bill opens his door to reveal Clarice, viewers realize with shock that their schema of time–space relations, constructed by the editing, is wrong. Clarice's situation gives the shock its emotional power. A character for whom the viewer cares deeply, she is now in mortal danger.

◻ ALTERNATIVES TO CONTINUITY EDITING

Although it predominates in popular cinema, continuity editing is not the only method of editing used by filmmakers. Several alternatives exist, some of which disrupt continuities of time and space to varying degrees. Filmmakers often seek to create vivid stylistic effects by breaking from the naturalistic rendering of time and space that continuity editing provides. To do this, they commonly employ jump-cutting and/or montage.

Jump Cuts

This type of editing produces abrupt breaks in the continuity of action by omitting portions of an ongoing action. Imagine that an editor is examining a strip of film that contains one shot showing a woman walking across a room and opening a door. If the editor removes several frames from the middle of that shot, it will produce a break in the action, which will seem to jump over the interval of missing frames. The editor has created a **jump cut.**

Inspired by the use of jump-cutting in such French films as *Breathless* (1959), U.S. filmmakers in the late 1960s and early 1970s experimented with the technique in *Easy Rider* (1969) and *Bonnie and Clyde* (1967), which was edited by Dede Allen. She has reported that the film's director, Arthur Penn, kept telling her to make the story go faster, and, to do this, she used jump-cutting to omit portions of the action and speed things along. The first scene of the film shows Bonnie (Faye Dunaway) in her bedroom. She paces restlessly about the room and lies down on the bed. Allen cuts from a shot of Bonnie walking over to her bed with her back to the camera to a shot in which Bonnie faces the camera and is already reclining on the bed. The cut between these two shots produces a jump, or discontinuity, in both her orientation relative to the camera and her position on the bed. This tiny break in the action creates a small acceleration in time, propelling the story forward a bit faster than standard continuity editing could accomplish.

The editors of *Easy Rider* used jump-cutting extensively to give many scenes a rough and jagged rhythm. In addition to jump-cutting, they employed a very unusual method of scene transition. Instead of using a dissolve, a fade, or a cut, they employed a unique technique that can best be described as flash cross-cutting. Cross-cutting is

Bonnie and Clyde (Warner Bros., 1967)
This jump cut shows Bonnie standing and looking down at her bed, then reclining on the bed. The intervening action is omitted. The result for the viewer is a brief moment of perceptual disorientation. Frame enlargements.

typically used within a scene to reference and compare two or more lines of action. As used in *Easy Rider,* flash cross-cutting is a method of scene transition in which the last shot of the first scene and the first shot of the next scene are intercut very rapidly. The viewer oscillates rapidly, back and forth, between the end of one scene and the beginning of the next.

Flash cross-cutting is a unique method of scene transition which, like the jump cut, produces a very noticeable break in continuity. These techniques disrupt the smooth flow of action and call attention to themselves as visual devices. While flash cross-cutting is a rarely employed device, jump-cutting is a standardly employed method of producing discontinuity. It tends to be used, however, within scenes that have been constructed according to overall continuity principles. The contrast with these makes the jump cut vivid and effective.

Montage

Montage editing builds a scene out of many brief shots, each of which typically presents a fragmentary view of action and locale. The shots are often edited to a very rapid pace, subjecting the viewer to a barrage of visual information. With each shot offering an incomplete view, the total picture of the event emerges from the montage as a whole. Montage editing is typically used (1) to fragment time and space and (2) to visually embody thematic or intellectual ideas.

The Soviet Montage Tradition

Soviet filmmakers in the 1920s first practiced this method of editing, and the most famous of these filmmakers is Sergei Eisenstein. Eisenstein was very familiar with the continuity editing of U.S. pictures, particularly the work of D. W. Griffith (*The Birth*

ARTHUR PENN

Along with Sam Peckinpah, Arthur Penn is one of the great poets of screen violence. Unlike Peckinpah, though, who treated violence as an essential and instinctual component of human behavior, Penn places violent behavior within a clear social context and uses it to illuminate the political atmosphere of an era. *The Chase* (1966) presciently treats the United States as a gun culture and studies its festering climate of violence. In its horrific climax, the town sheriff (Marlon Brando) is savagely beaten and cannot prevent the public assassination of a small-time criminal under police custody. Here, as elsewhere in Penn's films, the killing of John F. Kennedy provides the model and resonant reference point for explorations of U.S. social violence.

Penn trained as a television director and debuted as a feature filmmaker with an unusually psychological Western, *The Left-Handed Gun* (1958). *Mickey One* (1965) was a European-style, existential art film whose unconventional visual style and ambitious story were too far ahead of U.S. film culture when it was released. Penn applied the style of the French New Wave, primarily jump cuts and other unconventional edits and optical effects, to a mainstream U.S. film

Bonnie and Clyde (Warner Bros, 1967)
The slow-motion, bloody deaths of Bonnie and Clyde changed American cinema forever. Penn's gut-wrenching images established a new threshold of brutality on film, yet they seem almost tame by today's standards. Unlike later filmmakers interested in gore for its own sake, Penn used violence as a way of exploring the cultural climate of violence in American society. Frame enlargement.

of a Nation, 1915; *Intolerance,* 1916), who used it with great sophistication. *Intolerance,* for example, in telling four stories simultaneously, represents the pinnacle of parallel editing and cross-cutting. Eisenstein resolved to break with continuity principles, and he developed a montage style based on the creation of visual conflict between and among shots. His motivation was a sociopolitical one. As a Marxist, he believed that conflict was the essence of history, society, and art. In *Battleship Potemkin* (1925), *October* (1928), and other films, Eisenstein's elaborate montages created conflicts of movement, rhythm, tone, lighting, and graphical properties among the shots. In many scenes, the editing has a harsh and jagged quality, as Eisenstein pushes these conflicting visual elements to the limit.

The huge and extended massacre of civilians by Czarist troops in *Battleship Potemkin* is the most famous and influential example of Eisensteinian montage. Eisenstein's editing fragments space and time by fracturing it into a multitude of brief shots

with *Bonnie and Clyde* (1967), an important work of modern cinema. Using slow motion and multicamera filming for its scenes of violence, audaciously mixing high comedy and brutal violence, Penn's film captured the rebellious spirit of the times with its unconventional style and countercultural portrayal of Bonnie and Clyde as youthful heroes taking on the establishment. *Alice's Restaurant* (1969) and *Little Big Man* (1970) quickly followed, essential documents of late 1960s film and society.

Penn faltered in the 1970s. With the eclipse of the social idealism and political excitement of the 1960s, and with Watergate the dominant metaphor of social corruption in the next decade, Penn was disillusioned and cut off from the social ferment that nourished his films. However, he managed a stunning artistic expression of a bleak cultural period. *Night Moves* (1975), a detective film, brilliantly captures the national darkness, despair, and confusion experienced in the wake of the assassinations of John and Bobby Kennedy and Martin Luther King, Jr. and the collapse of the 1960s' social movements. It is, perhaps, Penn's best film.

Following *The Missouri Breaks* (1976), a big budget Western teaming Brando with Jack Nicholson and widely regarded as a failure, Penn worked infrequently and without commercial impact. *Four Friends* (1981) was barely released, *Target* (1985) was an efficient demonstration of Penn's ability to make a plot-driven thriller, and *Dead of Winter* (1987) was an effective, if cold-blooded, psychological chiller that Penn directed as a favor to friends who would have otherwise been unable to get their script produced.

Penn's checkered film career demonstrates the essential interconnection of film and society. Penn thrived during a period of social turbulence when the film industry welcomed innovative, cutting-edge work and when he could connect his artistic visions to the political dramas unfolding around him. Disillusioned with the 1970s and disappointed with the special-effects-driven blockbuster fantasies that dominated U.S. film from the latter half of that decade, Penn simply stopped working in films, except on an irregular basis, and has turned his energies to a deepening involvement with the New York-based Actor's Studio. But Penn remains hopeful that the industry may again welcome his kind of film.

that violate continuity principles. Actions are repeated, omitted, viewed simultaneously from multiple angles, slowed down, speeded up, and have their screen direction abruptly reversed. The editing is as violent as the drama that it visualizes. In this sequence and elsewhere, Eisenstein showed other filmmakers the power of montage as a tool for fragmenting time and space and, in this regard, it has been profoundly influential.

Eisenstein also practiced what he termed "intellectual montage," using the editing to suggest ideas and guide the viewer's thought process. The massacre sequence in *Battleship Potemkin* concludes with a vivid example of intellectual montage. To defend the massacre victims, a battleship fires its guns at the headquarters of Czarist troops. As their palace explodes, Eisenstein cuts together three quick shots of different statues of lions. The first stone lion sleeps, the second sits upright, the third roars. The montage, however, makes it look like a single, sleeping lion has awakened with

a

b

c

Battleship Potemkin (1925)
Eisenstein's thematic montage creates a symbol for
the people's revolution. Three separate statues of
lions, skillfully edited, become a single lion, roused
from its slumbers and roaring its defiance. Because
the shots are so brief, the editing imparts a sense of
movement to the statuary. Frame enlargements.

fury. The symbolic idea is that the wrath of the people against the Czar is now aroused;
the lion of revolution stalks the land.

We turn now to contemporary examples of these categories of montage.

Spatial Fragmentation

Montage editing used to create spatial fragmentation tends to forgo the use of a clear
master shot, the matching of action to that master shot, and the systematic repetition
of familiar camera set-ups. *Moulin Rouge,* for example, breaks almost all of the rules of
continuity in its editing. Eyelines, camera angles, and object positioning fail to match
from shot to shot. The cutting is so quick, though, that the viewer has little time to
concentrate on these continuity problems. Viewers probably notice them subliminally,
however, because the editing does feel wild and jagged, not smooth and flowing.

During the dance scenes in the Moulin Rouge, the editing fragments the club's
spatial layout by showering the viewer with visual information at a fast rate and by
showing many, many close-ups and few master shots. The club is a dizzying montage

offering glimpses of people, lights, signs, and faces. Editor Jill Bilcock said that her experience constructing the scenes out of so many close-ups was "like being given thousands of different kinds of colored beads and asked to make a necklace."

The editing builds the scene by accumulating details, bits and pieces of space and action. The editing aims to create a collage of discrete visual impressions rather than a spatially ordered, coherent, and stable environment. The scene is organized by a cumulative principle—the piling up of detail.

While the montage cutting of contemporary films descends from the Soviet model of editing, there are other clear historical precedents. In Alfred Hitchcock's *Psycho* (1960), the film's main character, Marion Crane (Janet Leigh), is murdered in her shower one third of the way into the film. The murder itself lasts for 40 seconds and is composed of 34 shots. These tend to fall into three categories: (1) shots of Marion struggling with her attacker, holding the killer's knife arm with her hand, (2) shots of Marion's face and hands as she writhes in the shower, and (3) shots of the killer stabbing towards the camera. By rapidly intercutting these categories of shots, Hitchcock and editor George Tomasini create a scene of extraordinary violence, but one in which most of the actual violence is suggested because viewers almost never see the knife actually touching flesh. The impression of the murder is built up in the mind's eye by virtue of the rapid editing.

As Eisenstein showed, montage can fragment space *and* time, and contemporary filmmakers have used editing in vivid ways to fracture space and distort time. In Sam Peckinpah's *The Wild Bunch* (1969), montage editing slowed action down, interrupted it with cutaways to parallel lines of action, and intercut normal speed and slow-motion footage to create stylish distortions of time and space. During the elaborate gun battle that opens the film, two snipers are shot from their rooftop perch. One man falls

---

Psycho (Paramount, 1960)
Rapid montage editing creates the sensation of a violent murder in *Psycho* by assembling flash cuts of murderer and victim. The violent pace of the editing intensifies the brutal nature of the scene. Frame enlargements.

The Wild Bunch (Warner Bros., 1969)
Two rooftop victims, two different film speeds, and the simultaneous resolution of these
lines of action. The editing reconfigures space and time. Frame enlargements.

from the roof to the ground in slow motion; the other falls forward and into the
rooftop ledge at normal speed. The editing intercuts these different time frames to
establish an impossible parallel. The man who falls off the roof—travelling a much
greater distance and in slow motion—strikes the ground at the same instant that the
other victim hits the ledge. The viewer accepts these manipulations as permissible
stylistic organizations of the action, despite their evident unreality.

Thematic Montage

Like Eisenstein, filmmakers may use montage to create ideas in the mind of the viewer.
The arrangement of shots cues intellectual, and sometimes emotional, associations by
the viewer. In *Strike* (1924), Eisenstein wants to convey the brutality of the Czarist
government's decision to use troops to put down a workers' strike, and he cuts from
shots of the troops attacking the workers to images of a cow being butchered in a
slaughterhouse.

Modern Times (United Artists, 1936)
Associational editing invites viewers to draw intellectual connections among images. Chaplin
compares factory workers and sheep at the beginning of *Modern Times*. Frame enlargements.

SAM PECKINPAH

Peckinpah's films are widely identified with the explicit screen violence that they helped popularize, but his handling of violence is remarkably complex and ambiguous. Peckinpah stylized screen violence through slow motion and montage editing to give it a seductive aesthetic beauty while simultaneously emphasizing its physical brutality and moral and emotional horror. As a result, viewers are caught in a disquieting push–pull dynamic, alternately drawn to and repulsed by Peckinpah's imagery.

Ride the High Country (1962), Peckinpah's second feature, was a classically beautiful Western emphasizing an old-fashioned, straightforward heroism that would never again appear in his increasingly ironic and cynical films. His breakthrough film, *The Wild Bunch* (1969), used montage editing of a complexity unprecedented in U.S. cinema to portray the spectacularly violent end of a band of Western outlaws. The film's extreme violence made it wildly controversial and established Peckinpah as an authentically roguish voice in the U.S. cinema and the most important director of Westerns after John Ford (*Stagecoach*, 1939; *Fort Apache*, 1948; *The Searchers*, 1956).

In the next five years, sustained by the social ferment of the late 1960s, Peckinpah embarked on a brief but highly productive and influential period of filmmaking. He alternated between ultraviolent explorations of male brutality and corruption (*Straw Dogs*, 1971; *Bring Me the Head of Alfredo Garcia*, 1974) and gentle, funny, melancholy portraits of losers and outsiders in a vanishing West (*The Ballad of Cable Hogue*, 1970; *Junior Bonner*, 1972).

Pat Garrett and Billy the Kid (1973) was an elegiac retelling of the legend and a meditation on the passing of the West. MGM recut the film against Peckinpah's wishes, deleting key sequences. Peckinpah had always had a tempestuous relationship with studio executives, but this was the beginning of the end for him. He made one more outstanding film (the weird *Alfredo Garcia*) and was then finished as a creative voice in the cinema.

His few subsequent films—*The Killer Elite* (1975), *Cross of Iron* (1977), *Convoy* (1978), *The Osterman Weekend* (1983)—are incoherent embarrassments that show all too clearly Peckinpah's rapid and sad decline. Crippled by personal demons and paralyzed by a cynical disdain for modern corporate America, Peckinpah lost his ability to direct. Considered unemployable by the studios, and unable to work well when he did find employment, Peckinpah was largely inactive in his last years.

But the films he made during that spectacular burst of creativity from 1969–1974 profoundly influenced the representation of screen violence and dramatically demonstrated the creative possibilities of bringing bad or reprehensible characters to the center of a screen narrative. Peckinpah's is an authentically abrasive cinematic voice. His films morally challenge their viewers with tragic visions of the destructive effects of violence in human life.

The Ballad of Cable Hogue
(Warner Bros., 1970)
In *The Ballad of Cable Hogue,* the former frontier hero is run over by an automobile and dies at the dawn of the modern era. Peckinpah loved outcasts, losers, and loners, and his best Westerns sadly contemplate the inability of these misfits to survive in a modernizing West. The car that runs over Cable kills not just Hogue but the old West that Peckinpah knew and loved.

Familiar with Eisenstein's work, Charles Chaplin, in *Modern Times* (1936), used a similar bit of associational editing (though it is not a montage because it consists of only two shots). At the beginning of the film, he cuts from a shot of sheep being herded into a pen to a shot of workers leaving a subway and crossing the street to enter their factory. The viewer is asked to draw the appropriate conclusions based on the comparison of the two categories of images.

In *Pat Garrett and Billy the Kid* (1973), director Sam Peckinpah used **thematic montage** to emphasize the irony in the fate of sheriff Pat Garrett, killed by the same politicians who hired him years earlier to kill the outlaw Billy the Kid. Peckinpah inter-cuts two time frames, one set in 1908 showing Garrett's assassination, the other set in 1880 showing Billy and his gang shooting the heads off of some chickens. The inter-cutting shows Billy firing from the 1880 time frame and seeming to hit Garrett in the 1908 frame. The historical irony is clear. By killing the Kid, Garrett unintentionally brought about a chain of events that ultimately led to his own death many years later.

Case Study: *The Graduate*

One of the most creative and imaginative sequences in *The Graduate* (1967) uses asso-ciational montage to show the hero, Benjamin (Dustin Hoffman), spending his days floating in his parents' backyard swimming pool and his nights making love with the next-door neighbor, Mrs. Robinson (Ann Bancroft), in a hotel room. The montage blurs time and place. The viewer knows that a great deal of time is passing, days, probably weeks, but can't say exactly how much. Most remarkably of all, different places and locations blend into one another in a dreamlike way.

In the first shot of the montage (**a**), Ben gets out of the pool, puts on a white shirt, and walks into his parents' house, pushing open the patio door. In shot 2 (**b–1**), Ben enters through a door wearing the white shirt, but has entered the hotel room where Mrs. Robinson awaits. The match in action—Ben exiting screen left in shot 1 and entering screen right in shot 2—implies, falsely, that these spaces are connected as part of a single location.

Ben sits with his head against the black headboard of a bed as Mrs. Robinson unbuttons his shirt (**b–2**). Shot 3 (**c–1**) is a close-up of Benjamin's head against a black background. The viewer assumes it to be the bed on which he was lying in the previous shot, especially because his facial expression matches in both shots. Ben then gets up, crosses the room, and closes a door, beyond which his parents are sitting at a dining room table (**c–2**). They glance at him as he closes the door. Ben then recrosses the room and sits in a black chair before a television set (**c–3**). Obviously, this cannot be the hotel room; he is at home with his parents.

Shot 4 (**d–1**) shows Ben's face against a black background, this time assumed to be the chair in front of the television. The camera then zooms out to reveal the hotel room with Mrs. Robinson dressing (**d–2**). She leaves. Again the viewer has been mis-led. The room in shot 4 is different than the one in shot 3. Shot (**e–1**) is another close-up of Ben's face against a black background. The viewer thinks it to be the bed on which he was lying in the previous shot, but the camera zooms out to reveal that he is in his bedroom at his parents' house. He glances out his window, puts on his swim trunks, and goes down the stairs. In shot 6 (not illustrated), his mother watches him dive into the pool. Shot 7 (**f**) is a close-up of Ben swimming underwater. In shot

a

b-1

b-2

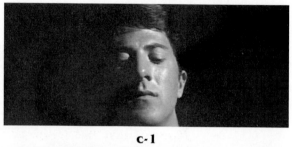

c-1

c-2

c-3

d-1

d-2

e-1

e-2

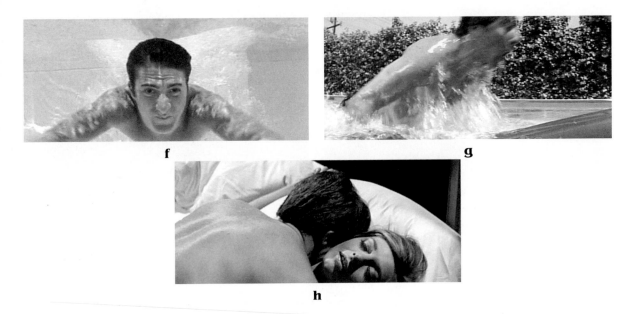

f

g

h

8 (**g**), he leaps up onto the pool's inflatable raft, and shot 9 (**h**) is a matched cut on action that shows Benjamin moving on top of Mrs. Robinson in bed.

The filmmakers use continuity principles, such as matching action, to create the disorienting, dreamlike effect in which times and places are indistinct and melt into one another. This is a slower, more seductive presentation of the breakdown of time–space than in the violent, hard-edged montages of contemporary action films. The editing invites the viewer to draw associations across the cuts. In this case, the associations are psychological, having to do with Ben's alienated frame of mind. He is in a daze, disconnected from all of his environments, lonely and unhappy, sleepwalking through his life, barely conscious of his connection either to his parents or to Mrs. Robinson.

Sequence Shots

In closing this chapter on editing, it is important to note the existence in cinema history of a stylistic tradition in opposition to montage and to the general contribution of editing in structuring a scene. This is the use of the **long take,** sometimes also known as the **sequence shot.** The term refers to a shot of very long duration which, in some cases, may last for the entire length of a scene. If a filmmaker chooses to construct a scene using the long take, this decision will substitute for the normative practice of building a scene by cutting among different camera set-ups. In other words, the long take becomes the foundation of the scene, not editing. In *Easy Rider,* as noted in an earlier chapter, the harvest prayer scene is composed of an extended 360-degree panning shot across the faces of the commune members. Because the scene is composed of one shot, there is no editing.

Long takes do not always have to be sequence shots. Sometimes a scene can be composed of several very lengthy takes. In Orson Welles's *Citizen Kane* (1941), Kane's parents strike a deal with a banker, Mr. Thatcher, in which the bank will act as Kane's guardian and assume control over his estate until he comes of age. The scene is largely presented in two long takes that, together, run for almost four minutes of screen time. Instead of relying on editing to maintain visual interest, Welles sustains it by choreographing elaborate moves by the characters and the camera. In the work of Welles, and such other directors as Woody Allen, William Wyler (*The Best Years of Our Lives,* 1946), and Miklós Jancsó (*Red Psalm,* 1972), the long take is a recurrent and essential feature of style that provides an alternative to film editing.

SUMMARY

Almost universally, filmmakers regard editing as the decisive phase of production, giving a film its distinct shape, organization, and emotional power. There is, however, no single way to cut a scene or a film.

Continuity editing is the predominant approach used in narrative cinema. It establishes a coherent and orderly physical world on screen, despite variations in the camera's placement and angle. The rules that deal with screen direction and matched visual elements are an essential means of creating this coherence and order. Continuity errors occur when mismatched visual elements violate the perceptual constancies that a viewer looks for in the world represented on screen. If Julia Roberts is eating a croissant for breakfast, it should not suddenly turn into a pancake.

Realism is an elastic concept, however, and the physical and perceptual laws that continuity editing seeks to honor can be subjected to distortion and manipulation. Viewers accept many such manipulations, regarding them as permissible expressions of style or artistry. Montage editing enables filmmakers to create striking distortions of time and space, some of which are inconsistent with strict continuity principles. The craft of editing is infinitely powerful in its ability to reorganize time and space, and many things are permissible under the rubric of style.

Whatever approach a given filmmaker might use, if he or she is making a feature film and telling a story, the option of completely avoiding editing does not exist. Even where a filmmaker like Woody Allen may shoot each of his scenes in a single master shot, he and his editor must still join these shots together and make decisions about the points at which to do so. Hitchcock, a director for whom editing was of great importance, once tried to do without it. In *Rope* (1948), he cut only when the camera physically ran out of film (approximately every 10 minutes) and tried through elaborate means to hide the cuts when they did occur. The result is an interesting experiment but a sluggish film that lacks the dramatic rhythms and intensity that only editing can create. To be a filmmaker is to select, manipulate, sequence, and cut!

SUGGESTED READINGS

Ken Dancyger, *The Technique of Film and Video Editing* (Stoneham, MA: Focal Press, 1996).
Sergei Eisenstein, *Film Form* and *The Film Sense* (New York: Harcourt, Brace and World, 1949).
Vincent LoBrutto, *Selected Takes: Film Editors on Film Editing* (New York: Praeger, 1991).

Walter Murch, *In the Blink of an Eye: A Perspective on Film Editing* (Los Angeles, CA: Silman-James Press, 1995).

Gabriella Oldham, *First Cut: Conversations with Film Editors* (Berkeley and Los Angeles: University of California Press, 1995).

Karel Reisz and Gavin Millar, *The Technique of Film Editing,* 2nd ed. (Boston: Focal Press, 1995).

Ralph Rosenblum, *When the Shooting Stops . . . the Cutting Begins: A Film Editor's Story* (New York: Da Caps, 1988).

Michael Rubin, *Nonlinear: A Guide to Digital Film and Video Editing* (Gainesville, FL: Triad Pub. Co., 1995).

Chapter 5

Principles of
Sound Design

Chapter Objectives

After reading this chapter, you should be able to:

- describe the development of contemporary multichannel sound

- describe the three basic types of sound in cinema

- explain the uses and functions of dialogue in film

- explain the functions of ADR

- describe sound effects design and Foley techniques

- describe five steps for creating movie music

- explain five basic functions music performs in film

- explain the nature of sound design, its expressive uses, and how it builds upon the viewer's real-life acoustical skills and experience

- distinguish between realistic and synthetic sounds

- explain the fundamental differences between sound and image

- explain five codes of sound design and their expressive uses

- differentiate direct sound, reflected sound, and ambient sound

- explain how sound establishes continuity in film as well as intellectual and emotional effects

- explain why switching between on-screen and off-screen sound helps makes camera positions more flexible

Key Terms and Concepts

sound field
soundstage
dialogue
effect
music
speech
voice-over narration
production track
ADR

ambient sound
Foley technique
spotting
temp track
cue sheet
leitmotif
sound design (designer)
realistic sound

synthetic sound
direct sound
reflected sound
room tone
sound perspective
post-dub
sound bridge
off-screen sound

Image editing employs standard rules and techniques that: (1) provide editors with methods for organizing shots, (2) establish constancies of time and space between the story world on screen and viewers' experiences of their physical environment, and (3) are based on correspondence with the viewer's perceptual experience and have become familiar to viewers through constant repetition over many films. Like image editing, film sound has its own rules (or codes) of structural design. One can speak

Celluloid film carries an optical soundtrack, positioned between the edge of the frame and the sprocket holes. The small space available for optically encoded sound information placed great restrictions on the frequency range of film sound, until the advent of Dolby Digital and other digital sound systems.

of sound fades, sound cuts, sound dissolves, and sound perspective. This chapter examines the three categories of sound in film: dialogue, effects, and music. It explains the concept of sound design and examines its rules and techniques.

◻ EVOLUTION OF FILM SOUND

Of all the components of film structure, sound has shown the greatest improvements in recent decades. Contemporary film uses multiple channels of sound information to envelop viewers in a dynamic, three-dimensional **sound field** (the acoustical area covered by speaker placement in a surround set-up and activated by multichannel sound coming from the speakers). In the 1930s and 1940s in contrast, film sound was essentially a monaural, single-channel experience, with each speaker in a theater auditorium receiving the same signal. Sound was encoded as an optical track on the strip of film, and directors and sound mixers were invariably disappointed at the loss of volume, limited frequency range, and distortion in the upper register that occurred when they encoded their sound onto the optical track. Low-volume sound effects vanished into the hiss of the track. High volumes produced a different problem. On optical tracks, the louder the sound, the larger its visual encoding (i.e., the more space it occupies on the track). Because the track space available between frame line and sprocket holes is fixed, volume levels that exhaust this space edge into harsh noise, a frequent problem with soundtracks from these years.

To compete with television in the 1950s, Hollywood moved to widescreen film formats, some of which carried multichannel stereo sound, utilizing magnetic stripes to encode the sound signal. To play such soundtracks, projectors had to be outfitted with special playback heads, much like a tape recorder. Widescreen formats such as Cinemascope (35mm) and Todd-AO (70mm) carried from four to six channels of sound. (In this regard, film stereo was distinct from home stereo, a two-channel system used for playing music.) Mag stripe stereo on widescreen film, however, was reserved for special appeal films, and, until the mid-1970s, the industry norm remained a single-channel optical track.

Armageddon (Touchstone, 1998)
Six-channel playback of digital film sound routes bass signals to a separate, dedicated channel. This gives the modern film sound stage an impressive acoustic floor and adds tremendous power to special effects imagery. Frame enlargement.

Debuting in 1976, Dolby Stereo carried two optical tracks that were encoded with four channels of sound information. These were configured for playback as left, center, right, and rear (surround) channels. With Dolby Stereo, multichannel sound gained widespread acceptance in the film industry. For the consumer market of home video, Dolby Surround debuted in 1982, enabling home viewers to play Dolby Stereo movies as stereo videocassettes. Initially, though, Dolby Surround only decoded the left, right, and surround channels, but Dolby Prologic decoders, marketed in 1987, enabled center channel decoding as well.

Cinema sound became even richer when Dolby moved to a digital six-channel system in 1992. Known as Dolby Digital, the system carried three channels across the front—left, center, right—plus two fully independent rear channels (left and right surrounds) and a dedicated channel for low frequency (bass) signals. The digital soundtrack data were placed between the sprocket holes on the film, which also carried an analog stereo soundtrack.

Dolby added yet another channel in 1999. Dolby Digital Surround EX is a seven-channel system, adding a third surround channel, positioned behind the viewer, in addition to the rear left and rear right split surrounds of the 5.1 system. This extra channel can be used to create flyover effects, useful in films like *Star Wars Episode 2: Attack of the Clones.*

Today, the industry uses several competing digital sound formats: Dolby Digital, Digital Theater Systems (DTS, using a CD for the soundtrack synched with time code printed on the film), and Sony Dynamic Digital Sound (SDDS). Each film print, however, still carries an optical soundtrack, as a backup in case a problem arises with the digital information and because many theaters are only equipped for optical playback.

Digital playback revolutionized the art of film sound. Filmmakers no longer had to contend with the restrictions imposed by an optical track. Spread across three channels in the front, the **soundstage** (the acoustical space established by the front

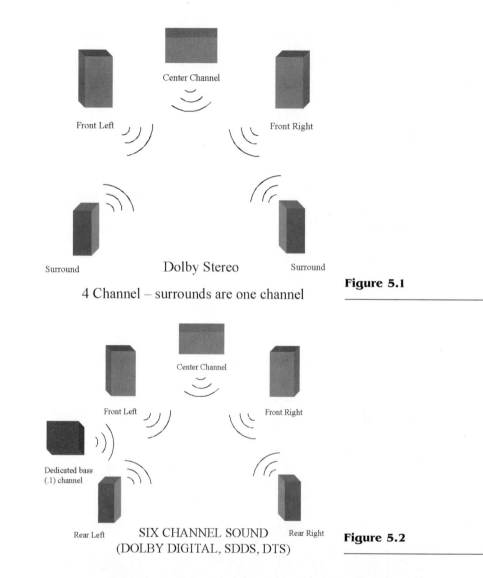

Dolby Stereo

4 Channel – surrounds are one channel

Figure 5.1

SIX CHANNEL SOUND
(DOLBY DIGITAL, SDDS, DTS)

Figure 5.2

speakers) is broad and expansive and is anchored with an impressive bottom register supplied by the dedicated bass channel. The thunderous explosions in contemporary action films illustrate the potential this channel has given cinema. The rear surround channels make the sound field dynamic and three-dimensional, enveloping the viewer in multidirectional sound. Until the 1990s, the surround channels were used infrequently for the occasional sound effect, but they are now used very aggressively, along with all of the other channels, to spatialize the sound field (that is, to render it in highly directional terms) and provide the viewer with an immersive sound experience. The Oscar-winning (for sound-effects editing) *The Ghost and the Darkness* (1996) boasts an exceptionally complex and aggressive six-channel mix.

Cinema is now oddly unbalanced. In sound, it is fully three-dimensional, but its picture remains two-dimensional. Viewers are surrounded by sound but must watch a picture on a flat screen, positioned in front of them. It seems likely that the ideal toward which cinema is evolving is a totally 3-D experience, in picture *and* sound. At some future point, cinema viewers will have an immersive visual experience, but, so far, the medium has achieved this ideal only with sound.

Dolby Digital brought six-channel sound to the home video environment on laser disk in 1995 and on DVD (digital video disk) in 1997. Indeed, the successful launch of DVD has encouraged studios and filmmakers to undertake six-channel remixes of older film soundtracks for release in this format. Warner Brothers' DVD of *Dirty Harry* (1972) carried an impressive Dolby Digital remix, and director Wolfgang Peterson supervised an outstanding six-channel remix of the track for *Das Boot* (1981) on DVD. The film portrays submarine warfare in World War II, and its new soundtrack creates a total sonic environment that places viewers inside a narrow, cramped German submarine deep in the Mediterranean. Other older films given six-channel remixes include titles newly restored for theatrical release and subsequent DVD distribution. These include Hitchcock's *Vertigo* (1958) and the classic musicals *My Fair Lady* (1964) and *West Side Story* (1961).

Sound in cinema has never been better than in the contemporary period. One cannot make similar claims for cinematography, editing, or many other elements of cinema structure. In this regard, sound is making a uniquely improved aesthetic contribution to cinema. Viewers today are privileged to enjoy a total sonic experience that was not available to moviegoers in earlier periods.

Das Boot (Columbia TriStar, 1981)
Digital, multichannel soundtracks create a spatial, three-dimensional sound field by surrounding the viewer with discrete, directional sound. Wolfgang Peterson's film about submarine warfare in World War II is one of the outstanding sonic experiences in contemporary cinema; sound is both the subject and structure of this film. The U-boat Captain and his officer listen anxiously for sonar signals warning of the approach of Allied warships. Frame enlargement.

☐ TYPES OF SOUND

Three basic types of sound figure in cinema. These are **dialogue, effects,** and **music.**

Dialogue

Since the late 1920s when synchronous sound became a permanent feature of the movies, two primary kinds of dialogue have been employed in the cinema. **Speech** is delivered by characters on screen usually in conversation with one another. **Voice-over narration** accompanies images and scenes but is not delivered by a particular character from within the scene. Voice-over narration typically is provided by an all-seeing, all-knowing, detached narrator or by a character in the story, usually from some time later than the events portrayed on screen.

Speech

Motion pictures use a wide range of dialects and speech types. Shakespearean adaptations faithfully transpose the Bard's language to the screen and frequently employ classically trained actors such as Laurence Olivier, Ralph Richardson, or John Gielgud. Kenneth Branagh's trilogy—*Henry V* (1989), *Much Ado about Nothing* (1993), and *Hamlet* (1996)—are among the most cinematic of these adaptations. By contrast, other films adopt a more playful attitude toward Shakespeare. Oliver Parker's *Othello* (1995) successfully casts an actor lacking classical training—Laurence Fishburne—in the title role, and Baz Luhrmann's MTV-style *Romeo and Juliet* (1996) grafted the play's language onto a thoroughly modernist visual style. More recently, *Shakespeare in Love* (1998) used naturalistic, nonpoetic language to portray a fictional episode from the playwright's life.

At the other extreme from the poetry of Shakespeare lies the colloquialism of modern life. The dynamic impact of sound in the late 1920s and early 1930s was due largely to the electrifying presence of a new generation of screen actors. James Cagney, for example, brought his scrappy, high voltage personality to a series of gritty, tough, urban

Much Ado about Nothing (Samuel Goldwyn, 1993) Kenneth Branagh and Emma Thompson play bickering lovers in this delightful version of Shakespeare's comedy. Branagh's Shakespearean films respect the Bard's language while giving it a completely cinematic showcase. Frame enlargement.

dramas that allowed him to draw on his boyhood experiences growing up in the slums of New York's Upper East Side. The way Cagney moved and spoke electrified audiences because it was so different from the mannerisms and speech of stage-trained actors. In the Cagney classic *Angels with Dirty Faces* (1938), he plays a good-hearted crook named Rocky who greets his friends with the salutation, "Whadda ya hear? Whadda ya say?," rattled off in rapid-fire delivery. Cagney got this greeting from a pimp he had known when he was a youth.

The screen appeal of many stars, like Cagney, resides partly in their distinctive manner of speaking. Will Smith's lilting voice, often barbed with a wisecrack, or Eddie Murphy's trademark laugh, have endeared them to audiences. In *Face/Off* (1997), actors John Travolta and Nicolas Cage swap each other's mannered speaking style in an impressive display of the connection between speech and star charisma.

By speaking to audiences in a colloquial, familiar manner, movies forge a strong rapport and powerful emotional bonds with viewers. In the 1950s, when Marlon Brando, playing an outlaw motorcyclist in *The Wild One*, was asked what he is rebelling against, he replied "Whadda ya' got?," and a young generation instantly understood his insolence and contempt for established society. In Spike Lee's *Clockers* (1995), the thick street dialects of Brooklyn gangs vividly establish their authority and authenticity.

Voice-Over Narration

While rarely used today, voice-over narration in earlier periods was an essential part of certain genres. In the 1940s and 1950s, many films noir—*Out of the Past* (1947), *Criss*

Angels with Dirty Faces (Warner Bros., 1938);
The Wild One (Columbia Pictures, 1954)
The electrifying impact of rough, colloquial speech helped propel James Cagney and Marlon Brando to stardom. Playing a gangster in *Angels with Dirty Faces*, Cagney drew from the vocal patterns of the city streets where he grew up. As the outlaw motorcyclist in *The Wild One*, Marlon Brando's slurred, insolent speech conveyed his rebelliousness and mockery of society.

Cross (1949), *The Killers* (1946)—told their stories through intricate flashbacks accompanied by voice-over narration. In voice-over, the tough private eye or the world-weary criminal delivered hard-boiled lines of dialogue. At the beginning of *Double Indemnity* (1944), with a bullet wound slowly leaking blood from his shoulder, a cynical insurance agent confesses his crime: "I killed Dietrichson—me, Walter Neff, insurance salesman—thirty-five years old, unmarried, no visible scars, 'til awhile ago, that is."

Voice-over narration can be used for ironic or playful effects. In one of the most famous films noir, *Sunset Boulevard* (1950), the narrator turns out to be a dead man. The film opens with shots of a man's body floating in a swimming pool. The police arrive and remove the body as the narrator, a screenwriter named Joe Gillis, tells how the murder occurred. It is not until the end of the movie that viewers realize the dead man *is* Joe Gillis. He talks wistfully about how it feels when the police fish him out of the pool and lay him out "like a harpooned baby whale."

Of course, in the case of *Sunset Boulevard*, the narration is unreliable and misleading. Dead men don't talk. Director Billy Wilder plays against an established convention of voice-over narration, which is that the character doing the narration must survive the events of the story. In this case, he doesn't, and it enabled Wilder to pull off one of his darkest jokes. In a similar manner, the narrator of *American History X* (1998) is murdered but continues his narration, commenting on the things that his death has taught him. *American Beauty* (1999) is another film that uses this device.

While voice-over narration is closely identified with U.S. films noir, it has also been used in documentary filmmaking, especially that subcategory of documentaries known as the newsreel. Newsreels routinely accompanied feature films, cartoons, and serials in the nation's movie theaters in earlier decades, and they typically employed the so-called "voice of God" narrator. Such a narrator was male and spoke with a deep, booming, authoritative tone.

Double Indemnity
(Paramount, 1944)
Hard-boiled, tough-guy dialogue, spoken as voice-over narration, coupled with dark, low-key lighting to establish the hard-edged, cynical atmosphere of classic film noir. Fred MacMurray, as the doomed Walter Neff, provides the gripping narration about a murder scheme gone awry. Frame enlargement.

American History X
(New Line, 1998)
Daniel (Edward Furlong)
narrates the film, and he is
murdered near its end. But he
continues his narration and
reflects upon the meaning of his
death. The film plays with the
movie convention that narrators
will survive the stories they nar-
rate. Frame enlargement.

In *Citizen Kane* (1941), director Orson Welles satirized the "voice of God" newsreel narrator. The film tells the life story of Charles Foster Kane, a rich newspaper
man who rose from humble beginnings. The film opens with Kane's death; a newsreel follows, viewed by newspaper reporters for background on their stories about
Kane's death. The newsreel features a "voice of God" narrator as director Welles expertly mimics the conventions of this kind of documentary.

Beyond the fake newsreel, however, *Citizen Kane* offers a host of other voice-over
narrators. *Citizen Kane* is a classic and superlative example of voice-over narration used
for complex effect and as an essential ingredient of film structure. The plot of the
film is constructed as a series of flashbacks, each one narrated by a different character, which makes the emerging portrait of Charles Foster Kane into a kaleidoscope.
Characters recollecting Kane include the millionaire banker, Walter P. Thatcher, who

Citizen Kane (RKO, 1941)
Jed Leland (Joseph Cotton),
one of the principal narrators
in *Citizen Kane,* explains why
Kane's first marriage failed. As
he begins his speech, the image
dissolves to the past to show the
first Mrs. Kane at breakfast. The
narrative voices are not easily
reconciled. Leland describes
events he couldn't possibly have
witnessed. Frame enlargement.

was given custody of Kane as a little boy; Susan Alexander, Kane's second wife; Jed Leland, the drama critic who worked briefly on Kane's newspapers; Mr. Bernstein, Kane's chief editor and close friend; and Raymond, Kane's personal valet.

Each of these characters narrates a section of the film, recalling events in ways that clash with the memories of the other narrators. For example, Jed Leland recalls the Charles Foster Kane who betrayed his ideals and principles, whereas Mr. Bernstein emphasizes those principles, remembering how Kane used his newspaper to fight crime and expose official graft and corruption.

The voice-over narration frames the various flashbacks and colors them with a variety of psychological perspectives. *Citizen Kane,* in part, is a mystery film. The mystery is Kane's personality, which ultimately remains unknowable. It is difficult to reconcile the various Kanes disclosed in the narrators' memories because each is so different from the others. In this way, the respective voice-over narrations deepen the emotional and psychological mystery of film, the nature of Kane's personality. Few films in cinema history have used voice-over narration so skillfully and with such profound structural and emotional effects.

ADR and Dialogue Mixing

Most of the dialogue heard in the average feature originates from the **production track** (the soundtrack recorded at the point of filming), but 30 percent or more of a film's dialogue is the result of **ADR** (automated dialogue replacement). Following shooting, actors recreate portions of a scene's dialogue in a sound studio, and this postproduction sound is mixed in with dialogue from the production track. The mixer must smooth out the audible differences of tone and timbre and make sure that no audio cuts are apparent to the listener. Digital software facilitates the ADR process, alleviating the need for an actor to speak in perfect synch with the picture; the software can match the ADR speech with the lip movements on screen.

ADR is typically used when portions of the production track are unusable or unsatisfactory, and some films, such as Sergio Leone's *Once upon a Time in America* (1984), have extraordinarily high amounts of ADR. All of the dialogue in that picture was done as ADR; none originated from the production track.

Camera placement can facilitate opportunities for using ADR. One of the highlights of *Pretty Woman* (1990) occurs when Julia Roberts goes on a Beverly Hills shopping spree. The ensuing montage is scored to the titular Roy Orbison song, and a dialogue exchange between Richard Gere and the shop clerk (Larry Miller) kicks off the start of the montage. Gere tells the clerk, "She has my [credit] card," and the clerk incautiously replies, "And we'll help her use it." The clerk's dialogue was dropped in as late-in-the-game ADR, an opportunity facilitated by the blocking of the scene, as the accompanying photos demonstrate.

Sound Effects

Sound effects are the physical (i.e., nonspeech) sounds heard as part of the action and the physical environments seen on screen. They include **ambient sound,** which is the naturally occurring, generally low-level sound produced by an environment (wind in the trees, traffic in the city). They also include the sounds produced by specific

a   b

Pretty Woman (Touchstone, 1990)
The blocking of a scene can create opportunities to add new dialogue using ADR. These two frames from a single shot show how changing character positions facilitated the addition in postproduction of the salesman's line, "And we'll help her use it." The salesman is visible at rear (a) between Julia Roberts and Richard Gere, but when Roberts walks out of the store, she blocks the salesman from the camera's view (b), at which point the new line of dialogue was inserted. Frame enlargement.

actions in a scene, such as the rumble of the spaceship Nostromo in *Alien* (1979) as it passes nearby or the crash of broken glass as Mookie throws a trashcan through the window of Sal's Pizzeria in *Do the Right Thing* (1989). Digital methods of sound recording and mixing enable sound engineers to achieve an impressive aural separation of individual sound elements. This gives the effects in contemporary film a richer texture than in decades past and enables selective emphasis of individual effects without a corresponding loss of the overall sonic context.

Virtually all of the sound effects that one hears in contemporary film are the results of postproduction manipulation. Sound effects recorded as part of the production track may be electronically cleaned and optimized, but most are recorded separately and in places other than the filming environment. Many effects are created using **Foley technique.** Foley technique refers to the live performance and recording of sound effects in synchronization with the picture. As the film is projected in a sound recording studio, a Foley artist watches the action and performs the necessary effects. A Foley artist might walk across a bare floor using hard shoes in synchronization with a character on-screen to produce the needed effects of footsteps. The Foley artist may open or close a door or drop a tray of glasses on the floor to create these effects as needed in a given scene.

Foley techniques require considerable physical dexterity, often verging on the acrobatic, from the artists creating these live effects. Foley is often needed because many of today's films involve the use of radio microphones that are attached to individual actors in a scene. Unlike mikes on a boom overhead, radio mikes fail to pick up natural sounds in the environment, and these often have to be dubbed using Foley techniques.

Because of the nonspecific nature of sound—taken out of context, many sounds are difficult to identify—Foley often uses objects that are not part of the scene. To create sound effects in *Star Wars Episode 2: Attack of the Clones* for the skin surfaces of alien creatures, when other aliens or objects touch them, the Foley artists used pineapples, coconuts, and cantaloupes. The rough texture of their surfaces proved to be ideally suited to evoking the imaginary sound of alien skin.

Whether or not Foley is employed to create a given effect, digital software enables sound engineers to electronically enhance effects and introduce changes in the sound-wave characteristics of a given source. The effects track of a film is the highly processed outcome of these electronic methods of sound manipulation. Leading the industry's transition to digital audio in 1984, Lucasfilm had a proprietary digital sound worksta-tion (ASP, Audio Signal Processor) that stored and mixed sound in digital format. For *Indiana Jones and the Temple of Doom* (1984), when Jones is surrounded by a bevy of arrows flying toward him, ASP electronically extended the arrows' whizzing sounds and added Doppler effects (Doppler is a means of spatializing sound by altering its pitch).

The simple, raw recording of a given effect usually lacks emotional impact, so audio engineers typically manipulate the effect, by layering in other components, to make it suitably expressive. In *Apocalypse Now,* during the scene where panicky Americans machine-gun a group of Vietnamese in their boat, sound designer Walter Murch wanted to affect the viewer's psychological and emotional response to the machine-gun sound. He wanted the viewer to feel that the sound was realistic even though it was not a live recording of a single source but a synthetic blend of multiple, separate recordings.

Murch backed the microphone away from the gun to get a clean recording and then, later, added supplementary elements such as the clank of discharging metallic cartridges and the hiss of hot metal. By layering these additional features over the softer sound of the gun firing, Murch artificially created a convincing realism in ways that were compatible with his recording technology. Doing this involved "disassembling" the sound rather than capturing it live and direct on tape.

Apocalypse Now (United Artists, 1979)
The sound of the machine gun in *Apocalypse Now* was actually a blend of multiple, separate elements expertly layered together to produce the psychological impression of a single, live source. Frame enlargement.

In *Terminator 2* (1991), for the gun battle in an underground parking garage, sound designer Gary Rydstrom recorded guns firing in this reverberant space. But to make the sound interesting, he also recorded the sound of two-by-fours slapping together in the garage and layered this echoing sound into the effect to "fatten" it up. In *Backdraft* (1991), Rydstrom gave blazing fires an audio presence and personality by layering in animal growls and monkey screams. Given the film's context—about deadly urban fires—he knew the audience would not hear these sounds as animal noises but as attributes of the fire. For the backdrafts, produced when a huge fire sucks in oxygen before exploding, he used coyote howls, which gave the backdrafts a subliminal personality and intelligence. Expressive sound effects are complex, artificial creations that transcend their live sound components.

Music

Music has always accompanied the presentation of films for audiences. During the silent period, film music was often drawn from public domain, noncopyrighted classical selections or from the popular tunes of the era. Numerous catalogues offered filmmakers or musical directors a guide for selecting appropriate music depending on the tempo of the scene and its general emotional content. In addition, some original symphonic scores were composed for silent films.

The original score composed especially for motion pictures became standard practice in the sound period. While many different musical styles can be employed in film scoring—jazz (*Mo' Better Blues*, 1990), rock (*Bill and Ted's Excellent Adventure*, 1989), ragtime (*Ragtime*, 1981), symphonic orchestral (*Star Wars*, 1977)—music is typically used to follow action on-screen and to illustrate a character's emotions.

Backdraft (Universal, 1991)
Taken out of context, the meaning of an isolated sound can be very fluid and difficult to identify. This enables sound designers to attach sounds to unrelated images to great effect. The fires in *Backdraft* were mixed with animal sounds, although viewers did not identify these sounds as such. This audio design suggested that fire was a kind of living organism, with intelligence and personality. Frame enlargement.

Creating Movie Music

The production of movie music involves five distinct steps: spotting, preparation of a cue sheet, composing, performance and recording, and mixing. The first stage is **spotting,** during which the composer consults with the film's director and producer and views the final cut in order to determine where and when music might be needed. Spotting determines the locations in the film that require musical cues, where and how the music will enter, and its general tempo and emotional color.

Much of this is left up to the composer, although detailed discussions with a film's director are not uncommon, especially when the director has strong preferences as to the style of scoring. Sometimes the director will impose a **temp track**—a temporary musical track derived from a score the director likes—onto the soundtrack of an edited scene, or even the entire film, and ask that the composer create something like the temp track. Not surprisingly, many composers find this stifling.

After the film has been spotted, the music editor then prepares a **cue sheet.** The cue sheet contains a detailed description of each scene's action requiring music plus the exact timings to the second of that action. This enables the composer to work knowing the exact timing in minutes, seconds, and frames of each action requiring music. As a result, musical cues can catch the action and enter and end at precisely determined points.

Once the cue sheet has been prepared, the third step is the actual composition of the score. This is done by the composer using a video copy of the film. The video contains a digital time code that displays the reel number and minutes, seconds, and frames into each reel for all of the action. Using the cue sheet and video the composer creates the score, carefully fitting the timing of music and action.

Computer programs known as "sequencers" enable the composer to lock the score onto the video's digital time code. Once this is done, any scene can be played back, and the computer can call up the score, enabling the composer to check timings. Tempo adjustments—speeding up or slowing down the music—can also be made by

Platoon
(Orion Pictures, 1986)
The score for *Platoon* deliberately avoids using conventional war-film music. Instead, composer Georges Delerue employed an already-existing classical composition—Samuel Barber's melancholy "Adagio for Strings"—and used it to emphasize the film's haunted, tragic tone.

computer to precisely match music with action. The sequencer can also generate a series of clicks that many composers use to establish a desired tempo for a given scene and that is then used as a guide for composition.

Digital technology has also altered the phase of composition in which the composer demonstrates the score for the director. Digital samplers enable composers to electronically simulate all needed instrumentation in their scores and play the results for the director, who can hear a close approximation of the film's score-in-progress. Before the age of samplers, composers demonstrated their scores on the piano, which required that directors be able to understand how the piano performance would translate into a full-bodied instrumentation. The disadvantage of digital sampling is that demonstrations now give directors more input into scoring—an area most are not qualified to handle—because, using a sampler's computer keyboard, anyone can easily manipulate the musical characteristics of a composition. Some directors, to their composer's dislike, find this an irresistible temptation.

Once the music has been composed, the next step is performance and recording of the score on a sound stage while a copy of the film is projected on a large screen or video monitor. Timing of music to film action is facilitated by the use of clicks to establish tempo, "streamers"—lines imprinted on the film or video—that travel across the screen and mark the beginning and end of each cue, and a large analog clock with a sweep second hand. The performance of the score is often attended by the director and producer of the film.

The final stage in the creation of movie music is the process of mixing, which is the blending of the various sound tracks, effects, music, and dialogue. The fact that movie music is mixed along with dialogue and effects has influenced the attitude of composers to the kind of music they create. Because dialogue is regarded as the most important sound in a movie, music is typically mixed at a lower volume when it accompanies dialogue. Composers know this and work accordingly.

Hollywood composer Miklos Rosza pointed out that when music accompanies dialogue it should be simple, without a lot of ornamentation, because this will be lost in the mix when the music is buried beneath the dialogue. He also recommended that music in dialogue passages be scored with strings rather than brass instruments because he felt strings blend better with the human voice. While there is much variation among composers in their approach to scoring, these remarks indicate something most would agree on—the film score is not autonomous. It should be written with the action in mind and be capable of blending with all other sound sources in the movie.

So much for the technical steps involved in producing movie music. What of its dramatic functions? Why is it used, and what does it accomplish in movies?

Functions of Movie Music

The great U.S. concert hall composer, Aaron Copland, occasionally ventured into the world of filmmaking to compose scores for such pictures as *Of Mice and Men* (1940), *Our Town* (1940), *The Red Pony* (1949), and *The Heiress* (1949). Copland discussed the functions of movie music as he saw them, emphasizing five basic functions.

Setting the Scene   Film music creates a convincing atmosphere of time and place. Movie music characterizes the locations, settings, and cultures where the story occurs.

Often, this may involve the use of special instrumentation that reflects regional or ethnic musical characteristics. Jerry Goldsmith, one of today's most prolific and respected composers, employed pan flutes in his score for *Under Fire* (1983), a film dealing with the revolution in Nicaragua in 1979. By using an instrument that was not specifically tied to Nicaragua, but was found in many peasant cultures in Central America, Goldsmith was able to create a musical score that tied the Nicaraguan revolution, musically, to its peasant origins, but in a way that included echoes of the peasant cultures of other Central American countries, much as the revolution itself did in the 1980s.

Sometimes the time and place that a composer wishes to create is not one that exists in reality. For his celebrated score for the science fiction film *Planet of the Apes* (1968), Goldsmith relied on the use of unusual instruments, such as ram's horns and brass slide whistles, and unusual musical techniques, such as clicking the keys of woodwind instruments directly on the microphone. The result was a score that many people thought was electronic, though Goldsmith has pointed out that he did not use any electronic techniques. He used existing instruments in an unusual fashion to enlarge the sound possibilities of the orchestra. These new and unusual sounds perfectly suited the film's futuristic fantasy set in an alien and frightening world.

Unfortunately, the scene-setting function of movie music sometimes draws on and fosters cultural stereotypes. Dimitri Tiomkin, who composed the score for Howard Hawks's Western *Red River* (1948), needed music for a scene in which Indians attack a wagon train. He wrote music with a stereotypical tympani beat in order to telegraph the idea that the Indians were about to attack. Tiomkin knew that this Indian music was quite artificial and without any real historical basis, but he believed that authentic tribal music would have been less effective because it was unconventional. Tiomkin elected to use the musical stereotype because the audience was familiar with it.

Under Fire
(Orion Pictures, 1983)
Movie music helps establish place and locale, often by employing regional or ethnic musical instruments and traditions. Jerry Goldsmith's score for *Under Fire* used pan flutes, associated with peasant cultures of Central America, to musically characterize the film's Nicaraguan setting and the popular basis of that country's revolution. Frame enlargement.

Adding Emotional Meaning   All motion picture composers stress the importance of this function. Composer Hugo Friedhofer pointed out that music has the special ability of hinting at the unseen, whereas images can only show what is visible. Music extends an image's range of meaning by adding psychological or emotional qualities not in the picture.

The tonal range of Western music, particularly the highly coloristic rendering used in the romantic period of the late nineteenth century, has become the model for orchestral movie music because the emotional content of this musical style is extremely familiar to audiences. Think of all the romantic melodramas in which the teary lovers are about to be parted and the violins are sawing away on the soundtrack, or the way the strings in John Williams's soaring score for *E.T.* capture the pathos of Eliot's goodbye to E.T. at the conclusion of that film.

Movie music emphasizes emotional effects most often by direct symbolization: the music embodies and symbolizes an emotion appropriate to the screen action. An alternative approach is to employ a contrast of image and music. Though less common than direct musical symbolization, it can be quite effective.

An especially impressive example occurs during the helicopter attack sequence in Ridley Scott's *Black Hawk Down* (2001). The Black Hawk helicopters in reality are very loud, but the film's sound editor minimized the realistic sound of the engines, sometimes eliminating it entirely. Hans Zimmer's music score substituted for the engine sounds and musically portrayed the whooshing of the helicopter blades. The result was subjective and psychological. The musical evocation of an absent sound effect worked to convey the stress and concentration of American soldiers about to land in a battle zone. Their minds on the upcoming battle, they were not "hearing" the helicopters. The film viewer does, but only indirectly, by way of the music.

Black Hawk Down (Columbia Pictures, 2001)
The sound design eliminates realistic sound from portions of the helicopter attack sequence and uses music to quietly imitate the whooshing helicopter blades. The design creates a subjective perspective that portrays the mental concentration of the American soldiers in the helicopters, about to go into combat. Frame enlargement.

A Clockwork Orange
(Warner Bros., 1971)
The thug Alex (Malcolm McDowell, center) dances and sings "Singin' in the Rain" while his gang assaults a husband and wife in their home. Director Stanley Kubrick's appropriation of this cheerful song, best remembered from the classic MGM musical that starred Gene Kelly, was an act of cruel subversion, placing the music in a new, horribly violent context. Frame enlargement.

Leaving Las Vegas
(MGM, 1995)
For this grim story about an alcoholic (Nicolas Cage) and a hooker (Elizabeth Shue) who have a brief affair while he drinks himself to death, the filmmakers used music to counterpoint the bleakness of the story. The main musical theme is the song "My One and Only Love," a tender and sentimental ballad given a lush, sweet orchestration for the film. The song creates a sharp counterpoint to the drama. Frame enlargement.

Director Stanley Kubrick famously combined picture and music in counterintuitive ways. In *Dr. Strangelove* (1963), the world ends in a nuclear holocaust, which is scored with the lilting 1940s melody "We'll Meet Again." More cruelly, in *A Clockwork Orange* (1971), Kubrick used the exuberant title song from MGM's beloved musical *Singin' in the Rain* (1952) as the accompaniment to a rape scene.

Japanese director Akira Kurosawa loved to contrast music and image. In *Drunken Angel* (1948), the central character of the film, a small-time gangster, loses control of the local neighborhood he dominated. Furthermore, he is dying of tuberculosis. He wanders the streets shunned by shopkeepers, coughing his life out. To emphasize the character's despair, Kurosawa instructed his composer, Fumio Hayasaka, to accompany the action with a silly and mindless cuckoo waltz. Kurosawa knew that the mindless optimism of the waltz, in its extreme contrast with the character's situation, would underline and emphasize the gangster's despair and sadness.

Serving as Background Filler   This use of movie music was more typical in older films than it is in contemporary filmmaking. During the Hollywood period in the 1930s and 1940s, films were distinguished by so-called wall-to-wall music. Music accompanied almost every scene, and it often assumed a kind of background filler function, just as Copland noted. Contemporary films tend to use music more sparingly, and composers like Jerry Goldsmith believe that less music is better because, when used, it becomes more significant.

Creating Continuity   Like dialogue and effects, music can bridge shots in ways that link and unify them. In montage scenes, for example, where many shots are edited together, music often supplies a unifying structure for the montage. When Julia Roberts goes on her shopping spree in *Pretty Woman*, the Roy Orbison song, from which the film derives its title, accompanies and unifies the montage.

A classic example of music unifying a montage occurs in Bernard Herrmann's score for *Citizen Kane*. A famous sequence in the film shows Charles Foster Kane and his first wife Emily in a series of brief encounters across the breakfast table. The montage telescopes many years of marriage into these breakfasts. Each encounter registers further decay and disintegration in their marriage. Herrmann wrote a little waltz for the montage, established it in the first scene and then used a series of variations for each succeeding scene in the montage, with the music growing colder and more forbid-

Citizen Kane (RKO, 1941) Composer Bernard Herrmann provided a waltz and variations to link musically the different shots of *Citizen Kane*'s famous breakfast montage. Frame enlargement.

ding as the montage progresses, in order to capture the deepening alienation between Charles and Emily.

One of the most important ways that film music creates continuity is by using a **leitmotif** structure. Indeed, this is one of the most common ways of scoring a motion picture. A leitmotif is a kind of musical label that is assigned to a character, a place, an idea, or an emotion. Once assigned, a leitmotif can be repeated each time the character or idea or emotion reappears. This helps make the music recognizable to an audience, especially after stretches of film where no music has been heard, and it also helps characterize the character, place, idea, or emotion. The leitmotif can be presented with great invention and variation, restated in differing rhythms and colors. Leitmotif is derived from the operas of Richard Wagner, who used it as a way of helping his audience recognize and understand the characters and their emotional situations.

The Italian composer Ennio Morricone's score for Sergio Leone's *Once upon a Time in the West* (1969) employs a very explicit leitmotif structure. Each of the four major characters in the film has his or her own theme, and the themes reappear as the characters do throughout the film so that one can easily follow the story and its conflicts simply by listening to the music. Almost every motion picture score is structured as a set of themes and variations, and this repetition of familiar musical material is a powerful means of creating continuity.

Music can also establish continuity by creating pacing and tempo within scenes. As soon as music is added to a scene, the images take on a rhythm and pace they did not otherwise possess because relationships are established musically across the shots. Elmer Bernstein, composer of the score for the popular Western *The Magnificent Seven* (1960), has pointed out that his music for this film is actually faster than the action on screen. He wanted the music to help speed along an otherwise slow film. Bernstein's now-classic score adds immeasurably to the pacing of the movie, providing excitement in scenes that would otherwise lack it.

Emphasizing Climaxes   Movie music emphasizes climaxes and concludes scenes or the end of a film with finality. Music in movies tends to begin and end on specific actions:

Once upon a Time in the West (Paramount Pictures, 1969)
Each character in this epic Sergio Leone Western has his or her own highly distinctive musical theme. The leitmotif structure of the score is especially explicit.

doors opening and closing, cars pulling away, monsters jumping out of the dark. In these ways, musical cues alert the audience to the climaxes and the emotional high points of scenes. Danny Elfman's score for *Batman* (1989) is exceptionally accomplished in catching action and emphasizing climaxes.

Music need not always be used to heighten action. Sometimes, its absence can be very effective. In *The Silence of the Lambs* (1991), the climactic confrontation in a dark basement between Clarice Starling (Jodie Foster) and serial killer Buffalo Bill features spooky ambient sounds and source music coming from Bill's boom box, but no film score. One had been composed for the scene, but the filmmakers elected to go instead with the ambient sound. In the police thriller *Bullitt* (1968), during the famous car chase, the music ceases early on. As detective Steve McQueen starts his pursuit of a pair of suspected killers, the music begins in a tense and ominous fashion, but then it stops so that sound effects—screaming engines, squealing tires—take over to carry the sequence. Most movies use music to make car chases more exciting, but the chase in *Bullitt* is historically important for avoiding this obvious strategem.

Contemporary Trends in Film Scoring

Although movie music today performs the basic functions noted by Copland, the styles employed, and the importance of music for the industry, have changed since his era. The use of romantic orchestral music to score films in the Hollywood period gave way in the 1950s to more modern approaches. Elmer Bernstein composed a jazz-oriented score for *The Man with the Golden Arm* (1955), and Leonard Rosenman composed an atonal, 12-tone serial score for *The Cobweb* (1955). Folk and rock scores in the late

---

The Silence of the Lambs (Orion, 1991)

Sometimes no music at all is more effective than a score. One mark of intelligent scoring is knowing when not to score. Composer Howard Shore wrote music for the climactic scene where an FBI agent (Jodie Foster) confronts a serial killer in a dark basement. Upon seeing the edited sequence, however, he felt it worked better, with more suspense, without the music. Frame enlargement.

1960s distinguished *The Graduate* and *Easy Rider* (1969). At this time, the symphonic orchestral score fell out of style, but it made a triumphant comeback in the mid-1970s in the work of John Williams. His scores for the *Star Wars* films and Steven Spielberg's pictures reestablished the symphony orchestra as an essential scoring resource.

Today, film music is a key part of the movie business. Studios often market films using contemporary music supplied by popular bands and singers and rely on sales of recorded film music as a supplementary source of income. (The parent corporations that own studios also own music publishing and recording businesses.) Because of this, studios are often interested in scores that can be marketed in the format of popular songs. This trend goes back at least to David Raksin's score for *Laura* (1944), and could be found in the 1950s with films like *High Noon* (1952), and in the 1960s in *The Magnificent Seven, Breakfast at Tiffany's* (1961), and *Dr. Zhivago* (1965). Today, it is firmly established and is extremely common. The soundtrack of *Forrest Gump* (1994) was essentially a collection of popular tunes from the 1960s, while *Natural Born Killers* (1994) featured the work of popular 1990s performing groups.

The crafting of movie music as a series of pop hits has become a permanent fixture of the industry and has had a detrimental effect on the art of film scoring. The artistry of film scoring aims to create a fusion of music and image rather than detachable songs that can be marketed on their own and have only a marginal relationship with the images on screen. It was this development that effectively ended the longtime partnership between director Alfred Hitchcock and composer Bernard Herrmann. Herrmann had composed extraordinary music for the Hitchcock films *The Trouble with Harry* (1955), *The Man Who Knew Too Much* (1956), *The Wrong Man* (1956), *Vertigo* (1958), *North by Northwest* (1959), *Psycho* (1960), and *Marnie* (1964), and had served as a musical consultant on *The Birds* (1963). Herrmann composed a score for Hitchcock's next film, *Torn Curtain* (1966), which was grim and foreboding, but the producers at Universal wanted a pop song that could be hummed and played on the radio. Responding to their pressure, Hitchcock threw out Herrmann's score and substituted a more conventional composition in its place. Miffed at this treatment, Herrmann never worked with Hitchcock again.

Psycho (Paramount Pictures, 1960)
Bernard Herrmann contributed brilliant scores for Alfred Hitchcock's pictures. The score for *Psycho,* for example, used only string instruments. The shrieking strings heightened the impact of the film's brutal violence. Frame enlargement.

Dr. No (United Artists, 1962) Composer John Barry has created some of the best-known scores in contemporary film. In the 1960s, his jazz-styled music for the James Bond series helped immortalize ultra-cool Agent 007 (Sean Connery). More recently, his sweeping orchestral scores for *Out of Africa* (1985) and *Dances with Wolves* (1990) gave those films a lush, epic tone. Frame enlargement.

Like Herrmann, most serious film composers think that the pop song approach compromises the integrity of their scores. Sometimes the application of pop songs is done in an almost schizophrenic fashion. *Robin Hood, Prince of Thieves* (1991), starring Kevin Costner, employed a score that utilized many period instruments, but at the end of the film, over the final credits, a pop rock love ballad provided the exit music, roughly jolting moviegoers out of the medieval period of the movie.

The cross-marketing of movies and pop songs is now a firmly established feature of the industry. To some extent, film scoring suffers from this emphasis. Many films feature scores that, musically, have little to do with the action or emotions on screen. But, despite this, the art of film scoring remains very much alive. Exciting, ambitious original scores by Hans Zimmer (*Black Hawk Down*, 2001; *The Thin Red Line*, 1998), James Horner (*A Beautiful Mind*, 2001; *Field of Dreams*, 1989; *Glory*, 1989), John Barry (*Out of Africa*, 1985; *Dances with Wolves*, 1990), Danny Elfman (*Planet of the Apes*, 2001; *Men in Black*, 1997; *Edward Scissorhands*, 1990), and others continue to make a distinguished contribution to modern movies.

☐ SOUND DESIGN

The complexity of modern film sound, and its increasing importance in the artistic design of a film, requires a new creative member of the production term: the **sound designer.** Walter Murch's brilliant work on *Apocalypse Now* elicited the credit "sound design" because of Murch's key contributions to the film's total artistic design. On *Apocalypse Now,* Murch and his crew manipulated 160 tracks of recorded sounds. These were mixed together to create the finished soundtrack. Since then, the term has come into general usage.

Sound design goes far beyond the routine technical challenges of getting audible sound and mixing effects and music with dialogue. Sound designers create a total sound environment for the film's images, an environment that not only supports the images but extends their meaning in dynamic ways. The sound design of a film builds a mix of **realistic** and **synthetic sounds.** Realistic sound matches the properties of a real source. Unlike realistic sounds, synthetic sounds are invented and have no counterpart in actual life, but they bond with the images on screen and extend their meaning. The voice of Steven Spielberg's character E.T. resulted from a mix of human speech and animal sounds, incorporating up to eighteen different sound elements. In *Return of the Jedi*, the sounds of the laser guns and the air motorcycles were created by electronically modifying and re-recording a mixture of sound sources.

The modern film audience is privileged to experience film soundtracks of unprecedented complexity and subtlety. Sound designers create highly sophisticated manipulations of sound information. These manipulations are rule-governed and exploit unique properties of sound that differentiate it from a film's image track.

Differences between Sound and Image

Sound and images uniquely differ from one another. Two kinds of differences exist: (1) What viewers notice about pictures and sound, and (2) How pictures and sound structure time.

Perception of Image and Sound

Obviously, images are visible and can be seen, and sound cannot. Image edits, whether cuts, fades, or dissolves, can be seen on screen. Sound edits are inaudible. Images can be touched. Sound cannot. As a result, viewers notice images, but tend to be less aware of sound design. Viewers tend to think of cinema as an essentially visual medium, with sound as the backup element, there to support the images.

Because of this, viewers think that they interpret sound in reference to images. In most instances, however, sound shapes the image as much as the image shapes the

---

Apocalypse Now (United Artists, 1979)
To this shot of a spinning ceiling fan, sound designer Walter Murch added the sound of a helicopter propeller. This audiovisual combination places equal stress on image and sound; each conditions the other. Frame enlargement.

sound. Walter Murch created a memorable image–sound juxtaposition in *Apocalypse Now* by adding a helicopter sound to a shot of a spinning ceiling fan. Viewers hear a helicopter engine and rotor blades but see the spinning blades of the fan. In this striking contrast, sound and image are equally assertive, equally important. Viewers may think of images as being more important, but in this instance the helicopter sound contextualizes the image as much as it contextualizes the sound.

Sound design is an extremely powerful but nearly subliminal element of film structure. Furthermore, sound has a fluid nature that images do not. Taken out of context, many sounds can be difficult to identify, which enables sound designers to use them with great freedom, attaching them, for example, to a variety of images, as in the sound effects used in *Terminator 2* and *Backdraft*. Sound can stimulate the imagination in ways images do not. In *The Conversation* (1974), Gene Hackman plays a surveillance expert, Harry Caul. He overhears a murder committed in an adjoining hotel room. The violence of the killing is conveyed in the noises that come through the wall into Harry's room. Sound designer Walter Murch knew that what the audience (and Harry) would imagine based on the sounds would be far worse than what any picture could show.

The Conversation (Paramount, 1974)

Featuring brilliant sound design by Walter Murch, Francis Ford Coppola's *The Conversation* is that rare film that deeply probes the psychological components of sound. Harry Caul (Gene Hackman) is a pathologically withdrawn man who works as a professional wiretapper. As he labors to discover the meaning behind a mysterious conversation he has taped, Murch and Coppola show the subjective nature of sound. Harry psychologically projects a meaning onto the audio information that proves to be tragically incorrect. In this scene, he crouches in a hotel bathroom to tape a conversation in the next room. Frame enlargement.

Structuring Time

Unless they contain explicit movement, many images are ambiguous with respect to time. They can be run forward or backward with little noticeable difference. A long shot of a forest or the exterior of a house is ambiguous in this way, but not a shot of traffic or joggers. Viewers can tell if the latter two images were run backwards, but not necessarily the first two.

Sound adds directional time to images. With sound, viewers perceive images as moving forward unambiguously. George Stevens's Western *Shane* (1953) provides an interesting illustration of this principle. Stevens realized that a man dismounting a horse looks more graceful than when climbing into the saddle. Accordingly, when the film's villain climbs into the saddle, the editor used a shot of the character *dismounting* but played it in reverse. The sound in the scene—a gurgling stream, wind, off-screen dialogue from other characters—gives the shot a clear forward momentum. Viewers who are aware of the trick can see that the shot is played backwards, but for most viewers, unaware of the editing magic at work, the sleight-of-hand passes unnoticed because of the way the shot is paired with sound that is clearly directional in time.

Sound gives images forward momentum or adds to the momentum that the shots already possess. Sound temporalizes images. This is the principle that underlies the codes of sound continuity. But creating continuity is only one of the achievements of sophisticated sound design, which, like image editing, is a rule-governed practice. What are the basic rules and procedures for manipulating sounds and for establishing relationships with images?

The Codes of Sound Design

To construct the finished soundtrack viewers hear when watching a movie, designers employ five essential codes: (1) the sound hierarchy, (2) sound perspective, (3) sound bridges, (4) off-screen sound space, and (5) sound montage.

The Sound Hierarchy

Because of the variety of sounds in the audio environment and the need to organize them to facilitate the viewer's understanding of story information, sound designers customarily treat them in terms of a hierarchy of importance. When filmmakers manipulate dialogue, sound effects, and music within a scene, the hierarchy of relationships typically emphasizes dialogue. As one sound mixer stated, "When an audience is sitting in the theater, you're taking them to another world. If they have to turn and ask the person next to them, 'What did he say?', then you've interrupted disbelief. Now they're back in their world, they're not in the story." In practice, dialogue is the determining element in a sound mix. It is generally the first element to be mixed, and the volume of effects and music is usually kept at a softer level to run underneath the dialogue.

Everyone has seen movies in which an important character dies during a noisy battle. Often, the character makes a little speech before dying. When this occurs, the volume of the battle sounds invariably drops below the dialogue. Once the character has died, the battle sounds rise again to their previous level. Prevailing assumptions stipulate that dialogue should always be clear, crisp, and understandable to the viewer.

On the Waterfront (Columbia Pictures, 1954)
Breaking the sound hierarchy can create startling effects. When Terry Malloy (Marlon Brando) tells Edie (Eva Marie Saint) that he was involved in her brother's murder, the sound mix eliminates nearly all of their dialogue, replacing it with loud, harsh sounds from the environment, the New York harbor. These piercing sounds portray the characters' anguish and stand in for the missing dialogue. These sounds are the most important and prominent ones in the scene and carry its emotion, a function more typically performed by dialogue or music. Frame enlargements.

Filmmakers do not always construct a standard sound hierarchy; some have deliberately sought to avoid it. In the early 1970s, one major U.S. filmmaker revolutionized sound recording techniques in ways that challenged the dominant place of the actor's voice in the hierarchy of sound. Beginning with *California Split* (1974) and *Nashville* (1975), director Robert Altman pioneered the use of multichannel, multitrack sound recording. Rather than using a boom mike—a microphone hung on a long pole suspended over a scene to record the voices of the actors—Altman employed radio mikes. Each actor was separately miked, their voices transmitted to a recording receiver.

In the sound mix, Altman aimed to produce a profusion of voices, much as one hears in a crowded room. In the crowd scenes in *California Split,* for example, many actors speak at once, and the dialogue is multilayered, full of overlapping speech. In addition, the radio mikes picked up ambient noises, like the rustle of clothing, that are usually not captured by more standard recording techniques. The resulting audio mix was extremely rich and multidimensional, and a single character's voice did not always predominate over other voices in a scene. The mix gave Altman an audio equivalent to what his images were showing, namely, many things happening at once.

Altman's approach frustrated critics because they were used to a more normative sound hierarchy in which all voices were clearly modulated and balanced to give a single speaker primacy of position in the audio mix. His films of the early 1970s were somewhat controversial, but multitrack recording methods are today an industry standard, even though most films do not aim for the audio density of Altman's pictures.

The Sound Hierarchy in Early Cinema   While contemporary sound design typically features a highly articulated mix of dialogue, effects, and music, films from the early sound period blended fewer elements to create the soundtrack. Rather than working with many tracks each of dialogue, effects, and music, early sound films mixed a couple of dialogue tracks, a mono music track, a few sound effects, and an ambient track. In contrast to the profusion of sound detail in contemporary film, the audio design of early sound films included less information. Occasionally, one finds an incomplete sound hierarchy in these films, a mix of dialogue, effects, and music that runs counter to the practices that would soon become normative in the industry.

In Sergei Eisenstein's first sound film, *Alexander Nevsky* (1936), about a Russian folk hero who repulsed a German invasion in the thirteenth century, music and dialogue tend to predominate in the sound structure of the film, with background ambient sound and sound effects used less extensively. Some scenes or shots completely lack the ambient sound and effects that are clearly denoted by the images and action.

At the beginning of the movie, for example, a group of Mongol warriors visits Alexander Nevsky's fishing village. Viewers hear the sounds of their horses and armor as they arrive, but, leaving, they make no sound at all. Their exit is completely silent. Later in the film, during the visually impressive sequence that details the burning of the city of Pskov and the slaughter of its inhabitants by the invading German army,

---

Alexander Nevsky (1936)
The soundtrack of many films in the early sound period have a minimal range of effects and ambient noise, even when images, such as these shots showing a screaming child, suggest highly specific sounds. Frame enlargements.

ROBERT ALTMAN

Though Altman directed his first feature in the mid-1950s (*The Delinquents*, 1955), the 1970s saw him gain prominence as a leading U.S. filmmaker. Unlike George Lucas, Steven Spielberg, or, in an earlier period, Alfred Hitchcock, Altman has never been at home in the studio system. His career exhibits considerable friction and tension between the cynicism and European-style ambiguities of his films, their offbeat audiovisual and narrative style, and the conventional norms of mainstream studio filmmaking.

With *M*A*S*H* (1970), Altman embarked on a series of revisionist genre films that displayed his own critical, questioning relationship with Hollywood norms. Ostensibly about the Korean War but really about Vietnam, *M*A*S*H* irreverently dissected war film clichés and became a counterculture hit. In short

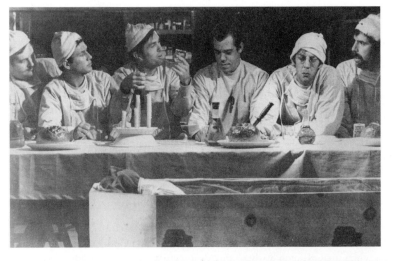

M*A*S*H (Twentieth Century Fox, 1970) Altman's films typically feature a large cast of performers, a multichannel sound mix with overlapping dialogue, and a loose, unstructured narrative. *M*A*S*H* is a dark comedy about Army surgeons during the Korean War, but everyone knew the film was really about Vietnam. The composition in this scene alludes to DaVinci's *Last Supper*.

viewers hear only music and dialogue without any sound effects. Close-ups of screaming, crying children lack these sound effects.

During the climax of the film, the epic battle on a frozen lake between Nevsky's armies and the invading Germans, music and sound effects alternate one at a time. The music plays for a while and then stops, and viewers hear sound effects (swords clashing, men shouting). Then the sound effects stop, and the music begins again. These manipulations of sound may strike a modern moviegoer's ears as rather crude and unrealistic because of the peculiar manner in which effects and music have been

order, Altman self-consciously revised the Western (*McCabe and Mrs. Miller,* 1971), the detective film (*The Long Goodbye,* 1973), and the gangster film (*Thieves Like Us,* 1974).

Founding the Lion's Gate production company in 1970, Altman began in these films to explore multi-track sound recording, but obtained mixed results until teaming with production mixer James Webb on *California Split* (1974). Henceforth, an uncommonly dense audio track distinguished Altman's work, featuring multiple, overlapping, layered effects and dialogue. In a clear departure from studio style, Altman's preferred sound design stressed complexity and ambiguity of speech and effects.

Altman reached his summit in the 1970s with *Nashville* (1975), a kaleidoscopic, multinarrative portrait of politics and country music that was an enormous critical success. Following this, Altman rapidly fell from grace in the studio system. His next films—*Buffalo Bill and the Indians* (1976), *A Wedding* (1978), *Quintet* (1979), and *A Perfect Couple* (1979)—were deemed excessively uncommercial by their studios and barely released. *Health* (1979) was shelved by its distributor.

Despite landing the assignment to direct *Popeye* (1980), Altman was now deemed unemployable by Hollywood. But instead of fading away or descending into bitterness, he simply continued working, but as an independent. For the next decade, he made

mostly small-scale adaptations of theater plays (*Come Back to the Five and Dime, Jimmie Dean, Jimmie Dean,* 1982; *Streamers,* 1983; *Fool For Love,* 1985), but scored a triumphant return to prominent feature filmmaking with *The Player* (1992), a trenchant, caustic satire of a deal-driven, sequel-oriented Hollywood system. Ironically, the film was a hit inside Hollywood, which, oddly enough, welcomed Altman back. He followed *The Player* with another critical hit, *Short Cuts* (1993), an acidic, cynical adaptation of Raymond Carver short stories about Los Angeles. Altman was back on top.

Since then, Altman has worked steadily and, with *Gosford Park* (2001), found his biggest popular and critical success since the early 1970s. Despite the wayward turns of his career, Altman's work has been consistently intelligent and stylistically experimental. His multitrack sound recording and kaleidoscopic, fragmented narratives are among his most recognizable features of style. In addition, Altman approaches each film as a collaboration among cast and crew. Minimizing directorial ego, he openly solicits ideas and input from others on the set and views his job as a facilitator and coordinator of the team's effort. Accordingly, his reputation among actors and crew is outstanding. Major stars eagerly accept cameo roles in his films because they want the experience of participating in the unique atmosphere of an Altman production.

edited so that they are never copresent and because of the lack of detail in the film's audio space when compared to its often striking images.

While most films establish a clear hierarchy of sound relationships that gives the voice a privileged pride of place and surrounds the voice with music and important sound effects, Altman's work and Eisenstein's *Alexander Nevsky* are significant alternatives to this practice. Their deviant structure demonstrates, by its omission, the prevalence of the conventional hierarchy in which voice, effects, and music are copresent but in carefully regulated volumes.

Sound Perspective

Sound perspective designates the ways that sound conveys properties of the physical spaces seen on-screen. Sound perspective in film is based on correspondences with the viewer's acoustic perception of space in everyday life. The sound of an approaching or receding object, for example, changes its pitch in a predictable way depending on its direction of movement, a phenomenon known as the *Doppler effect.* Sound designers routinely use Doppler effects to accoustically convey the movement of a sound-producing object through three-dimensional space. Recall that the sound engineers at Lucasfilm added Doppler effects to the arrows whizzing at Indiana Jones to give them a convincing three-dimensional presence in the scene. In the *Star Wars* films and other science fiction pictures, Doppler spatializes the approach of CGI or miniature-model spacecraft and helps sell these special-effect images to viewers.

Sound perspective can also be created by using reverberance and changes in volume. **Direct sound** is sound that comes immediately from the source. It is spoken or recorded directly into the microphone and, because of this, it typically carries minimal or no reverberance and conveys little environmental information. By contrast, **reflected sound** carries reverberance. It reflects off of surrounding surfaces in the environment to produce reverberation. Differing surfaces reflect sounds in differing ways, and these differences convey important information about the kind of physical environment in which the sound is occurring. Hard surfaces like glass or metal tend to bounce sound very quickly and very efficiently whereas softer surfaces, like carpeting or cushioned furniture, are less reflective. They tend to absorb sound and, in extreme cases, may deaden sound. In *The Conversation,* the noises of the murder that Harry Caul hears through an adjoining hotel room wall are muffled and deadened.

Sound environments, then, can be characterized in terms of their sound-reflective or sound-deadening properties. Sound designers pay close attention to these features so that the audio environments they create for a film match the physical conditions of the scene or shot. Sound needs to reverberate in Edward Scissorhands's huge, vacant castle, but not on the western plains in *Dances with Wolves.*

Another, very important characteristic of sound in the audio environment is ambient sound. As explained earlier, this term refers to generalized noises in the recording environment. If shooting takes place out-of-doors, ambient sounds may include the airplane traveling overhead, the cries of children playing in the distance, or the sound of wind in the trees. Ambient sound is found in all recording environments, even in an empty room. When a scene occurs in an empty room, the soundtrack will not be dead or silent. It will carry **room tone,** the acoustical properties of the room itself, the imperceptible sounds that it makes. Room tone is a very low level of ambient noise, and it indicates that the audio environment created by contemporary sound design is never silent or dead but always conveys some audio information.

Sound perspective often correlates with visual perspective. If the action is presented in long shot, viewers also hear the sound as if in long shot. As the sound source gets more distant from the camera in a reverberant environment, the properties of reflected sound increase. As the sound source comes closer to the camera, the amount of reflected sound decreases. By varying the amount of reflected sound, filmmakers establish the location of a sound source within the visual space on screen.

The Others (Miramax, 2001)
Digital, multichannel sound creates tremendously vivid sound perspective. When Grace (Nicole Kidman) is terrorized by what she believes are ghosts, disembodied voices fly around the room, jumping from channel to channel, speaker to speaker, across the front soundstage and into the rear surrounds. As the unseen spirits flutter about the character, the sound reproduces this action in three-dimensional audio space. The effect becomes subjective, immersing the film viewer into the character's experience. Frame enlargement.

If the action is presented to the viewer in close-up, direct sound should predominate over reflected sound. The actors' voices should be intimate and sound as if they are spoken closely to the microphone. Sound designer Walter Murch has stated that he records not just sounds in the environment, but also the spaces between the listener and those sounds. In actual practice, however, microphone placement does not exactly parallel camera placement. While the difference in camera placement between a close-up and a long shot may be very great, the difference in actual microphone placement may only be a matter of several feet. Moreover, many contemporary films invert visual and sound perspectives by filming actors in long shot and miking them for direct sound. Peter Weir's *Dead Poets' Society* (1989) deals with the relationship between an unconventional English teacher (Robin Williams) and his students in an elite prep school in 1959. One of the boys discusses with his friend his excitement over getting the lead role in the school play. The two boys stand on a pier next to the water and are filmed in extreme long shot. Their voices, however, are miked in intimate terms. The audio space is very close. The visual space is very distant.

Sound Perspective in Early Cinema   As with other attributes of film structure, filmmakers did not grasp the complexities of sound design all at once. Sound technology came to the movies in the late 1920s, and filmmakers gradually discovered the creative possibilities of sound and how to use it in a rich and naturalistic fashion. As a result, and because early sound technology was quite limiting, the soundtracks in many early films tend to be less detailed and less reflective of the realities of sound space.

French director René Clair's *Under the Roofs of Paris* (1930), for example, is a mixture of pantomime, music, and dialogue. Much of the film was shot silent, with a few talking sequences added later. At the beginning of the film, the camera booms down from the rooftops to the streets of Paris where a song salesman is performing a new tune for a group of onlookers. Viewers hear the song throughout the camera movement, and, as the camera draws closer, the song's volume increases. There is, however, no apparent change in reverberation.

At the end of the scene, the camera booms back up to the rooftops. This time the volume of the song does not decrease as much as it should given the amount of physical space the camera crosses. Again, there is no change in reverberation. The perspectives established by visual space and audio space do not correlate very well.

Pointing out this feature of *Under the Roofs of Paris* does not imply that René Clair is an inferior filmmaker. Clair, in fact, was one of the most important early practitioners of sound and a filmmaker whose career straddled the silent and sound periods. He devised many inventive gags in his films where the humor depends on a particular manipulation of sound. Moreover, his work was a decided influence on the U.S. master Charlie Chaplin. Clair's film, *À Nous la Liberté* (1931), was the inspiration for Chaplin's *Modern Times* (1936). The point here is to emphasize that these codes of sound design are learned applications of style that filmmakers gradually discovered as a way of creating credible audiovisual relationships on screen. The design differences between an early film like *Under the Roofs of Paris* and more contemporary films shows the development and maturation of sound aesthetics.

Under the Roofs of Paris
(1930)
Correct sound perspective is not a feature of every film. The relationship of audio space and camera perspective often proves to be quite flexible. In *Under the Roofs of Paris*, as the camera travels from the rooftops to the street below, the appropriate changes in audio space do not occur. Frame enlargement.

Case Study: Jacques Tati

As with all rules and conventions of film structure, sound perspective can be satirized and played with by smart filmmakers. French director Jacques Tati was one of the masters of sound cinema. Tati was a pantomime comedian whose films bear some relationships to silent comedies. Dialogue in his films is minimal, and the sound space is dominated by a multitude of carefully organized environmental sounds. Tati **post-dubbed** his soundtracks to achieve a maximum of control over their sound design.

In Tati's masterpiece, *Playtime* (1967), he playfully distorts standard sound perspective. Early in the film, the main character, Mr. Hulot (played by Tati himself), is trying to keep an appointment with an official named Mr. Giffard. When Hulot tries to meet the official, he is instructed by the building's doorman to wait beside a bank of elevators while Mr. Giffard is paged. Hulot waits patiently, framed at screen left, while, on-screen right, a vast, receding hallway extends into the distance. Hulot is seated around the edge of the wall, however, so he cannot look down this hallway. But the viewer can.

As Hulot waits, loud footsteps occur off-screen. Because of their loud volume, the viewer assumes the person these feet belong to must be very near. In the next moment, however, a tiny figure appears in the distance at the end of the hallway. This is joke number one, reversing the expectation viewers developed based on the probable sound space–image space relation. The glass, metal, and tile hallway conveys the reverberant footsteps very effectively; they remain loud and only grow slightly in volume as the man approaches. This is joke number two. The third joke in the scene occurs as Tati, hearing the man but unable to see him, keeps trying to get up, assuming that he must be close given the loudness of his steps. The doorman, however, who can look down the hallway, keeps gesturing for Hulot to stay seated.

This scene is composed of a single shot, and the three distinct jokes that occur in it are based on Tati's playful manipulation of the sound space–image space relation. In this case, sound perspective is an unreliable indicator of visual space and of the physical relations in the scene. It illustrates the cinema's transformational property, its

Playtime (1967)
Director Jacques Tati satirizes sound perspective by making it an unreliable indicator of visual space. The sound of Mr. Giffard's footsteps remains extremely loud and distinct despite his changing location in a long hallway. Frame enlargement.

ability to alter and play with perceptual realities in ways that viewers readily accept. The cinema records *and* transforms audiovisual information, and filmmakers are constantly negotiating the creative possibilities of these functions.

Sound Bridges

Sound may be connected to a source on-screen or disconnected from an on-screen source. In the latter instance, the sound-producing source is off-camera. It is source-disconnected sound because, though viewers hear the sound, they cannot see its source. In any given scene, sound designers employ both categories. Source-connected sound occurs if viewers see Daniel Day-Lewis, as Hawkeye in *The Last of the Mohicans* (1993), tell a British officer that he will not serve in the English army. If, by contrast, the camera stays on the British officer while Hawkeye speaks off-screen, the sound is source-disconnected.

Switching between on-screen and off-screen sound gives filmmakers enormous flexibility in the editing of their films. Not everything that is heard needs to be shown. This frees the camera from being a slave to dialogue or other sounds and enables it to reveal aspects of the scene independently of what viewers hear on the soundtrack. All a filmmaker need do is return periodically to source-connected sound in order to sustain the viewer's sense of the important audiovisual relationships. Filmmakers often "cheat" in the editing of dialogue scenes by using reaction shots of a character's face taken from other points in the scene or film. The editing encourages viewers to read the expression as a reaction to the immediate dialogue, which is heard off-camera.

Filmmakers use sound to establish continuity across shots by alternating between on-screen and off-screen sound. Because sound gives images a clear direction and orientation in time—with sound, film images clearly move forward—sound can establish continuity of time across the shot changes in a scene. This often occurs through the use of a **sound bridge** in which dialogue or effects carry over, or bridge, two or more shots, unifying them in time and/or space. Sound bridges are one of the most powerful and important ways of creating continuity in film. In *Glory* (1989), Col. Robert Shaw (Matthew Broderick) must tell his African American regiment that the War Department has ordered that black soldiers in the Union army will receive less pay than their white counterparts. As Shaw speaks, the editor cuts to reaction shots of the black soldiers, showing their dismay at this insulting decree. Shaw continues to speak off-screen during these shots, establishing the sound bridge and creating continuity among the shots. The sound information tells viewers that all of the shots, which show completely different groups of characters, are part of a common space and within a single moment of time.

In the early German sound film *The Blue Angel* (1930), as the schoolmaster (played by Emil Jannings) removes his handkerchief to blow his nose, the action cuts to a reaction shot of the schoolboys. While looking at them, viewers hear the sound of Jannings blowing his nose. The editing switches from source-connected to source-disconnected sound. Sound flows over the cut, establishing a continuity that links up the different images. In dialogue scenes using the shot-reverse-shot technique, passages of spoken dialogue will flow over the cuts to establish continuity across the shot changes.

Glory
(Columbia TriStar, 1989)
The voice of Col. Robert Shaw (Matthew
Broderick) provides the sound bridge
unifying these reaction shots of African
American soldiers. The sound bridge
connects the space and time of these
shots, which contain no visual elements
in common. Frame enlargements.

In contemporary films, filmmakers often employ a modified sound bridge in which
the switch to source-disconnected sound occurs before the cut, rather than after it.
In other words, the sound cut precedes the visual transition. In Mike Nichols's *The
Graduate* (1967), a striking sequence expresses the social and emotional alienation
of the young hero, Benjamin (played by Dustin Hoffman), when he dons a scuba
suit and seeks refuge at the bottom of his parents' swimming pool. The camera films
him alone and isolated in the depths of the pool. As the camera tracks slowly away

The Graduate (Avco-Embassy, 1967)
A creative noncorrespondence between image and sound in *The Graduate*. The sound bridge to the next scene begins well before the end of the final shot in this, the previous scene. As the camera pulls away from Benjamin (Dustin Hoffman) in the swimming pool, viewers hear him talking on the telephone in the next scene. Frame enlargement.

from him, viewers hear sound from the next scene (which occurs in a phone booth) for 13 seconds before the image cuts to that scene. It is Benjamin talking on the telephone to invite Mrs. Robinson, his next-door neighbor, to meet him at a local hotel.

The sound of Benjamin on the phone, asynchronous with the shot of him in the pool, technically violates the time and space of the pool scene, but viewers accept the sound editing as a novel, interesting, and offbeat way of signaling the transition to the next scene. When *The Graduate* was released in 1967, this was an innovative way of making the transition, but it has become a fairly standard technique today.

Off-Screen Sound

Just as the distinction between source-connected and source-disconnected sound is relevant for understanding principles of sound continuity, it also helps explain how sound can extend the viewer's perception of visual space. **Off-screen sound** is part of the dramatic action of a scene, but its source is off-camera. This kind of sound enlarges the coordinates of the world represented on screen. That world is not coextensive with the images on screen. Instead, through sound information, it extends into an indefinite, acoustically defined area of off-screen space.

Filmmakers quickly grasped the creative possibilities. Produced only a few years into the sound era, Fritz Lang's classic *M* (1931) brilliantly uses off-screen sound to signal the lurking, unseen presence of a serial killer. The murderer compulsively whistles the theme from the *Peer Gynt* suite, and his rapid, repetitive whistling occurs off-camera in many scenes throughout the film as a means of building suspense, anxiety, and mystery. As a little girl looks in a store window and then runs down the street, the off-screen whistling conveys his stalking presence and desperate hunger for a new victim. Lang had quickly grasped the power of sound to fire the audience's imagina-

M (1931)
Director Fritz Lang's classic film vividly demonstrated the power of off-screen sound space. The whistled leitmotif of the serial killer (Peter Lorre) suggests his lurking presence as he stalks his victims from off-screen. Here, frustrated in his hunt, he pauses by a store window. Rows of knives reflected in the glass encircle his body, suggesting that he is a prisoner of his lethal desires. Frame enlargement.

tion. The unseen, conveyed through sound, is far more frightening than how the killer proves to look when the camera finally shows him. This sonic extension of the frame into off-screen space would become an essential technique in horror films in which monsters lurk just out of sight.

The famous ending of *All Quiet on the Western Front* (1931) shows the hero—a German soldier in the trenches of World War I—killed by a sniper as he reaches tenderly for a butterfly that has alighted on the fields of carnage. In close-up, the viewer sees the hero's hands reaching for the butterfly, then hears an off-screen gunshot and sees the hands drop lifelessly to the ground. At this moment, the ambient (and off-screen) sounds of battle cease, as the soundtrack deadens to convey the hero's passing.

Case Study: Robert Bresson

French director Robert Bresson used off-screen sound as a major component of his film aesthetic. Bresson's style is based on reduction, on paring away details until only the essentials remain. In line with this, he believed that images and sounds must not duplicate one another. He noted that "sound must never come to the help of an image, nor an image to the help of a sound," pointing out that when sound can replace an image, the image should either be cut or made less explicit in its dramatic or emotional content. Accordingly, in Bresson's films, the information conveyed by image and sound is carefully controlled and restricted. Bresson tried to avoid audiovisual redundancy by ensuring that his images and sounds would say different things.

One of the ways he avoids redundancy is by using sound to create off-screen space, to imply the existence of things that he does not then need to show. In *Pickpocket* (1959), for example, an early sequence shows the thief trying to rob spectators at a race track.

All Quiet on the Western Front (Universal, 1931) As the hero (Lew Ayres) reaches tenderly for a butterfly, a sniper's bullet, fired off-screen, abruptly ends his life. To simulate his passing, the soundtrack goes dead, all ambient noise ceasing. Frame enlargement.

Bresson, though, never shows the track or any horses. He uses sound to establish the location and the event and create the implied images. The shot shows people watching something off-screen, standing side by side, looking toward the camera while the soundtrack carries a race announcer's voice and the pounding of horses' hooves. These sounds create in the viewer's mind the images and impressions of a horserace. Having provided the sounds of a race, Bresson believed he did not need to show pictures.

Filmmakers routinely use off-screen sound to extend the frame in ways that are consistent with visual information presented in the shot or scene. In *Blade Runner,* for example, the futuristic city is conveyed through an abundance of off-screen sound information; it is also shown in spectacular long shots. By contrast, in the exceptional case of Bresson's cinema, sound creates images in the minds of viewers that are never shown on screen and are, Bresson believes, richer than any screen image could be.

Sound Montage

Contemporary multitrack sound design is based on montage, the editing of sounds into highly intricate and complex patterns that create meaning and emotion. *Apocalypse Now* features an exceptionally creative sound montage during the opening scene as Captain Willard (Martin Sheen) lies on his bed in a Saigon hotel. Willard longs to be back in the jungle where he can safely satisfy his violent appetites in combat and by working as a paid assassin. As he lies in the hotel, Willard imagines himself in the jungle. The soundtrack carries an audio representation of this inner fantasy. Sound designer Walter Murch systematically replaced city sounds with a series of jungle sounds. Urban noises—a policeman's whistle, the engines of cars and motorcycles—give way on the soundtrack to the squawk of jungle birds, the buzzing of insects, and the cries

Apocalypse Now (United Artists, 1979)
The beginning of *Apocalypse Now* shows Captain Willard (Martin Sheen) in a Saigon hotel room. A complex sound montage replaces Saigon's city sounds with jungle sounds to suggest Willard's desire to return to the jungle. Frame enlargement.

of monkeys. Murch pointed out that these sound manipulations convey the idea that, although Willard's body is in Saigon, his mind is in the jungle.

Visual montages arrange shots to express meanings not contained in any single shot taken in isolation. This scene from *Apocalypse Now* uses the same principle, transposed to sound. The total arrangement of sounds expresses the reality of Willard's fantasy in a way that the individual sounds, taken in isolation, cannot.

The six-channel systems used for playback in theater auditoriums and consumer home video have accentuated the montage structure of contemporary sound design. By spatializing sound—sending discrete elements to different speakers positioned about the viewer—six-channel playback emphasizes the richness and density of sound montages. The expanded dynamic range provided by digital sound has enabled filmmakers to construct ever more complex audio montages and has helped make this an essential feature of contemporary sound aesthetics.

SUMMARY

Though moviegoers may not be explicitly aware of sound design, its contribution to film cannot be overstated. The next time you watch a favorite movie on television, turn off the sound and see how impoverished the pictures become. Without sound, a movie loses much of its emotional impact.

Sound design works with the three types of sound—dialogue, music, and effects. Dialogue in film tends to be either voice-over narration or character speech. Sound effects are created using Foley techniques or more elaborate electronic manipulations as part of a comprehensive sound design. Music in film tends to be composed within a late romantic style, whose musical conventions and range of coloring are familiar to most moviegoers. Movie music helps set the locale and atmosphere of time and place in the story, adds psychological and emotional meaning to a scene, provides background filler, establishes continuity, and calls attention to climaxes and conclusions of scenes.

Sound design creates a complex audio environment to accompany film images, establishing dynamic audiovisual relationships and shaping in subtle and almost subliminal ways the viewer's interpretation of those images. Sound design is orderly and rule-based, following a set of basic codes, some of which establish perceptual correspondences with the viewer's real-world audio experience.

Dialogue, music, and effects are controlled to establish a hierarchy of sound relationships with dialogue being given primary importance. Direct, reflected, and ambient sound levels are carefully related to camera position to create sound perspective. Editors alternate between establishing on-screen and off-screen sound–image relations to keep camera perspective flexible and to maintain continuity. Sound editing establishes continuity across cuts, primarily by allowing sound to flow over the cut, as in the use of sound bridges. Sound is also used to prepare viewers for visual transitions, as when a sound cut precedes a visual cut, and to establish off-screen space that extends the viewer's physical sense of the image. Finally, sound montages may establish intellectual and emotional associations that go beyond the content of the images.

SUGGESTED READINGS

Rick Altman, ed., *Sound Theory/Sound Practice* (New York: Routledge, 1992).

Michel Chion, *Audio-Vision*, ed. and trans. Claudia Gorbman (New York: Columbia University Press, 1994).

Kathryn Kalinak, *Settling the Score: Music and the Classical Hollywood Film* (Madison: University of Wisconsin Press, 1992).

Fred Karlin, *Listening to Movies: The Film Lover's Guide to Film Music* (New York: Schirner Books, 1994).

Vincent LoBrutto, *Sound-on-Film: Interviews with Creators of Film Sound* (Westport, CT: Praeger, 1994).

Michael Schelle, *The Score: Interviews with Film Composers* (Los Angeles, CA: Silman-James Press, 1999).

Elizabeth Weis and John Belton, eds., *Film Sound: Theory and Practice* (New York: Columbia University Press, 1985).

Chapter 6

The Nature
of Narrative in Film

Chapter Objectives

After reading this chapter, you should be able to:

- explain why a script serves as the foundation for a film
- explain why the storytelling function came to film early in its history
- explain the relationship between narrative and the mass production of film
- explain the three basic elements of narrative
- differentiate between story and plot and explain how filmmakers may creatively manipulate this distinction
- explain the concept of authorship in cinema and why it is a problematic concept
- distinguish between real and implied authors

- explain how point of view operates in film narratives
- describe the classical Hollywood narrative
- distinguish explicit causality from implicit causality and explain their different narrative effects
- explain the antinarrative tradition in cinema
- describe the viewer's contribution to narrative
- define the nature of film genre
- describe the types of stories found in the major film genres

Key Terms and Concepts

story	antinarrative	point of view
plot	explicit causality	real author
deviant plot structure	implicit causality	implied author
the classical Hollywood narrative	suspense	genre
	surprise	convention
subjective shot		

Stories are found in all cultures. Narrative is a universal human activity used for entertainment, instruction, and socialization. It is also an essential way that people think about themselves and their world. To explain how things change, or how they got to be, people tell stories. Given the universality of narrative, it is not surprising that cinema, in its popular forms, has been a narrative medium.

Commercial filmmakers use the camera, light, color, sound, and editing to tell stories. Fiction films are distributed internationally to chains of theaters and video stores where fans of Westerns, science fiction films, and other genres turn to them for pleasure and enrichment.

The importance of narrative for popular movies cannot be overestimated. What, then, is narrative, and what are its structural elements in film? This chapter explains when and why narrative came to the movies, examines some of the basic elements of narrative structure, and concludes by examining what the viewer contributes to the experience of narrative.

☐ STORY AND SCRIPT

Though cinema is an audiovisual medium, it begins with the written word. The initial step in the production of a film is the completion of a script. Much like a play, the script tells the story in a scene-by-scene fashion, with dialogue and character interactions written out in detail. The script furnishes the basic structure of story and dramatic action that filmmakers will transform into picture and sound. There is no substitute for these attributes at the scripting stage; filmmakers find it difficult to develop them once a production has commenced and is before the cameras. Shekhar Kapur, the director of *Elizabeth* (1998), joined that project when the script was in its third revision, and nothing went before the cameras until the script was in its thirteenth draft. The resulting film is uncommonly rich and well designed, in large part because of its solid, scripted foundation.

The elegance of structure found in such exquisitely told narrative films as Hitchcock's *Rear Window* and *Vertigo* originated in outstanding scripts. (For *Vertigo,* Hitchcock went through three screenwriters before he got what he wanted.) Because of the structural complexity of filmmaking, a great deal about the medium must be preplanned and predetermined. As a result, filmmakers cannot simply improvise shots and action and

Time Code
(Screen Gems, 2000)
In this unusual film, a split-screen technique divides the frame into four grids, with each conveying a separate storyline, but all centering on the same events and characters. The plots even move from grid to grid, and the narrative becomes a kaleidoscopic mosaic. Changes in the sound mix "tell" viewers which grid to concentrate on. Director Mike Figgis shot on digital video in extended takes running almost 90 minutes. The only "editing" is that which occurs when the viewer compares the picture information across the four grids. Frame enlargement.

expect their finished film to have a sophisticated and intricate visual and narrative design. This design must be planned in advance. As we shall see in subsequent chapters, filmmakers use camera, sound, and editing to shape stories and bring them to life as cinema. But all of this begins with a script, even though the screenwriter, in practice, will specify few details of camerawork. (That is an area left to the director.) The audio-visual design of a film falls outside the domain of the screenwriter. The script, however, furnishes the narrative, dramatic action, and dialogue that a director then has the job of visualizing, using all of the tools that the craft of filmmaking offers.

☐ THE TURN TO NARRATIVE IN EARLY FILM HISTORY

The storytelling function in cinema arrived quickly. Public exhibition of projected motion pictures dates from 1895, when the photographic equipment manufacturers Auguste and Louis Lumière held a public screening of their short films. Called "actualities," they focused on everyday life and did *not* assume a narrative format. Subjects included parents feeding a baby, workers knocking over a wall, a train pulling into a station, and workers leaving a factory.

One film on the early program, however, *The Gardener Gets Watered* (1895), anticipated the use of film as a storytelling medium. A gardener watering his lawn is tormented by a mischievous boy who kinks the hose and then straightens it, spraying the gardener's face. He retaliates by chasing and spanking the boy. The film thus shows a series of events that were clearly staged for the camera and which present an episode of narrative action ordered in time, with a beginning and an end.

The Gardener Gets Watered (1895)
The use of film to tell stories followed soon after the invention of cinema. This early Lumière film, *The Gardener Gets Watered,* staged events for the camera and sequenced them as narrative. Frame enlargement.

In the United States, movies were an early attraction on the vaudeville stage, where motion picture presentations coexisted with slapstick comedians, singing performances, dramatic recitations, and animal shows. By 1902, however, narrative films, particularly comedies, began to appear on stage, where they were greeted enthusiastically by the public.

They coexisted, however, with a vast amount of nonfiction film material, including travelogues (films showing beautiful, exotic, or faraway places) and films focused on topical events such as a yacht race or political parade. Narrative film, though, quickly became the predominant form, displacing these nonfiction formats. The public was enthusiastic about story films, including comedies, dramas, chases, or trick films (films favoring such special optical effects as characters appearing and disappearing or moving in fast or slow motion). Nickelodeons—storefront theaters where the public could see an entire program of films for 5 or 10 cents—sprang up in great numbers, by 1910 attracting about 26 million Americans per week (a little less than 20 percent of the national population).

The nickelodeon boom demonstrated the explosion of popular interest in the movies, and it challenged producers to optimize film production so that it could meet the growing popular demand for motion picture entertainment. In this regard, story films offered decisive advantages over nonfiction production. Stories could be written as fast as films were needed, and they could capitalize on the scenic features of a given production company's locale. By contrast the documentary filmmaker was a hostage to events. Production had to wait for the interesting yacht race or parade to occur. The only limit on the production of story films was the imagination of the writers and the physical resources of the production companies.

The Birth of a Nation (1915) By 1915, cinema had reached artistic maturity and attained great narrative sophistication. *The Birth of a Nation* presented an epic (and intensely racist) narrative of unprecedented structural complexity. The circular masking on this shot is an iris—commonly used in silent cinema—which director D. W. Griffith employs to focus the viewer's attention upon the Little Colonel (Henry B. Walthall) as he defiantly rams a flag into the barrel of an enemy cannon. Frame enlargement.

D. W. GRIFFITH

In early film history, D. W. Griffith perfected (though he did not invent) the essential techniques of motion picture narrative. Griffith's understanding of the principles of film structure and the methods of cinematic storytelling was uncommonly sophisticated. Viewed today, the camerawork and editing in his films seem thoroughly modern, even though the melodramatic stories appear somewhat dated.

Griffith was born in Kentucky in 1875, into a family ruined and impoverished by the Civil War and Reconstruction. Determined to become an actor and playwright, Griffith loved the theater and considered it to be a legitimate art. By contrast, he thought the movies were a bastard offspring, and he came to them reluctantly after failing to launch a successful theatrical career. In 1908, Griffith made his first film at the Biograph Studio in New York, where he continued to

work until 1913. In his Biograph films, Griffith developed an increasingly complex and expressive visual style that he used to punch his stories across with maximum emotional impact. He perfected this style by directing a huge number of films. He directed 86 films in 1910, for example, and 70 films in 1911. Their subjects fell into categories that would define the basic Hollywood genres: gangster films, Westerns, biblical films, and war films.

At Biograph, Griffith strained against the narrative restrictions imposed by the one-reel format (one reel was approximately 10 minutes). In 1911, he made *Enoch Arden* in two reels, and in 1913 he made the biblical epic, *Judith of Bethulia*, his final Biograph film, in four reels. By moving to longer forms, Griffith was able to tell increasingly complex stories. After leaving Biograph, Griffith made two epics, *The Birth of a Na-*

The Birth of a Nation (1915)
Griffith was a director of remarkable visual brilliance. In this moment of quiet intimacy from *The Birth of a Nation*, a soldier returning from the Civil War is greeted by his mother and sister. Their arms encircle and draw him into the house. The image is eloquent in its restraint and simplicity. Frame enlargement.

Historian Robert Allen has argued that the shift to narrative films can be explained in part by these advantages and points out that by 1909, fiction films represented 97 percent of the industry's total output. Public interest and the needs of the expanding industry decisively shifted film production into the narrative mold. The narrative sophistication of early film rapidly matured. The work of di-

tion (1915) and *Intolerance* (1916), which masterfully wove together multiple plotlines and featured huge casts of characters. At silent speeds, each film ran approximately three hours.

Griffith's films are a virtual catalogue of modern motion picture technique. By using multiple camera positions and fluid editing, he fractured a scene into its constituent shots, intercutting freely to create smooth continuity. Each shot was dramatically incomplete, recording just a fragment of the action and acquiring meaning in relation to the other shots that made up the scene. He drastically varied camera position and angle, freely incorporating low- and high-angle shots, as well as long shots, medium shots, and close-ups. In *Enoch Arden*, Griffith used a psychological image to show what a character is thinking. The camera draws close to the character's face, then Griffith cuts to another scene that represents the character's mental image.

Griffith skillfully placed his cameras to frame shots in highly expressive ways. In *The Birth of a Nation*, when the Little Colonel returns home from the Civil War, he is greeted by his mother. Rather than showing the mother's face, Griffith discreetly shows only her arms reaching out from inside the house to embrace him. This discreet framing, with its use of off-screen space, intensifies the emotions of the reunion by emphasizing their private nature.

By 1915 and 1916, when Griffith completed his epics, *The Birth of a Nation* and *Intolerance,* he had perfected the essential building blocks of modern motion picture narrative: rapid changes of camera position and angle, close-ups used to intensify the drama and reveal emotion, complex editing used to fracture a scene into a series of dramatically incomplete shots, camera movement used to extend the frame and follow action, and cross-cutting of multiple story lines.

Unfortunately, Griffith's brilliant grasp of film structure accompanied racist and reactionary attitudes. Most notoriously, *The Birth of a Nation* portrayed the Civil War and Reconstruction as catastrophes that destroyed the happy plantation life of the South and, by freeing Southern slaves, unleashed a tide of black villainy against virtuous white aristocrats. In the film's climax, the Ku Klux Klan saves Southern honor and white virtue by restoring order throughout the South. Because of its virulent racism, *The Birth of a Nation* remains as inflammatory today as when it was first screened. Its explosive nature is evidence of Griffith's filmmaking skill. Its visual power and emotional manipulation of audiences make its racism all the more vicious and repugnant.

Griffith tried to rebut charges that he was a racist and calls for censoring the movies with *Intolerance,* a complex film weaving together a modern story of crime and gangsters with stories about the fall of Babylon, the massacre of the Huguenots in medieval France, and the crucifixion of Christ. Griffith drew an epic portrait of social intolerance by telling these stories simultaneously, cutting back and forth among them to create dramatic and emotional connections. Its elaborate narrative structure made *Intolerance* a film far ahead of its time. Even today, it remains a challenging film.

Griffith continued to make several more outstanding films (*Broken Blossoms,* 1919; *True Heart Susie,* 1919; *Way Down East,* 1920; *Orphans of the Storm,* 1922), but during the 1920s his melodramatic stories seemed increasingly old-fashioned, and, except for two productions, the coming of sound put an end to his career. His last picture was the undistinguished *The Struggle* (1931). On his death in 1948, at age 73, he was a lonely, forgotten man who spent his last years living on the fringes of a Hollywood that had passed him by.

rector D. W. Griffith, beginning in 1908, displayed a special narrative brilliance and an unprecedented sophistication of visual design. Since the first decade of the medium's history, then, narrative has been an essential ingredient in the popular appeal of cinema, and it furnished the key basis on which the industry could flourish.

☐ ELEMENTS OF NARRATIVE

Narratives have three fundamental characteristics: (1) an understanding between viewers and the filmmaker about how the story should be judged; (2) a story and plot sequencing events into a particular order that forms the narrative; and (3) a narrator and narrative point of view.

The Fictive Stance

Audiences evaluate fictional stories differently from nonfictional ones, and they generally want to know to what degree a story is fiction or nonfiction. With fiction, the audience willingly suspends its disbelief in order to experience the pleasures of an imaginary world. The audience agrees to accept the contents of the story as real at one level of make-believe, while knowing, at another level, that it is only a story. Critic Peter Lamarque has termed this agreement "the fictive stance."

If a story is clearly fiction, the audience does not hold the filmmaker accountable for its truth or veracity. Instead, the audience applies a different set of criteria dealing with the artistic structure and organization of the story. Is it compelling, convincing, thrilling, entertaining, or amusing? By contrast, with nonfiction, audiences measure the tale according to notions of factual truth and honesty.

This seems like a clean and clear distinction, yet many stories and movies occupy gray areas. Are they fiction or nonfiction? How does one decide? In a movie like *Star Wars* (1977), viewers clearly have a fictional story. The events in George Lucas's film do not exist in this world or in any easily imaginable world of the near future. By contrast, Oliver Stone's *JFK* (1991) seemed to want to play both ways with its audience, mixing fact and fiction in ways that were often hard to detect. On the one hand, the film presents an exhaustive summary of the facts surrounding the assassination of President Kennedy, supported by real, archival news footage. The film uses this fact-

Star Wars (Twentieth Century Fox, 1977)
Star Wars is a clearly fictional story. The setting is futuristic, the characters have no real-life counterparts, and the story events are entirely imaginary. Viewers of this film have no difficulty deciding whether to evaluate it and experience it as fiction.

JFK (Warner Bros., 1991)
Kevin Costner as District Attorney Jim Garrison in *JFK*. Oliver Stone's
film created controversy because of its fluid mixture of real archival
footage of the Kennedy years, faked footage made to look archival,
and fictional characters who had no counterpart in the historical record.
Director Stone meticulously sifted through the factual record surrounding
the assassination, questioned the official findings that a lone assassin killed
Kennedy, but often described his film as a myth. As a result, viewers could
not tell where the film's factual ambitions turned into the fictions of myth
or be sure the filmmaker knew where the differences lay. In comparison
to a film such as *Star Wars*, the fictional status of this film is more
ambiguous and harder to evaluate.

---

based history to critique and debunk the Warren Commission's finding that Lee Har-
vey Oswald acted as a lone assassin. On the other hand, Stone intermixes the archival
footage with reenactments filmed so they would look like part of the documentary
record, and he concocts an entirely speculative explanation for the assassination based
on the unproved premise that Kennedy intended to withdraw U.S. forces from Vietnam and was killed by those committed to escalating the war. There is virtually no
evidence to support this contention, and Stone said that he was offering a counter-
myth to oppose what he regarded as the dominant mythology of a lone assassin. Where
did that leave the film: fiction, nonfiction, myth, history? *JFK* is an uncomfortable
mixture of these modes that leaves the audience unable to tell where the filmmaker
believes their differences lie.

Audiences want very much to know the truth value of the tales they are told. When
filmmakers, like Stone, fudge the distinctions between fiction and nonfiction, they
often stir up controversy. When Robert Zemeckis used real footage of President Clinton speaking about the Oklahoma City bombing victims in a fictional context in *Contact* (1997)—the film makes it seem as if Clinton is addressing a space shuttle
explosion—many people criticized what they regarded as the unethical use of the news

footage. Filmmakers, though, can work in the other direction quite successfully, presenting a clearly fictional story as if it were the record of real events. *The Blair Witch Project* (1999), for example, is a horror movie about the disappearance of a film crew that left footage of its terrifying last moments, and the film is constructed as a documentary that examines this footage and tries to reconstruct the story it tells.

Narrative Structure: Story and Plot

How the story is told is every bit as important as its content. **Story** and **plot** are fundamental characteristics of every narrative, and their relationship determines its structure. Plot refers to the sequencing of events as shown in a given film. It designates the way narrative events are arranged in the film. Story designates the larger set of events of which the plot is a subset. Any given narrative points beyond itself to imply a set of events that are not directly portrayed, as well as those that are shown. Story refers to the true chronological sequencing of all the classes of events, shown or implied, that make up the narrative.

Unlike the events of one's daily life, which often appear to be somewhat unstructured, random, and in flux, events in a narrative have a clear shape and sequence. Not all events need to be included in the plot, and this is where the distinction between story and plot arises. Many events can be implied or do not need reference at all. In the case of mystery or suspense films, events are withheld from the audience to be revealed at a later time. Viewers enjoy mysteries, for example, because they try to figure things out before the detective does.

In many films there is little structural distinction between a film's plot and a film's story. Often, a plot is linear, presenting the true chronology of a story from start to finish. The vast majority of commercially produced movies are told in a linear, chronological fashion. However, many films make use of flashbacks, a narrative structure that was especially common in Hollywood films of the 1940s (*Casablanca*, 1943; *Double*

Brute Force
(Universal, 1947)
Hollywood films of the 1940s used flashbacks—often lengthy and extended ones—to add richness and complexity to their narrative design. *Brute Force* portrays the frustrations of prison inmates by using flashbacks to show their former lives, outside of prison. Each of the film's main characters is alloted an extended flashback sequence. Frame enlargement.

Indemnity, 1944; *Sunset Boulevard,* 1950). *Passage to Marseilles* (1944), starring Humphrey Bogart, boasted an uncommonly intricate flashback structure, with flashbacks inside of flashbacks. The plot of *Citizen Kane* (1941) is structured as a series of flashbacks, which portray overlapping events narrated by different characters. In all of these cases, the flashbacks change the sequencing of story events in the films' plots.

Many contemporary films cleverly exploit the story–plot distinction. Quentin Tarantino's *Pulp Fiction* (1994) constructs a narrative composed of three relatively separate plots, each peopled by the same gallery of characters (primarily, two professional killers, played by John Travolta and Samuel L. Jackson, and a washed-up boxer, played by Bruce Willis). These characters and their separate plots cross paths at several strategic points in the film, most significantly when the boxer murders one of the hired guns (Travolta). Writer–director Tarantino stages this killing midway through the film, during the second plot segment, then brings Travolta's character back in the third, concluding plot. The viewer realizes, with a jolt, that this last episode is occurring earlier in story time than the second and watches Travolta with some sadness, already knowing how that character will die.

Sliding Doors (1998) shows how differently the life of Helen (Gwyneth Paltrow) would turn out, depending on whether she took a subway train home early one day or missed it. The film intercuts these two scenarios and shows how this seemingly minor difference sets in motion chains of events that produce alternate fates for the character. Intercutting the alternate storylines suggests the existence of parallel worlds.

In a similar fashion, *Run Lola Run* (1998) shows a desperate, twenty-minute sprint by Lola to retrieve a stolen bag of cash to save her boyfriend. If she can't retrieve it, gangsters will kill him. The plot shows the episode of her run three separate times, with seemingly chance events each time altering the outcome and changing the fates of the characters. The plots of *Annie Hall* (1977) and *Memento* (2001) jump around in many different time frames, leaving it to the viewer to assemble events in proper chronology.

Pulp Fiction
(Miramax, 1994)
John Travolta's hit man in *Pulp Fiction* is killed off midway through the film only to re-appear in the concluding plot segment. Quentin Tarantino's film playfully exploits the story–plot distinction by re-arranging its narrative events in a nonchronological way.

Mulholland Dr. (Universal, 2001)
The narrative in David Lynch's mysterious film is like a dream that becomes a nightmare. Betty (Naomi Watts) is a chirpy, aspiring actress, and Rita (Laura Elena Harring) is a mystery woman tormented by amnesia. They may or may not be the same person, and the entire story may represent Betty/Rita's last moment of consciousness before death. Lynch demolishes the classical Hollywood narrative in order to achieve a surreal poetry. Frame enlargement.

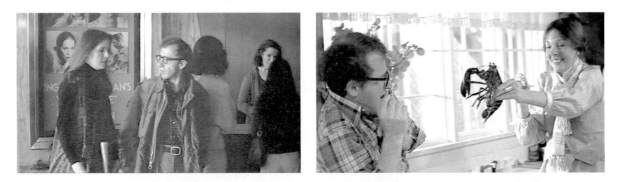

Annie Hall (United Artists, 1977)
Story and plot do not correspond in *Annie Hall*. The plot scrambles story events in a nonchronological way. In the plot, Annie and Alvy's tense date at the movies precedes their loving, funny adventure with the lobsters even though, in chronological story time, the latter comes first. Frame enlargements.

Case Study: *Annie Hall*

Woody Allen's film portrays the relationship between a playwright named Alvy Singer (Allen) and an aspiring singer, Annie Hall (Diane Keaton). The story is about the meeting of these characters, the growth of their love for one another, and the loss of that

WOODY ALLEN

Born Allen Stewart Konigsberg in Brooklyn, in 1935, Woody Allen adopted his now famous comic name when he began sending jokes to syndicated columnists while still in high school. The jokes and the name began appearing in national celebrity newspaper columns, giving Allen a measure of success very early in life, which he rapidly extended into a respected career as a writer for television comedy (*The Sid Caesar Show*, 1952) and stand-up comic and Broadway playwright (*Don't Drink the Water*, 1966; *Play It Again Sam*, 1969).

By the time he directed his first film, *Take the Money and Run* (1969), Allen was a successful comedy writer. Unlike many other leading U.S. directors, Allen is a writer first—he crafts a polished screenplay and only then takes a project into production. The result is a body of work that is extremely literate, thoughtful, and intelligent and that subjects human relationships and moral issues to the kind of sustained comic examina-

tion that can only be accomplished by having outstanding scripts as the foundation for a production.

Annie Hall (1977) was Allen's breakthrough film. The sophistication of its cinematic structure, its blending of comedy and pathos, and its complex and bittersweet portrayal of a love affair placed it leagues apart from the earlier films—*Bananas* (1971), *Sleeper* (1973), *Love and Death* (1975)—which tended to be collections of slapstick gags and one-liners strung together along a thin narrative line. *Annie Hall* built on the enduring Allen comic persona: a bumbling nebbish neurotically tormented by life but whose anxieties brilliantly expose the moral dilemmas of modern society.

Characteristically, Allen demonstrated his versatility, and his controversial preference for drama over comedy, by following *Annie Hall* with a sober, psychological

(continued)

Hollywood Ending (DreamWorks, 2002)

Woody Allen frequently appears as a performer in his own films. His fumbling, neurotic comic persona is instantly recognizable, whether it be in a period film such as *A Midsummer Night's Sex Comedy* (1982) or a contemporary comedy such as *Annie Hall* (1977), set in Allen's beloved New York City. He works quickly, making one or two films per year. Here, in a satire of contemporary cinema, he plays a blind Hollywood director who makes a hit film. Frame enlargement.

WOODY ALLEN *(Continued)*

drama, *Interiors* (1978), in which he did not appear and that he intended as an homage to Swedish director Ingmar Bergman, whom Allen greatly admires.

Allen established an extraordinary directing career in the next two decades. Working swiftly and economically, he released one film every year, establishing an extensive and stylistically diverse body of work. His comic films—*Manhattan* (1979), *Hannah and Her Sisters* (1986), *Bullets over Broadway* (1994)—have been the most popular with critics and audiences.

Artistically more daring and offbeat films include the black-and-white study of a human chameleon (*Zelig,* 1983); a bitter exploration of movie stardom (*Stardust Memories,* 1980); a bittersweet look at the power of cinema to alleviate the dullness and despair of life (*The Purple Rose of Cairo,* 1985); a loving, semi-autobiographical homage to radio shows and Rockaway Beach, Long Island in the 1940s (*Radio Days,* 1986); a probing psychological drama (*Another Woman,* 1988); and cynical, bitter portraits of marital conflict and human ruthlessness (*Husbands and Wives,* 1992; *Crimes and Misdemeanors,* 1990; *Deconstructing Harry,* 1997; *Celebrity,* 1998).

Creating a rich, artistically ambitious and consistently intelligent body of work, Allen demonstrates the virtues of inexpensive, small-scale filmmaking. He works regularly and often, with total artistic freedom and continually reinvents himself and his film style with each new production. By contrast, blockbuster directors, mired with huge budgets and difficult special effects work, cannot be so artistically adventurous or provocative.

love as the relationship breaks apart. At the end of the story, Alvy and Annie split up and go on to lead separate lives.

The story is chronological, dealing with the growth and decay of a love affair. The film's plot, however, imposes a structure on this story that breaks up and rearranges the actual chronology of events. The plot jumps around in time to show Alvy and Annie's affair at very different points in their relationship. In the first scene, Alvy explains that he and Annie have broken up and that he's having a hard time coping with the split because a year ago they were in love.

This acknowledgment cues a series of flashbacks showing Alvy's life as a child growing up on Coney Island, his relationship with his parents, a few episodes from his elementary school years, and then, as an adult, a conversation he has with a friend named Max. Annie does not figure in any of this material despite the fact that these episodes are cued by his recollection of their breakup.

Annie appears in the next scene. She meets Alvy outside a theater for a screening of the French documentary, *The Sorrow and the Pity* (1970). This scene apparently occurs quite late in their affair because they are tense with each other and hostile. Annie makes a reference to Alison, Alvy's first wife, and this cues a flashback to Alvy first meeting Alison and to a subsequent scene between them indicating that that relationship, too, is doomed. The next scene returns to Annie and Alvy but this time at a very early point in their relationship. It is a romantic moment, full of loving good humor and joy. They are spending the weekend at a beach house and have a minor disaster when several live lobsters escape the cooking pot and scatter across the kitchen floor.

From this happy scene, the film next goes into Annie's past and shows a little bit of her childhood in Chippewa Falls. Annie makes a reference to Alvy's second wife, which cues another flashback to that relationship and its particular tensions. The narrative then returns to Annie and Alvy at a point late in the relationship. They are in bed together, tense, angry, unable to make love. From this, the film cuts directly to the scene that shows their first meeting at a tennis club and then to a few scenes showing Alvy's early courtship of Annie.

The editing of the film creates a kind of kaleidoscope through which the viewer sees Annie and Alvy's affair. The story is broken into many different pieces, all arranged out of chronology. Watching the film, the viewer mentally reconstructs the actual story from the jumbled scenes provided by the plot. The story is never directly depicted in its actual chronology. Instead, the plot imposes a fragmentary structure on the story, inviting the viewer to reassemble implied material not actually seen, as well as the true chronology of events.

Case Study: *Memento*

Christopher Nolan's *Memento* (2001) features an especially clever and complex narrative structure in which the story is told backwards, beginning with the end and working in reverse back to the beginning. Leonard Shelby (Guy Pearce) suffers from a brain disorder that robs him of short-term memory. He knows who he is (or once was—he was married and worked as an insurance investigator), but he can't remember any details of his present life or recent past.

Leonard is obsessed with finding his wife's killer, but to do so he must struggle with his memory disorder. When he finds a clue, he tattoos it onto his body, photographs it, or writes it on the back of the photo so it will not be forgotten. The movie becomes a mystery in reverse, opening with Leonard's execution of a man he believes is the killer and then moving backwards to explain how he found his victim.

This main story line is woven together with three other narrative frames: scenes of Leonard alone in his hotel room, flashbacks of his married life, and flashbacks of an insurance case he investigated involving a man named Sammy Jenkis, who lost all short-term memory following a traffic accident. The case foreshadows Leonard's fate. Intercutting these narrative frames throughout the film produces a plot structure that is rich and kaleidoscopic, but the film's main line of action—Leonard's efforts to find his wife's killer—is a linear one (though in reverse order). No scenes could be removed from it, or placed in a different order, without damaging its clarity. Each scene is a crucial link in the narrative chain of events.

The film's story is further enriched by the ambiguities that accumulate as the plot moves backwards and in and out of Leonard's memories. He is, it turns out, an unreliable narrator because he cannot remember the things he has already done or said. He has killed other men, believing them to have been his wife's killer, but he doesn't recall doing so. Natalie (Carrie-Anne Moss), the girlfriend of a drug dealer, and Teddy (Joe Pantoliano), a cop, offer him help but may, in fact, be manipulating him for their own purposes. Memories can deceive and distort. Where does the truth lie?

Director Nolan gives the ingenious narrative structure a careful visual design. The opening credits appear overtop a Polaroid photo that begins to undevelop and

Memento (Newmarket, 2001)

This ingenious film mixes a linear narrative running in reverse with flashbacks and with a present tense time frame that shows Leonard Shelby (Guy Pearce) in his hotel room. Tracking his wife's killer and with no short-term memory, he relies on photographs to recall important details. The story develops great mystery as it progresses. Natalie (Carrie-Ann Moss) may be manipulating Leonard for her own ends; without a working memory, he is an easy victim and an unreliable narrator. To accentuate Leonard's isolation from people and places, the filmmakers shot in anamorphic widescreen 2.35:1, taking advantage of that format's shallow depth of field to focus on Leonard and make the backgrounds soft. Frame enlargements fade to white, and the first scene—Leonard's killing of Teddy—plays in reverse action. These strategies tell the viewer about the way the film will be organized.

Furthermore, the visual design of the different narrative frames always makes it clear which one the viewer is in. The main story line is in color, and the scenes of Leonard in his hotel room (these form the present tense of the story) are in high contrast black and white and are filmed with a handheld camera. The Sammy Jenkis flashbacks are also in black and white, but these are more brightly lit, are less grainy, and do not feature a handheld camera.

The narrative design is clever, highly organized, and is visually marked to assist the viewer in making sense of it. The pleasures of *Memento* lie in *how* the story is told, revealing the mysteries and ambiguities of the worlds that we believe our memories contain.

Authorship and Point of View

One of the peculiar characteristics of cinema is that it is often difficult to determine the author of a film. In literature, the author of a novel is generally understood to be a single individual, the writer. Films, by contrast, are made by groups of people, and it is often difficult to say with any certainty which member of the production team— director, cinematographer, editor, sound designer—is responsible for a particular effect on screen. In this sense, films have multiple authors. Films do have writers, but the author of a screenplay typically furnishes dialogue, narrative, and dramatic action, but not a film's visual or audio design. Cinematography, editing, sound—these vital areas of filmic design fall outside the domain of a screenplay.

Some years ago, the critic Pauline Kael attempted to argue that the real "author" of *Citizen Kane* was Herman J. Mankiewicz, the author of its screenplay. While Mankiewicz's script was undeniably brilliant, he had nothing to do with the film's extraordinary audiovisual design. The cinematography (by Gregg Toland), the art direction (by Van Nest Polglase), the music score (by Bernard Herrmann), and the editing (by Robert Wise) are all world-class accomplishments, and director Orson Welles was the key person organizing and integrating the contributions of these individuals. Kael's intentions to honor the film's writer were noble, but her case for Mankiewicz's authorship of the film failed to account for many of the features that have made *Citizen Kane* an outstanding and classic work of cinema.

Because the director typically has the controlling creative authority on a given production, the convention has evolved of treating the director as the author of a film. This should be done, however, in a cautious and conservative manner, with the understanding that no director is ever a film's sole author, as the writer of a novel is.

Real and Implied Authors
The collaborative nature of filmmaking gives the distinction that has existed in literary theory between the **real** and the **implied author** a special intensity. Literary critic Wayne Booth developed the notion of a real versus an implied author as a means of avoiding the biographical trap that sometimes ensnares a critic. In discussing the novels of Ernest Hemingway, for example, one cannot reduce their stylistic and literary structure to the facts of biography.

In other words, for Booth, "Hemingway," the literary persona (and the implied author) seemingly present in the writings, is distinct from Ernest Hemingway, the man, who was born in Illinois in 1899, served as a reporter on the *Kansas City Star*, fought

Psycho (Paramount Pictures, 1960) Director Alfred Hitchcock transformed his personal experiences, interests, and anxieties into brilliant film images and narratives, but the richness of these films transcends any biographical basis they might have. Moreover, Hitchcock depended on the collaboration of his regular cinematographer (Robert Burks), editor (George Tomasini), and composer (Bernard Herrmann). As an implied author, "Hitchcock" designates the creative result of these collaborations: a cinematic world of crime, guilt, terror, and madness. Norman Bates (Tony Perkins) inhabits such a world at his motel in *Psycho*. Frame enlargement (right).

in World War I, settled in Paris after the war, and died in Idaho in 1961. The novels have their own emotional logic and power, and one can speak of "Hemingway," the literary persona that hovers in the shadows of the writings, as being relatively distinct from Hemingway, the man.

A film critic might study the work of such filmmakers as "Hitchcock," "Ford," "Spielberg," "Godard," "Bertolucci," or "Kurosawa," and treat these as implied rather than real authors, the names as labels given to bodies of film and used to describe the characteristics of those films rather than the characteristics of those individual people. In this way, "Hitchcock" designates a narrative world characterized by a certain Catholic conception of sin, guilt, transgression, and punishment, and a visual design marked by such recurring features of style as high-angle shots used in moments of dramatic crisis.

The difficulty with maintaining a hard and complete distinction between the implied and the real author is that many directors do draw on personal experience in crafting their films so that a correlation does exist between who they are as people and the content of the films. Directors such as Ingmar Bergman, Steven Spielberg, and Alfred Hitchcock have undeniably based aspects of their films on personal experiences. Knowing something about their personal history can help clarify structural features of their films. But biographical correlations can be misleading and are easily overemphasized. Because of this, the distinction between real and implied authors is useful to maintain, not in any fixed or absolute sense, but as a way of keeping clear the many ways in which film structure, produced as a collaborative enterprise by teams of filmmakers in a medium that has multiple authors, may transcend the facts of an individual filmmaker's biography.

Point of View in Cinematic Narratives

As with authorship, narrative **point of view** has special conditions in cinema that differentiate it from its literary context. Literary narratives customarily use the first-person or third-person points of view. If point of view is in first-person, then the narrator employs the first-person pronoun. "I went there." "I did that." Third-person pronouns help produce a third-person narrative. "He went there." "She did that." While novels may use either, movies almost always use third-person narration. In most films, the camera assumes a point of view that is detached and separate from the literal viewpoint as seen by each of the characters.

However, there are times when filmmakers wish to suggest a character's literal point of view. To do so, the filmmaker would use a **subjective shot** or point of view shot in which the camera literally views through the eyes of the character. This kind of shot creates a brief interlude of first-person perspective. Generally, the shift from third- to first-person in film is signaled by showing the character reacting to something off-screen, then cutting to a view of what the character sees, the subjective view, and then closing the subjective moment with a cut back to the character from a third-person perspective.

In cinema, first-person point of view is more commonly present in an *implicit* way. In *Memento,* although we see Leonard Shelby on camera, the story is told from his point of view. We share his confusion and difficulty piecing events together, and our knowledge of the story is restricted to what he knows. We learn new information only when he does.

Through performance, production design, lighting, color, editing, the use of sound and camera, directors can suggest the emotional or psychological perspective of a character in a scene. George Stevens's *Shane* (1953) deals with the arrival of a mysterious gunfighter in a farming community in Wyoming. He stays at the home of farmer Joe Starrett and is revered by Starrett's young son, an impressionable little boy whose father is somewhat distant and who yearns for an attractive male authority figure to worship. He finds this in Shane, and it is implied very strongly that the story of the film is filtered through the point of view of young Joey Starrett.

There are, however, few subjective shots from Joey's perspective. Instead, the systematic visual presentation of Shane as an extremely romantic and idealized figure, clad in golden buckskins, establishes an implicit first-person narration, one that correlates with Joey's point of view. Shane's idealized visual and emotional presentation makes him precisely the sort of hero a young boy, starved for attention, might desire.

Extended First-Person Narration   Although *extended and explicit* first-person point of view is rare in film, there are a few spectacular exceptions to this rule. *Lady in the*

Strangers on a Train (Warner Bros., 1951)
First-person perspective typically occurs in cinema for brief intervals through the use of a subjective shot, representing what a character sees. Hitchcock often used subjective shots in remarkable ways. Guy (Farley Granger) and Bruno (Robert Walker) quarrel, in a camera set-up (third-person perspective) that represents neither character's viewpoint (a). When Guy punches Bruno, however, Hitchcock abruptly inserts a subjective shot (b, c), showing this action from Bruno's perspective. Thereafter, he returns to a more normative, third-person framing (d). Frame enlargements.

Lake, a detective film made in 1946 from a Raymond Chandler novel, is distinguished by the novelty of having the camera take the detective's first-person point of view throughout. Viewers see the detective when he pauses in front of a mirror or examines his reflection in a store window. At other times his hand or an item of his clothing might intrude into the frame.

Shane (Paramount
Pictures, 1953)
Shane's (Alan Ladd) smooth,
handsome face, golden buckskins, and refined manner
establish an implicitly first-
person perspective in *Shane*.
It is a boy's view of a romantic
and idealized Western hero.
Frame enlargement.

More recently, *84 Charlie MoPic* (1989) presented its narrative entirely through a subjective camera as MoPic, a combat cameraman, follows and films a dangerous seven-man reconnaissance mission to the Central Highlands during the Vietnam War. The action is presented as he sees it through the lens of his camera, and the gimmick works well in making the viewer a participant on the mission.

Filmmakers rarely employ subjective point of view so extensively, and the reason is clear. It becomes awkward and interferes with a flexible presentation of narrative information. First-person perspective ties the camera to a character's physical position, and filmmakers customarily want to film scenes from a variety of camera positions. Filmmakers therefore find it more effective to employ third-person camera positions but to use light, color, sound, performance, and composition to imply the emotional and psychological points of view of characters in a scene. Taken together, these elements of structure help create the cinema's distinctive narrative point of view: explicit third-person narration with implied first-person components.

◼ THE CLASSICAL HOLLYWOOD NARRATIVE

A plot is not a random collection of events. It places events in a time sequence that usually imparts a clear sense of purpose. The story seems to be moving in a certain direction, and in most cases, the viewer understands that it will come to a deliberate end, reach a purposeful and satisfying conclusion. Causality is the glue that holds the various events and episodes in the story together. One event in the story causes another event. Some plots are tightly constructed with events chained in a strong causal sequence. By contrast, other plots are loose, open-ended, or almost shapeless, with causality present in a minimal or implicit way.

The **classical Hollywood narrative,** named after the films produced by the Hollywood studios in the 1930s–1950s, is still prevalent in popular cinema. *The Lord of the Rings* (2001) and *Star Wars: Episode II: Attack of the Clones* (2002), for example, are classical Hollywood narratives, as are almost all popular film entertainments.

Such films feature a main line of action and one or more subordinate lines of action (subplots) tied to it. The plot is directional—activated by a main character pursuing a goal—and one event follows another in tight causal relationships, as links in a chain. The goals of the action are announced early in the film, and the plot follows a line of rising interest and tension as the characters confront impediments to their goals. The conclusion of the film sees the characters either achieving or failing to achieve their goals in a way that brings the narrative to a satisfying conclusion that resolves all outstanding story issues. It is this sense of completeness, resulting from the resolution of all lines of action, which gives the classical narrative its satisfying quality. In the cases of *The Lord of the Rings* and *Star Wars*, the story lines arc across several films before achieving complete resolution.

Case Study: *The Searchers*

John Ford's *The Searchers* (1956), a renowned and prestigious Western, illustrates the goal-directed, highly motivated action of the classical Hollywood narrative. At the beginning of the film, Ethan Edwards (John Wayne) returns from the Civil War to his brother's cabin in Texas. Ethan has been away for a number of years, engaged in activities that remain mysterious. He arrives at Aaron and Martha's homestead where relations between the brothers are tense and where it is hinted that Ethan and Martha share an unspoken love. Shortly after Ethan's arrival, Indians attack the homestead, burn the cabin, and wipe out the family, except for Aaron and Martha's two daughters, whom they abduct. Driven by a powerful hatred of Indians, Ethan becomes obsessed with returning his nieces to the white community.

This is the goal-directed activity that generates the remainder of the film's narrative and takes the character on a five-year search. The opening act of the film served to define the essential conditions—Ethan's love for Martha, his rootless and stubborn nature, and his pathological hatred for Indians—that motivate the ensuing action. As the plot progresses, however, Ethan encounters impediments to his goal, chief among them being his own savagery. Ethan's hatred for Indians poisons his feelings for Debbie (the one abducted niece who survives) once he realizes that she is living among the Comanche as a member of their culture. His original goal of rescuing Debbie is replaced by another and darker quest: to destroy her.

In its last act, *The Searchers* generates considerable excitement as Ethan finds Debbie and chases her down a ravine to the mouth of a cave. He lifts her in his arms and the viewer is afraid that he is going to bash her brains out, but in a last-minute turn of events he forgives her, forgives himself, and honors his original quest, returning her to the white community of Texas settlers.

Ethan's quest for Debbie is the main line of action in the film, but it is conjoined with a subplot showing the relationship of Marty, a relative accompanying Ethan, with a family of settlers, whose domestic lives hold more attraction for him than they do for Ethan. The subplot is interrelated with the main line of action—Marty decides that his real task will be to prevent Ethan from killing Debbie when he finds her—and both lines of action are resolved at the end. Debbie is rescued. Marty joins the family of

The Searchers (Warner Bros., 1956)

The highly motivated and goal-oriented classical Hollywood narrative. Ethan (John Wayne) returns from years of wandering to visit his brother's family and Martha, whom he loves (a, b, c). Comanches massacre the family and abduct the children. Ethan views the carnage with horror (d) and resolves to find and rescue the children. After years of searching, he returns with one child (e). In the last image (f), he stands alone, now without purpose in his life, turns and walks away, into the desert. Frame enlargements.

settlers and will (it is implied) marry their daughter. In the last scene, he enters the family's home, while Ethan chooses not to do so, walking away from the cabin, into the desert and back to the rootless existence from which he appeared at the film's beginning.

The classical Hollywood narrative makes use of **explicit causality.** One event clearly causes another in the chain that forms the narrative. The Indians' attack on the cabin prompts Ethan's quest. Ethan swears to return Debbie to her rightful community. He undertakes a five-year search. During the course of the search, he comes to hate Debbie. What will he do when he finds her? The tension surrounding this latter question generates the climax of the film and its surprising last-minute turn of events in which the character redeems himself in a way that allows him to honor the original goal, the one that had driven the narrative from its beginning.

Because of its explicit causality, classical Hollywood cinema features a clear hierarchy of narrative events. Certain episodes stand out as the most important links in the narrative chain, while others are less decisive and less important. If viewers are asked to summarize this kind of highly motivated film narrative, they can easily identify the most important narrative events. Asked to summarize *The Searchers,* a viewer might say that a band of Indians attacks a Texas homestead, one of the survivors vows revenge, searches for many years for a young girl, and finally locates and rescues her. These events could not be subtracted from the film without radically altering or damaging the story.

Alternatives to the Classical Narrative

While classical Hollywood narratives have proven to be very popular with audiences, and a great many films each year are produced in this format, alternative narrative forms have been an important and vital part of cinema. The examples cited earlier in the chapter of narrative structure in *Annie Hall* and *Memento* are clearly cases of nonclassical narrative.

Films made outside of mainstream Hollywood production often use alternative narrative structures. In these cases, causality may be minimized in favor of ambiguity. No clearly dominant line of action may emerge. The sequence of events may be loosely organized, giving the viewer a weaker sense of the direction in which the story is moving.

Many European films, for example, prize ambiguity over causality in structuring their narratives. Bernardo Bertolucci's *Last Tango in Paris* (1972) is a French-Italian coproduction that portrays the emotional devastation of an American named Paul (Marlon Brando), living in Paris, whose wife has just committed suicide. Her suicide is the fundamental motivating event for all of the film's action, but the film does not reveal what has happened until well into the narrative. As a result, considerable ambiguity surrounds Paul's behavior.

Unlike *Annie Hall* or *Memento,* where the plot rearranges the chronology of story events, Bertolucci does not alter the chronology of events in *Last Tango.* But he omits key scenes and delays giving the viewer important information needed to understand the story. Thus the viewer cannot at first comprehend the reasons for Paul's extreme emotional distress. The reasons for his distress (namely, his wife's suicide) are not made

Last Tango in Paris
(United Artists, 1972)
The narrative structure of *Last Tango in Paris* withholds key pieces of story information. As a result, first-time viewers have great difficulty piecing the story together. Paul's anguish is, at first, unexplained. When he visits the scene of a suicide, viewers struggle to grasp its significance for him. The film's narrative design deliberately poses interpretive challenges for its viewers. Frame enlargements.

clear until thirty minutes into the film. This gives many scenes during the intervening period an unclear and ambiguous status. In one, Paul stands in a bathroom as a maid cleans a tub full of blood. He waits silently as the maid describes how she was questioned by the police. At this point in the narrative, though, the viewer doesn't know what happened here, why the police are involved, or what relationship this has to Paul.

The important questions in the narrative—who Paul is, where the blood in the bathroom has come from, why he is in such distress—are answered slowly and incompletely. As a result, the narrative in *Last Tango* presents the viewer with serious interpretational challenges. Bertolucci's viewer must sort out the particulars of Paul's distress and his wife's suicide and their marital relationship by working through a plot structure that is not organized to facilitate the answering of these questions.

Independent filmmaking is another mode of production in which classical Hollywood narrative is often conspicuously absent. The narrative in many independent films is often very episodic, with events joined in a loose fashion, with minimal or **implicit causality.** John Sayles is one of the most successful independent filmmakers, with a long and respected filmography (*Return of the Secaucus Seven*, 1980; *Lone*

Star, 1996; *Men With Guns,* 1998). Although he has used linear, classical narrative in *Matewan* (1987), in other films he has moved far from it. *City of Hope* (1991) contains one of his more radical narrative structures. The film portrays a decaying urban economy and community in the 1990s. The narrative is not driven by the personal goals of a protagonist or a main line of action. Sayles instead follows an ensemble— a group—of characters as the narrative winds through the city to reveal a cross-section of its inhabitants: a corrupt city contractor, his disillusioned son, an idealistic city councilman, a group of cynical policemen, and citizen groups of various racial and ethnic backgrounds. Summarizing the story of this film is much more difficult than with *The Searchers* because narrative events are not tightly chained together and no single line of action predominates. The narrative focus is diffuse, unified by the common theme of showing a multitude of responses to urban decay.

The Antinarrative Tradition

The most extreme alternatives to classical Hollywood narrative can be found in the **antinarrative** tradition. Radical attempts at narrative deconstruction—at making films that decompose and take apart their own narratives—have been popular among more philosophically inclined directors. In their work, narrative is treated as a problem, as something to be refused or attacked.

Case Study: *Last Year at Marienbad*

French director Alain Resnais, in the classic modernist film *Last Year at Marienbad* (1961), presents a narrative that deliberately refuses to organize itself. *Last Year at Marienbad* deals with a murky, cloudy, unclear set of events taking place at a luxurious hotel. During the film, an unnamed man attempts to persuade an unnamed woman that they have met the year before at a fancy spa. Whether they actually did or not is never resolved.

Resnais's editing prevents the emergence of clear space and time relationships between scenes. For example, a number of shots are joined with matched cuts and continuous dialogue, which imply that no time has elapsed, but the characters' costumes change, as do the locales. These are contradictory cues that indicate time is both changing and not changing.

Last Year at Marienbad self-consciously studies the creation of narrative. In the film, a story tries to organize itself but never quite does. The movie opens in a kind of prenarrative state without characters and without a clear setting. The camera tracks through empty hotel hallways, past doors, friezes, columns, paintings, and tapestries. Voice-over narration, of unidentified origin, poetically states that this is an environment of soundless rooms where voices sink into rugs so deep that no step can be heard, where halls and galleries are from another age, where hallways cross other hallways that endlessly open onto deserted rooms.

During the course of the camera's movements through this poetically and mysteriously defined environment, a group of individuals appears in frozen, still-life postures, characters existing as sculptures in this strange hotel. Gradually the characters unfreeze, begin to move, and start delivering dialogue during which the mysterious man attempts to convince the unnamed woman that they have met the year before. The narrative comes to life.

Last Year at Marienbad (1961)
Antinarrative in *Last Year at Marienbad*. Characters move through richly detailed settings, but the narrative fails to emerge.

Last Year at Marienbad is a film that deliberately sets out to provoke, puzzle, challenge, and undermine assumptions about what narrative is and how it operates in film. There is no sense of direction to the plot, and no real conclusion is reached either. Instead, endless repetition—of images, camera movement, dialogue—is the defining structural characteristic. In this respect, *Last Year at Marienbad* stands as an extreme departure from the terms of narrative in popular, mass-market movies, and it can be classified as a modernist film in that it does not wish to tell a story so much as to talk about what stories are and how they may be structured on film.

Jean-Luc Godard's *Le Gai Savoir* (1969) is another example of the "antinarrative" narrative film. Here, two characters gather in an empty French television studio to inquire into the nature of images and to understand better how television and other visual media communicate. They meet for seven nights, and their comings and goings, and their philosophical reflections about the nature of pictures, constitute what plot there is. The soundtrack is punctuated by the noise of static and by Godard's own voice in a kind of running, anxious commentary about the nature of images and his own film. *Le Gai Savoir* reduces narrative to a minimum in order to construct a film that functions more on the lines of an essay than a story. In this respect, like *Last Year at Marienbad*, *Le Gai Savoir* illustrates the impatience with stories felt by many modern, stylistically radical directors.

Le Gai Savoir (1969)
Godard's *Le Gai Savoir*
perversely offers poetry and
philosophy in place of a narrative. Many modern, stylistically
radical directors believe that all
the stories have already been
told in cinema, and they reject
or deform the medium's storytelling function.
*(Museum of Modern Art
Film Stills Archive)*

Such filmmakers regard narrative as an obstacle to their creative interests. Telling
a story gets in the way. It obligates them to create, delineate, and motivate characters
and to emphasize the story, treating other, non-narrative elements as background components. Filmmakers whose interests are essayistic, poetic, or didactic often take the
medium in a non-narrative direction when they consider narrative to be incompatible with their artistic goals. Viewers of popular movies may find this antinarrative
orientation difficult to understand or seemingly perverse because the basic pleasure
offered by popular cinema is precisely the storytelling function. Such viewers may
find the antinarrative films to be a strange experience or to offer little of the familiar
pleasures they are accustomed to finding in movies. But the antinarrative tradition in
cinema is very real, and it has influenced many important filmmakers whose work has
enlarged the creative boundaries of cinema.

☐ THE VIEWER'S CONTRIBUTION TO NARRATIVE

Viewers participate in the storytelling process, and filmmakers design narratives in ways
that encourage this participation. In his choice of narrative technique, Hitchcock
preferred suspense over surprise because the former condition drew viewers into the
story as participants, whereas surprise tended to exclude them. **Suspense** as a narra-

tive technique depends on giving viewers information, whereas **surprise** depends on withholding it. If Hitchcock began a scene by showing viewers a ticking bomb under a table around which a group of friends were playing cards, he could then film the card game for 5 or 10 minutes of excruciating suspense, during which the audience is saying to the cardplayers, "Stop playing cards, there's a bomb under your table!" Conversely, if he did not show the bomb and it then exploded, it would produce a brief moment of shock and surprise.

Filmmakers use the elements of narrative structure to encourage the viewer's active contribution. The action of the popular thriller *The French Connection* (1972) deals with a New York cop's obsessive hunt for a powerful French drug smuggler. At the end of the film, the cop corners the smuggler in a warehouse. The cop chases him into a back room, but the camera stays outside the room, leaving both characters off-screen. After a pause, a gunshot is heard off-screen, and the image fades out. The film is over, and the viewer is left wondering who fired the shot and whether the cop got his man. As the end credits roll, that final gunshot reverberates in the viewer's mind. What did it mean, and why was it presented in such a mysterious way? How does the story *end*? Its structure challenges the viewer to make sense of the film's puzzling conclusion, its final withholding of information, and its lack of explicit narrative closure.

As the ending of *The French Connection* illustrates, storytellers can hook the audience by deliberately omitting important pieces of story information. The audience infers and fills in this information as its contribution to the story, binding storyteller and audience in a close creative relationship. In a mystery film, viewers will try to guess the identity of the murderer before the detective or the narrative reveals it. The final shot of the ice pick under the bed in *Basic Instinct* (1992) teases the audience with the possibility that the real killer in the narrative is still at large and may strike again.

Basic Instinct (Carolco, 1992)
The open ending of *Basic Instinct* suggests that the killer is still at large and invites the audience to imagine what happens next. The narrative conclusion is ambiguous and does not tie up all loose ends.

The Sixth Sense vividly illustrates this storytelling partnership between filmmaker and audience. Its narrative is uncommonly clever, and, in its closing moments, it springs a last-minute surprise on the viewer that completely changes everything the viewer has assumed about the characters and story. The film's phenomenal box-office success was due to the pleasure that its remarkable twist gave viewers and to repeat business. Viewers came back to see the movie again, intrigued by its clever design, curious to see how the twist was accomplished and whether there were any clues to the ending that they had missed. *The Others* (2001), a ghost story starring Nicole Kidman, works in a similar fashion.

The viewer's participation in a narrative activates a basic operational principle of the human mind—the search for pattern. Perception and interpretation are not mechanical responses to information, but are active, goal-directed processes. Narrative activates these processes by inviting the audience to search for the overall pattern within a given narrative structure, the story to which the plot points. The desire to see the completed pattern is experienced by viewers as the need to find out "what happens next" in a story. The clear causality and motivation in a classical Hollywood narrative like *The Lord of the Rings* stimulates this desire by organizing the story in a linear fashion that points forward, with great momentum, toward its completion. The more fragmented structure of *Memento* or *Last Tango in Paris* stimulates this desire by burying the master pattern—the story—inside a narrative structure—a plot—that hides it. In each case, the act of storytelling binds the audience to the narrative as participant and co-creator, strengthening the bond between audience and storyteller as they both help create the story.

The Sixth Sense (Hollywood Pictures, 1999)
This uncommonly clever ghost story sprung an unforgettable twist ending on its viewers, many of whom felt compelled to return to the film for a second viewing to see how it was done. The story is psychologically rich and has a slow, meditative pacing. These are not the typical characteristics of a box-office blockbuster, and they demonstrate that the pleasures offered by a well-told story do not go out of fashion. Frame enlargement.

These considerations point to an important conclusion: Meaning is not "in" the film but is formed by the interaction of the film's audiovisual and narrative design with the viewer's own horizon of perceptual and social experience—the viewer's interpretive contribution. The implication of this is enormous. It means that filmmakers cannot control the meaning of their films because the experiences, values, and assumptions that viewers bring to those films, and that establish their frameworks of interpretation, are incredibly diverse and variable.

Obviously, viewers use a variety of criteria to evaluate the aesthetic qualities of a narrative. Is it coherent? Is it pleasurable? Is it convincing? Does it make sense? These are evaluations of narrative structure—how the story is aesthetically organized and told.

In a story where events are linked in a tight causal chain, with few digressions, viewers tend to expect an ending that ties up the loose ends by resolving all outstanding story issues. If they are given, instead, an ambiguous ending, as occurs in *The French Connection*, some viewers may feel frustrated while others find the ambiguity exciting and are stimulated to fill in the missing information. Viewers routinely evaluate how the story is told and whether, given the type of film it is, the story is told in a satisfying way.

Because so many movies establish screen worlds that are recognizably similar to their own, viewers also evaluate narratives using standards borrowed from personal and social experience. Here, it is not so much the narrative design that is evaluated as the way the narrative portrays people or situations. Arab Americans protested the Arnold Schwarzenegger thriller *True Lies* (1994) because of its portrayal of Arabic groups as terrorists. Some African Americans felt that the hyenas in Disney's *The Lion King* (1994) were unpleasantly close to a caricature of black people. The mannerisms and Caribbean accent of Jar-Jar Binks in *The Phantom Menace* (1999) aroused similar complaints. Viewers assess the narrative portrayals against their own understanding of the issues, situations, or groups. Does the narrative square with their own sense of things, or does it seem unreasonably biased or distorted in a way that style cannot justify?

The standards viewers apply when evaluating narratives, then, are quite broad, and they range from judgments about the artistic design of the story to judgments about its success in representing familiar things or people. Filmmakers can influence but they cannot control these evaluations. Filmmakers *can* control the audiovisual design of their films, but viewers are the essential cocreators of the meanings that arise from those designs.

◻ FILM GENRES

Many popular films fall into **genres,** which are sets of interrelated stories and their associated images. The most popular and historically significant American film genres include the Western, the gangster film, the musical, film noir, and the science fiction film. One of the most important characteristics of genres is that the stories are repeated again and again, with rules, or **conventions,** about what can happen within the genre. Moreover, many conventions are unique to a given genre. What viewers accept in a musical film might appear ridiculous in a gangster film.

The repetition of story situations throughout a genre produces two effects: it enables viewers familiar with the genre to anticipate likely narrative developments and outcomes, and it enables filmmakers to achieve highly concentrated meanings within the genre. Consider these simple terms common to Westerns: *gunfighter, Indian, cowboy*. Each word conjures up a host of associated images and potential story situations for viewers who are familiar with the genre.

A viewer critical of genres, who objects that all Westerns or all horror films are the same, is missing the point. Film scholar Robert Warshow has pointed out that "one does not want too much novelty" from a genre film. Fans of a genre derive pleasure from the small variations that are worked out within the preestablished order of story and setting. Repetition of familiar material is very important, and too much novelty or originality can place a film outside a genre's framework.

The Western

The Western is one of the oldest screen genres. Indeed, the Western as a cultural category predates the cinema. It emerged near the end of the nineteenth century and was established in a variety of precinematic forms: the dime novel, the Puritan captivity narratives, the Leatherstocking tales (1823–1841) of James Fenimore Cooper, theatrical plays and shows (e.g., Buffalo Bill's Wild West Show), and painting (ethnographic studies of Indian cultures as well as Frederic Remington's action scenes).

The Western, then, already existed when the cinema was invented at the turn of the century. The cinema supplied movement and exciting visual images to flesh out existing cultural stories about westward expansion and conflict between settlers and Native Americans. The Western rapidly established its popularity in cinema. By 1910, 21 percent of all U.S. pictures were Westerns. During the next decades, Hollywood pro-

The Toll Gate (1920)
The Western is one of the oldest screen genres and quickly achieved enormous popularity. William S. Hart was one of the most popular Western stars in the silent period. Hart aimed to portray the West with realism and with a serious, adult outlook that contrasted with the adolescent appeal of stars like Tom Mix. Frame enlargement.

duced Westerns in great quantities, and many of the industry's most popular stars were closely identified with the genre: Gary Cooper (*The Virginian, The Westerner, High Noon*), John Wayne (*Stagecoach, She Wore a Yellow Ribbon, Hondo*), Clint Eastwood (*High Plains Drifter, The Outlaw Josey Wales, Unforgiven*). John Ford, perhaps the finest director of the Hollywood period, made many of the genre's enduring classics: *Stagecoach, My Darling Clementine, Fort Apache, The Searchers, The Man Who Shot Liberty Valance.*

Beginning in the 1970s, however, the genre's popularity notably diminished, and since then it has never recovered the close relationship with a mass audience that it once enjoyed. Important and fine Westerns continue to be made—*Tombstone, Unforgiven*—but the genre's high period of creativity and appeal to a wide audience seems to have ended. It remains, though, the quintessential U.S. genre, the one most closely tied to the theme and mythology of the U.S. experience and identity.

The Western is defined by period, setting, and theme. The period is that interval of time between the Civil War and World War I, and the setting is west of the Mississippi River, on the plains, the desert, or the mountains. Films that fall outside these specifications may lie on the periphery of the genre but they are not Westerns. This period and setting contain the great historical stories that have furnished the genre with its material: waves of migration via the overland trails, the Indian wars, the building of the railroads, the cattle drives, the gold rushes.

While the genre has many themes, the one at its heart is the conflict between cultural ideas about civilization and the wilderness in stories that explain why violence is necessary for the preservation of community. The theme is linked to an enduring pattern of imagery. In the highly conventionalized opening typical of many Westerns, the central character, a man of violence, rides in to a town or settlement from the wilderness. A narrative situation—the approach of a violent individual to a community—is linked to a particular setting and image, the wilderness of desert or

---

Unforgiven (Warner Bros., 1992)
Clint Eastwood is the Western's last big star, and his work as director–producer demonstrates genuine mastery and feeling for the genre. In *Unforgiven*, he probes the destructive consequences of violence and offers a revisionist treatment of his star image. Frame enlargement.

The Gunfighter (20th Century Fox, 1950);
Shane (Paramount Pictures, 1953);
El Dorado (Paramount Pictures, 1967)
Violent showdowns at the saloon's bar. Gregory Peck
(background) faces down an impudent young gunman in *The Gunfighter.* Shane (Alan Ladd) protects
his honor in a brutal fistfight. Robert Mitchum cleans
out the saloon in *El Dorado.* Frame enlargements.

mountain. The long shots integrate the character with the surrounding wilderness,
and, by showing how large and expansive the wilderness is, they stress the fragility
and vulnerability of the settlement or community. The struggle between violence and
law is embodied in this visual contrast. As a figure of violence, the gunman comes from
the wilderness to the community, and, frequently at the end of the films, he must leave
the settlement to return to the mountains or plains.

The Western is among the most rule-bound of film genres. It links specific story
situations to particular settings. In many Westerns, the violent skills of the protagonist are tested in a public arena. This arena is typically a saloon, where armed and violent confrontations occur in close proximity to the bar. The genre has coded this
location for violence. By contrast, schoolrooms and churches are impermissible locations for violent confrontations. Gunfights or brawls almost never occur there.

The regularity of story in the Western is most apparent in the necessity for a gunfight at the conclusion of the film. The gunfight resolves the narrative conflicts by

granting that, at this moment of primitive social development, violence is needed on behalf of the community. Because genres *are* so rule-bound, too much variation from the formulas can produce **deviant plot structures** that viewers may deem unsatisfying. Howard Hawks's 1948 production of *Red River* is a case in point. It deals with the first cattle drive over the Chisholm Trail. Tom Dunson (John Wayne) leads his cattle on this perilous trek, assisted by his adopted son, Matthew Garth (Montgomery Clift). During the drive, Dunson grows tyrannical and becomes a borderline psychopath obsessed with preventing cowboys from quitting the drive and threatening to hang those who do. Eventually, he becomes unbearable, and the men revolt. Matthew Garth takes the herd and leaves Dunson behind. Dunson swears revenge and tells Matt that he will kill him when they next meet.

The plot moves in traditional Western fashion toward the promise of a climactic gunfight. But it never occurs. Instead, a comical fistfight between Matt and Dunson leads to their reconciliation. Many viewers have felt somewhat cheated by this ending, which is at odds with the genre. (From the standpoint of the director's other films, however, this ending seems less deviant because in most of his work Hawks tended to prefer comedy and comradeship over tragedy.)

The Western makes an excellent tool of study for students who wish to understand how genre works. It has a long history, is extremely rule-bound and precise in the application of those rules, and yet it shows an impressive diversity of style and subject matter. This is the essential and fascinating aspect about a genre: it shows diversity within constraint, variations within an abiding master pattern.

Red River (United Artists, 1948)
The abrupt conclusion of *Red River*, in which John Wayne and Montgomery Clift trade punches rather than bullets and then become friends again, strikes many viewers as an implausible turn of events. The formulaic nature of genre films, such as Westerns, conditions viewers to expect certain kinds of narrative events. Because of this, genre filmmakers are often more tightly bound in their work by what an audience expects and what a genre requires than are filmmakers whose work places them outside genre boundaries.

The Gangster Film

The gangster film is nearly as old as the cinema, having clear precursors in the early silent era. The genre emerged as a powerful force in U.S. film, however, at the time of the Great Depression. In the years 1930–1932, three films—*Little Caesar, The Public Enemy,* and *Scarface*—defined the essential narrative patterns, settings, images, and types of social conflicts that would characterize the genre during the next decades.

In the classical gangster structure, the narrative focuses on the rise and fall of a career criminal, from his early, humble, frequently immigrant origins to the zenith of his success, and then to his decline from power and violent death. This narrative pattern characterizes *Little Caesar, The Public Enemy,* and *Scarface,* as well as many later gangster films, including the *Godfather* films, the 1983 remake of *Scarface* by Brian De Palma, and Mario Van Peebles's *New Jack City* (1991). Other gangster films, of course, deviate from the classical narrative. Mike Newell's *Donnie Brasco* (1997) foregoes the epic style of a rise-and-fall story in its low-key account of the last days of a small-time New York hood (Al Pacino). Martin Scorsese's *Goodfellas* (1990) has elements of the rise-and-fall story in its tale of a young Brooklyn man's aspirations to join the local mob, but its main focus is a kind of ethnography of mob behavior and ritual.

In the classical structure, the gangster hero represents a perverse version of the American myth of success. He is an inverted and dark embodiment of the Horatio Alger myth, which stipulated that opportunities to advance were open to everyone, no matter how humble their origins. His determination and persistence enable him to achieve great economic success, but he must use harsh and violent tactics to do

Little Caesar (Warner Bros., 1931)
One of the biggest in a long line of movie gangsters, the snarling Rico Bandello (Edward G. Robinson) in *Little Caesar.* Rico is so smug and self-centered that when death finally comes he can scarcely believe it. Riddled by a police machine gun, he asks in disbelief, "Mother of Mercy, is this the end of Rico?"

Donnie Brasco (Columbia TriStar, 1997)
Much distinguished work in the genre lies outside its classic narrative structure. Small-time hood and hanger-on Lefty Ruggerio (Al Pacino) is not the stuff of a rise-and-fall story. Rather than an epic hero like Little Caesar or The Godfather, he's a nobody, a foot soldier in the neighborhood mob. But he is a compelling character who illuminates the low end of gangsterdom, and the film invests the story of his last days with compassion. Frame enlargement.

so, and his appetite for power, wealth, and violence is boundless. As Scarface (1931) says, "Do it first, do it yourself, and keep on doing it." As Scarface (1983) says, "Me, I want what's coming to me. The world and everything that's in it."

The roots of the gangster film in U.S. culture include this Horatio Alger myth of success, as well as the example of the 19th-century robber barons, who, like the film gangster, amassed great fortunes through frequently ruthless methods. The genre's cultural roots also include the impact of the Great Depression and its demonstration of economic injustice, and the influence of Prohibition, which eroded respect for law and order and generated popular sympathy for the rum-running gangster.

Each of these cultural factors helped make the movie gangster what he was and ensured that the genre offered a sustained critique of society. If society, after all, created gangsters like Little Caesar or Scarface, how healthy could it be? Francis Ford Coppola's *The Godfather* (1972) opens with a dark screen, as a voice intones, "I believe in America." As the lights come up, Don Corleone confers with an Italian man who has come to him because the courts have not provided justice. His daughter has been raped and assaulted, and the legal system failed to convict her assailants. He seeks from Don Corleone a more primitive kind of justice, one that involves violent retribution.

With his ability to exercise this kind of justice and his rejection and repudiation of established society, with his attainment of wealth and power, the gangster character appeals to an implicit dissatisfaction on the part of movie audiences with their social and economic status. By succeeding and becoming wealthy, the gangster fulfills the culture's deepest ideals, but he does so by violating its norms. This appeal is nowhere more apparent than in the conventions that surround the death of the movie gangster. As dictated by the rules of the genre, the gangster's death must be spectacular, and it often contains a powerful social critique. In *High Sierra* (1941), Roy Earl (Humphrey Bogart) is a romantic and sympathetic gangster, with great compassion and empathy for the poor and downtrodden. The film presents his death as a cowardly act by the legal authorities.

Earl is not simply killed; he is shot off a mountaintop and falls from a great height, a hero of legendary stature brought down by callous authority. Shot in the back, he is felled by a police sniper. His death is witnessed by Marie, the woman he loved, and in the closing moments of the film she murmurs, "Freedom," equating Earl's death with a final escape from unjust social authority. The end credits are presented on a scroll that moves toward the top of the frame in a visual design that echoes the distant High Sierra mountains and symbolizes the idea of transcendence and escape that Earl's death embodies in the narrative.

At the conclusion of *White Heat* (1948), the psychopathic gangster Cody Jarrett immolates himself atop a huge gasoline storage tank. In one of the most famous moments in all U.S. cinema, he screams, "Made it, Ma, top of the world!" just before he and the tank explode. The erupting mushroom cloud, which is the film's final image, situates Jarrett's crazed violence within the postwar atomic age and its nuclear anxieties. Jarrett is a violent psychopath, yet the energies of violence embodied in modern society and represented by the atomic weapon and the mushroom cloud are infinitely greater. The ending of the film suggests a nuclear apocalypse. Jarrett has made it to the top of the world, and now the world ends.

The famous montage that concludes *The Godfather* (1972), in which editor Peter Zinner cuts back and forth between the baptism ceremony for Michael Corleone's infant son and the execution of Corleone's enemies, suggests Michael's own violent and corrupt nature and also the violence and corruption at the heart of established

---

High Sierra (Warner Bros., 1941)
Cornered in the Sierra Nevada Mountains, Roy Earle (Humphrey Bogart) dies a noble death, and the film's credit design, with titles rolling toward the heavens, suggests that in death Earle has at last found freedom and transcendence. Frame enlargement.

White Heat (Warner Bros., 1948)
Cody Jarrett (James Cagney) seconds before his explosive death in *White Heat*. Jarrett's fiery end is a cautionary note for the nuclear age. Jarrett's spectacular death is a moment of such visual brilliance that it has become part of cinema's folklore, comparable to King Kong's last stand atop the Empire State Building. Both monsters, Kong and Jarrett, find an unforgettably poetic death. Frame enlargement.

society. Michael has attained a position of eminence, wealth, and political power and commands sufficient social prestige to ensure a proper baptism for his son in one of the city's largest and most prominent churches, even as he wipes out his enemies.

At the conclusion of Brian De Palma's *Scarface*, Tony Montana (Al Pacino) is gunned down by a small army of South American narco mercenaries but not before he engages them in a prolonged, hyperviolent gun battle. Although Tony has the appetites and moral sensibility of a shark, the ferocity with which he fights lends his death,

Scarface (Universal, 1983)
Defiant to the end, Tony Montana (Al Pacino) finds a flamboyant death in a hyperviolent gun battle with South American narco bandits. One of the most unredeemable of movie gangsters, he nevertheless gains a savage stature in the manner of his death.

when it comes, a stature befitting the genre, even though as a character he lacks the romantic appeal of Roy Earle or the sentimental rendering given Cody Jarrett or the Godfather. The film ends by invoking the social critique inherent to the genre: the camera moves past Tony's body to a statue bearing the inscription, "The World is Yours."

Each of these films presents the gangster's death in a spectacular manner that contains an implicit social critique. The genre stipulates that the gangster must have a great deal of charisma. The gangster's appeal invites the viewer to ask about the kind of society that produces such seductive forms of corruption and violence. Like the cowboy, the movie gangster is a highly charged cultural symbol. He embodies the danger of chaotic lawlessness as well as popular resentment of legal authority. The movie gangster represents a highly complex social fantasy about the prize and price of success. As such, in its uniquely American rendering, the gangster is a figure tied closely to a capitalist economy and is an expression of social ambivalence toward such an economy. In this respect, unlike the Western, the gangster genre remains timely and contemporary, its appeal never fading or going out-of-date.

The Musical

Unlike the Western and gangster films, which appear in cinema during the silent era, musicals owe their origin to sound filmmaking. Indeed, the film that is popularly credited as being the first "talkie," *The Jazz Singer* (1927), is a musical built around the singing of star Al Jolson. Sound made the cinema a receptive medium for the talents of the singers and dancers who would proliferate in musicals, and the genre flourished from the 1930s to the 1960s.

In the 1930s, Busby Berkeley choreographed and/or directed a string of hit musicals—*Footlight Parade* (1933), *42nd Street* (1933), *Gold Diggers of 1935* (1935)—that were enlivened with extravagant sets and his trademark manner of filming a chorus line as if it were a visual kaleidoscope. Dance partners Fred Astaire and Ginger Rogers epitomized grace and elegance in a long film series including *Flying Down to Rio* (1933), *The Gay Divorcée* (1934), *Top Hat* (1935), *Swing Time* (1936). In the 1940s and 1950s at MGM, producer Arthur Freed established a production unit that turned out a steady stream of the genre's classics, many of which starred Astaire, Gene Kelly, and Judy Garland: *The Wizard of Oz* (1939), *Meet Me in St. Louis* (1944), *An American in Paris* (1951), *Singin' in the Rain* (1952), *The Band Wagon* (1953). These decades, and Freed's work in particular, may be regarded as the genre's classical period.

During this period, the genre's essential narrative centered on the courtship rituals of a romantic couple who sang and danced to express their desire for each other. Viewers knew that the characters played by Astaire and Rogers were right for one another because they moved so uniquely well together. At the same time, the genre broke its visual style into two domains. Dialogue scenes were shot in a realist style, while the musical sequences take filmmaker and viewer far from realism. These scenes include the wild geometric forms of Busby Berkeley, popular in the 1930s, and the aggressive color design of the ballet sequences from Vincente Minnelli's *The Band Wagon* (1953) and *An American in Paris* (1951). In the latter film, the compositions and color schemes evoke the style of French Impressionist painters. For filmmakers who

With their joyous optimism and happy romance, the musical couple is in love with love and each other. Dance expresses this celebration. Ginger Rogers and Fred Astaire are the most famous couple in musical film history. They courted each other on the dance floor in ten films.

wanted to experiment with radical color and image styles, the musical was an ideal genre, offering them possibilities unmatched by any other film format.

Contemporary audiences frequently have trouble accepting the genre's bifurcated style. The transition points from everyday reality to the musical scenes with their extravagant song, dance, color, lighting, and camerawork often seem jarring to contemporary viewers, who may react nervously when a character in a classic musical suddenly breaks into song and dance.

Once again, though, it is important to understand the connection between these visual and narrative conventions and the underlying social values they express. The classical musicals—*Singin' in the Rain* (1952), *Meet Me in St. Louis* (1944), *The Band Wagon* (1953), and *An American in Paris* (1951)—belong to a less cynical age, and they express a cultural optimism and innocence that contemporary viewers find quite foreign. The musical is a joyous celebration of life, romance, and desire, whereas modern audiences may be more accustomed to cynical representations of life on movie screens.

Singin' in the Rain
(MGM, 1952)
The relatively naturalistic presentation of dialogue scenes in the musical gives way to elaborately stylized musical sequences, which gave filmmakers opportunities to explore color, light, and movement with complete imagination. The musical's antirealism is the most extreme of any film genre, and narrative is relatively unimportant. Frame enlargement.

Moulin Rouge (20th Century Fox, 2001)
Director Baz Luhrmann tried to revive the movie musical with this fanciful, energetic tale of Satine (Nicole Kidman), a popular singer at the famous nineteenth-century French club. The movie's frantic pace and self-conscious use of wildly different musical sources, including Madonna, Elton John, and *The Sound of Music,* make this a very untraditional musical and show how flexible genre can be. Frame enlargement.

Furthermore, the musical is an antirealist, antinarrative form. A semblance of realism only prevails during the dialogue scenes. By contrast, the musical interludes are about the possibilities for stylizing color, sound, and movement in cinema, freed from the necessity to ground those styles in anything that smacks of realism. The story line in a musical is often the least important of its elements. The stories are typically very slight, without much elaboration, and serve mainly as a way of connecting the musical sequences, which is where the heart of the genre really lies. The musical genre is about the pure poetry of image and sound, freed from all literal consideration. Like the Western, this genre has notably diminished in recent years. The cinema is a poorer medium for its loss.

The Horror Film

Like Westerns and gangster films, horror has roots in the early silent period and existed as a literary and theatrical genre long before the invention of cinema. In the silent era, Lon Chaney (known as the "man of a thousand faces") used horrific makeup to create memorably grotesque characters in *The Phantom of the Opera* (1925) and *The Hunchback of Notre Dame* (1923). Actor John Barrymore played a strikingly repellent Mr. Hyde in *Dr. Jekyll and Mr. Hyde* (1920). Using distorted sets and compositions, the German expressionists created hauntingly bizarre worlds, such as that in F. W. Murnau's vampire classic *Nosferatu* (1922).

In the 1930s, Universal Pictures gave the cinema its classic monsters: *Frankenstein* (1931), *Dracula* (1931), *The Mummy* (1932), and *The Wolf Man* (1941). The brilliant makeup and set design, and the classic visual conceptions given to the monsters, have made these 1930s Universal productions the golden age of movie horror, and they have exerted an enduring influence on popular conceptions of Dracula, the Frankenstein monster, and werewolves. During this period, producer Val Lewton at RKO made a series of poetic and atmospheric horror films—*Cat People* (1942), *Isle of the Dead* (1945), *I Walked with a Zombie* (1943)—in which horrible or uncanny things were suggested rather than shown. Since then, horror has been big box office, an enduring genre that has never been long out of favor with audiences.

Critic Robin Wood defines the basic narrative situation in horror films as one whereby "normality" is threatened by the monster. Monster films from *Frankenstein* (1931) and *Dracula* (1931) to *Halloween* (1978) and *The Fly* (1988) often define normality in terms of the romantic, heterosexual couple or the family, particularly parent–child relationships (*The Exorcist,* 1973; *The Omen,* 1976). This is not, though, an invariable pattern. John Carpenter's remake of *The Thing* (1982), for example, is set amidst an all-male community of scientific researchers based in Antarctica.

Aside from the obvious physical danger it typically poses to ordinary, normal characters in the films, the monster poses a larger and more profound threat to the classification systems that define reality and on which culture and society rest. Whether a vampire, a mummy, a werewolf, or a vengeful psychopath, the monster represents a confusion—a violation—of social categories that specify boundaries between normal and abnormal, human and animal, living and dead. The monster typically occupies an uncertain middle ground between these distinctions, neither living nor dead, neither fully human nor fully an animal, abnormal but bearing disturbing traces of the human. Stories in the horror genre address the fragility of human identity by showing, through the monster, the loss, destruction, or violation of humanity.

The screen's most famous monsters—Bela Lugosi's Dracula, Boris Karloff's Frankenstein's monster, Lon Chaney's wolfman, Freddie Kreuger, Jason Voorhees—demonstrate that the monstrousness of the monster lies in its display of both human

The Mummy
(Universal, 1932)

The Mummy (Universal, 1999)
In its golden age, the horror genre created its enduring monsters using brilliant makeup designs applied to the face and body of actors Boris Karloff, Bela Lugosi, and Lon Chaney. Lacking a comparable generation of monster movie actors, today's films use high-tech effects and digital animation. Karloff's classic mummy used makeup and lighting to give the actor a sinister look; by contrast, the remake featured a monster created and animated in the computer. Frame enlargements.

and inhuman characteristics. As such, the horror film questions the viewer's most deeply cherished notions about what it means to be a human being. By centering on imaginary creatures who dwell in the margins of human life and consciousness, the horror film terrifies viewers by undermining their secure sense of where human identity lies in relation to the world of the dead, of animals, or of things.

The greatest and most enduring monsters are those that remain recognizably human while being undeniably monstrous. This recognition that human identity and monstrosity are one is the genre's deepest secret and most profound source of terror.

The monsters in the *Alien* series, for example, are genre classics, genuinely creepy creatures, from which audiences recoil with primordial fear and disgust. The "face huggers," blending arachnid and crustacean anatomy, seed their human hosts, and the baby aliens gestate inside the human victim, destroying their host as the human gives birth to the monster. The narrative arc of the first three films brings the creatures ever closer to Ripley, the series heroine, until it transpires that she, too, has been seeded and is no longer fully human. The third film ends with her destruction.

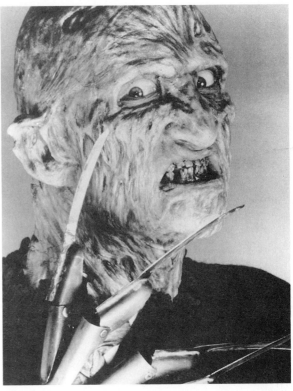

Alien 3 (20th Century Fox, 1992)
One of the monsters inspects Ripley (Sigourney Weaver) and then gives her a tender caress because she is no longer fully human. Gestating inside her is a baby alien. The horror genre terrifies by violating the conditions that define human identity. Frame enlargement.

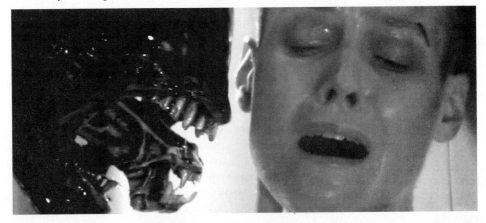

Evolution of the Horror Film

The evolution of the horror film demonstrates how genre conventions change. Old conventions become exhausted, and filmmakers search for new ones in their neverending challenge to retain the interest of the audience. Horror films of the 1930s and 1940s depicted the monster using an actor in (often brilliant) makeup, whereas contemporary films often use computer-based special effects to visualize the creatures. Moreover, horror films during their golden age tended to end on a very comforting note. The monster was destroyed, and the romantic couple reached safety unharmed. Horror was often left to the viewer's imagination in contrast with the graphic gore of modern films, which use contemporary effects technology to visualize the elaborate violence that is now basic in the genre. (In this respect, *The Blair Witch Project* [1999], *The Sixth Sense* [1999], and *The Others* [2001], all of which work through suggestion rather than graphic violence, are a return to the golden age of horror.)

By the 1970s and 1980s, in such films as *Halloween* and the neverending *Nightmare on Elm Street* and *Friday the 13th* series, the monster became indestructible and undefeatable. These monsters—Freddy, Jason, Michael Myers of the *Halloween* films, and the aliens in the *Alien* series—remain alive at the end of each episode, and viewers know they will come back again to haunt and terrify. Contemporary horror films, therefore, are more disturbing and unsettling than horror was in previous decades, when narrative conventions insisted that normality be restored and secure at film's end. Perhaps because the modern viewer's sense of what is normal is more precarious and more easily undermined, the destruction of order and security may strike contemporary audiences as a more authentic vision of life. The monsters today are everywhere, and they cannot be defeated, a perception that the narrative design of contemporary horror emphasizes.

SUMMARY

In their most popular form, movies tell stories, yet the film medium can also inform and instruct by observing real events (these movies are called documentaries) or it can represent pure shape, line, color, and form rather than real things (these are experimental, "underground," or avant-garde films). Yet it is narrative films that have captured the popular audience. The turn toward narrative emerged very early in film history and has been present ever since.

Present in all cultures, narrative thinking is an essential human ability. Fictional narratives, the kind movies typically employ, grow out of a particular context in which the storyteller and the audience agree to play make-believe in a way that grants the fictional story a special status: its truthfulness is not counted to be as important as its artistic organization and its power to delight and to compel belief.

Filmmakers create narrative structure by establishing discrepencies between plot and story. Using flashbacks, the omission of detail, or other devices, filmmakers can rearrange the proper order of story events and/or create obstacles to the viewer's assimilation of story information. If skillfully done, this will arouse the viewers' interest and make them keenly interested in seeing the full outcome of events. Among the most popular of plot structures is the classical Hollywood narrative, which offers a clearly dominant line of main action and one or more interrelated secondary lines of action. This narrative type is clearly motivated, forward moving, and establishes explicit causal relationships among its story events. Alternatives to the classical Hollywood narrative may feature implicit or minimal causality or, in extreme cases, an anti-narrative orientation.

All stories are told by someone, although the collaborative nature of cinema makes it difficult to identify a single or sole author. In film, narration is produced by the complex of structural elements—the camera, lights, sound, color, set design, costumes, and other elements of structure. While these can be used to imply a character's subjective perspective, point of view in the cinema is usually third-person, with implicit first-person components.

SUGGESTED READINGS

Rick Altman, *Film/Genre* (London: BFI, 1999).

David Bordwell, *Narration in the Fiction Film* (Madison: University of Wisconsin Press, 1985).

Seymour Chatman, *Coming to Terms: The Rhetoric of Narrative in Fiction and Film* (Ithaca, NY: Cornell University Press, 1990).

Seymour Chatman, *Story and Discourse: Narrative Structure in Fiction and Film* (Ithaca, NY: Cornell University Press, 1978).

John L. Fell, *Film and the Narrative Tradition* (Norman, OK: University of Oklahoma Press, 1974).

Avrom Fleishman, *Narrated Films: Storytelling Situations in Cinema History* (Baltimore: Johns Hopkins University Press, 1992).

Jane Gaines, ed., *Classical Hollywood Narrative: The Paradigm Wars* (Durham, NC: Duke University Press, 1992).

Barry K. Grant, *Film Genre Reader II* (Austin: University of Texas Press, 1995).

Andrew Horton, *Writing the Character-Centered Screenplay* (Berkeley: University of California Press, 2000).

Kristin Thompson, *Storytelling in the New Hollywood: Understanding Classical Narrative Technique* (Cambridge, MA: Harvard University Press, 1999).

George M. White, *Narration in Light: Studies in Cinematic Point of View* (Baltimore: Johns Hopkins University Press, 1986).

Chapter 7

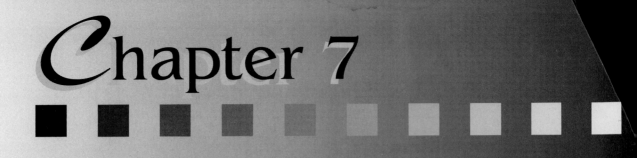

Modes of Screen Reality

Chapter Objectives

After reading this chapter, you should be able to:

- explain the basic modes of screen reality
- describe the principles of narrative, character behavior, and audiovisual design that operate in each mode of screen reality
- differentiate ordinary fictional realism, historical realism, documentary realism, and fictional documentary realism
- describe how the cinema functions as a medium that can record properties of the visual world before the camera as well as transform the appearance of that world

- explain how this double capacity for recording and transforming relates to the basic modes of screen reality
- explain the importance of production design for the mode of fantasy and the fantastic and how fantasy settings achieve credibility
- distinguish two modes of cinematic self-reflexivity
- explain why multiple modes of screen reality are possible in cinema

Key Terms and Concepts

screen reality
realism
expressionism
fantasy and the fantastic

cinematic self-reflexivity
ordinary fictional realism
historical realism
documentary realism

documentary
fictional documentary
  realism

This chapter examines how filmmakers use the elements of structure (lighting, editing, camera position, etc.) to create versions of representational reality on screen. Audiences routinely view a wide variety of films, ranging from comedies and Westerns to serious dramas, science fiction, and gangster films. The worlds represented on screen vary considerably among such films. Each possible screen world establishes its own validity, and a filmmaker must convince the audience that what they are seeing is plausible and is, taken on its own terms, real.

The concept of **screen reality** pertains to the principles of time, space, character behavior, and audiovisual design that filmmakers systematically organize in a given film to create an ordered world on-screen in which characters may act and in which a narrative may unfold. Obviously, different kinds of films create different representational realities on screen and relate in different ways to the actual social worlds inhabited by their flesh-and-blood spectators. A film's screen world is a systematic, artistic transformation of the viewer's personal and social frames of reference. This process of transformation is complex and multileveled. This chapter explains the basic modes or types of screen reality, and why there are several different but equally acceptable modes.

The cinema can configure physical, social, or psychological reality in many different ways or modes. Cinema persuades film viewers to believe in the validity of various uniquely constituted on-screen worlds. There are four fundamental modes of representational reality on screen: **realism, expressionism, fantasy and the fantastic,** and **cinematic self-reflexivity.** (For the purposes of the discussion, each mode will be treated as an ideal type. In practice, however, a given film may draw on elements from several modes.) How do these modes operate and how are films constructed from within them?

☐ REALISM

This is one of the most commonly encountered modes of screen reality, but one must be careful in discussing it. The term *realism* is probably the most overused and overworked item in critical discussion and daily conversation about film. *Realism* is a slippery term, with meanings that can be difficult to pin down or with connotations that ill-fit the medium of cinema. Nevertheless, it is an essential term for describing some of the attributes and functions of cinema, provided one is clear and cautious in using it.

The difficulty that the cinema poses for the term *realism* is that the medium involves so much artifice. What these chapters have termed the *transformational function* of cinema is its ability to go well beyond the viewer's visual and social experience, to create novel images that have no counterpart in life, and to do so using structural elements—wide-angle lenses, for example—that transform normal vision. On the other hand, though, the camera is a recording mechanism that produces images of the things that once were in front of its lens, and these images can correspond very closely to the viewer's experience and sense of the world. Recording the things and events that were before the camera connects the cinema in a powerful way to the real world. The camera can take pictures of that world. Thus, the realistic components of cinema are generally those that accord with the medium's abilities to record and correspond with experience. As these are very important attributes, one or more concepts of realism become essential to understanding the medium. Three broad types or categories of realism clearly exist in film: **ordinary fictional realism, historical realism,** and **documentary realism.**

Ordinary Fictional Realism

In this mode, the world on-screen closely resembles the one that the viewer inhabits. Time and space operate much as they do in viewers' ordinary lives. Characters belong to readily recognizable social worlds and communities (though these may differ from the viewer's), and they do not have magical powers or behave in ways that are exotic, strange, or incomprehensible. In other words, films in this category seem to have an ordinary, everyday kind of realism. This mode characterizes a large number of films. Among them is *A Beautiful Mind*, the 2001 Academy Award winner for Best Picture. Russell Crowe portrays John Nash, a brilliant mathematician whose mind was clouded by schizophrenia. Three fundamental components of ordinary fictional realism operate in *A Beautiful Mind*, as in other films belonging to this mode.

Case Study: *A Beautiful Mind*

Naturalistic Visual Style   The first of these components is the lack of overly pictorial, expressive interventions in the visual style of ordinary fictional realist films. Explicit, readily recognized stylistic manipulations are generally absent. These might include extreme lighting effects, elaborate camera movements, editing for discontinuity, or elaborate production design. Such elements will call the viewer's attention to a film's formal design, emphasizing surface and texture. By contrast, the visual style of ordinary fictional realism is relatively unobtrusive. As a film's formal design becomes more elaborate and insistent, the film begins to move out of this mode.

The camerawork in *A Beautiful Mind* serves the characters, the dialogue, and the story, providing viewers with compositions that focus attention on the emotional meaning of scenes and on important events and turns in the narrative. Doing so, the camerawork does not announce its presence with stylistic flourishes. Instead, it observes the characters and their doings, and most viewers would find it difficult to recall details of the cinematography, though not details of the story that the cinematography has illuminated.

Like most films in this mode, *A Beautiful Mind* employs continuity editing to replicate, on-screen, basic perceptual cues that viewers use to infer relations of time and space in their daily lives. The film uses the eyeline match, shot-reverse-shot cutting, inserts matching the master shot, the 180-degree rule, and transitional material to prepare for changes of screen direction. As a result, the editing creates very strong visual and narrative continuity. The action flows over the cuts, and the screen world built from shot to shot links up in a physically coherent way.

The editing creates a realistic impression of time and space in which the physical constancies in the world on screen do not depart in fundamental ways from those that viewers observe in their own lives. The physical positioning of characters does not change arbitrarily from shot to shot. In a similar fashion, the lighting, set, and costume design all aim for an unobtrusive naturalism. Visual design and shot construction in *A Beautiful Mind* achieve an impression of ordinary realism by avoiding cinematic designs that look excessively artificial or elaborately arranged.

Linear Narrative Structure   Films in this mode often employ a linear narrative in which the sequence of events has a clear logic, that is, in which events are chained together as a series of causes and effects. The action at the beginning of the film sets in motion events that lead to the final outcome. The narrative thus moves forward, in one predominant direction. The story traces Nash's life from the onset of his schizophrenia, when he is a student at Princeton in 1947, to his winning of the Nobel prize in 1994. The story has a linear and chronological structure, and it shows the viewer how Nash battled his psychological disorder and ultimately triumphed over it. His victory, and his winning of the Nobel prize, gives the story a satisfying and upbeat resolution.

A Beautiful Mind (Universal/DreamWorks, 2001)
Balanced compositions and camera positions that facilitate continuity
editing—note how the close-ups match the master shot and use the
eyeline match—help give *A Beautiful Mind* its naturalistic visual style.
The visual design serves the characters and dialogue and calls little overt
attention to itself. In this scene, Nash's wife (Jennifer Connelly) visits
him when he is confined to a psychiatric hospital. Frame enlargements.

Nonlinear Designs   Narratives that are nonlinear tend to move films out of the mode of ordinary realism. Nonlinear designs emphasize a film's style and structure, and, in cases where the designs are especially elaborate, they may require the viewer to work actively to make sense of the story. The kaleidoscopic structure of Woody Allen's *Annie Hall* (1977), for example, presents the story of Alvy Singer's affair with Annie in a nonchronological fashion, leaping in and out of different time periods in the lives of the characters. This doesn't prevent the audience from enjoying the movie, laughing at the gags, or feeling sad when Annie and Alvy finally break up. But the film's complex design sets some challenges for the audience. Because it is so fragmented, the story is not as easy to follow as it is in *A Beautiful Mind*. Furthermore, viewers notice the fragmented narrative as a *design;* the film's structure announces itself in an assertive manner.

Multiple flashbacks are a common way of breaking up what would otherwise be a linear narrative. One of the most famous films to employ multiple flashbacks is Akira Kurosawa's *Rashomon* (1950). The film's story is set in Japan's twelfth century and centers on the details surrounding the rape of a noblewoman and the death of her samurai warrior husband. The events of the crime are recalled differently by four separate narrators: the bandit accused of the rape, the noblewoman herself, the spirit of the dead samurai accessed through a medium, and a woodcutter who was an unseen witness to the tragedy. As each narrator presents a different version of the events under question, the film flashes back to the crime, but each time the story told in the flashback changes. In the case of *Rashomon*, the multiple flashbacks signal a didactic intent on the part of the filmmaker and encourage the viewer to extract the following lesson: that truth is relative and that people will perceive those versions of reality that best suit their own self-images.

Rashomon (1950)
The complex flashback structure of *Rashomon* creates a nonlinear narrative. The film's multiple flashbacks present contradictory versions of the same events. Through its narrative design, the film suggests that memory is selective and truth is relative.

Plausible Character Behavior   Characters should behave in believable ways. This is one of the most important constituents of the viewer's sense that films in this mode are realistic. When characters act in ways that are unmotivated or improbable, the viewer's level of belief in the fiction suffers, and such a viewer is likely to say that the film was not very realistic. Viewers are scrupulous judges of character behavior. If that behavior is not dictated by the demands of genre or story formula, viewers expect that it will conform with their own sense of what is right and appropriate under the circumstances.

Nash's schizophrenia becomes worse—he becomes delusional and sees people who aren't there—when he stops taking his medication. Although it has very destructive consequences, his decision not to take his pills seems entirely plausible because they dull his mind, making it difficult to work out scientific problems. Even worse, the pills have made him physically unresponsive to his wife.

Because images and stories in this mode seem so accessible, critics and viewers sometimes regard ordinary fictional realism as an easy accomplishment or as synonymous with no style at all. On the contrary, the elements of linear narrative, unobtrusive visual design, and plausible character behavior do not denote the absence of cinematic style. They should not be misunderstood as indicating a zero-degree level of style, nor should one assume that a filmmaker can readily achieve these attributes. Like the others, this mode is a highly constructed one, involving the deliberate design and manipulation of elements of structure. The appearance of ordinary realism is one that is *constructed* and *created*. That this is a paradox in no way diminishes the achievement.

Historical Realism

Ordinary fictional realism generally represents a time or place not too far removed from the social world of the film's audiences. Many films in the realist mode, however, aim at the recreation of a more distant past. Such films include Martin Scorsese's *The Age of Innocence* (1993), set in late nineteenth-century, aristocratic New York society, James Ivory's *The Remains of the Day* (1993), set among the British aristocracy circa World War II, and Steven Spielberg's Oscar-winning *Schindler's List* (1993), which aims at a visual and cultural recreation of Poland and Germany during the Nazi era. The most prolific filmmakers to work consistently in this mode are director James Ivory and producer Ismail Merchant, a team whose literate and nuanced films include *The Bostonians* (1984), *Room with a View* (1986), *Howard's End* (1992), *The Remains of the Day* (1993), and *Jefferson in Paris* (1995).

The historical realist mode works by accumulating authentic period detail. Meticulously decorated sets and costumes evoke now-vanished eras. Production design, therefore, is extremely important in this mode. Nominees for Academy Awards in the categories of art direction and costume design are often dominated by historical realist films. In 1994, for example, these included *The Age of Innocence, The Remains of the Day,* and *Schindler's List.*

To achieve this detail, filmmakers often conduct extensive historical research. Janusz Kaminski, the cinematographer for *Schindler's List,* based the visual design of his images on the photography of Roman Vishniac, who photographed European Jewish communities in the 1920s and 1930s and published these photographs in a book called *A Vanished World.* Seeking to re-create these communities for the film, Kaminski emulated

The Age of Innocence
(Columbia Pictures, 1994)
Production design is a key element of style that helps establish the period setting of films in the mode of historical realism. Sets and costumes in *The Age of Innocence* embody with fine detail the aristocratic world of late nineteenth-century New York society.

Vishniac's photographs. To do so, Kaminski tried to work as if he were photographing the film using the technology of fifty years ago, with no fancy lights, dollies, or tripods.

Robert Altman's *Gosford Park* (2001) portrays the codes of social etiquette that bind a house full of English aristocrats in the 1930s with the service staff that waits on them and tends to their every need. An American filmmaker, Altman knew little about this historical period and the behaviors appropriate to it, but he wanted to get it right. He therefore hired a former butler, a housemaid, and a cook, all of whom, now in their eighties, had entered domestic service in the 1930s. They became technical advisors on the film, instructing the actors and filmmakers on the precise ways to prepare meals,

Gosford Park (USA Films, 2001)
To recreate the social world of English high society in the 1930s, the filmmakers hired special consultants to advise on details of setting, dress, and behavior. The consultants, now in their eighties, had been domestic servants in the period that the film portrays. Their advice helped bring to life a now vanished period in English history. Frame enlargement.

Ali (Columbia, 2001)
This film biography of the world champion boxer includes very stylized camerawork but weaves elements of historical realism into its account of Ali's life. For the scene depicting the assassination of the Rev. Martin Luther King, the filmmakers modeled their composition on a well-known news photograph showing King's associates clustering around his body and gesturing to a rooftop where the gunfire that killed King originated. The movie image (shown here) acquires its impression of realism through its close visual relationship with the news photograph. The filmmakers intend for viewers to make this comparison. Frame enlargement.

clean shoes, set a dinner table, and for the actors to carry themselves properly as service staff in this period. Arthur Inch, the butler advisor, for example, corrected errors of costuming. He pointed out that a livery footman always wore a white bow tie, not a black one. This and other advice helped the filmmakers capture the small, accurate details of dress and behavior that helped the film achieve its vivid historical realism.

The weight of such detail, in conjunction with characters whose behavior must conform to different social norms than those that prevail today, works to persuade viewers of the authenticity of the screen world. Many such films—*Sense and Sensibility* (1995), *Howard's End, Titanic* (1997)—depict the confining nature of social class by showing the conflict between what a person desires to do and what his or her station in life demands. Construed according to the dictates of a historical period, character behavior furnishes an important index of historical realism, provided the norms of the era are clearly understood and the behavior is plausible within those norms.

An especially powerful depiction of such a conflict, *Elizabeth* (1998), portrays the accession to the throne of Queen Elizabeth I in sixteenth-century England, from which she commenced a forty-year rule known as England's golden age. The film was shot on location in a variety of historical settings throughout the United Kingdom, including Durham Cathedral, Haddon Hall, and Bamburgh Castle, providing the film with regional authenticity. Director Shekhar Kapur envisioned the core of the film as Elizabeth's journey from youth and love to ruthlessness, power, and the renunciation of her personal needs and feelings, and he stylized the film so as to bring out this core meaning. He used white light—as in several fades to white—to suggest the transcendent religious meanings on which she would model her image as Queen. To embody the ruthlessness and cruelty of the political world she inherits, Kapur chose sets made of stone. English castles at the time included wood in their design, but Kapur felt that stone would better convey the coldness and harshness of power and would imply that these structures—castles and halls—would outlast the people living in them. To emphasize the forces of history and destiny, he also shot from extremely high angles, with the camera looking sharply down on the figures below. The climactic sequence late in the film, in which Elizabeth consolidates her throne by assassinating her political enemies, is modeled on a comparable, famous sequence in *The Godfather* (1972) wherein Michael Corleone (Al Pacino) violently rids himself of his enemies. These choices of light, set, camera position, and narrative structure demonstrate that filmmakers who aim for historical realism need not be shackled by an overly literal depiction of the past. They are free to invent and to stylize their materials in ways that clarify the core meanings that are inherent in the past being depicted. Historical realism, therefore, is compatible with inventive methods of visual stylization.

Documentary Realism

Concepts of realism in the cinema are closely tied to traditions in which the camera is used as an instrument of reportage and documentation. Films that fall into this tradition are frequently termed **documentaries,** although such films may employ a wide range of styles. While the topic of documentary filmmaking is an extremely broad one, and generally falls outside the confines of this textbook, a word on the subject is in order in relation to concepts of realism.

While the camera can be used as a recording instrument to capture events, situations, and realities that may be transpiring independently of the filmmaker, the camera is also an instrument of style. A filmmaker's choices about lenses, film stocks, and camera positions and angles alter the raw material of the event unfolding before the camera so that it becomes a cinematic event that has a stylistic organization and design. It is naive, then, to believe that documentary filmmaking is the equivalent of raw reportage. A filmmaker's structural choices transform the raw material before the camera into an organized cinematic design.

Basis of Documentary Realism

Documentary films exist in a state of tension, caught between the camera's recording and transformative functions. The documentary filmmaker aims to report on an event that has occurred, yet, to do so, he or she must transform that event into cinema. How, then, does the concept of realism operate within the documentary tradition? How can realism be squared with a filmmaker's need to shape structure? Are documentary films essentially like fiction films in that they speak a language of structure and style that is unique to the cinema?

To some extent, documentaries *are* like fiction films. In each, a filmmaker confronts the same array of choices: where to put the camera, where to cut the shot, how to join several images together, whether and how to impose a narrative logic on the events to be depicted. Despite these similarities, however, two unique characteristics distinguish documentary realism from ordinary fiction films. First, audiences and most documentary filmmakers assume the existence of a noncinematic referent, some person, event, or situation that exists prior to, and independently of, the film that is being made. This assumption does not hold for fiction films in which the characters are clearly made up for the purposes of the story.

The second basis on which documentary realism rests is the perceived absence of fictionalizing elements. These might include the presence of actors performing a role or a narrative structure which alters the time chronology of the event. Audiences and most documentary filmmakers assume that fictionalizing tendencies begin with the presence of actors and an invented narrative structure. Critics charged that the documentary about the collapse of the auto industry in Flint, Michigan, *Roger and Me* (1989), violated documentary ethics because it rearranged and reordered the chronology of events leading to the demise of the General Motors auto plant. The film condensed events that occurred over a long period of time so that they seemed to happen virtually overnight. Assumptions of a noncinematic referent and the absence of key fictional elements are central to the mode of documentary realism, but, in practice, there is considerable flexibility for individual films to negotiate their own unique approaches with reference to these issues, particularly when a filmmaker wants to offer a stylistic commentary on the events or people the film depicts.

Documentary Poetics

Case Study: *The Thin Blue Line*

Some documentaries make no claim of reportorial objectivity and come close, instead, to a form that might best be described as an extended poetic essay. Errol Morris's *The Thin Blue Line* (1988) reexamines the 1976 murder of Dallas policeman Robert Wood

---

The Thin Blue Line (Miramax, 1988)

The Thin Blue Line mixes standard documentary elements, such as interview footage with real people, and highly stylized crime scene reenactments. The poetic results show how imaginative and creative documentary style may be. Interview footage with Randall Adams, filmed in a straightforward manner, contrasts with the visually expressive crime reenactments. Note the tight framing of the gun and the dark, low-key lighting. Frame enlargements.

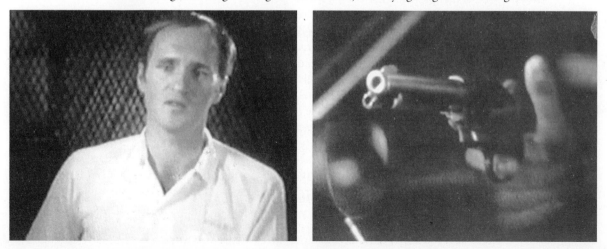

through interviews with Randall Adams and David Harris. Harris was originally arrested for the killing, but he swore that hitchhiker Randall Adams was the killer. Adams was arrested, convicted, and sentenced to death while Harris was released. Harris subsequently confessed to the crime. Adams, who maintained his innocence all along, was exonerated as a result of this film.

The Thin Blue Line powerfully illustrates the flexibility of documentary realism. It portrays an actual event through interviews with the principal people involved. This interview footage, however, is intercut with re-creations of the shooting employing actors, an original, moody musical score by celebrity composer Philip Glass, and very stylized editing.

Morris wanted to avoid the style of such popular journalistic documentaries as *60 Minutes*. That show intercuts different speakers to explicitly compare and contrast the claims that they make. Witness A claims that condition X is true, and then a direct cut shows witness B claiming that condition Y is, in fact, true.

On *The Thin Blue Line*, Morris forbid editor Paul Barnes from employing this type of editing. Barnes could not cut from shots of Adams to shots of Harris or vice versa. On the soundtrack viewers could hear one man speaking after the other but would never see them together in adjacent shots. Adams and Harris are interviewed separately, and each talks about what brought him to Dallas on the eve of the fatal shooting. Moving back and forth between the recollections of each man, the film establishes two parallel lines of action in the double series of events that brought them to the city. Imposing a calculated visual design, the editing separates interview footage of each man from footage of his antagonist. Barnes does not cut from one to the other without first interspersing shots of the Dallas skyline or other transitional material.

The editing imposes a preplanned visual design on the narrated events and also an ethical structure. The ethic, in this case, emerged from Morris's wish to avoid what he perceived as the exploitative journalistic practice of setting a person up to be contradicted by another witness. Does this design violate documentary realism? As we have seen, documentary realism must coexist with a filmmaker's inherent need to impose structural design on his or her materials. In this case, the editing does not falsify the noncinematic referent or invalidate the contents of the interview footage with the actual participants.

What about the crime scene reenactments? These are clearly fictionalizing elements. Director Morris and editor Barnes tried to avoid the typical style of fake dramatizations in which the actors are cleanly lit and clearly photographed. Accordingly, they chose to play the reenactments in dark light with very tight (close-up) camera framings that prevent viewers from seeing many details. This design creates a style for the reenactments that tells viewers that these belong to a different order of reality than the interview footage and that the filmmakers know the difference between the two. The reenactments unquestionably place fictionalizing elements within the film. The shooting is portrayed by actors. In principle, this is a violation of documentary realism, but the film uses its structural design to alert viewers that the reenactments belong to a manipulated and stylized level of reality.

Fictional Documentary Realism

The Thin Blue Line demonstrates that documentary filmmakers can use realistic designs to report on events as well as nonrealistic designs to create emotional and poetic effects. While the stylized reenactments in the film have an arty, unreal quality to them, the sequences with Harris and Adams utilize two fundamental codes of documentary film practice, interview footage with the people involved in an event and voice-over narration.

Suppose, however, that a filmmaker deliberately uses the codes of documentary filmmaking but applies them to a wholly fictitious event. To the extent that documentary is a film *practice*—specifying a method of working as well as stylistic designs that are permissible and those that are not—there is nothing to prevent a filmmaker from imitating this practice, that is, from making a fake documentary such as *The Blair Witch Project*. **Fictional documentary realism** describes the style and effects of such films. Rob Reiner's *This Is Spinal Tap* (1984) is a well-known example of a fake documentary. In the film, director Reiner plays fictitious director Marty DiBergi who is making a documentary film about British rock group Spinal Tap. No such group exists, of course, except in the pretend world of this film parody, which accurately skewers many of the conventions of rock documentaries.

The film opens with Reiner, as DiBergi, seated by a camera and lighting equipment as he tells viewers about his first meeting with Spinal Tap in 1966 and explains the genesis of "the documentary, the, if you will, rockumentary you are about to see." DiBergi talks directly into the camera with cinema equipment prominently displayed behind him. Because viewers think documentaries are more real than fiction films, shrewd filmmakers can emphasize this impression by displaying the cinema equipment used to create the images on screen. Such an on-screen display of camera equipment is unthinkable in the mode of ordinary fictional realism, but, within documentary realism, it serves to authenticate the special nonfiction status of the film by communicating to the audience that the filmmaker is not trying to "fool" viewers into mistaking the film's images for reality itself.

Other codes of rock documentaries that the film employs include people-on-the-street interviews with fans talking about what Tap means to them. These interviews

This Is Spinal Tap (Embassy Pictures, 1984)
This Is Spinal Tap applies documentary techniques to completely fictitious events and characters. The film looks like a documentary but is really an elaborate hoax. Representational reality may be unreliable or ironic. In the case of *This Is Spinal Tap,* the filmmaker expects the audience to recognize the irony.

Best in Show
(Warner Bros., 2000)
Filmmaker Christopher Guest has specialized in fake documentaries. This one is a hilarious comedy about a group of oddballs who've entered their dogs in a prestigious show. Fake interviews and apparently impromptu situations abound. Frame enlargement.

are intercut with faked concert footage and faked behind-the-scenes glimpses of backstage preparation for concerts. Other faked documentary codes include a series of interviews with the band members (all of whom, of course, are actors) and even faked black-and-white kinescope footage, supposedly from 1965, dramatizing an early television appearance by Tap (like the Beatles on Ed Sullivan).

The popularity of *This Is Spinal Tap* has led to other films in the fake documentary mode. Among the best are a pair by Christopher Guest—*Waiting for Guffman* (1997), about a small-town theater troupe putting on a show, and *Best in Show* (2000), about the nutty contestants in a prestigious dog show. Like *Spinal Tap*, these films imitate many of the rules of documentary filmmaking, but much of their humor depends on the viewer getting the ironies and appreciating the elaborate fakery.

☐ EXPRESSIONISM

Expressionism is an extremely stylized mode of screen reality in which filmmakers use visual distortion to suggest emotional, social, or psychological disturbances or abnormalities. The distortions may be subtle but most often they are manifest and explicit. In this regard, expressionism is an antirealist mode that aims to move far from naturalism, emphasizing instead strange or bizarrely poetic designs using lighting, color, lenses, camera position, and set design. Expressionism in its pure form, as it characterized German cinema in the 1920s, is distinct from expressionism as it survives in contemporary cinema.

Classic German Expressionism

The expressionist mode in its purest form is found in 1920s German cinema. Expressionism began in German painting and theater in 1908 and, by the 1920s, had spread to the cinema where it characterized a series of classic films including *The Cabinet of Dr. Caligari* (1919), *Nosferatu* (1922), an early version of Dracula, and the science fiction classic *Metropolis* (1926).

Nosferatu (1922)
Expressionistic integration of character and decor in *Nosferatu*. Expressionist distortions included architectural design as well as the human figure. Note how the vampire's elongated body fits within the arched doorway. The expressionist style linked people and settings to form a uniquely stylized screen reality. Frame enlargement.

In these and other films of the early German cinema, the expressionist style was overtly opposed to realism; it emphasized elaborate distortions in the mise-en-scène. Lighting designs employed a prevalence of shadows and violent visual contrast. Decor and set design utilized aberrant architectural forms to create dwellings whose off-kilter, skewed designs embodied decentered, anxiety-ridden screen worlds. Normal, rectilinear architectural forms (dwellings where walls, floor, and ceiling are at right angles to each other and in parallel planes) were replaced with skewed structures built with diagonals and nonparallel planes.

These filmmakers integrated the actors' physical appearance and movements with the architectural forms. In the accompanying illustration from F. W. Murnau's *Nosferatu,* the vampire's thin, elongated body is linked at a visual level with the arched door frame in which he lingers before pouncing on his victim. Expressionist acting frequently employed a distorted physical appearance, and, as the image from *Nosferatu* illustrates, these strange body types functioned as expressive forms and were integrated seamlessly with the shapes and textures of the set design.

Expressionist filmmakers often used odd camera angles to enhance the decentering of the screen world. The camera's positioning, the lighting design, and the decor all work together to achieve maximum distortion in expressionist mise-en-scène. These distortions were often correlated with a particular kind of subject matter. Characters might be grotesques as in the vampires of *Nosferatu* or the mad doctor in *Metropolis.* They inhabited fantasy realms of myth as in Fritz Lang's *Seigfried,* or futuristic worlds as in Lang's *Metropolis.* Correlated with these extrahuman or subhuman characters were their extreme and sometimes deranged emotional states. The terror of the victim of the sleepwalking killer in *The Cabinet of Dr. Caligari,* and the killer's own anxiety-laden flight across the rooftops, are expressively conveyed in the wild decor pictured in the accompanying illustration.

The Cabinet of Dr. Caligari
(1919)
Expressionist set design created a bizarre, strange, off-kilter world in the classic *The Cabinet of Dr. Caligari*, the first expressionist film. Note the disturbing diagonal lines suggesting disorder and instability throughout the set in place of normal rectilinear architecture. Frame enlargement.

German expressionism entered the United States via a wave of émigré German filmmakers working in Hollywood, and the style was popularized in the series of horror films produced in the 1930s at Universal Studios. James Whale's 1931 production of *Frankenstein* features the grotesque characters and diagonal visual forms that link it closely with the German horror and fantasy films that flourished in the 1920s. In the opening scene, Dr. Frankenstein and his evil assistant Fritz hide in a

Frankenstein (Universal Studios, 1931)
Expressionist set design—note the sloping diagonals—in the Universal horror genre.
Dr. Frankenstein (Colin Clive) digs up a fresh corpse for his experiments. Subsequently, his monster rages against confinement in a castle cell. Frame enlargements.

graveyard, waiting until the gravediggers have finished burying a body. They plan to dig it up and steal the corpse for use in their gruesome medical experiments. Visual designs emphasizing extreme antirealism and distortion effectively convey the film's horror content.

Contemporary Expressionism

While the pure expressionism characterizing German cinema of the 1920s is rarely found in contemporary filmmaking, modern directors often employ the visual distortions of expressionist style.

Case Study: Alfred Hitchcock

Alfred Hitchcock was probably the best-known filmmaker to use expressionism as an ongoing feature of his work. In *Psycho* (1960), a striking low-angle shot of Norman Bates, the psychopathic killer, dehumanizes his face. By emphasizing the working of his gullet as he chews on some candy, it transforms him visually into a birdlike creature. This is appropriate as Norman is a taxidermist by hobby and keeps his office stuffed with birds of prey, which he has mounted on the walls. Hitchcock said that these birds are perfect symbols of Norman himself. They are birds of the night—predators— and he sees his own guilt mirrored in their eyes.

In *Strangers on a Train* (1951), a demented fan of a famous tennis player kills the athlete's greedy and selfish wife, believing that he is doing the celebrity a favor. Hitchcock films the killing from a memorably distorted perspective, as the image refracted by the wife's eyeglasses, which have fallen to the ground in her struggles with the killer. After she is dead, the killer reaches for the glasses, and the refracted image gives him giant lobster hands, dehumanizing him in a poetic manner (in the film's first scene, he wears a vulgar, lobster-print necktie).

In *Notorious* (1946), about a woman who is coerced into spying for the U.S. government, an early scene shows her waking up with a hangover. She looks up and sees a government agent hovering in the doorway of her bedroom. Hitchcock employs a subjective expressionistic shot to represent her point of view and to make the agent seem very threatening and sinister. The agent appears as a silhouette. As he walks toward her and she turns her head to look up at him, tracking his movements, his figure pirouettes upside down across her field of vision.

In *Vertigo* (1958), to suggest the approaching despair and madness of the detective hero (James Stewart), Hitchcock included a completely artificial sequence. The detective's nightmare hallucination is represented, in part, through animation. A bouquet of flowers, held by a ghostly character in the film, suddenly splits apart and the petals fly menacingly toward the viewer. Hitchcock departs from realism here so thoroughly that it sometimes confuses modern viewers, uncertain whether they are seeing an example of inferior visual effects or a genuinely radical visual design.

As these examples from Hitchcock's cinema illustrate, the director learned from the expressionists about the power of a distorted visual image and employed such designs systematically throughout his career when he needed to suggest intensified states of emotional disturbance.

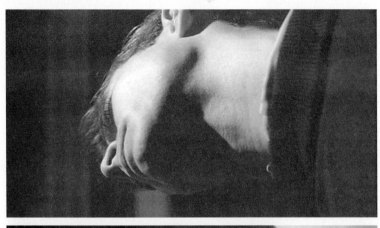

Psycho (Paramount Pictures, 1960)
This strange, low-angle shot of Norman Bates (Anthony Perkins) in *Psycho* turns him into a bird. This adds a symbolic dimension to the narrative since Norman is a taxidermist specializing in stuffing predatory birds. The bizarre image suggests that Norman, too, is a predator, a creature of the night, like his birds. Hitchcock appreciated the special power of expressionistically distorted images to transform normal visual reality. Frame enlargement.

Notorious (RKO, 1946)
In *Notorious,* Cary Grant, as an American government agent, appears in this bizarre, upside-down perspective. The angular distortion represents the anxious point of view of a character reclining on a bed. In this respect, the visually unstable point of view replicates the original aims of German expressionism, which were to visually represent subjective states of mind. Frame enlargement.

Notorious (RKO, 1946)
With a subtle expressionistic touch, Hitchcock designs this shot from *Notorious* so that the cup of poison (*foreground*) looms gigantically beside the woman who is being poisoned (Ingrid Bergman, *background*). To get the shot, Hitchcock instructed his prop crew to construct an enormous cup and then placed the camera in this low-angle position to emphasize its size. Frame enlargement.

Strangers on a Train
(Warner Bros., 1951)
Hitchcock shows a murder as
the distorted reflection in the
lens of a pair of discarded eyeglasses. Having finished with his
victim, the killer then reaches
for the glasses, and the optical
distortion turns his hand into a
giant lobster claw. Frame
enlargements.

Other Recent Cases

More recent productions have drawn on the expressionist heritage. Spike Lee's *Crooklyn* (1994) features a 20-minute sequence shot with uncorrected anamorphic perspective— making the characters and settings look thin and elongated—to visualize a city girl's disorientation at living in the suburbs. One of the chief villains in Tim Burton's *Batman*

Crooklyn (Universal, 1994)
Uncorrected anamorphic perspectives squeeze the characters in this distorted fashion. Used throughout a lengthy episode detailing a young woman's disorientation while visiting surburban relatives, they mark the episode off from the rest of the film and provide a way to visualize the character's anxieties. Frame enlargement.

Returns (1992) is the industrialist Max Schreck (Christopher Walken). In name and appearance, he evokes the 1920s German classics. "Max Schreck" was the name of the actor who played the vampire in *Nosferatu*, and as the character appears in Burton's film, he sports a flamboyant shock of white hair that makes him look like the mad scientist Rotwang in Fritz Lang's *Metropolis*. In other respects, as well, Burton's film evokes classic expressionist mise-en-scène. The huge fireplace in Bruce Wayne's mansion strongly resembles the giant fireplace used in *Bride of Frankenstein* (1935). These details of design and character are explicit homages to the German cinema, used to explicitly evoke some of its best-known stylistic features.

Martin Scorsese's *Cape Fear* (1992) employs a number of striking expressionistic motifs in the opening title design. The film deals with a vengeful psychopath, newly

Cape Fear (Universal, 1992)
The diagonal shadow of a murderer haunts the river's surface in the expressionistic title design of *Cape Fear*. Frame enlargement.

MARTIN SCORSESE

Martin Scorsese is one of the most accomplished and respected directors in contemporary U.S. cinema. His work glances self-consciously off established genres like the musical and gangster film and brings to them a European-styled openness of narrative, ambiguity of character and moral perspective, and extraordinary cinematic styling. Scorsese has an encyclopedic knowledge of old films and voraciously views other directors' work. He fully understands the traditions from which his own films derive. Because of this love for the medium and its past, he has been especially active in efforts to preserve and restore old films, such as *Lawrence of Arabia* (1962), and (during the 1980s) to persuade Eastman Kodak to develop film stocks with more stable dyes to protect against color loss. He shot *Raging Bull* (1980) in black and white because of the then-unresolved problem of color fading.

Educated at New York University, where he subsequently taught from 1968–1970, he directed his second feature, *Boxcar Bertha* (1972), under legendary B-movie producer Roger Corman. Scorsese then displayed a startling cinematic maturity in *Mean Streets* (1973), a vivid portrait of four male friends in New York's Little Italy that combined a diffuse narrative, an aggressively moving camera, and improvisatory, unpredictable performance styles. The film marked the beginning of Scorsese's remarkable collaboration with actor Robert De Niro. Together, they form one of the most striking actor–director relationships in cinema history. De Niro's mercurial, quicksilver, threatening persona is an essential part of Scorsese's accomplishments in his revision of Hollywood's musicals (*New York, New*

York, 1977), gangster films (*Goodfellas*, 1990), suspense films (*Cape Fear*, 1991), and boxing films (*Raging Bull*). In addition, De Niro contributed indelible portraits of a psychopath in *Taxi Driver* (1976), and of a nebbishy fan in *The King of Comedy* (1983).

Because of his unconventional visual and narrative style, Scorsese labored for many years without due recognition from the Hollywood industry. The late seventies and early to mid-1980s were an especially difficult period for him when he was uncertain that he could continue to support himself as a director. However, he enjoyed great critical acceptance with *Goodfellas* in 1990 and immediately followed that with two shrewd career moves. *Cape Fear*, executive-produced by Steven Spielberg, demonstrated his ability to manufacture a mainstream (if highly unpleasant) suspense film, and *The Age of Innocence* (1993) dramatically expanded his screen domain beyond the familiar urban milieu of crooks, psychopaths, and losers. This lavish, sensitive portrait of nineteenth-century New York aristocratic society

(continued)

Taxi Driver (Columbia Pictures, 1976)
In *Taxi Driver*, Scorsese and actor Robert De Niro collaborated to produce their most powerful and chilling creation—the psychopathic cab driver Travis Bickle and the hellish urban world he inhabits. Scorsese's expressionistic style visualizes Bickle's dementia with astonishing and disturbing vividness, and De Niro supplies some of his most brilliant improvisations.

MARTIN SCORSESE *(continued)*

demonstrated that Scorsese was not only a major film-maker (many already knew that) but that he possessed a surprising artistic range. He continued to expand this range with *Kundun* (1997), a visual poem about the Dalai Lama.

After many years of laboring in the wilderness, Scorsese has at last earned respect and acceptance from the Hollywood industry. Like John Ford, Alfred Hitchcock, and William Wyler, old-time Hollywood directors he greatly admires, Scorsese is today an acknowledged master of his medium and a re-spected member of the industry, which accords him the privilege—like Ford, Hitchcock, and Wyler—of making personal films.

This level of success led him, as it has other film-makers (Coppola and *Apocalypse Now*), to pursue a highly personal but grandly ambitious project—*Gangs of New York* (2002), a nineteenth-century period piece about New York gangsters that was shot in Italy and went over budget and over schedule. At the height of their careers, and with all of Hollywood's resources before them, few filmmakers resist the temptation to dream big.

released from prison, who wreaks a terrible plan of destruction on the family of the lawyer he blames for his conviction. The film's title is derived from the river in North Carolina where the climax occurs. The title also evokes, in a poetic and symbolic manner, the climate of terror and anxiety that is established in the story when the psychopath begins stalking and tormenting the lawyer's family.

During the opening credits, the waters of the Cape Fear River reflect several distorted expressionistic forms. A predatory bird swoops down near the surface of the water, its shadow extended and disturbed by the river's rippling surface. Super-imposed over the water is a terror-stricken eye, glancing about with extreme agitation. Later in the sequence, a screaming mouth appears, the teeth fearsomely exposed. Next looms a dark, ominous figure of a man, skewed on a diagonal. Finally, a drop of blood drips from the top to the bottom of the screen, bringing with it a wave of red color.

A dissolve links the end of the credit sequence to a close-up of the eyes of the lawyer's young daughter, viewed as a negative image. Here, Scorsese revived an expressionist technique from Murnau's vampire classic *Nosferatu*. To suggest the phantom world, Murnau showed Dracula's coach and horses as film negatives. Scorsese pulls viewers out of the expressionist title sequence and inserts them into the world of the narrative proper by using negative imagery, suggesting, at a visual level, what the narrative will establish, a world in which human behavior and values are dangerously inverted.

Used by filmmakers as diverse as Hitchcock, Burton, and Scorsese, expressionism constitutes a powerful mode of screen reality permitting a filmmaker to break with re-alism and skew images and characters in ways expressive of social or psychological abnormality. In this regard, the style has transcended the context (silent German cinema) in which it first flourished to become an essential and ongoing mode of screen reality.

☐ FANTASY AND THE FANTASTIC

This mode of screen reality sometimes overlaps with expressionism (as, for example, in the case of *Batman Returns*). There are, however, important distinctions between them. Expressionism can be employed within a relatively naturalistic framework, as in the films of Alfred Hitchcock, where the expressionistic elements are of relatively brief duration and occur within scenes whose overall style is more naturalistic. By contrast, in films employing a fantasy or fantastic mode, settings and subjects, characters, and narrative time are often displaced from the viewer's own realm into other realms, sometimes futuristic ones, where normal laws of time and space may not apply. Characters might have super-powers, like Superman, or advanced technology that lends them super-powers, like Robocop. Adventurers can pilot starships to new galaxies as in *Star Wars*, and artificial beings, created by mad inventors, can become suburban hairdressers, like Edward Scissorhands. Angels can assume material form and fall in love with humans, as in *City of Angels*.

This mode is as old as cinema. One of the earliest films was Georges Melies's *A Trip to the Moon* (1902), which took viewers on the titular journey and depicted the moon as inhabited by a species of lizard people who chase their visitors from Earth merrily about. *A Trip to the Moon* is a science-fiction fantasy, but the mode of fantasy in cinema transcends genre. Fantasy is essential to science fiction but it also can characterize romance

A Trip to the Moon (1902) One of the cinema's fundamental roots lies in fantasy. Since the inception of the medium, filmmakers have used it to picture the imagination. Early filmmaker Georges Melies filmed a band of intrepid astronomers traveling to the moon and dreamed up this memorable image, picturing their spaceship landing in the eye of the man in the moon. Frame enlargement.

Batman (Warner Bros., 1989) Production design is critically important in establishing the fantasy mode of *Batman*. The gigantic and grim Gotham City is a fanciful transformation of modern cities and provides the visually striking setting for the story. Indoor sets, mattes, and miniature models suggest a monumental urban landscape that is dark, cold, gray, largely devoid of color, light, open space, or human values. Suffocatingly dense and heavy, Gotham City chokes its inhabitants with architecture that suggests an absence of freedom or hope.

(*Always, The Ghost and Mrs. Muir, City of Angels, Ghost*), drama (*Stairway to Heaven*), the war film (*A Guy Named Joe*), and Arthurian legend (*Excalibur, First Knight*).

Ways of Making Fantasy Credible

Viewers are willing, even eager, to suspend disbelief in order to enter an enchanting, amusing, or thrilling fantasy world. Filmmakers, though, have to work to sustain this willingness and make the unreal seem credible for the duration of the film. One way of doing this is to set the fantasy within recognizably real surroundings, as in *City of Angels* (1998), where well-known Los Angeles settings (and some in San Francisco) provide a convincing locale for the action. So intent were the *City of Angels* filmmakers on evoking the realities of an urban setting that they placed the actors (Nicolas Cage and Dennis Franz) high atop a real skyscraper construction site for a dialogue scene that has the characters sitting on a girder overlooking the city. Having evoked place in this detailed manner, the film shifts easily into its moments of explicit fantasy—angels defying time and space to move with lightning speed, angels guiding the dying into a transcendent realm of light, an angel's hand unharmed by a knife that has sliced through his finger.

Another effective way to establish the credibility of a fantasy world is through the sheer accumulation of narrative detail. The more thoroughly a filmmaker can render the fantasy world, the richer its tapestry of detail—characters, places, events—the more convincing it will come to seem to viewers. George Lucas is a master at working in this manner. The hugeness of his *Star Wars* project—encompassing to date four films produced over more than two decades—and the expanse and wealth of story information that he gave to his mythopoetic world are quite unprecedented in modern cinema. By beginning his saga in the middle of the story (*Star Wars* is episode four), Lucas abruptly plunged his viewers into a well-defined fantasy universe, and each subsequent film elaborated on the intricate network of characters and locations that the films were constructing, installment by installment. By the end of *Return of the Jedi*, this imaginative universe contained a galaxy of uniquely differentiated and vividly rendered planets where critical episodes of the story line occur. *The Empire Strikes Back* opens on the ice world of Hoth and a deadly clash between the Empire and the rebel forces, which have gone into hiding after launching (from the planet of Yavin 4) their assault on the first Death Star in *Star Wars*. The heroes, Luke, Han, and Princess Leia, escape the battle, with Luke journeying to the jungle world of Dagobah, where he encounters the Zen-like but diminutive Yoda. Han and Leia seek refuge on Bespin in the Cloud City run by Lando Calrissian. Darth Vader, though, sets a trap, freeze-dries Han, and sends him to Tatooine, the desert world where Luke grew up and where the toad-like gangster Jabba the Hut has his headquarters. The climax of the Empire–rebel struggle occurs in *Return of the Jedi* on Endor, a forest planet that is home to the Ewok, a race of furry, cute but fierce Rebel allies. Filling out this remarkably detailed gallery of places and characters are bounty hunters (Boba Fett, Greedo), monsters (the sand-dwelling Sarlacc), and Wild West cantinas (Mos Eisley). The elaborate effects that Lucas and his artists created for the films is certainly a major part of their appeal. But the intricately layered narrative details extending across four films arguably have done more to establish the fantasy and make it convincing.

A third way of establishing credibility in this mode is by using production design to make unreal settings seem tangible and convincing. Consider the work of Tim Burton, one of the most popular filmmakers currently working in fantasy. His films include *Batman* (1989), *Edward Scissorhands* (1990), *Batman Returns* (1990), *Beetlejuice* (1988), *Mars Attacks,* and *The Legend of Sleepy Hollow* (1999), and, as producer, *The Nightmare Before Christmas* (1993). *Batman* features a brilliant production design by Anton Furst that evokes Gotham City as a dark, congested metropolis rife with crime. As in other films about dark cities of the future—*Blade Runner* (1982), *Dark City* (1998), *The Matrix* (1999)—the metropolis of *Batman* is one of the stars of the film, taking a commanding visual presence alongside the major characters. Rendered

Edward Scissorhands
(20th Century
Fox, 1990)
All things are possible in fantasy, even a gothic castle perched in the middle of suburbia.

with sets, mattes, and miniature models, Gotham is a wholly imaginary creation, but its visual design is so powerful that it comes convincingly to life.

In *Edward Scissorhands*, production designer Bo Welch daringly drops Edward's medieval castle into the middle of suburbia, even showing it perched ominously at the end of a street of trim houses with manicured lawns. It's an ostentatious design concept, almost daring the audience to react with disbelief. Yet, when a saleswoman (Dianne Wiest) calls on its occupant, the castle proves to be adorned with so much Gothic detail that it becomes unquestionably *real*.

In fantasy, the real is limited only by a filmmaker's imagination, and whatever an audience can be persuaded to believe in becomes real for this mode. In this regard, fantasy offers filmmakers tremendous flexibility of style and freedom of invention be-cause audiences do not require plausibility in the way that they ask it from a filmmaker working in the realist mode. An enduring cliché of science-fiction films demonstrates the freedom to invent that fantasy offers its filmmakers. Except mainly for Stanley Kubrick's *2001: A Space Odyssey* (1968), which showed spacecraft gliding silently through space, most science-fiction spacecraft emit loud, powerful rumblings from their engines. In *Star Wars'* first scene, for example, a series of spaceships approaches the camera, and then, in a reverse angle cut, the group flies away. The roar of the engines gives these special-effects creations an impressive physicality. Multichannel sound, with the dedicated bass channel, has accentuated this cliché because now spacecraft can emit wall-shaking low-frequency sound as they pass by. Doppler effects are routinely employed to create the changes in pitch (higher pitch for approaching objects, lower for receding ones) correlated with movement.

While the Doppler effects are accurate for Earth-bound experience, in the outer space context they are impossible. In space there is no sound because there is no medium, such as the air or atmosphere on Earth, to transport sound waves. Consequently, spaceships should make no perceivable noise at all. But this would be dramatically flat and uninteresting. Thus, the cliché has developed—which viewers happily endorse—that spaceships traveling through a void make noise.

Fantasy and Cinema Technology

The fantasy mode is tremendously popular throughout the world. *Harry Potter and the Sorcerer's Stone* (2002), *Lord of the Rings: Fellowship of the Ring* (2002), *Spider-Man* (2002), and *Star Wars Episode II* have generated billions of dollars in global markets. To take advantage of this popularity, fantasy films now showcase the indus-try's most important technological advances. Digital, multichannel sound (discussed in Chapter 5) debuted in three high profile fantasy films. Dolby Digital premiered its system in *Batman Returns* (1992). Digital Theater Systems (DTS) unveiled its CD-playback system with *Jurassic Park* (1993). Sony Dynamic Digital Sound (SDDS) came on line in *The Last Action Hero* (1993).

George Lucas is a major figure in modern movie fantasy and in pushing the indus-try to develop the next generation of effects technology. These two attributes are in-terconnected. In 1975, he created Industrial Light and Magic (ILM), which became the industry's premiere effects house, creating effects for dozens of major productions—

GEORGE LUCAS

Though he has directed very few films, Lucas's influence on contemporary film is enormous. He is the industry's technological visionary, fixed on the digital future of cinema and helping transition the industry toward all-digital production methods. A graduate of the University of Southern California Film School, Lucas took one of his student projects and expanded it into his first feature as director. *THX-1138* (1971) is a grim, science-fiction vision of a totalitarian future. Its sober and somber tone is galaxies removed from the spirited hi-jinks of his subsequent *Star Wars* series.

Lucas followed *THX-1138* with the hugely popular *American Graffiti* (1973), portraying the bittersweet antics of high-school graduates at summer's end on the threshold of the sixties. Its complex sound design resulted from Lucas's collaboration with sound designer Walter Murch, who also worked on *THX-1138*. Committed to optimizing cinema sound, Lucas teamed with another top sound designer, Ben Burtt,

on the *Star Wars* trilogy and built a state-of-the-art postproduction sound facility at Skywalker Ranch, his corporate headquarters.

Released in 1977, *Star Wars* was one of two films in the mid-1970s that changed Hollywood. The other was Steven Spielberg's *Jaws* (1975). These films made more money than anyone dreamed a film could make and inaugurated the blockbuster era. Lucas planned *Star Wars* as a kind of old-time Hollywood cliffhanger and took extraordinary care with the special effects. He formed Industrial Light and Magic at San Rafael, California, in 1976 to do the effects work. ILM is now an established leader in the effects industry, breaking new ground in digital effects for Spielberg's *Jurassic Park* (1994). Through ILM, Lucas has exerted a profound influence over the effects design of contemporary films. Through the mix of adventure and effects-driven fantasy he perfected in *Star Wars,* Lucas helped shape the very definition of a Hollywood blockbuster.

(continued)

Star Wars (20th Century Fox, 1977)
With *Star Wars,* Lucas embraced the cliffhanger style of old movie serials and aimed to fashion a modern mythic parable. The film's extraordinary success helped change Hollywood filmmaking forever. Over the next two decades, Lucas's work and production facilities would help spearhead the digital effects revolution in contemporary film.

GEORGE LUCAS *(continued)*

Following *Star Wars*, Lucas stepped out of the director's chair and turned his attention to getting ILM and his production company, Lucasfilm, into good financial condition and to producing films for other directors. In this capacity, he oversaw completion, and cowrote, the other two films in the trilogy (*The Empire Strikes Back*, 1980; *Return of the Jedi*, 1983) and each of the three Indiana Jones films directed by his pal Steven Spielberg (*Raiders of the Lost Ark*, 1981; *Indiana Jones and the Temple of Doom*, 1984; *Indiana Jones and the Last Crusade*, 1989).

Lucas returned to directing, and to his *Star Wars* project, with *The Phantom Menace* (1999) and *Attack of the Clones* (2002). He believes that celluloid film is now a relic of history and that the medium will be moving in the all-digital direction that he wants to take

it. All-digital filmmaking, Lucas feels, will give filmmakers total freedom to make images conform to their ideas, rather than (as at present) trying to make their ideas conform to the world as it can be photographed.

Lucas has changed the face of U.S. film. His work embraces the simplicities of formulaic melodrama and avoids the thematic complexity and nuances found in the work of other leading U.S. directors such as Sidney Lumet, Robert Altman, Martin Scorsese, and Woody Allen. This has led some critics to charge that his films perpetuate an adolescent hunger for spectacle and constant visual thrills. But there is no denying the enormous popular acceptance of his work or its tremendous trend-setting importance for mainstream filmmaking. Lucas's digital paradigm is, in all probability, the future of cinema.

the *Star Trek* series, the Indiana Jones series, *Who Framed Roger Rabbit* (1988), *Jurassic Park* (1993)—and doing research on the next generation of effects tools, those that would be supplied by digital imaging and digital methods of production. By the mid-eighties, Lucasfilm had a computer-assisted electronic editor (EditDroid) on line and an all-digital sound editor (SoundDroid) used to mix and create effects for *Indiana Jones and the Temple of Doom*. To achieve cutting-edge sound in the films that he produced, Lucas constructed the industry's state-of-the-art postproduction sound facility, the Technical Building at Skywalker Ranch, Lucas's corporate headquarters in Marin, California.

As with sound, the revolution in digital imaging developed in cinema for films in the fantasy mode. Computer-animated sequences first appeared in *Future World* (1976), *Tron* (1982), *The Last Starfighter* (1984), and *Star Trek II: The Wrath of Khan* (1982), but the box-office failure of the first three pictures delayed the widespread application of digital imaging for several years. But, by the late eighties and early nineties, 3-D digital imaging had attained new levels of sophistication, and the next generation of digital effects films created tremendous interest in the technology throughout the industry and excited audiences with fantasy creatures that seemed impossibly real: the

Who Framed Roger Rabbit (Disney, 1988); **Jurassic Park** (Universal, 1993); **The Mask** (New Line, 1994)
Fantasy has been on the cutting edge for new developments in cinema technology. Traditional (nondigital) methods of compositing special effects images reached their zenith in *Who Framed Roger Rabbit,* an expert blend of live action with animated characters. The widespread application of digital imaging in the years following *Roger Rabbit* took the visual potential of cinema into new dimensions. Fantasy films showcased these breakthroughs.

slithery water alien in *The Abyss* (1989), the gleaming, shape-shifting *Terminator 2* (1991), and the dinosaurs of the *Jurassic Park* series (1993, 1997, 2001).

The vividness of Spielberg's dinosaurs—created by ILM—convinced George Lucas to return to his *Star Wars* series now that digital effects offered a new arsenal of powerful tools for envisioning anything a filmmaker could imagine. Lucas had long wanted to shift the industry toward all-digital methods of filmmaking, and he has pursued this ambition with the new *Star Wars* films. *Attack of the Clones* (2002) was shot on digital cameras that were custom-built for Lucas by Sony, and the film was exhibited theatrically in digital format at selected locations around the country. Lucas's ambitions are big ones, and the industry is transforming itself to meet them. The long-term result will be comparable to the coming of sound in the late 1920s; that is, it will change everything. It will cut the industry off from the photomechanical technology to which it has been wedded since its inception and take it into an all-electronic realm.

The fantasy mode has been a key player in this drama. It is now synonymous with state-of-the-art cinema technology. In this regard, fantasy is tremendously important for contemporary cinema. It generates huge box office and is propelling the industry into its all-digital future.

☐ CINEMATIC SELF-REFLEXIVITY

However unusual or fantastic their settings and design, the other modes of screen reality aim to persuade the viewer that the world depicted on screen is real, that it is, for the purposes of the narrative, a valid world whose premises are not questioned within the body of the film. The fantasy world that George Lucas creates in the *Star Wars* films is, taken on its own terms, a self-enclosed and internally valid one.

By contrast, the self-reflexive mode makes no pretense that the world represented on screen is anything other than a filmic construction. Films in this mode remind viewers that what they are watching is, after all, a movie. Self-reflexive films tell the viewer that the reality on screen is a movie reality. These acknowledgments take a variety of forms. Typically, they fall into two categories. They tend to be either comic or made with didactic intent.

Comic Self-Reflexivity

The tradition of self-reflexivity most commonly found in popular, mass market movies employs a comic design. Throughout *Annie Hall*, director and star Woody Allen continually interrupts the narrative with a series of humorous asides and confessions made to the camera. By speaking to the camera, of course, he speaks directly to the film's audience. Looking at the camera lens, he looks directly at the eyes of the viewer. During one scene, when Alvy Singer (Woody Allen) and Annie Hall (Diane Keaton) quarrel over whether she said going to psychoanalysis will change her life or change her wife, Alvy breaks off the argument, turns to the camera, and reminds the film's viewers that they know what was said because they have been there all along, listening to the quarrel. Likewise, in a subtle way, the tradition established by director Alfred Hitchcock of making guest appearances inside his films reminds viewers of his controlling presence as director and, therefore, of the film's status *as* a film.

Annie Hall (United Artists, 1977)
Woody Allen, as Alvy Singer, turns toward the camera and speaks to the film's viewers in this scene from *Annie Hall*. Allen breaks the illusion of make-believe in a moment of comic self-reflexivity. In popular films, self-reflexivity is quite common in comedy but rare in drama. Frame enlargement.

Case Study: *Austin Powers* and *Charlie's Angels*

Contemporary screen comedy often makes use of a self-reflexive style. *Scary Movie* and *Scary Movie 2,* for example, play with the viewer's familiarity with the horror movie conventions that are being satirized. Like Woody Allen, Mike Myers has made playing to the camera an integral part of his ironic comic persona. His *Austin Powers* films (1997, 1999, 2002) include numerous moments of self-conscious comedy, in which Myers jokes with the camera, making humor by acknowledging its presence. He winks at it, grins broadly to it, and uses it to make a formal introduction of key scenes, as when he leans forward, smiles, and says into the camera, "Ladies and gentlemen, Mr. Burt Bacharach," introducing cameo appearances by the composer, who then performs selections from his songs. Bacharach's songs were very popular in the 1960s and 1970s, and their catchy melodies are major emblems of the popular culture of those periods. Myers's introductions of Bacharach, then, are moments of nostalgia and affection, and his use of a self-reflexive camera emphasizes them.

A secret agent from the 1960s, Austin Powers is based on the many screen spies who had popular film series in that era. These include James Bond, Derek Flint, and Matt Helm. Myers weaves numerous references to those movies into his own.

Austin Powers
(New Line, 1997)
Austin Powers (Mike Myers), the international man of mystery, jokes and confides with the camera and viewers, thereby acknowledging the presence of each. Here, he offers an affectionate introduction to a cameo appearance by composer Burt Bacharach. Frame enlargement.

Charlie's Angels
(Columbia, 2000)
How do you update a notoriously sexist 1970s television show for a modern audience? With a wink, and an ironic attitude that says, "These aren't the same old Angels you thought you knew." The irony invites a hip, self-reflexive attitude from the viewer. Frame enlargement.

Austin Powers in Goldmember (2002), for example, costars Michael Caine as Powers's father. Caine is an actor closely identified with the sixties spy craze, having played secret agent Harry Palmer in several pictures (including *The Ipcress File* [1966]). His presence in *Goldmember* evokes this history. Furthermore, *Goldmember* plays with the title and character of one of the most famous James Bond films, *Goldfinger* (1964).

The recent popular hit, *Charlie's Angels* (2000), starring Cameron Diaz, Drew Barrymore, and Lucy Liu, was based on a notoriously sexist 1970s television show in which three glamorous women work undercover as secret agents. The show was criticized as "jiggle" television because the prime appeal seemed to be watching the Angels jiggle and flounce around as sex objects.

By contrast, the movie winks self-consciously at its audience. It keeps the babe factor, through the casting of Diaz, Barrymore, and Liu, but brings the characters in line with contemporary society by making them more assertive, independent, and self-aware as women, qualities the TV characters had lacked. This is a delicate balancing act, and it works by inviting the audience to play along with the joke. The new Charlie's Angels may still be sex objects, but they kick butt big time, like male screen action heroes have always done.

The self-reflexive mode works extremely well for comedy because it promotes the intimate relationship with an audience that is integral to effective humor. *Austin Powers* and *Charlie's Angels* invite the audience to play along and be as hip as they are by enjoying the jokes. The comic possibilities of the self-reflexive mode assume that the viewer will understand the social norms, movies, and movie characters that are being referenced. Only viewers who "get" the references will enjoy the humor these films offer.

Didactic Self-Reflexivity

The second category of self-reflexive film style is used for didactic purposes and falls within the aesthetic tradition identified with the theater of playwright Bertolt Brecht. Brecht was an active playwright and poet from the 1920s until his death in 1956, and his plays include such classics as *The Threepenny Opera, Galileo,* and *The Caucasian Chalk Circle.* As a Marxist, Brecht sought in his art to have a direct impact on his social world and historical period, and to do so he developed a unique and very influential approach to drama.

Impatient with the conventions of the theater of his day, Brecht created his own theatrical forms that he termed "epic" and that tried to break down the barriers that separated spectators from the play they were watching. Brecht considered the illusion of naturalism or realism, as created in theater or film, to be an obstacle preventing play-goers or film viewers from reflecting on the connections between their own lives and the events depicted on stage or screen.

He wanted his plays to become a stimulus to social action and reform, to have direct real-world consequences, and so he deliberately broke with realist and naturalist traditions by incorporating explicitly didactic techniques into his theater. Actors on stage might speak directly to the audience, or the social contradictions dramatized by the action of a play might be announced directly via titles projected on a screen above the stage. These methods were anti-illusionist in that they sought to dispel the illusion of a self-contained fictional world created by conventional drama and stagecraft.

The Brechtian Legacy in Film

Case Study: *Weekend*

Brecht's work in the theater continues to exert an enormously powerful influence on filmmakers. French director Jean-Luc Godard is probably the most famous Brechtian filmmaker currently working. Godard's films offer a virtual catalogue of Brechtian cinematic techniques, that is, techniques that break the illusion that the spectator is watching a real, authentic world on screen rather than a movie. These techniques enable Godard to speak directly to his audience as author, rather than indirectly through the characters and action of a film. *Weekend* (1967), Godard's savage satire of modern consumer society, employs three kinds of didactic, self-reflexive techniques. These are the use of printed titles, nontraditional camera techniques, and the incorporation of imaginary characters and moments of performance self-disclosure.

Titles Title cards break up the narrative action of *Weekend*, which follows the comic and violent misadventures of a middle-class couple journeying across France on holiday. The printed titles offer ironic and poetic commentaries on the narrative. During the opening credits of the film, two title cards proclaim, with some irony, that this is "a film adrift in the cosmos" and "a film found on a dump." A long musical sequence in the middle of the film, during which a pianist performs a Mozart sonata as the camera tracks three times around the perimeter of a farmyard, is introduced by flash-cut inserts of the title "Musical Action."

Weekend (New Yorker Films, 1967)
Storybook characters dressed in fairy-tale costumes help shatter realism in Godard's *Weekend*. Dressed in these outlandish costumes, Emily Brontë and Le Gros Poucet step into the film from some alternate poetic reality. They quarrel with Corrine and Roland, who promptly burn them for violating the standard of realism. Frame enlargement.

Throughout the film, title cards serve to: (1) introduce and set off a given scene from the surrounding context of the narrative, (2) tell viewers what it is they are about to see, (3) remind viewers of the filmmaker's intrusion on the narrative, and (4) emphasize the way the filmmaker has chosen to shape and organize the structure of the film. By calling attention to the film's methods of constructing its images and narrative, each of these functions is consistent with the Brechtian goal of breaking the illusion of reality exerted by the screen world.

The title card "Totem and Taboo" prefaces the film's most horrific sequence, dealing with the cannibalism and mutilation of English tourists at the hands of a guerrilla army based in the countryside. This title derives from a famous book by Sigmund Freud dealing with primitive social organization and behavioral taboos in human ancestry. Here, the self-reflexive qualities are multiple. In addition to the four functions described above, the title card tells the viewer that the scenes that follow will contain shocking and taboo imagery, as indeed they do, and, for viewers who know the reference, this acknowledgment positions the scenes in relation to Freud's famous work.

Nontraditional Camera Techniques   These are a second method used by Godard to create self-reflexive style in *Weekend*. Two sequences stand out for their use of radical camerawork. The tracking shot along the row of stalled cars (described and discussed in Chapter 2) and the circular tracking movements around the farmyard during the musical interlude extend the length of these shots and scenes to a point many viewers find unbearable, especially because no new narrative information is being disclosed. However, the tracking shots go on for so long that the visual device—camera movement—becomes the subject of the shots. By elaborating camera movement at such length, the style becomes self-reflexive by making the viewer acutely aware of the visual design. As in comic uses, however, self-reflexiveness depends on the viewer's knowledge of the norm that is being violated. In this case, the norm is that camerawork is subordinated to the action of a scene rather than vice versa.

Imaginary Characters and Performance Self-Disclosure   *Weekend* is filled with imaginary storybook characters. These establish a third area of self-reflexive technique. During one episode in the middle of the film, the vacationing couple, Corinne and Roland, encounter poet Emily Brontë and a companion dressed in storybook costumes.

Corinne and Roland ask for directions to their destination, Oinville, but Brontë and her companion reply with metaphysical riddles. When Roland asks for the directions, Brontë inquires if he is interested in poetical or physical information. When Roland tells her that they only want to know how to get to Oinville, Brontë tells him that physics doesn't really exist, only individual sciences, prompting Roland to mutter, "What a rotten film. All we meet are crazy people." His remark is a moment of performance self-disclosure in which the actor steps out of character to evaluate the quality of the film in which he appears. Of course, Godard does not believe he's making a rotten film and so the evaluation is ironic. In another instance of performance self-disclosure, Corinne grabs Brontë and says angrily, "This isn't a novel. It's a film. A film is life."

For the Brechtian tradition, this is precisely the attitude to be combatted, and it is what motivates the use of self-reflexive techniques. By breaking the spell of reality cast by film or play, these techniques point to the enormous differences between life and the constructed spectacles on stage or screen.

The scene culminates in a moment of horror. Roland drives away Brontë's companion and then sets her on fire. As the poet burns and cries, a shaken Corinne says that this is bad, that they shouldn't have torched her, prompting Roland to remark, "Can't you see they're only imaginary characters?" Godard, the director, then reveals the emotional paradox on which cinema rests. Corinne replies, "Why is she crying, then?"

Brontë's fiery destruction by Roland illuminates the emotional paradox. Though the film presents Brontë as a storybook character dressed in a fairytale costume, her violent death strikes the viewer as a terrible crime. Despite her obviously fictional status, her death is disturbing. This paradox—a film's ability to compel emotion and belief from the viewer despite the fictional artifice of its characters—is the phenomenon that the Brechtian tradition seeks to control, understand, and influence.

The Legacy of Godard   Godard's self-conscious, radical cinematic techniques have exerted an enormous influence on other filmmakers, as has the Brechtian tradition that nourished his work. Spike Lee is a contemporary director who freely mixes modes of screen reality in his films, incorporating ordinary fictional realism, fantasy sequences, and modes of self-reflexivity. The black and white narrative of *She's Gotta Have It* (1986), for example, is punctuated by one striking color sequence, a musical fantasy, that departs greatly in tone and style from the surrounding narrative.

In *Do the Right Thing* (1989), Lee displays a precise understanding of how Brechtian techniques can be used to contain and control the emotions generated by the story on screen. During the famous racial slur sequence, a gallery of characters

Do the Right Thing
(Universal, 1989)
Mookie (Spike Lee) in the famous racial slur sequence from *Do the Right Thing*. Director Lee uses a self-reflexive technique to maintain artistic control over the sequence's inflammatory stream of racist insults. By alternating between different modes of screen reality, Lee evokes the poisonous intensity of racial hatred and then contextualizes it with a clear and direct condemnation. Frame enlargement.

hurl obscenities and insults at targeted social groups. A young Italian man (John Tur-turro) insults African Americans, Mookie (Spike Lee) insults Italian Americans, a Hispanic gang member insults Koreans, a cop insults Hispanics, and a Korean merchant condemns Jews. Each character is filmed in an identical fashion: The camera quickly tracks from long shot to medium close-up to add visual emphasis to the verbal invective.

The sequence is emotionally powerful and inflammatory because it gives full-throated voice to various racisms. Spike Lee realized that he needed to break down and contain the emotions unleashed in the scene and that were likely to be aroused in the film's audiences. Accordingly, he breaks the hypnotizing power of the racist rhetoric with an explicitly didactic, Brechtian conclusion. A black radio deejay breaks into the montage, telling the characters to cool down, shut up, and break that nonsense off. The deejay heartily condemns the racial antagonisms of the characters, restoring calm and sanity.

Filmmakers like Lee or Godard use self-reflexive techniques in a didactic manner to maintain a measure of control over the social impact of their films and the messages inside those films. These techniques enable the filmmakers to insert editorial remarks into the film, offering the viewer explicit guidance about how a scene should be interpreted or understood. The Brechtian tradition is a major aesthetic influence on filmmakers who want to speak directly to their audience and who wish to assert maximum control over the impact of their social messages.

Impact on Viewers of Self-Reflexive Techniques

The comic and didactic modes of cinematic self-reflexivity tend to pull viewers out of the reality represented on-screen by reminding them that it is a cinematic construction. The illusion created by a screen world, however, is very powerful. It can sustain the digressions and intrusions of self-reflexive techniques. Such techniques typically dispel, *momentarily,* the emotional pull the viewer experiences from the screen world, but it is difficult to disrupt this emotional pull for very long. It tends quickly to reassert itself.

In *Weekend,* for example, despite all of the title cards, the radical camera movements, and the moments of performance self-disclosure, the basic spectacle of Corinne and Roland's comic and increasingly violent car journey across France is exceptionally compelling. While one appreciates the social responsibility that Lee demonstrates as director when he brings on the calm deejay to conclude the racism scene in *Do the Right Thing,* one nevertheless remembers the scene for its extraordinarily hypnotic stream of racial insults.

The represented world on screen can be manipulated by filmmakers using self-reflexive techniques, but, for spectators, the screen world tends to retain its emotional integrity and validity. Viewers know that Austin Powers and Charlie's Angels are just movie characters. They admit this themselves, but viewers still want to spend time with them. The cinema compels emotional belief in its modes of screen reality even when filmmakers admit to viewers that it's all just a movie.

SUMMARY

Because the camera has a double capacity, functioning as a medium that can both record properties of the visual world set before it and manipulate and transform the appearance of that world, filmmakers can create differing styles or modes of screen reality. The mode of ordinary fictional realism employs an audiovisual and narrative design that aims to replicate on screen, with a fair degree of resemblance, the spectator's understanding of space, time, causality, and the dynamics of human behavior.

The expressionistic mode makes available to filmmakers a range of extremely explicit stylistic distortions and manipulations that are used to express heightened, extreme, or abnormal states of feeling, thought, or behavior. The mode of fantasy and the fantastic establishes a realm of time and space far removed from ordinary reality in which character behavior can retain recognizably human dimensions or possess magical and extraordinary powers and abilities.

Finally, the mode of cinematic self-reflexivity is available to filmmakers who wish to reveal and display the constructed and artificial basis of the cinema. Typically, filmmakers employ this mode for either a comic effect or for communicating an urgent social message directly to their audience. In the latter case, filmmakers will use this mode if they feel that the necessity of having to speak indirectly through characters and a story will prevent them from getting their message across or may leave the message itself muddied and muddled.

While the cinema has four distinct stylistic modes available to it, the divisions and boundaries between these modes are not hard and fast. In fact, many films incorporate one or more distinct modes. Musicals like *Singin' in the Rain* or *An American in Paris,* for example, typically draw on ordinary fictional realism as well as fantasy and the fantastic. These stylistic modes are extremely flexible, and filmmakers can move in and out of several different modes.

Screen reality is constructed partly by the manipulations of film design discussed in this chapter, and it can vary widely across films. It is, however, also constructed by viewers. Representational reality seems real only when a viewer decides that it does. Representational conventions change over time, as does the viewer's response to them. Contemporary audiences react with disbelief when gunshot victims in 1940s movies clutch their stomachs, double over, and slowly sink out of frame. Screen reality exists in relation to viewers who judge its perceived levels of credibility and validity. By manipulating film structure, filmmakers hope to influence viewers' judgments, but their ability to control viewer response is limited. Like so much else about film, the creation of screen reality is a collaborative production.

SUGGESTED READINGS

Jonathan Bresman, *The Art of Star Wars: Episode I: The Phantom Menace* (New York: Del Rey, 1999).

Lotte Eisner, *The Haunted Screen: Expressionism in the German Cinema* (Berkeley: University of California Press, 1989).

Bill Nichols, *Representing Reality: Issues and Concepts in Documentary* (Bloomington: Indiana University Press, 1992).

Irving Singer, *Reality Transformed: Film as Meaning and Technique* (Cambridge, MA: MIT Press, 1998).

Robert Stam, *Reflexivity in Film and Literature: From Don Quixote to Jean-Luc Godard* (New York: Columbia University Press, 1992).

Mark Cotta Vaz, *Industrial Light and Magic: Into the Digital Realm* (New York: Del Rey, 1996).

Chapter 8

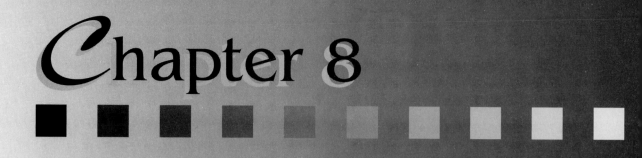

Hollywood International

Chapter Objectives

After reading this chapter, you should be able to:

- identify the Hollywood majors
- describe how a film's box office success is measured
- explain why box office gross is a misleading indicator of a film's economic performance
- identify the ancillary markets and explain their significance
- describe the box-office performance of U.S. films in world markets
- explain how the U.S. film industry facilitates the marketing of its product
- describe three key forms of Hollywood's stylistic influence on world cinema

- explain how contemporary filmmaking operates within an integrated market
- define blockbuster production
- define product tie-ins and product placement
- describe the international marketing of *Jurassic Park*
- explain how Hollywood absorbs and transforms foreign film style by comparing and contrasting the original European version of *The Vanishing* with its U.S. remake

Key Terms and Concepts

majors
limited release market
domestic theatrical market
gross

rental
negative cost
ancillary markets
blockbuster

diversification
product tie-ins
product placement
homage

Movies are a business as well as an art, and the industry's business structure greatly affects the kind of films that it makes. Furthermore, in both an artistic and an economic context, the cinema is a global phenomenon. Movies are seen by millions of people throughout the world, and filmmakers have an enormous opportunity to communicate cross-culturally to viewers in different countries and diverse social communities. In turn, this means that a film's profit potential is not restricted by national borders. The box office champions perform well in a global market that is dominated by the U.S. cinema. In response to this influence, foreign filmmakers alternatively accept and reject the model of filmmaking promoted by the Hollywood system.

This chapter and the next one place the cinema within an international frame, artistically and economically. This chapter examines the global economic dominance of Hollywood film, how the U.S. industry facilitates the international marketing of

MAJOR STUDIOS Motion Picture Producer/Distributors	**OWNED BY**
Columbia—Tri-Star	Sony (Japan)
Disney (Buena Vista)	Walt Disney Co.
MGM/UA	
Paramount	Viacom
20th Century Fox	News Corp. (Australia)
Warner Bros.	Time Warner
Universal	Vivendi

Figure 8.1: The Hollywood majors.

Titanic (Paramount/20th Century Fox, 1997) The size of the global film market is staggering, and overseas revenues can dwarf a film's earnings from the domestic U.S. market. *Titanic,* for example, grossed $500 million domestically and $1 billion overseas.

its product, and Hollywood's stylistic influence on world cinema. The next chapter examines important stylistic alternatives to Hollywood in the international cinema. Filmmakers seeking to develop an indigenous national style often search for alternatives to the style of U.S. film. The greatest international box-office popularity has been achieved by a fairly narrow range of film styles and subjects. Though seen by the greatest numbers of people, these should not be misidentified as representing all that the cinema has to offer.

☐ THE GLOBAL DOMINANCE OF HOLLYWOOD

The Majors

The Hollywood industry is composed of the **majors** (large studio–distributors that fund film production and distribute films internationally) and a number of small, independent production companies and distributors. The Hollywood majors are Columbia Pictures (*Spider-Man* [2002], *Men in Black 2* [2002], *Cruel Intentions* [1999]), Warner Bros. (*Harry Potter and the Sorcerer's Stone* [2001], *A.I.: Artificial Intelligence* [2001], *LA Confidential* [1997]), MGM (*Hannibal* [2001], *Legally Blonde* [2001]), Disney (*Pearl Harbor* [2001], *Monsters, Inc.* [2001], *A Bug's Life* [1998]), 20th Century Fox (*Moulin Rouge* [2001], *Cast Away* [2001], *Star Wars Episode II: Attack of the Clones* [2002], Universal (*The Scorpion King* [2002], *American Pie 2* [2002], *The Fast and the Furious* [2001]), and Paramount Pictures (*The Sum of All Fears* [2002], *Lara Croft: Tomb Raider* [2001], *Saving Private Ryan* [1998]). Each year the majors fund ten to fifteen productions and distribute an additional ten to twelve films produced by other companies, usually the independents.

The soaring costs of film production prevent the majors from expanding their production activities beyond this relatively modest number of films. At the same time, however, low-budget independent films (*The Deep End* [2001], *Memento,* [2000], *The Blair Witch Project* [1999]) have performed well at the box office, and this has made the independent market attractive to the majors. Accordingly, they have created subsidiary companies to distribute independent film: Fox Searchlight, Paramount Classics, New Line (Time Warner), and Miramax (Disney). As a result, the majors effectively control the markets for both mainstream and independent film.

The two markets are quite different in size and scale. Production costs are much lower for independent films, as are publicity costs because the films are not distributed as widely or promoted as aggressively. A *Lord of the Rings* will saturate theaters

---

Clerks (Miramax, 1994)
Because of their low production costs, independent films don't have to be blockbusters to perform well at the box office. Shot in grainy black-and-white, *Clerks* found a sizeable audience. The relative popularity of pictures like *Clerks* has attracted the majors to the independent market, most of whom now distribute such pictures through their own subsidiaries. Miramax, the distributor of *Clerks,* had been unaffiliated with the majors for most of its operating history. Disney now owns it. Frame enlargement.

Shrek (DreamWorks/Universal, 2001)
Computer-animated characters, voiced in this film by big Hollywood stars like
Eddie Murphy and Mike Myers, are often today a key ingredient in the success of
a blockbuster. Most blockbusters are showcases for special effects, and the blend of
CGI and warm, witty characters made Shrek a huge hit in the global film market,
where it grossed nearly $500 million. Frame enlargement.

nationwide; a *Memento* will be released only in selected regions of the country. Thus,
the industry refers to independent film distribution as the **limited release market.**

Partly because of limited publicity and distribution, independent films typically
earn far less at the box office than the majors' productions. *Memento*'s total box office

The Blair Witch Project
(Artisan, 1999)
Because of its extremely low production cost and huge box-office
earnings, this independent film has
been called the most profitable film
in history. Frame enlargement.

earnings were $25 million, which is extremely high for the limited release market. More typical are pictures like *Tadpole* (2002), with $2.5 million after two months in release and *13 Conversations about One Thing* (2002), with $3 million after six months in release. By contrast, *The Sum of All Fears* (2002), a big-budget film based on a Tom Clancy novel, earned $31 million in its first *three days* of national release. Independent films do occasionally become box office hits. *My Big Fat Greek Wedding* (2002) grossed over $200 million, and *The Blair Witch Project* (1999), over $100, but most have modest earnings that match their modest budgets.

For the majors, the **domestic theatrical market** (U.S. and Canada) is but a small part of their total box-office earnings. The world cinema market is huge, and overseas revenue can be enormous. Hollywood films produced by the majors dominate this market. In 2002, *Spider-Man*'s global revenues of $822 million made it the biggest film in U.S. *and* in overseas markets. Of the top 125 films worldwide in 2001, only four were foreign pictures unreleased in the United States. In other words, American film production/distribution accounted for 99.9 percent of the world's top earning films that year. Many films earn more overseas than domestically. After twenty-four weeks in release, *Harry Potter and the Sorcerer's Stone* earned $300 million in the domestic market and $650 million overseas. At the twenty-four-week mark, *Lord of the Rings: Fellowship of the Ring* had earned $300 million domestically and $540 million overseas. The world market for these pictures is more important in terms of box-office revenue than the domestic U.S. market. The highest earning picture in world markets remains *Titanic* (1997), with a global **gross** of $1.8 billion.

The overseas market is a vital source of revenue for Hollywood because the cost of producing and marketing a film has exploded in the last two decades. Since 1999, costs have hovered around $75–80 million. In 2001, for example, the average production cost was $48 million, plus $31 million for advertising.

Furthermore, domestic box office falls off very quickly, with films earning most of their revenue in the first week or two. *Pearl Harbor* (2001) earned nearly 40 percent of its total domestic box office during the opening weekend. *Harry Potter* earned 41 percent of its total during the first week. By the third week of release for *Star Wars Episode 2: Attack of the Clones,* its domestic box office had fallen by 65 percent. This is a typical pattern for nearly all films today.

Because production costs are rising and box office declines rapidly once a film is in release, the industry needs its overseas markets. The larger problem that the industry faces is that it is very hard to make money from film production. How can this be, the reader justifiably wonders, given the millions earned by top grossing films? Nevertheless, profits are hard to find, and this essential fact explains much about how the industry presently operates and is organized.

Splitting the Box-Office Dollar

Where does the money go? The popular media report box-office grosses but these are distinct from the **rentals,** which are the revenues returned to the studio distributor and from which profit arises after expenses. Information about gross earnings, taken out of context, is nearly meaningless. *Pearl Harbor,* for example, grossed $450 million in world markets, but it cost $140 million to make. By contrast, *Traffic* (2001) cost

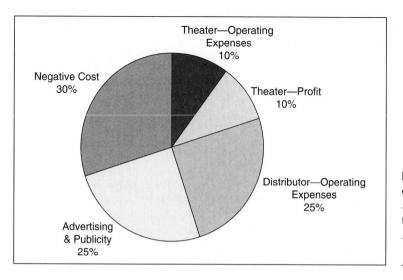

Figure 8.2: Where the box-office dollar goes.
Source: Harold L. Vogel, Entertainment Industry Economics, *2d ed. (New York: Cambridge University Press, 1990)*

$45 million to make and earned $200 million in world markets, a better cost-to-earnings ratio. *The Blair Witch Project* (1999), which only cost $35,000 to produce, grossed over $120 million, leading many to describe it as the most profitable film in history.

Gross earnings must be evaluated in relation to a film's production cost, which, in the industry's vocabulary, is known as its **negative cost.** This is the expense the production has incurred, which includes the salaries for everyone from stars to the production crew, the costs of printing the film in the lab, and all of the resources involved in the production (set design, costuming, special effects, etc.). Expensive star salaries will drive up negative costs. For *The Matrix,* which had a negative cost of $60 million and grossed $350 million worldwide, Keanu Reeves earned 10 percent of the film's gross, which likely earned him in excess of $30 million. That is money the studio distributor will never see.

Box-office earnings are diverted at multiple points by individuals and groups that have a claim on those moneys. To illustrate this, let's consider where your money goes when you buy a ticket. Of every dollar, the theater keeps 10 percent (ten cents) for its operating expenses and an additional 10 percent for its profit. The distributor keeps 25 percent to cover its operating expenses (studio distributors operate worldwide organizations). Advertising and publicity for a film will consume 24 percent of the box-office dollar. This leaves approximately 30 percent to cover negative costs and, after that, to begin to generate profits. However, with average negative costs now around $50 million, that thirty cents on the dollar hardly begins to cover these expenses.

High-priced stars who take a percentage of the gross (a practice known as taking "points") further diminish the revenues remaining for profit. For *K-19: The Widowmaker* (2002), star Harrison Ford earned a salary of $25 million *plus* 20 percent of the gross. Furthermore, studios often rely on outside investors to finance the cost of a production, and these profit participants will be paid before a studio sees its profit. Fifty percent of the gross was promised to participants on *Terminator 3* (2003)! That fact, plus the film's huge production cost—$200 million—virtually guarantee that this film will never earn a profit.

The paradox, therefore, is resolved—despite the industry's seemingly impressive yearly earnings, the high cost of producing and promoting films leaves little profit from theatrical revenues. For this reason, Hollywood relies heavily on earnings from ancillary markets.

Ancillary Markets

These are all of the nontheatrical markets in which viewers watch movies or from which studios derive revenues. Warner Bros.' *Batman* earned money as a motion picture, a comic book character, a soundtrack album, a book about the making of the film, a Saturday morning cartoon series, and a wide range of toys, games, clothing, and other associated products carrying the Batman logo. Revenue earned by the Batman character from these products, both domestically and overseas, returns to AOL Time Warner, the parent corporation that owns the rights to the character and that controls the media in which the Caped Crusader is marketed.

Ancillary markets include broadcast and pay cable television (both domestically and worldwide), home video royalties realized through rental and sale of videotapes and DVDs, and the licensing of film characters and logos to merchandisers and retailers.

Since the mid-1980s, revenue from home video and cable television has surpassed box-office earnings. Since that time, the majors have earned more from sales

---

Harry Potter and the Sorcerer's Stone (Warner Bros., 2001)
The biggest box-office film of 2001, it earned nearly $1 billion in global revenue by the end of its theatrical release. And that's just box-office revenue. The movie also drove a global wave of merchandizing based around the popular characters. Author J. K. Rowling created those characters, but AOL Time Warner now owns the copyright, enabling it to generate profits in multiple media markets. For the film industry, this is the key element of a blockbuster—its ability to drive consumer spending on a wave of related products in the ancillary markets. Frame enlargement.

of films to video and cable markets than from ticket sales in the nation's theaters. *Shrek* (2001) grossed $268 million at the domestic box-office, but earned $470 million in VHS/DVD sales and rentals. The DVD market, in particular, generates huge revenues. *Spider-Man* sold $145 million of DVDs in its first week of home video release.

The markets for motion picture entertainment are now integrated—the theatrical market exists in conjunction with the ancillaries—and corporate survival depends on the control of these markets. This environment creates a distinct rationale for **blockbuster** production. The blockbuster film, whether *Spider-Man, Harry Potter, Lord of the Rings,* or *Star Wars,* has enormous audience appeal that spreads across a variety of media categories. These films do a huge business in the theatrical market, which, in turn, generates big revenues in ancillary markets. But to create blockbusters and to market them across the ancillaries requires that a film studio be **diversified,** with its business activities spread across a range of products, media, and associated markets. Diversification positions a film studio to compete within the integrated entertainment market, enables it to perform in overseas markets, and facilitates the marketing of blockbuster films.

Case Study: AOL Time Warner

Warner Bros. belongs to parent company AOL Time Warner, which is the largest media and entertainment company in the world. In January 2001, America Online, Inc., the on-line computer subscription service with 34 million members, merged with Time Warner, Inc., a vast media empire with holdings in film, book publishing, and music recording. AOL Time Warner's revenue in 2001 was $38 billion, a huge figure that provides some idea of the size of this corporation. Hollywood film is only one of many entertainment media controlled by AOL Time Warner, which are grouped in

---

Lord of the Rings (Warner Bros., 2001)
Parent company AOL Time Warner had a very good year with its subsidiary New Line Cinema. *Lord of the Rings* and *Austin Powers in Goldmember* were two hits carried by New Line, and their earnings, therefore, stayed in-house at AOL Time Warner. The global media market is ruled by a relative handful of giant companies, like AOL Time Warner. Frame enlargement.

six core areas: America Online (interactive services, Web properties, Internet technologies, and electronic commerce services), film entertainment (film production) Networks (cable television and broadcast network programming), Cable (hardware for cable television systems), Music (recorded music and music publishing), and Publishing (magazines, books, direct marketing).

Entertainment includes the Warner Bros. studio–distributor (*Harry Potter, Ocean's 11, Cats and Dogs*) and the smaller film companies New Line Cinema (*Lord of the Rings, Austin Powers in Goldmember*) and Castle Rock Entertainment (*The Last Days of Disco, Mickey Blue Eyes*). Warner Home Video releases Warner Bros., New Line, and Castle Rock films to this ancillary market. Warner Home Video was the most aggressive champion among the majors of the DVD format, having released by 2002 nearly 900 titles on DVD, including *The Matrix,* which produced revenues of $11 million.

Warner Bros. Television (*ER, Friends, The Drew Carey Show*) is the leading supplier of television programming in the world, in more than 175 countries and 40 languages. It owns a library of material for distribution to television systems that includes 6500 feature films, 36,000 television programs, and 14,000 cartoons. The WB Television Network airs eleven hours of series programming to 90 percent of U.S. households from Sunday to Thursday nights, including *Dawson's Creek, Buffy the Vampire Slayer,* and *Felicity.*

The Entertainment group also includes Warner Bros. Consumer Products, which licenses film characters and logos to retailers and merchandisers, including superheroes from D.C. Comics (Batman), Hanna-Barbera (Flintstones), and Harry Potter merchandise. Warner Bros. also owns movie theaters, some 800 screens in seven foreign countries.

Recorded music operations are conducted through Warner Bros. Records, and the Atlantic, Elektra, and Sire labels, and companies that make CDs, audio- and videocassettes, CD-ROMs, and DVDs. Warner Music International operates in sixty countries worldwide. Other entertainment operations include theme parks and ownership of D.C. Comics and *Mad* magazine.

To conduct cable network programming, Time Warner owns TBS, TNT, Cable News Network (CNN), CNN International, Turner Classic Movies, the Cartoon Network, HBO (Home Box Office), and Cinemax. These holdings make Time Warner the leading supplier of cable programming in the United States. CNN, for example, has 85 million subscribers, and TBS has 87 million.

Publishing operations include 139 magazines, featuring such leaders as *Time, People, Sports Illustrated, Money,* and *Entertainment Weekly,* and, in terms of books, the Book-of-the-Month Club and publishing houses Warner Books and Little, Brown.

America Online operations include two worldwide Internet services (AOL and CompuServe), America Online's music properties (AOL Music Channel and Winamp), and Web ventures that include the Netscape browser, the Moviefone movie ticket service, MapQuest, and AOL Instant Messenger.

As this brief profile indicates, AOL Time Warner creates media programming *and* controls the distribution systems (the Internet, theaters, video, cable and broadcast TV) needed to get that programming to its audience. What are the advantages of such diversification? One advantage is that AOL Time Warner can offset the loss accruing to any one area of business operations from profits associated with others.

The major advantage, however, is that AOL Time Warner keeps in-house all revenues from the performance of its products across a wide range of media markets.

Harry Potter and the Sorcerer's Stone was the biggest box-office film in the world in 2001, and AOL Time Warner owns the trademarks and copyrights to the characters. Thus, it can market Harry as a movie, a soundtrack album, a DVD, and video-cassette, and receive revenue from the tidal wave of Harry Potter merchandise.

Similarly, Batman was a hugely successful comic book, movie, video, record, and line of toys. The Batman character originated in D.C. Comics, which AOL Time Warner owns and publishes. The *Batman* film was produced by Warner Bros., a book about the making of the *Batman* movie was published by Warner Books, the soundtrack album appeared on Warner Bros. Records, and revenue from the release of the film to the home video market was generated through Warner Home Video.

Thus, regardless of how the Harry Potter or Batman characters appear—as a movie, record album, book, video viewed in the home, comic strip, or toy model or board game—AOL Time Warner is assured a steady stream of money. Revenues from the theatrical market are insufficient to cover today's high cost of film production. As a result, the Hollywood majors are held by larger firms that operate in multiple media markets. This is the only way that expensive film production can be a winning game for the industry.

Film and Product Merchandising

Film-based product merchandising as an extremely important revenue source for the industry is a direct function of diversification into multiple media markets. Blockbuster films—*Harry Potter, Lord of the Rings, Jurassic Park*—often feature mechanical or fantasy characters that lend themselves to manufacture and merchandising across diverse product lines. There is a direct correlation between these mechanical characters and the imperatives of product merchandising. As the licensing director of Amblin Entertainment (the production company responsible for *Gremlins*) remarked, "Whenever you have a non-human type of character, it lends itself to merchandising." Film-based merchandising takes two forms: the product tie-in and product placement.

Product Tie-ins

With their skyrocketing box-office gross, Steven Spielberg's *Jaws* and George Lucas's *Star Wars* in the mid-seventies announced the onset of the blockbuster era. The phenomenal impact of *Jaws* in the summer of 1975 was intensified by the enormous range of **product tie-ins** marketed around the release of the film. These products included T-shirts, plastic tumblers, the soundtrack album, a paperback about the making of the movie, beach towels, bike bags, blankets, costume jewelry, shark costumes, hosiery, hobby kits, inflatable sharks, iron-on transfers, games, posters, sharks' teeth necklaces, sleepwear, children's sweaters, swimsuits, ties, and water pistols.

The majors derive huge revenues from licensing movie characters and props to merchandisers. Hollywood's product licensing revenues totaled $70 billion in 2001, and the contemporary blockbuster is designed to maximize this revenue. In 2002, *Spider-Man, Scooby-Doo, Stuart Little 2, Men in Black 2,* and *Star Wars Episode 2* were designed for maximum product tie-ins.

Jaws (Universal, 1975)
While *Jaws* terrified summer audiences, it was accompanied by a marketing blitzkrieg pushing shark products. Blockbuster films are huge engines driving the leisure-time economy. They stimulate massive cycles of consumer purchasing. Their economic impact is far more significant than the artistic merits they may possess.

This kind of marketing is now a standard feature of film distribution. The *Star Wars* movies have grossed more than $1 billion at the U.S. box office, but merchandising related to the films has generated more than four times as much money! The James Bond adventure *Die Another Day* (2002) carried $120 million worth of advertising by twenty brands, a promotional windfall for the film's distributor, MGM, which spent $30 million to promote the film. All of the extra advertising was a virtual freebie for MGM. As an industry analyst has remarked, "The entertainment business is impacting so many other parts of our economy today. It's driving traffic in fast-food chains, it's selling toys, it's selling cars, it's selling sneakers. Consumers are making choices on everything from french fries to pajamas based on entertainment properties."

Product Placement

A second category of film merchandising illustrates the deep connection between modern film and the consumer economy. **Product placement** is a form of product advertising that appears inside a motion picture. Today, if Mel Gibson or Cameron Diaz

Cast Away
(20th Century Fox, 2000)
This scene from *Cast Away* shows especially blatant product placement. In terms of the composition, the Wilson soccer ball is visually more important than the film's main character, played by Tom Hanks. "Wilson," the ball, even becomes a character in the film. Note how the product's positioning ensures high visibility for the brand label. Frame enlargement.

Wayne's World
(Paramount, 1992)
Product placement became so prominent and enduring a feature of contemporary film that Wayne and Garth could not resist making fun of it. In this scene, while pretending to complain about big stars who "sell out," they happily push products by Coke, Pizza Hut, and others. Frame enlargement.

drinks a can of beer in a movie, it is not going to be a generic fictitious label such as Ajax beer. It will be a popular, commercially available beer such as Budweiser or Michelob. Famous brand labels don't just accidentally appear on screen. They are there because manufacturers paid a placement fee to studios to guarantee their labels a visible spot on-screen. The size of the fee depends on how prominently the product is displayed. Studios count on income from product placements to offset expensive production costs, which accounts for the growing frequency of product placements.

In 1990, The Center for the Study of Commercialism, based in Washington, DC, conducted a study to determine the pervasiveness of product placement. They found that the year's top-grossing film, Paramount Pictures's *Ghost,* contained twenty-three references to sixteen different brand-name products. The second highest-grossing film that year, Disney's *Pretty Woman,* contained twenty references to eighteen brand names. *Total Recall,* the sixth highest-grossing film that year, was the champion. It contained

Total Recall
(Tri-Star Pictures, 1990)
Total Recall, starring Arnold Schwarzenegger, featured more product placements than any other film of 1990. The film's satirical content suffered from the constant on-screen product advertising.

fifty-five references to twenty-eight brand-named products including Heinz ketchup, *U.S.A. Today,* Ocean Spray juices, the Hilton Hotel, Pepsi, Fuji Film, Hostess snacks, Panasonic T.V., Nike shoes, Coca-Cola, Kodak film, Sony television, Beck's Beer, Campbell's soup, Northwest Airlines, Killian Red Beer, Miller Light Beer, Miller Genuine Draft Beer, Gordon's Liquor, Jack-in-the-Box restaurants, ESPN, and Evian water.

Given the emphasis on product placement in today's Hollywood, obvious issues of creative control arise. Do paid advertisements within the context of a film narrative subtly alter the shape and focus of that narrative? At least with certain films, the answer is an unqualified "yes." *Total Recall* is a science-fiction thriller in which the villains are ruthless futuristic corporations in league with gangsters running a brutal mining operation on Mars. The film's satire and criticism of corporate control is compromised by its massive reliance on product placements. These render the film's anti-corporate satire less than coherent. At a minimum, product placements will tend to bias the social perspective of a film toward an unquestioning or unexamined acceptance of the contemporary consumer economy with its engineered leisure-time markets and products. This subverts the effort by a film such as *Total Recall* to satirize a future world overtaken by for-profit leisure-time industries. Its massive reliance on product placement makes *Total Recall* into the very thing it would satirize.

Case Study: *The Phantom Menace* and *Jurassic Park*

Sometimes, an aggressive product-licensing campaign can have an unintended effect. Even with a big box-office hit, efforts to license products can fail if the merchandise and the film provide a poor fit. *Star Wars Episode 1: The Phantom Menace* sold more than $2 billion of merchandise worldwide, but many millions of unsold toys and products remained on retailers' shelves, leaving retailers feeling burned and believing that the film had been oversold and overhyped. Accordingly, Lucasfilm acknowledged its

---

The Phantom Menace (20th Century Fox, 1999)
Although this film was a major hit worldwide, many of its product tie-ins failed to move off of store shelves. *Phantom Menace* merchandise over saturated the market, and many of the items for sale—clip on hair braids, for example—were poor fits with the film. Lucasfilm scaled down its merchandising efforts with the next installment in the series. Frame enlargement.

mistake and reduced the number of product tie-ins for *Episode 2: Attack of the Clones,* concentrating on core items like action figures, video games, and books and eliminating fringe items like the Anakin Skywalker inflatable chair and the Obi-Wan Kenobi clip-on hair braids.

The performance of *Jurassic Park,* the number one film in world markets in 1993, offers a more successful example of product licensing. Products associated with *Jurassic Park* included ice cream, frozen pizza, cakes, juices, cookies, key rings, chairs, sneakers, and, of course, toy dinosaurs. Video and computer games were a huge chunk of the product merchandising conducted with the film. Ocean Software paid $2 million as an advance royalty in exchange for worldwide rights to all *Jurassic Park* video games. It was a good deal. In France the film opened on October 20, and, by the end of December, Ocean Software had already sold 250,000 video games there. So stunning was the early performance of *Jurassic Park*-themed computer games, food, clothing, books, and toys that the vice-president of International Merchandising for MCA/Universal, the studio conglomerate that produced the film, predicted that international sales of *Jurassic Park*-licensed products would out-perform domestic U.S. sales.

Long-term planning before the film's release helped ensure the successful marketing of the film and its associated products. The previous international box-office champion was another Spielberg film, 1981's *E.T.: The Extra-Terrestrial.* Studio marketing executives believed they had fumbled the ball with *E.T.* more than a decade ago. Because the main character in *E.T.* is an ungainly little alien, the executives underestimated the market potential for product tie-ins, and they actually had difficulty finding manufacturers who were interested in bringing out *E.T.*-themed lines of merchandise.

Marketing executives were determined not to repeat this mistake with *Jurassic Park.* Accordingly, two years before the film's premiere, the studio put teams of licensing, promotional, and manufacturing personnel to work preparing for the film's global launch. A major component of the marketing strategy was the *limited* disclosure of information about the film. Spielberg did not want to reveal too much about

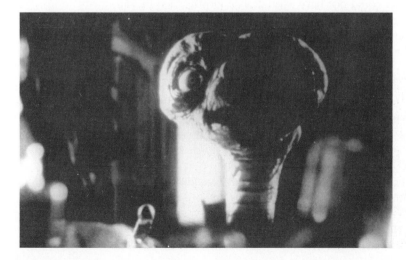

E.T. (Universal Studios, 1982) Despite its longtime position as box-office champ before being dethroned by *Jurassic Park* and then *Titanic,* *E.T.* never realized its full potential as a catalyst for product marketing. In comparison with the early 1980s, the film industry today heavily depends on product placement and marketing for additional revenue streams. Throughout the 1980s, the industry carefully reorganized itself to capitalize as much as possible on the profit potential of diverse leisure-time markets. Frame enlargement.

the film in early trailers and publicity. The secrecy was designed to keep the audience in suspense about the mysterious film prior to its release. Marketing programs were drawn up in countries throughout the world using only one graphic illustration from the film, an image showing the head of a dinosaur tipping over a Park vehicle.

As the film's premiere drew closer, minimal, teasing information gave way to full media blitzes. For example, the film premiered September 3 in Sweden, Finland, and Norway and two weeks later in Denmark. Television was the major media form promoting the picture in these Scandinavian countries. Massive advertising campaigns saturated television viewers with promos for the film. In Norway, ninety-seven commercials were presented in the nine days before the film's premiere. Heavy television advertising also whet viewers' appetites in Sweden, Denmark, and Finland. As a result, from the less than 24 million people inhabiting these countries, the film grossed $15 million.

Spielberg's Assessment

Surveying the extraordinary performance of his film in global markets, Spielberg likened its appeal to the magic of a compelling story told around a campfire. In earlier times, communities would sit by the campfire and listen attentively as a storyteller cast a spell with tales of magic and fantasy. Today, Spielberg pointed out, the gathering around the campfire is the entire world. From Europe to Asia to Central and South America, people gather in multiplex theaters. "That's what has thrilled me most about the *Jurassic Park* phenomenon. It's not domination by American cinema, it's just the magic of storytelling and it unites the world, and that is truly gratifying."

Spielberg's feeling of satisfaction was deserved. He has made some of the most popular pictures of all time and even his serious, adult-themed films (*Schindler's List, Saving Private Ryan*) have reached wide audiences. But more than the magic of good storytelling was at work in the global performance of *Jurassic Park*. Without American corporate control of a global media industry, and control of revenue from interlocking media formats (movies, books, records, home video, and retail merchandising), the *Jurassic Park* phenomenon could not have existed. The global reach of U.S. media industries is fundamental to the success of blockbuster films. Despite what Spielberg has said, this economic framework cannot be easily dismissed.

Economic Significance of the Blockbuster Film

Besides being super profitable, blockbuster films have two additional characteristics. Their stories frequently depend on fantasy or special effects (this is the magic that Spielberg referred to), and their characters are often superhuman or mechanical and nonhuman (the shark in *Jaws*, the robots in *Star Wars*, the alien in *E.T.*, the robot in *Terminator 2*, and the dinosaurs in *Jurassic Park*). Special effects promise to provide audiences with visions of things never before photographed, and this is a big part of the allure of blockbusters. Furthermore, as we have seen, mechanical characters lend themselves quite well to reproduction across diverse product lines. (Not all blockbusters have each of these elements. *Forrest Gump* [1994], *Home Alone* [1990], and *Beverly Hills Cop* [1984], for example, are not dependent on mechanical or nonhu-

Forrest Gump (Paramount Pictures, 1994);
Men in Black (Columbia TriStar, 1997)
Blockbuster films typically showcase state-of-the-art special effects and fantasy narratives populated by eccentric or mechanical characters. Tom Hanks's *Forrest Gump* was a charming simpleton who, courtesy of digital wizardry, managed to meet nearly every significant historical figure of the 1960s. *Men in Black* portrayed an Earth overrun by aliens, including the giant, and mean-spirited, Edgar bug.

man characters. *Gump,* though, is a special effects showcase, while *Home Alone* and *Beverly Hills Cop* boast cartoonlike plots with ultrapowerful heroes [played by Macaulay Culkin and Eddie Murphy] at their center.) Blockbuster filmmaking crosses a wide range of media sources and merchandise lines. As such, the shark frenzy generated by *Jaws* in 1975, the dinosaur craze created by *Jurassic Park,* and the wave of *Phantom Menace* toys that swept retailers in 1999 represented cultural phenomena far greater than the films themselves. The shark and dinosaur and *Star Wars* markets extended well beyond the revenues created by motion picture ticket sales.

Here lies the most important principle represented by blockbuster production. The blockbuster motion picture is merely the hub of a giant wheel of interconnected services and products. The film provides the stimulus for a huge array of merchandising and marketing in the nation's and the world's restaurants, toy stores, and other retail outlets, and it creates audience interest that sustains revenues in the cable and home video markets. Blockbuster filmmaking, therefore, is about more than just the making of a single film. Successful blockbuster production stimulates the creation of a huge network of associated products and productions. This is why the integrated market is so important. Because the appeal of blockbuster film characters crosses media classes and product lines, parent corporations who own the film studios that produce those characters must also control all of the other markets in which the film and its characters will appear.

This is accomplished by controlling the multiple ways that consumers will encounter the film and/or its characters. Whether consumers view it as a theatrical motion picture, as a video on home television or by way of pay cable, whether they listen

STEVEN SPIELBERG

Judged by box-office receipts, Steven Spielberg is the most popular filmmaker in the world. *Jurassic Park* (1993) broke world box-office records, and the top grossing film it displaced was *E.T.* (1982), another Spielberg creation. His other hits—*Jaws* (1975), *Raiders of the Lost Ark* (1981), and *Indiana Jones and the Last Crusade* (1989)—are among the highest grossing films of all time. But unlike Spielberg's public, until recently critics have remained divided over the merits of his work.

During the 1970s and early 1980s, he seemed to be essentially a maker of popcorn movies, built around special effects and basic emotions. The mechanical shark, the spacecraft and aliens of *Close Encounters of the Third Kind* (1977) and *E.T.*, these evoke a narrow range of

uncomplicated feelings, mainly awe and wonder, issuing from unexpected encounters with fantasy creatures.

As a filmmaker, Spielberg was a genuine boy wonder. Unlike his contemporaries, he did not attend film school but went straight into the industry. Born in Cincinnati in 1947, he was just twenty-one when hired as a television director by Universal Studios, where he was in charge of episodes of *Night Gallery, Marcus Welby,* and *Columbo.* His first feature film, *Duel* (1971), made for television, was a gripping thriller of a traveling salesman menaced on the road by a mysterious, anonymous truck driver.

At the age of twenty-six, Spielberg began filming a similar story about a confrontation between ordinary

Jaws (Universal, 1975); **E.T.** (Universal, 1982)
Spielberg's films are among the top moneymakers of all time. *Jaws* was an efficient thrill machine that terrified summer audiences, and *E.T.* cast a potent spell of childlike wonder and mystery. These effects-driven films represent one side of Spielberg the filmmaker, while *Schindler's List, Amistad,* and *Saving Private Ryan* represent his more ambitious and complex achievements.

to the film's music on a soundtrack album, or read a paperback book about the making of the movie, or buy dolls, games, or clothing tied-in to the film's characters, the revenue streams generated by these media markets stay in-house. By licensing the use of the blockbuster characters to other manufacturers, the potentially huge rev-

people and the unknown, but this time with an aquatic setting. *Jaws* (1975), the work of a hungry young filmmaker eager to prove himself, caused a sensation the summer of its release. People were afraid to go in the water, just as they had been afraid to take showers when Hitchcock had finished with them in *Psycho* (1960), a decade and a half earlier. A ferocious thrill machine, *Jaws* evoked a primitive terror in its audience that Spielberg never again attempted to duplicate. He quickly turned to spirited evocations of childlike wonder and adolescent adventure: *Close Encounters of the Third Kind* (1977), *Raiders of the Lost Ark* (1981), *E.T.* (1982), *Indiana Jones and the Temple of Doom* (1984). Their spectacular success obliterated his only early career misfire, *1941* (1979), an overblown and unfunny attempt at a World War II slapstick comedy.

But Spielberg was more ambitious than the critics recognized. He now began to expand his range with more mature subjects. With *The Color Purple* (1985), he adapted Alice Walker's novel about an African American woman's experiences with an abusive husband. *Empire of the Sun* (1987), another World War II film, and *Always* (1989), a remake of a classic 1943 Hollywood film, were critical and commercial disappointments, but in both cases Spielberg conspicuously stepped away from popcorn moviemaking. Moreover, they demonstrated something that was hard to see at the time, that World War II had special resonance for Spielberg and that he would become one of its most important cinematic chroniclers.

He next broke the digital threshold with *Jurassic Park*, providing not the first but the most spectacular demonstration of next-generation computer-based effects. It was *Schindler's List*, though, released the same year, that earned Spielberg the critical respect that had, until now, eluded him. This grim black-and-white film portrays the horrors of the Nazi extermination camps in Poland with a depth of emotional feeling and an adult sensibility that Spielberg had never before demonstrated in his work. Moreover, he extended his historical and moral sense of obligation by helping launch a vast project documenting and recording the oral histories of Holocaust survivors, accounts that will be digitized and become part of the world's historical record. He felt a special urgency in carrying out this project because many of the survivors are now quite elderly.

Beginning with *Schindler's List*, Spielberg came into his own as a filmmaker of considerable artistic and moral ambition. Fashioning brilliant images, he now used film to examine issues of human evil and moral redemption. *Amistad* (1997) graphically showed the horrors of slavery in its portrait of a historic rebellion of African slaves in Colonial America. *Saving Private Ryan* (1998) showed the D-Day invasion of the Normandy beaches in a way that caught the savagery of the combat with a ferocity unprecedented in commercial cinema. Intended to dramatize the heroism of that generation of U.S. soldiers, the film aroused tremendous interest in their example and public respect for their sacrifice.

Spielberg's somber historical dramas are his most artistically ambitious films; most encouraging in this respect, they have performed solidly at the box office. The greatest strength of U.S. film has always been its conjunction of popular appeal with work of artistic distinction. More than many other directors now working, Spielberg exemplifies this principle.

After *Saving Private Ryan*, Spielberg took an unusual (for him) break from filmmaking. His next two features, *A.I.: Artificial Intelligence* (2001) and *Minority Report* (2002), were an ambitious and challenging return to the genre of science fiction, but without the children's orientation of *E.T.* and *Close Encounters*. Both are grim and disturbing films, aimed for adults, and suggest that Spielberg, who has always been a visionary director, is now pursuing his artistic ambitions as vigorously as he once courted the box office.

enue stream generated by product tie-ins throughout the world helps enlarge corporate earnings.

In its truest sense, then, blockbuster filmmaking is about the production and manufacture of commodities on a national and global scale. Film is only a means toward this pattern of global production. Blockbuster films are the engines that drive the global entertainment markets. Understood in economic terms, the blockbuster film's importance is measured only in its ability to stimulate a huge wave of consumption of film-themed leisure-time products and services. With their blockbuster productions and aggressive promotional campaigns, U.S. film studios have made the world their marketplace. The danger in this is that global film production becomes increasingly homogenized, increasingly the same from country to country, given over to special effects-driven fantasy narratives or violent action spectacles featuring superhuman heroes. To escape this influence, as the next chapter shows, many filmmakers in other countries have explored alternative film styles. But these alternatives coexist with the Hollywood influence. The U.S. cinema absorbs, modifies, and influences the work of foreign directors, some of whom eventually come to work in the U.S. industry.

◻ INTERNATIONAL INFLUENCE OF HOLLYWOOD STYLE

The U.S. cinema influences foreign directors in three key ways: (1) it stimulates filmmakers to absorb selected aspects of U.S. cinema into their own work; (2) it employs émigré directors; and (3) it remakes foreign films and then distributes these overseas.

Influence on Foreign Filmmakers

Hollywood films are popular throughout the world. Directors in other countries incorporate examples and quotations from U.S. films in their own work to demonstrate their affection for Hollywood film. French directors Francois Truffaut and Jean-Luc Godard include extensive **homages** to Hollywood in their films. Truffaut paid his respects to his beloved Hollywood director, Alfred Hitchcock, in *The Bride Wore Black* (1968), and Godard's first film, *Breathless* (1959), is styled as a riff on U.S. gangster pictures and Hollywood star Humphrey Bogart. Virtually the entire career of fellow French director Claude Chabrol is a variation on Hitchcock-style films of crime and psychological suspense.

Case Study: Akira Kurosawa
While he is a master of cinema in his own right, Japanese director Akira Kurosawa was extraordinarily receptive to the example of Hollywood. In *The Bad Sleep Well* (1960), a thriller about corrupt corporations, Kurosawa borrows from Warner Bros. crime films of the 1930s in using montages of newspaper headlines to announce major plot developments. *Yojimbo* (1961), a samurai film about a warrior who manipulates two criminal gangs into annihilating each other, uses for its main set a dusty, wide street in a T-design that recalls the main street of many a Hollywood Western. The climatic showdown in *Yojimbo* occurs here just as it has in countless Westerns. *Yojimbo* also includes a reference to the well-known Western *High Noon* (1952) and a scene lifted directly from the 1942 crime drama, *The Glass Key*.

At the conclusion of *Sanjuro* (1962), two samurai confront each other. They draw their swords like guns from holsters, and the faster draw wins. Quicker to get his sword out of its scabbard, the hero kills his opponent. Kurosawa has clearly modeled this

Yojimbo (Toho, 1961)
Kurosawa's popular samurai film
makes reference to the design of
classical Hollywood Westerns
and was, in fact, remade as a
Western, *A Fistful of Dollars*
(1964). It concludes with a
"high noon" style showdown
on the town's dusty main street.

showdown on Western gunfights. In *Kagemusha* (1980), another samurai drama, the film's horizon shots of samurai on the march were modeled on the Monument Valley compositions of John Ford's classic Hollywood Westerns (these included *Fort Apache* [1948], *She Wore a Yellow Ribbon* [1949], and *The Searchers* [1956]).

Kurosawa borrowed from Ford, but he also played against Hollywood tradition. The climax of *Kagemusha* features a charge by samurai mounted on horseback against

Last Man Standing (New Line, 1996)
Walter Hill's remake of *Yojimbo* shifts its locale to Depression-era Texas but incorporates a great deal of Kurosawa's original imagery. Bruce Willis plays the outsider manipulating two criminal gangs into destroying each other. Frame enlargement.

an opposing clan armed with rifles. The scene visualizes an important Japanese battle that has historic significance because it was the first demonstration of the effects of organized firepower on an army carrying only swords and lances. As the riders charge, they are mowed down and wiped out by their enemy.

Kurosawa had the riflemen shoot the horses out from under the riders, deliberately reversing a well-known Hollywood convention in which one invariably fired to hit the rider and not the horse. This convention can be seen in Ford's classic 1939 Western, *Stagecoach*. During the climax, a band of Apache Indians, armed with rifles, chases the stagecoach and its inhabitants across the plains. The chase is long and thrilling, mainly because the Indians never shoot the horses pulling the coach. Ever since the film was made, critics have pointed to the artificial quality of this chase in which the Indians never do the logical thing by shooting the horses to stop the coach. In *Kagemusha*, Kurosawa deliberately departed from this time-worn convention. In this regard, Kurosawa's relationship with the U.S. cinema is by no means unique. He is one of many directors who defined their work with and against Hollywood filmmaking.

Absorption of Foreign Filmmakers

Because of its prestige, the U.S. cinema continually attracts and absorbs talented filmmakers from abroad, who, in turn, help modify and change U.S. film style. Beginning in the late 1920s, a major wave of émigré filmmakers arrived in Hollywood from Germany. These included cinematographer Karl Freund, directors Fritz Lang, F. W. Murnau, and Ernst Lubitsch, scriptwriter Carl Mayer, and actors Emil Jannings and Conrad Veidt. Lang had directed such classic German films as *Metropolis* (1926) and *M* (1931), and he went on to have a long career in Hollywood, frequently specializing in dark crime films before he returned to Germany near the end of his career to direct his final films.

Many of Hollywood's enduring classics were created by filmmakers who began their careers in other countries. The jaunty adventure classic *The Adventures of Robin Hood* (1938), the popular romantic drama *Casablanca* (1942), and the super-patriotic portrait of composer George M. Cohan, *Yankee Doodle Dandy* (1944), were all directed by Michael Curtiz, who was born in Hungary and worked in Germany during the early part of his film career. Hollywood's superstar director Alfred Hitchcock arrived in the United States in 1939 after a lengthy and distinguished career as a director in the British cinema. While apprenticing in the British system as an assistant director, Hitchcock worked and studied in Germany for two years, absorbing the style of expressionism, then prevalent in German cinema. Hitchcock's subsequent U.S. movies are strongly marked by the elements of German expressionism that he found so impressive while studying in Germany in 1924 and 1925.

Recent Émigré Filmmakers

In recent years, émigré directors have created some of the U.S. cinema's most distinguished or popular films. Based on a series of stylish, frenzied action films—*A Better Tomorrow* (1986), *The Killer* (1989), *Bullet in the Head* (1990), *Hard Boiled* (1992)—Hong Kong director John Woo emigrated to Hollywood but found the U.S. system unable to accomodate his audacious style. Thus, his initial U.S. films—*Hard*

Target (1993), *Broken Arrow* (1996)—were disappointments, but Woo eventually prevailed with a critical and popular success in *Face/Off* (1997).

Peter Weir established his career in Australia with such memorable films as *Picnic at Hanging Rock* (1975), *The Last Wave* (1978), and *Gallipoli* (1981), the latter film starring Australian actor Mel Gibson, who subsequently became a major Hollywood star. Weir then went on to direct the well-regarded U.S. films *Witness* (1985) and *Dead Poets' Society* (1989) with such established U.S. celebrities as Harrison Ford and Robin Williams. Weir's colleague in the Australian cinema, George Miller, established his international reputation with the hits *Mad Max* (1979) and *The Road Warrior* (1981), both starring Mel Gibson. In the U.S. cinema, Miller directed one segment of *Twilight Zone—The Movie* (1983), *The Witches of Eastwick* (1987), and *Lorenzo's Oil* (1992).

The Hollywood career of Dutch director Paul Verhoeven has created much notoreity. He established his reputation with the well-regarded Dutch films *Soldier of Orange* (1977) and *The Fourth Man* (1983) before embarking on a string of popular U.S. hits. These include *Robocop* (1987), *Total Recall* (1990), *Basic Instinct* (1992), and *Starship Troopers* (1997). *Robocop* is that rare example of a thinking person's action film. Verhoeven studied the contemporary action thrillers of Sylvester Stallone and Arnold Schwarzenegger and determined to beat them at their own game by providing ultrakinetic, supercharged thrills and extreme violence. This he did while infusing the action spectacle with a sharp and biting satire of a U.S. media culture dominated by infotainment programming and a caustic portrait of early 1980s economic and social policies. Seeing the excesses and irrationalities of contemporary U.S. culture as only the outsider can, Verhoeven skewered the culture with a remarkable satire.

To do so he employed the spectacular violence and supercharged action narrative that are standard formulas of contemporary U.S. film. In this regard, his career illustrates one of the ironies resulting from absorption into the Hollywood industry.

Robocop (Orion Pictures, 1987)
The critical and popular success of *Robocop*, a savage social satire of 1980s America, launched the Hollywood career of Dutch director Paul Verhoeven. Like many foreign filmmakers before him, Verhoeven found the huge resources and popular impact of Hollywood filmmaking to be powerful lures. Unlike some of his less-successful predecessors, though, Verhoeven enjoyed great popular success with his American productions.

Émigré directors in the U.S. cinema rarely work with the kind of artistic freedom or produce the stylistically unusual works that drew Hollywood to them in the first place. Woo's initial U.S. productions were frustrating experiences, and Verhoeven has yet to produce for U.S. screens anything like the haunted, surreal dreamworld he captured in his Dutch film *The Fourth Man* (1979).

Remakes of Foreign Films

In its constant search for story material, Hollywood often turns to other, older films, even from overseas. For his follow-up to *Memento,* director Christopher Nolan selected a 1997 Norwegian film, *Insomnia,* and "Americanized" it by switching the setting from Norway to Alaska and casting actors Al Pacino, Hilary Swank, and Robin Williams.

Many recent star vehicles are foreign film remakes. *Vanilla Sky* (2002), starring Tom Cruise, was based on a 1997 Spanish film called *Open Your Eyes. K-Pax* (2002), with Kevin Spacey, was an unofficial remake of another Spanish film, *Man Facing Southeast* (1986). *Twelve Monkeys* (1995), with Bruce Willis, was a feature-length remake of the classic French short, *La Jetée* (1962). The Richard Gere–Jodie Foster vehicle, *Sommersby* (1993), was a remake of a popular French film, *The Return of Martin Guerre.* The comedies *Three Men and a Baby* (1987) and *The Man with One Red Shoe* (1985) were also remakes of popular French hits. The Nicolas Cage–Meg Ryan romance *City of Angels* (1998) was an Americanized remake of Wim Wenders's German production, *Wings of Desire* (1986). *Last Man Standing* (1996), starring Bruce Willis, was

---

Insomnia
(Warner Bros., 2002)
Flush with the success of the independent hit, *Memento,* and for his first mainstream film with major stars, director Christopher Nolan turned to a 1997 Norwegian film that he admired and proposed an American remake. The result was critically acclaimed and starred Al Pacino as a cop tracking a serial killer (Robin Williams) while suffering a progressive psychological breakdown. Hollywood regularly turns to foreign film as a source for remakes, but the results are not always so distinguished as *Insomnia.*

a remake of Kurosawa's *Yojimbo*. While remakes of foreign hits have been especially common in recent years, it is not a new trend. The classic Western *The Magnificent Seven* (1960) Americanized Akira Kurosawa's magnificently filmed Japanese epic, *Seven Samurai* (1954).

The challenge Hollywood faces in remaking foreign films is to translate story material from one cultural context to another. In some cases, the translations are fairly successful, as with *Three Men and a Baby,* mainly because the original was a piece of comic fluff not bound closely to a particular cultural context. By contrast, the Americanized Western *The Magnificent Seven* simplifies and eliminates much of the historical and philosophical complexity of the Japanese original. This is because no parallel cultural relationship exists in the American West with that between the samurai warrior and the peasant farmer in medieval Japan. Unable to translate the class conflicts and historical framework of Kurosawa's feudal drama to the American West, the screenwriters working on the remake simply eliminated large chunks of the original film. As a result, while the U.S. remake is somewhat entertaining, it has never achieved the international stature of Kurosawa's film. In a similar fashion, *Last Man Standing* could not translate to its depression America setting the complex historical symbolism in *Yojimbo*.

Case Study: *The Vanishing*

What changes when Hollywood remakes a foreign film? The recent case of *The Vanishing* shows Hollywood's impact on the original material as it tailored the film to fit the U.S. market.

Both versions of the picture were directed by George Sluizer. Originally, *The Vanishing* was a French/Dutch coproduction released in 1988. The film did very well in international distribution and won several top awards at film festivals. Noting

The Vanishing (1988)
In the original version of *The Vanishing,* Raymond Lemorne is a vicious, inhuman sociopath who looks perfectly normal. The film's special creepiness comes from its suggestion that beneath this outward normality lies unspeakable evil. By contrast, in the American version, the killer looks quite sleazy and unpleasant. This establishes a less-disturbing philosophical outlook in the remake. Frame enlargement.

the film's success, Hollywood felt it could be a viable commercial property as a remake. Director Sluizer came to the United States to oversee the project. The U.S. version of *The Vanishing*, starring Jeff Bridges, Kiefer Sutherland, and Nancy Travis, was released in 1993. The distinguishing features of his original picture were revised to fit contemporary U.S. horror film conventions. These revisions reduced the uniquely disturbing psychological power of the original and made it, instead, into a more standard and formulaic horror film.

Narrative in the Two Versions   The story in each version of *The Vanishing* is superficially similar, turning on the mysterious disappearance of a young woman and the determined efforts by her lover to find out what happened to her. In the original version, while vacationing in France, Rex Hofman and Saskia Wachter stop for gas at a local station. Saskia goes inside to buy drinks while Rex waits by the car. When she fails to return, Rex goes into the station looking for her, but she has vanished without a trace. During the next three years, Rex relentlessly papers the city with posters carrying Saskia's photograph, soliciting information about her whereabouts. He also appears on local television shows pleading his case. A parallel narrative in the film follows Raymond Lemorne, a university chemistry professor, family man, and sociopath who is compelled to prove that his behavior exceeds ordinary moral categories. He devises an elaborate scheme in which, posing as a weak man with an arm in a cast, he will lure a naive woman into his car, sedate her with chloroform, and abduct her. The film implies that Saskia has fallen victim to Lemorne's plan.

Intrigued by the spectacle of Rex and his determined efforts to learn the answer to Saskia's fate, Lemorne contacts Rex and promises that if Rex accompanies him to the site of Saskia's disappearance, he will tell Rex everything. With diabolical calculation, Lemorne plays on Rex's desperate need to know the answer to Saskia's fate. He persuades Rex to drink coffee laced with a sleeping pill, telling Rex that, if he does so, he will experience exactly what Saskia experienced. Fearing that drinking the coffee will lead to his death, as apparently it did for Saskia, Rex nevertheless complies. In the final scene, Rex awakens, entombed in a coffin, buried alive. In the final moments of the film, Rex scratches vainly at the wooden lid and cries out Saskia's name.

The story in the U.S. remake begins in a similar fashion, but eventually it veers off in a contrived and unsatisfying direction. Jeff (Kiefer Sutherland) and Diane (Sandra Bullock) are vacationing in the northwestern United States. Diane disappears, Jeff spends three years trying to find out what happened to her, and, eventually, Barney (Jeff Bridges), Diane's abductor, contacts him. Jeff drinks from Barney's cup of coffee, and he awakens, buried alive. Earlier in the film Jeff had found a new girlfriend, Rita (Nancy Travis). At the climax of the story, she tracks Barney to his secluded cabin and rescues Jeff. Rita and Jeff kill Barney. In the final scene of the film, they dine in a restaurant and laugh about the whole affair.

Alterations for the Hollywood Market   The disturbing narrative in the original French/Dutch production of *The Vanishing* is recast in the remake to fit contemporary U.S. narrative formulas. Three major changes are imposed on Tim Krabbe's original novel and screenplay. These result in emphases on (1) romance, (2) a reassuring, "happy" ending, and (3) standard horror film conventions.

Romance   The entire middle section of the remake focuses on the relationship between Rita and Jeff and adds considerable narrative complications in place of the elegant simplicity of the original film's narrative. In a convoluted subplot, Jeff tries to write a book dealing with Diane's disappearance while preventing Rita from learning the contents of the book. Jeff has promised Rita that he will try to forget Diane, and Rita exerts considerable pressure on him to coerce Jeff's loyalty. But as Jeff writes his secret book, he slips away one weekend a month, donning a fake uniform and telling Rita he is in the Army Reserves, in order to continue his hunt for Diane's abductor. Eventually, Rita catches on to Jeff's plans and this leads to many additional scenes in which the couple argues over Jeff's obsession with Diane and Rita's need for an exclusive commitment to their relationship.

In the original version, Rex did find a girlfriend, Lieneke, in the middle section of the film. However, this relationship remained a minor and subsidiary part of the narrative, the major focus of which was the psychological cat-and-mouse game between Raymond and Rex. Eventually, Lieneke leaves Rex, realizing that a relationship with him is impossible because of his obsessions, and they reach this decision without any of the melodramatic emotional fireworks expended by the couple in the U.S. remake. Indeed, the acting by the cast in the original production is much cooler and more emotionally distant than the theatrical and somewhat overwrought styles employed by the U.S. performers.

A major alteration, then, in the remake of *The Vanishing* emphasizes elements of traditional romance because these are lacking in the original production, at least after the disappearance of Saskia at the beginning of the film. The story is reconfigured to bring a new love interest into Jeff's life and to have that occupy the long middle section of the film. Romantic love is an enduring characteristic of Hollywood films, and belief in the power of romance to reconfigure one's life and improve one's destiny is

The Vanishing (20th Century Fox, 1993) The American remake of *The Vanishing* emphasizes a romantic subplot between Jeff (Kiefer Sutherland) and Rita (Nancy Travis). The romance is formulaic and uninspired. Its comforting presence replaces the disturbing spiritual perspective of the original. Frame enlargement.

an essential part of the mythology of the couple constructed in U.S. cinema. Accordingly, the narrative of *The Vanishing* was overhauled and retrofitted with these elements. In the end, love—in the form of Rita—saves the day.

A Happy Ending   The most striking difference between the two versions is the last-minute rescue of Jeff in the U.S. remake, whereas Rex, in the original, perishes. The ending of the U.S. version is comforting and reassuring while the original holds real psychological terror. In the original, the camera remains in the coffin, with Rex gasping for breath as the image fades out and the end titles appear, leaving the viewer in a state of acute anxiety and considerable psychological tension.

The last-minute rescue in the U.S. remake alters not only the outward structure of the narrative. It changes the philosophical and metaphysical design as well. In the original version, the narrative is a grim meditation on the inevitability of death, derived from the symbolic imagery of a golden egg. (The story is based on a novel called *The Golden Egg* by Tim Krabbe.) None of this symbolism survives in the remake.

Both films include an opening scene in which the lovers drive through a dark tunnel and run out of gas. In the original version, this scene introduces the imagery of the golden egg. As Rex and Saskia drive through the tunnel, she describes a recurring nightmare in which she is inside a golden egg, unable to get out, flying through space for eternity. She adds that lately she dreams about a second golden egg flying in space. At this early point in the narrative, the viewer cannot know that this is a death dream. However, the enclosure of Saskia and Rex by the darkened tunnel clearly prefigures their final, if separate, entombment. During the tunnel sequence, a soprano vocal on the soundtrack adds an element of mystery and mysticism and marks the scene as significant.

When Rex and Saskia run out of gas, they quarrel because he ignored her earlier warnings about low fuel. She tells him she is scared, and a truck approaches them from

The original version concludes in the most terrifying way possible. Buried alive, unable to escape, Rex suffocates in a frenzy of panic. It is a ferociously grim ending that nothing in the remake matches. Frame enlargement.

Jeff and Diane run out of gas in a dark tunnel in the American remake, but the scene remains mundane and without metaphysical mystery. Frame enlargement.

behind. She turns, sees its looming lights, and cries out, "the golden egg!" Saskia stays to look for a flashlight to guide their way out of the tunnel, while Rex angrily leaves her behind, determined to walk to a station to refill their spare can. She cries after Rex, imploring him not to leave her alone. The camera stays inside the car with Saskia, and the viewer sees her thrashing about, looking for the flashlight in the car's confined space. This, too, prefigures her protracted struggles in the final, confined space of her life, the coffin provided by Lemorne. Rex returns with the gas, and Saskia extracts a promise from him never to abandon her again.

In the original version, this promise is binding. By drinking Lemorne's drugged coffee and submitting to Saskia's fate at the end, Rex honors this promise and rejoins Saskia in oblivion. Before this, however, Rex has begun to share Saskia's dream. One afternoon with Lieneke, Rex has a seizure. He seems possessed, thrashes in place and cries out, "the golden egg" and Saskia's name. This, too, prefigures death, because he will struggle and cry out like this in the coffin. Rex subsequently tells a television interviewer that he regularly has Saskia's dream and believes that they will meet each other again inside a golden egg. The golden egg and the dream shared by Rex and Saskia, and the imagery of the enclosing dark tunnel at the opening of the film, establish the entire narrative as an advance toward a delayed but prefigured death.

In the U.S. remake, the altered ending in which Rita saves Jeff from death entailed that the underlying symbolism of the original narrative be abandoned. Accordingly all reference to dreams of the golden egg were removed from the narrative. It was a costly choice because it meant that the narrative in the remake would work only on a literal and mundane level, whereas the original enriched the anxiety and terror with a cosmic, mystical dimension. In the remake, Jeff and Diane do drive through a tunnel and run out of gas, but there is no dialogue about a shared dream. There is no prefiguration of a final entombment. The tunnel sequence in the remake fails to evoke the mystery and sense of metaphysical predestination that the original accomplishes.

By contrast with the original's evocation of cosmic horror, the final scene in the remake concludes the narrative on a trivializing note. Jeff and Rita enjoy a dinner in a restaurant with Jeff's publisher. A waiter arrives offering them coffee, and Jeff and

Rita look at each other, laugh, and reply that they don't drink coffee any more. On this comic note, the end credits roll. Their laughter is meant to comfort the audience and end the film in a reassuring way, but it winds up trivializing the narrative.

Horror Film Conventions   Among the most unfortunate changes made in adapting *The Vanishing* to a U.S. market are the use of contemporary horror conventions. *The Vanishing* contains extensive stalking sequences in which the killer hunts his prey. Whereas the original film began with Rex and Diane stuck in the tunnel, the remake opens with a series of lengthy scenes that show Barney perfecting his plans and methods for abducting a woman. The film's initial focus is on Barney, and Jeff and Diane do not appear until much later. When they arrive at the gas station, extensive crosscutting shows Diane going inside for drinks and Barney stalking her. Viewers know the killer is lurking at the station and wait uneasily for Diane to fall into his clutches.

This narrative design reduces the terrifying sense of mystery evoked by the original film, where the killer is slowly and gradually revealed. By contrast the U.S. version immediately identifies the killer, shows viewers how he plans to abduct his prey, and then he waits for Diane to walk into the trap. As a result, the remake generates suspense instead of mystery and gives viewers a clear and anticipated *abduction*, rather than a *vanishing*. Viewers know what will happen to Diane before it happens. In the original version, viewers learn Saskia's fate only at the end of the film. Prior to that, she simply vanishes from the face of the earth. Instead of mystery, the remake offers a literal, ordinary crime.

Other stalking sequences show Barney hunting Rita at Jeff's apartment and the extended hunt and chase between Rita and Barney at the cabin during the film's climax. During this sequence, the film conforms to the most unfortunate of contemporary horror conventions, namely, a gratuitous emphasis on explicit violence. While the elegant psychological narrative of the original contained little overt violence, the remake degenerates into a routine bloodbath. Struggling with Barney, Rita clubs him, stabs him, and burns him with a cigarette lighter, while Barney, in turn, tries to cut Rita's head off with a handsaw. Eventually, Rita frees Jeff, and Jeff clubs Barney to death with a shovel. Gross-out physical effects replace the psychological emphasis of the original.

Unlike the original version, the American remake reveals the killer (Jeff Bridges) right at the beginning, and he looks very creepy. Frame enlargement.

The elegant psychological suspense of the original, in which no overt violence occurs, degenerates into the usual horror film bloodbath in the remake as Rita goes after the killer with a variety of weapons. Frame enlargement.

Conforming to the Hollywood Market   This case study of two versions of *The Vanishing* demonstrates the costs of the way that Hollywood lures foreign filmmakers with the promise of access to its glamour and resources. The chance to make a U.S. picture in Hollywood with popular U.S. stars is extraordinarily tempting because the scale of the technical resources and cultural power available in the Hollywood system is so high. Furthermore, the global reach of its product ensures that the successful émigré director, such as Paul Verhoeven, can have a much larger potential audience.

In return, however, the industry imposes its own demands. Both versions of *The Vanishing* are directed by George Sluizer, but this is less important than one might at first think. Comparison of the two films shows that it is not the director, but the U.S. production system—with its assumptions about what audiences want to see, how horror film narratives should be designed, and how much violence is necessary to ensure marketability—that exerts the determining influence over the film's design.

These dynamics are enduring ones. Many émigré filmmakers arriving in Hollywood find that, in crucial respects, they are accorded less freedom than in their home industry and that the unique or unusual features of their work, which attracted Hollywood to them in the first place, may not be welcomed in their U.S. productions. Sluizer's original version of *The Vanishing* is sophisticated and inventive. Its merits, though, did not survive the cross-cultural transformation into a Hollywood product. Because it would become a standard U.S. horror film, Hollywood needn't have hired Sluizer to direct the project. These dynamics illuminate the reciprocal influences prevailing between Hollywood and the international cinema. Hollywood absorbs influences from overseas, and, at the same time, transforms and domesticates those influences according to the perceived demands of the U.S. market.

SUMMARY

U.S. filmmaking exerts a global influence throughout world markets. This influence has a clear economic basis. U.S. film studios are owned by diversified parent corporations whose holdings equip them to compete in an integrated world entertainment market. Blockbuster filmmaking, driven by special effects and mechanical or superhuman characters, is an ideal means of dominating domestic and world cinema markets. The blockbuster film is enormously popular, generates huge overseas interest, and lends itself to extensive lines of product merchandising. With its multinational corporations, and blockbuster productions, the U.S. cinema is able to perform very aggressively in global markets.

Hollywood exerts strong international influence not just economically, but stylistically as well. The style and content of U.S. films have a major impact on world cinemas in three ways: (1) foreign filmmakers borrow images, characters, and story situations from the U.S. cinema; (2) filmmakers who have established their careers in other countries come to Hollywood to make U.S. films; and (3) Hollywood remakes foreign films according to the norms and standards of U.S. film and popular culture.

Despite its very real impact on world markets, the reach of the U.S. blockbuster cinema is limited. Although blockbuster films may threaten to homogenize the tastes of world cinema audiences, U.S. and international film culture remain extraordinarily diverse and contain many film styles and approaches to filmmaking that differ from the norms of blockbuster production. The next chapter demonstrates several of these alternatives.

SUGGESTED READINGS

Tino Balio, ed., *The American Film Industry,* rev. ed. (Madison: University of Wisconsin Press, 1985).

John W. Cones, *Film Finance and Distribution: A Dictionary of Terms* (Hollywood, CA: Silman-James Press, 1992).

Peter Cowie, *Variety International: Film Guide 2000* (Los Angeles, CA: Silman-James Press, 2000).

Peter Lev, *The Euro-American Film* (Austin: University of Texas Press, 1993).

Barry R. Litman, *The Motion Picture Mega Industry* (Boston: Allyn and Bacon, 1998).

Stephen Prince, *A New Pot of Gold: Hollywood Under the Electronic Rainbow, 1980–1989* (New York: Scribner's, 2000).

Jason E. Savire, ed., *The Movie Business Book* (NY: Fireside, 1992).

Justin Wyatt, *High Concept: Movies and Marketing in Hollywood* (Austin, TX: University of Texas Press, 1995).

Chapter 9

The Cinema in an
International Frame

Chapter Objectives

After reading this chapter, you should be able to:

- explain how visual and narrative designs in the international cinema differ from the norms of U.S. filmmaking
- describe two key features of the international film art movement of the 1950s
- identify and describe the basic film styles of five key international auteurs
- explain the aims of Italian neorealism and describe its cinematic techniques
- assess the legacy of Italian neorealism and its influence on subsequent filmmakers
- describe the theoretical and historical origins of the French New Wave and

- discuss the stylistic approaches of key New Wave directors
- explain the origins of New German Cinema and compare the film styles of its key directors
- explain the social conditions that motivated the emergence of the new Hong Kong cinema
- describe the artistic and generational dynamics at work in the emergence of new wave film styles
- recognize and appreciate the diversity of artistic styles in the international cinema

Key Terms and Concepts

auteurism (auteur)
neorealism
surrealism

new wave
"white telephone" films
the camera-pen

"auteur theory"
jump cut
melodrama

The cinema is a global medium. As such, it displays an extraordinary diversity of styles. A familiarity with the norms of U.S. filmmaking is but a first step toward a comprehensive understanding of the cinema's broad range of artistic styles and accomplishments. Previous chapters emphasized mostly U.S. films and filmmakers. The international context should now be stressed. It presents an astonishing range of cinema styles and approaches and demonstrates the medium's great flexibility in its methods of storytelling and image design. In an international context, Hollywood becomes one reference point amid many others.

A survey of milestones in the international cinema turns up unique visual and narrative designs and many filmmakers whose work is a distinct departure from the styles of U.S. filmmaking. This chapter examines some of these alternatives within two major categories: international auteurism and the phenomenon of national film movements.

■ THE INTERNATIONAL AUTEUR CINEMA

Auteurism, the belief that certain directors can function as independent artists whose films display a unified personal style and design, characterized French film criticism throughout the 1950s and inspired the French New Wave directors in the 1960s. In turn, auteurism influenced U.S. film criticism and film production from the late 1960s onward. In some ways, though, auteurism was not a new insight. Throughout cinema history, many directors exerted controlling artistic influence on the style and themes of their films. These included Frank Capra and John Ford in Hollywood, Alfred Hitchcock in the British and Hollywood industries, Carl Dreyer, a Danish director who worked in a variety of European countries, and Sergei Eisenstein, Fritz Lang, and F. W. Murnau, from the classic silent era in Russian and German cinema.

What was distinctive, though, about the international auteur period beginning in the 1950s was (1) a new insistence on the (old) idea that film was an art and the director its key visionary, and (2) the emergence into worldwide distribution of an international cinema dominated by key superstar directors. International film culture in the 1950s and 1960s emphasized the recognition of outstanding international auteurs.

The auteur filmmaker, of course, was not a European phenomenon. Hollywood had its own auteurs. In an earlier period, these included John Ford, Alfred Hitchcock, and Orson Welles, while contemporary figures include Martin Scorsese, Francis Ford Coppola, Tim Burton, and Steven Spielberg. The film art movement of the 1950s, though, tended to privilege the international auteur. Because this chapter examines cinema in an international context, these figures are discussed here. (Hollywood auteurs are discussed and profiled throughout the other chapters.) Among the most important of the international auteurs were Michelangelo Antonioni, Ingmar Bergman, Luis Buñuel, Federico Fellini, and Akira Kurosawa.

Michelangelo Antonioni

Italian director Antonioni's earliest films were documentary shorts made within the tradition of **neorealism** that dominated Italian cinema of the period. These included *People of the Po* (1943) and *Dustmen* (1948). Consistent with neorealism, these were bleak, unsentimental portraits of working-class life.

In his feature films, however, beginning with *Story of a Love Affair* (1950), Antonioni began an examination of lovelessness and alienation among the middle and upper classes. From *Story of a Love Affair* to *Il Grido* (1957), Antonioni develops the distinctive visual and psychological coordinates of his soon-to-be-famous cinematic style. These include: (1) the use of long takes and sequence shots, (2) silent stretches within scenes during which the narrative is suspended while the film concentrates on moments of emotional stillness and psychological alienation between the characters, and (3) an increasingly precise compositional design that describes, through the positioning of characters and objects, the spatial coordinates of alienation.

Antonioni gained international prominence with *L'avventura* in 1960, honored with a special jury award at the Cannes Film Festival for the beauty of its images and for its invention of a new cinema language. Beginning with *L'avventura,* the distinct

Red Desert (1964)
Antonioni's films offer precise visual statements on the theme of human alienation. In his pessimistic vision, the structures and architectural forms that people have created displace them. *Red Desert* deals with industrial pollution. In this shot, looming outside his window, huge chemical storage tanks dwarf an industry executive. Frame enlargement.

components of Antonioni's style, this new cinema language—the use of long takes, moments of silence and narrative suspension, and the refinement of visual strategies for embodying states of psychological alienation—achieve a strikingly sophisticated and elaborate design.

Visual Design in *L'avventura*

L'avventura presents a deliberately mysterious and unresolved narrative. Set among the wealthy Italian leisure class, the film examines a boating party consisting of Anna, her boyfriend Sandro, her friend Claudia, and other guests. The group interrupts its swimming to go ashore on a rocky Mediterranean island. On the island, Anna tells her boyfriend that she no longer feels anything for him and wants to go away. Shortly thereafter, she vanishes. Her comrades find no trace of her on the island. She has completely disappeared.

The island is rocky and barren, and Antonioni explores this landscape with a distinctive visual brilliance. After Anna's disappearance, he spends an extraordinary amount of time, with little dialogue, examining the visual and spatial relations of isolated characters placed against rocks, sea, and sky. The narrative is nearly suspended during these long scenes, as the imagery emphasizes the isolation of small characters dwarfed against an immense, forbidding, and empty landscape. The scenes are virtually silent, with long hiatuses between passages of dialogue. These are the empty moments so common in Antonioni's films during which the fragile emotional connections among characters break down. His compositions during the island search display the most famous feature of his cinematic design, his extraordinary ability to create visual environments in which architectural design or features of landscape displace, obliterate, or swallow up the human figure.

The story in *L'avventura* remains an enigma. Anna is never found, nor does the viewer ever learn why and how she vanished. Her friends Claudia and Sandro become lovers but they are estranged at the film's end. No answers are forthcoming, and all of the characters seem to have reached an emotional dead end. By leaving the narrative profoundly unresolved and celebrating ambiguity, Antonioni implicitly pointed to the huge distance between his cinematic style and the tidy and reassuring

L'avventura (1960)
A barren island landscape and images of human isolation and anguish in Antonioni's *L'avventura*. Antonioni's special cinematic skill lay in placing his characters in physical settings where the visual design externalizes the characters' psychological problems. Frame enlargement.

conventions of storytelling of the U.S. cinema, in which all the narrative questions tend to be neatly resolved before the final fade-out.

Case Study: L'eclisse

Antonioni continued to explore his concerns about lovelessness and psychological alienation in the modern world in a pair of films which, along with *L'avventura*, are regarded as his trilogy. These are *La Notte* (1960) and *L'eclisse* (1962). His visual and narrative designs had reached a point of extreme concentration and emphasis by the time he made *L'eclisse*. The film begins with the disintegration of a love affair

L'eclisse (1962)
Changing compositions in the opening shot of *L'eclisse*. After lingering on the image of the table lamp and books, the camera pans right to reveal Ricardo. Note how the composition splinters his body. Frame enlargements.

between Vittoria (played by Monica Vitti, who starred in all three films of the trilogy) and Ricardo. In the first scene, Vittoria announces to Ricardo that their affair is over and she is leaving. Later, she has a brief relationship with her mother's stockbroker but that, too, dissolves by the end of the film, as the viewer, again, is left with a powerful vision of human disconnection.

The opening scene of *L'eclisse* demonstrates the extraordinary complexity and power of Antonioni's compositions. The first shot of the film is a close up of a lamp and books with a white object resting on top of the books. Significantly, this composition lacks any apparent human presence. After a few seconds, though, the camera pans right to reveal Ricardo sitting at his desk. The white object on top of the books turns out to be his elbow. His body is bisected by a pyramid sculpture and bordered by a second lamp on the right of the frame.

This compositional design is typical of Antonioni. In his cinema, human beings are enclosed or dwarfed by the structures that surround them. The looming physical presence of their material environment overwhelms their attempts at love and communication. Antonioni's compositions are precise, visual statements of this sad psychological condition.

Shot two shows Vittoria, with her back to the camera, standing in front of some curtains. She turns to face the camera and reaches for something out of frame. The visual design of the scene proceeds differently from the continuity principles of the U.S. system. Antonioni uses no establishing shot to clarify the spatial connections between the fields of view presented in shot one and shot two. The viewer assumes, for the sake of the narrative, that the two characters inhabit the same room, but the visual information does not specify their actual physical relation to one another.

Shot three presents another composition that the viewer cannot integrate into the established spaces. A picture frame encloses an ashtray and a series of porcelain

---

The second and third shots of *L'eclisse* present more fragmentary views of the scene. Unlike Hollywood's continuity editing, Antonioni's visual designs prevent the viewer from integrating shot information in a perceptually satisfying way. Frame enlargements.

figurines. A hand, which the viewer assumes is Vittoria's, reaches through the picture frame and rearranges these objects.

Antonioni frustrates the viewer's desire for psychological (and visual) integration and closure. This is a significant point. By withholding the establishing shot, by building the sequence out of fragmented details, Antonioni frustrates the viewer's desire to integrate those details into a larger pattern or environment, and this ensures that the viewer begins to feel disconnected and cut-off, just like the characters.

Without any dialogue, Antonioni spends two and a half minutes visually describing the emotional distance between Vittoria and Ricardo and the way that this psychological distance is externalized into their relationship with the environment. The images are very eloquent, from the opening shot of Ricardo's body fragmented by the everyday objects of his room to later imagery of Vittoria staring lifelessly into space, with her presence and body dehumanized to become one more object of visual decor in the room. By withholding establishing shot information and by extending the long, dead silences between Vittoria and Ricardo, Antonioni creates a series of fractured, splintered spaces that do not cohere.

Antonioni ends the film with an even more dazzling example of visual form. Vittoria's affair with the stockbroker has become sterile and unfulfilling. She leaves his apartment and walks off into the city. A five-and-a-half minute montage follows, concluding the film without reference to any of its characters. In this montage of 44 shots, Antonioni explores the city's empty, nonhuman spaces and evokes a disturbing and anxiety-provoking environment, placed within the shadow of nuclear extinction by alluding to the era's fears about the Bomb. The narrative is suspended, the main characters have been removed from the stage, yet the film goes on during the final montage to evoke in a poetic and non-narrative way a cluster of visual impressions and accumulating anxieties.

Antonioni's Later Career

On the basis of his growing international reputation, Antonioni made several films in English, the first of which, *Blow Up* (1966), was a popular and critical hit. Its successor, *Zabriskie Point* (1969), was less successful with audiences and critics. Stunned by this failure, he returned to documentaries and made a nearly four-hour film about the Chinese revolution, *Chung Kuo cina* (1972).

He did not return to narrative features until making *The Passenger* in 1975. In this film, Antonioni reprised his familiar themes of alienated identities and disrupted lives. A television news reporter (Jack Nicholson) in the Middle East assumes the identity of a dead man found in a Moroccan hotel and is drawn unwittingly into violent political intrigue. At the end of the film, Antonioni executes a dazzling seven-minute tracking and zoom shot. The camera pulls away from the reporter in his hotel room to move through the street and courtyard, then returns to the hotel window to reveal that a narrative ellipsis has occurred—the reporter is dead. The lengthy tracking shot worked to pull the viewer's attention away from the character at precisely the moment where a turning point in the narrative occurs. The film implies that he may have been murdered by the agent responsible for the death of the original political operative found in the Moroccan hotel, but the death remains ambiguous and unexplained because the camerawork prevented viewers from seeing what occurred. The conclusion of *The Passenger* shows Antonioni working with undiminished visual brilliance and continuing to experiment boldly with narrative, as when he moves the camera away from the major action during the film's climax.

Unfortunately, however, he suffered a stroke in 1985, which effectively ended his filmmaking career. (He did, however, make a brief return, directing *Beyond the Clouds* [1995] in collaboration with German director Wim Wenders.) But Antonioni's place in cinema history was already secure. *L'avventura, L'eclisse,* and *The Passenger* established him as an international director of the first rank. His distinguished work uses composition and landscape to decenter the human figure and show characters who lead emotionally dislocated lives in stories whose coherence is disrupted and attenuated and in which a psychology of alienation prevails. Each of these features marks an immense distance from the style of the U.S. cinema.

Ingmar Bergman

Ingmar Bergman established his career in the small state-subsidized Swedish industry. Because the state guaranteed to underwrite the production and distribution costs of projects that failed to turn a profit at the box office, Bergman worked in a relatively pressure-free artistic environment, without the commercial worries of Hollywood directors. As a consequence of this relative freedom from box-office pressures, Bergman's films are extremely severe, often unrelentingly grim, and focus on human spiritual problems and crises of religious faith. Light humorous moments are rare in Bergman's films (except for his few comedies). Bergman felt compelled to use film to explore some of humankind's deepest spiritual and emotional problems, and this led him to make films whose stark tone and extremely austere visual design would seem to be box-office poison, at least when measured by Hollywood's standards of what an audience would want. Bergman, though, found an astonishing popular success, and it was greeted with respect by critics. As a result of these factors, he became a giant figure of the international cinema.

After training in the theater, Bergman, the son of a Lutheran minister, began his directing career with *Crisis* (1946), but he did not achieve significant international recognition for a decade. It was *Smiles of a Summer Night* (1956), a light-hearted sex comedy (somewhat uncharacteristic of Bergman) that brought him to prominence as an internationally recognized director. Following that production, he launched into a series of sober and challenging examinations of spiritual crises and religious dilemmas. *The Seventh Seal* (1956) is an extraordinary evocation of the plague years of the Middle Ages and tells an allegorical tale of a wandering knight engaged in a desperate chess game with Death (personified as a figure in black whose face is strikingly rendered with white clown makeup). Death has come to claim the knight, but the warrior uses the game as a delaying tactic. Death agrees to spare him as long as the game goes on, and the knight uses this temporary respite to try to find, in the closing moments of his life, an answer to the question of why suffering must exist in a world presided over by a presumably benevolent God.

The cinematography is by Gunnar Fischer, and the cast includes Max von Sydow, Gunnar Bjornstrand, Bibi Andersson, and Gunnel Lindblom, all of whom became regular members of Bergman's stock company. Bergman shot his films very quickly and

The Seventh Seal (1956)
By playing chess with Death,
the Knight (Max von Sydow)
hopes to uncover the mysteries
of life. The stark lighting and
elegant composition are hall-
marks of Bergman's work in this
period. Frame enlargement.

worked with a small cast of technicians and performers. Subsequent additions to this
stock company included the actors Liv Ullmann and Erland Josephson and cinematographer Sven Nykvist, replacing Fischer on the later productions.

Bergman followed *The Seventh Seal* with *Wild Strawberries* (1957), one of his most
famous films, about a science professor, traveling to receive an honorary doctorate,
who is overwhelmed by memories and dreams of his youth, his parents, and his children. Late in life and with great anxiety, he confronts the ultimate question about
whether his life has had meaning.

Wild Strawberries (1957)
An elderly professor, en route to
receiving an honorary degree,
reevaluates his life in *Wild
Strawberries,* one of the best
of Bergman's introspective,
psychologically probing films.
Victor Sjostrom, who had been
a major Swedish director during
the silent era, plays the professor. Frame enlargement.

The Trilogy

In the early 1960s, Bergman commenced a stark trilogy of films focusing on the religious and philosophical problems of God's silence in a world torn by cruelty and violence. These films were *Through a Glass Darkly* (1961), *Winter Light* (1963), and *The Silence* (1963). In each of these works, the narrative covers a very short period of time, the cast is very small, and the range of emotions evoked is restricted but intense. *Through a Glass Darkly* deals with the schizophrenic breakdown of a young woman and the detached, cruel response of her father who studies her disintegration in order to write about it in a novel. *Winter Light* deals with a village pastor's personal crisis when he is called on to give communion but lacks faith himself. *The Silence* deals with the fate of two sisters in a strange, mythical city where the inhabitants speak an unknown language. The two sisters become progressively more estranged from one another and from the world about them. These films enabled Bergman to bring to an end the religious issues that his filmmaking had examined for a decade, and their spare, austere design pointed toward the control and minimalism that was increasingly becoming his cinematic signature and would be on display in his masterpiece, *Persona*.

Case Study: *Persona*

In 1966, Bergman made one of the most distinguished films of his long and illustrious career, *Persona*, a drama about the exchange of identities between a theater actress and the nurse attending her. For inexplicable reasons, the actress decides to stop speaking. The nurse entrusted to her care is obsessed with uncovering the mystery behind the actress's willed silence. This silence creates a void that eventually engulfs the personality and mind of the nurse. The two women merge identities, a moment Bergman captures in a mystical and mysterious image where each woman's face is superimposed on top of the other, creating a composite, third, yet nonexistent, persona.

Persona (1966)
The human personality as enigmatic, seductive, and destructive. Bibi Andersson and Liv Ullmann merge identities in *Persona*.

Persona is Bergman's most cinematically self-conscious and assured film. Many of his other films contain exquisite cinematography by Gunnar Fischer and Sven Nykvist but have a literary quality due to a primary reliance on dialogue and acting performances. In *Persona,* in contrast, Bergman draws attention to the apparatus of the cinema and points to the illusions that the cinema creates—illusions of time, space, and movement—in developing the film's story about the exchange of identity and the breakdown of language.

Bergman establishes this self-conscious referencing of cinema at the film's beginning. The story begins when a doctor assigns the nurse to care for Mrs. Vogler, the actress who has stopped speaking. This scene, though, occurs 7 minutes into the film. Before this, Bergman has offered a poetic and non-narrative montage (during which the opening credits appear). The montage is mysterious and dreamlike, constructed out of brief, kaleidoscopic visual impressions that resist the viewer's effort to make them cohere.

The first image of the film is the firing of the carbon arc inside a motion picture projector. Bergman analogizes the beginning of his film with the beginning of the cinema. As *Persona* begins, the shots evoke the beginning of the projection apparatus. The viewer sees images of film running through the gate of a projector and a countdown leader flashing on a screen. A brief cartoon image follows and then an image of a hand signing in the language of the deaf.

A kaleidoscope of disjointed images follows, including shots of a tarantula crawling on a glass screen, a sheep with its throat being cut and its organs removed, a crucified hand with a nail pounded into it, a landscape with trees, an iron-spiked fence, a mouth, an old woman's face, a boy lying on a platform covered by a sheet, a dangling hand, an old woman's hands at rest, feet, a face with eyes closed jump-cut with a shot of the eyes opening. On the soundtrack, dissonant music alternates with a phone ringing and dripping water. The boy under the sheet changes positions and then he sits up and turns

In the poetic and mysterious prologue of *Persona,* an unidentified boy touches a screen containing the luminous image of the nurse (Bibi Andersson). Bergman's images are often symbolic and nonliteral, and they challenge viewers to interpret their mystery. Frame enlargement.

toward the camera. He runs his hand across the lens of the camera. A reverse angle cut shows the boy in front of what appears to be a motion picture screen. On this screen, the faces of the nurse and Mrs. Vogler dissolve one into the other. Their superimposition suggests the merging of consciousness that will be the theme of the film.

At this point, *Persona*'s credit sequence begins with white letters on a black screen. Brief shots flash as subliminal images between the credits—a Vietnamese monk on fire, the boy's face, women's faces, lips pressed against glass, various landscapes, and, fading in from a white screen, a door through which the nurse emerges to receive her assignment from the doctor. At this point the narrative proper begins.

This complex, kaleidoscopic montage preceding the narrative in *Persona* virtually defies analysis. Its poetic, non-narrative qualities are far removed from the methods of U.S. popular cinema. The images are evocative, disturbing, anxiety-provoking, taboo (the imagery of the sheep with its throat cut), and constitute a poetic and radical digression from the narrative of the film. That narrative, however, never establishes the kind of driving causal force that propels events in a Hollywood film. Bergman's narrative is a small, slender thread from which he creates mysterious images and an elliptical drama of psychological breakdown.

Bergman's Later Career

Bergman followed *Persona* with a series of internationally acclaimed films. *Hour of the Wolf* (1968), *Shame* (1968), and *The Passion of Anna* (1969) present elliptical, mysterious, and metaphorical narratives about the process of artistic creation, the proximity of artistic perception to madness, and the relation of the artist to a world in which violence and war are normal conditions. *Cries and Whispers* (1972), one of Bergman's most famous films, focuses with unbearable psychological intensity on the relationship among four women brought together in a turn-of-the-century manor house by one's impending death from cancer.

After *Cries and Whispers,* Bergman continued to work prolifically, realizing an adaptation of Mozart's opera, *The Magic Flute* (1975), a difficult and intense study of the breakdown of a marriage, *Scenes from a Marriage* (1974), a nightmarish vision of a female psychiatrist's descent into madness, *Face to Face* (1976), and, as his farewell to filmmaking, *Fanny and Alexander* (1982), with sumptuous costumes and art direction in a story about a young boy and his family in turn-of-the century Sweden. The film's magical atmosphere, wider-than-usual emotional range, and vivid production design made it very popular. It earned four Academy Awards for Best Foreign Film and for its costumes, art direction, and cinematography. Bergman announced that this was his final film. Although he made one additional 16mm project for Swedish television, he has apparently retired from the world of cinema.

Like Antonioni, Bergman is a giant of the international screen, one who created a unique, distinctive, and unmistakably personal world on film. Bergman's characters suffer psychological and spiritual anguish, and he is relentless in using the camera to probe the nuances of emotional torment, spiritual despair, and the mysteries of artistic creation. His psychological poetry, minimal narratives, grim subject matter, and spare, stark visual style are in sharp contrast with the style of popular commercial films. Beyond this, however, lies their greatest significance. Bergman's designs demonstrate that, paradoxically, the inner life of the mind and heart is entirely cinematic, despite the fact that the camera must photograph matter rather than spirit. Bergman used the camera to reveal the spirit and feeling in and behind things that the camera could not directly capture. This was a true gift and one that very few filmmakers possess.

Luis Buñuel

While Antonioni and Bergman achieved fame in their native countries of Italy and Sweden, Luis Buñuel was an itinerant filmmaker, working alternately in Mexico, Spain, France, and the United States. He was a true freelancer, not at home for very long in any national cinema industry. But irrespective of the country in which he worked, Buñuel honored the surrealist impulse to explore, and even celebrate, the forces of social anarchy and the subconscious, irrational mind.

Presaged by the Dadaist movement (1916–1920) in modern art, which was committed to anarchy and the breakdown of order in art and society, surrealism appeared as a fully-articulated movement in 1924 when Andre Breton in Paris issued his Surrealist Manifesto. **Surrealism** intended to overthrow social and artistic conventions by evoking the logic and desire of dreams. Influenced by Freudian psychoanalysis, surrealism tried to access the subconscious and irrational mind by creating art whose content and style was frankly fantastic and dreamlike. Long after the surrealist wave had crested in modern art, Buñuel continued to explore the collison of dream and reality, social decorum and irrational impulse.

Un Chien Andalou

In 1928 Buñuel teamed with the surrealist artist Salvador Dali to make *Un Chien Andalou,* one of the most scandalous films of its time. A determined assault on the conventions of good taste and bourgeois morality, Buñuel and Dali's film is a catalog of sexual and religious taboos and anticontinuity approaches to narrative construction. From an editing standpoint, correct continuity matches fail to occur. The implied

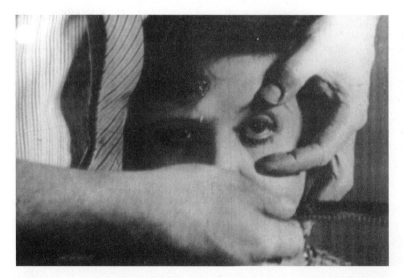

Un Chien Andalou (1928) The most shocking and audacious act in the history of cinema. To make his artistic intentions perfectly clear, at the beginning of *Un Chien Andalou,* director Buñuel slices into an eye. Frame enlargement.

angles of a character's line of sight are incoherent, and characters improperly appear inside their own point-of-view shots. From a social and moral standpoint, the film attacks the act of seeing that underlies cinema and, by extension, attacks the institution of cinema itself. In the film's opening moments, Buñuel performs one of the most shocking and famous acts in the medium's history. He stands behind a young woman, takes out a straight razor, and brings it close to her eye. The film cuts to a long shot of thin clouds slicing across a full moon and then to an extreme close-up of the razor slicing into an eye which disgorges a dollop of viscous fluid.

The shot, of course, depends on a trick effect. Rather than the actress's eye, Buñuel slices the eye of a dead animal photographed in extreme close-up. Nevertheless, the act is shocking and never fails to provoke a gasp even from jaded, contemporary audiences. For once, the camera does not cut away from the promised, outrageous event. This assault on the eye, both literally and figuratively, is an emblematic gesture indicating Buñuel and Dali's aims in *Un Chien Andalou*—to shock and to provoke, to sear the eyes of their audience. The film's disjointed, dreamlike, and irrational narrative frustrates the audience's desire to draw a coherent interpretation of its dissociated events and scandalizes viewers (more so in 1928 than today) with a catalog of outrageous images that violate decorum and propriety.

A Cinema of Subversion

The assault on the eye emblemizes Buñuel's entire career in which he challenges the viewer's social values and perceptions of reality. Buñuel was a humorist who celebrated the power of the irrational and the force of the unexpected, intending to subvert the spectator's trust in an ordered and reassuring universe. Buñuel's films delight in strange juxtapositions of unusual objects, as when, in *Un Chien Andalou,* the protagonist suddenly appears strapped to a piano, on top of which is a bleeding animal carcass, and, with great effort, tries to pull it across the room.

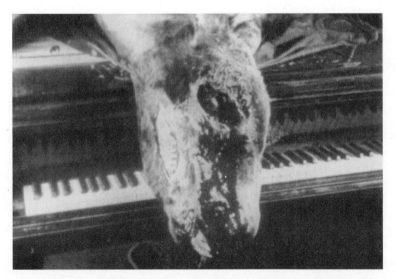

Buñuel's subversive assault on order, rationality, art, and religion compelled his use of surreal, antirational imagery. A bleeding animal carcass is draped over a piano in *Un Chien Andalou.* Frame enlargement.

Because dreams and unconventional erotic practices are, in their nature, opposed to the everyday world of ordinary logic and social morality, Buñuel regarded them as having a liberating potential. This assumption was consistent with his surrealist belief that subversive art could shake up time-worn social perceptions and attitudes, and this was his reason for including such material in his films. As a surrealist, Buñuel felt that by exploding the logic and conventional practices of everyday life, he could open a space for freer and less-inhibited human behavior and perception.

Because his films were anticlerical and portrayed sexual perversions, Buñuel and his cinema were long an enemy of the Catholic church, especially in Spain where the authorities tried to destroy all copies of *Viridiana* (1961), a parable about the attempts of a devout and saintly young woman to lead a Christian life but which ends in disaster for herself and for everyone in her life. In the mid-1950s Buñuel worked in France and then returned again to Mexico in 1958 to direct *Nazarin*, about a saintly priest whose efforts to conduct a spiritual life and follow the example of Christ, ironically, lead to his being hunted by the police as a criminal and thrown into jail. Buñuel's point was that, in present-day society, efforts to lead a genuinely Christian life end in failure. *Viridiana* (1961), shot in Spain, was a continuation of this idea and aroused the wrath of the Spanish authorities even though it won the top prize at the Cannes Film Festival.

Case Study: *The Exterminating Angel*

In 1962, Buñuel returned to Mexico to film *The Exterminating Angel,* one of his most famous and surreal films. The narrative focuses on twenty dinner guests who gather for a sumptuous banquet hosted by a wealthy socialite. After dinner, the guests find they cannot leave. They take off their jackets and bed down for the night on furniture and the floor. In the morning, they are still trapped in the room and remain so for several weeks. Paradoxically, no one from the outside can break in.

During their confinement, the veneer of polite bourgeois manners gradually crumbles. Desperate for water, the guests break through the ornate walls of the mansion with a pick axe, rupture a water line, and gather in a frenzy for the available water. Searching for food, they find a flock of sheep inexplicably running through the house and butcher and eat them. One guest, in delirium, sees a disembodied hand scuttle across the floor. With unexpected aggression, it grabs her neck and attempts to strangle her. All pretense to civilized manners gone, the guests smash the furniture in the room and build a bonfire on the living room floor. Two guests are found dead, suicide victims, and the remaining guests decide to kill a scapegoat victim in an effort to break the mysterious spell that holds them in the mansion.

Eventually, the guests find that they are in the same positions as on the original night. They retrace their steps, trying to recreate their words and gestures from the original evening in an effort to undo the spell. This formula works, and they can now leave the room. They go outside where the authorities cheer them as if they were refugees from a prison camp. To give thanks, they enter a church, but Buñuel's universe remains irrational. Following the ceremony, along with the other members of the congregation, they remain trapped inside the church. A huge flock of sheep breaks into the building, while violence in the streets erupts outside.

In this film, as in his other works, Buñuel's style lacks the visual complexity of Antonioni or Bergman. The secret to his surrealist style lies not in an elaborate or refined usage of the camera, sound, or editing but in his matter-of-fact approach to the absurd. He presents the most illogical and outlandish events as if they were completely normal. *The Exterminating Angel* opens on a world that initially obeys normal laws of time and space, but the narrative gradually escalates the illogical and the irrational until the viewer completely accepts the absurd premise of the film. As a surrealist, Buñuel aims to depict the chaotic emotional and social impulses that he believes lie beneath the artificial order established by social conventions and propriety. To get at these chaotic impulses and desires, he proceeds gradually and with a completely logical presentation of the illogical.

Case Study: *The Discrete Charm of the Bourgeoisie*

This method distinguishes one of his best and most famous films, *The Discrete Charm of the Bourgeoisie*, produced in France in 1973. A group of wealthy and cultured friends repeatedly tries to have a civilized dinner party, alternately at restaurants and at their respective homes. A series of strange events frustrates each of their attempts. Patronizing a restaurant, the dinner party discovers that the manager has just died and is laid out in the very next room. They lose their appetites. The party attempts to dine at a friend's house, but a group of soldiers, taking a break from maneuvers, comes to the house expecting to be fed. Accepting a dinner invitation from another friend, the group arrives at the home, only to find themselves mysteriously on stage in front of an auditorium of restless spectators.

Buñuel presents these strange and bizarre events as if they were completely natural occurrences. Moreover, he interrupts the narrative with scenes showing various characters waking from sleep and announcing that everything just seen in the film was a dream. This continually reframes the narrative as a series of dream episodes with the result that the order and structure required for a coherent narrative break down. Dreams are embedded within dreams so many times that the viewer is no longer sure who dreamt what or what level of reality governs events. This peculiar structure enables Buñuel to mount an attack on the logic and structure of realist narratives and places the film very far in style from the Hollywood model, in which the rela-

The Discreet Charm of the Bourgeoisie (1973) A violent, unrealistic, irrational universe constantly disrupts the efforts of the bourgeoisie to complete their dinner party. Nevertheless, they persist, and the film leaves them on the road, still looking for their dinner. Frame enlargement.

tions of time and space in a film narrative tend to be clearly established. Under the Hollywood model, dream episodes have explicit boundaries, often established by explicit visual cues, that clearly mark them off from the body of the narrative.

In Buñuel's final film, *That Obscure Object of Desire* (1977), he assaults conventional narrative and cinematic representation by casting two different actresses with similar features in the same role of a young Spanish woman who tempts and teases a French widower. Accordingly, the young woman continually changes her appearance, despite being the same character, depending on who plays her, and no one else in the film seems to notice. With this tactic and typical surrealist wit, Buñuel calls into question not just the integrity and unity of the personality, but also conventions of cinematic representation that have always required that a character be portrayed by a single performer unless the character is being shown at different stages of life.

Buñuel's Legacy

Buñuel's surrealistic film style assaults virtually all of the continuities of time and space, of narrative logic, and character presentation that prevail in commercial cinema. His work in this regard is a major source of inspiration for contemporary specialists of the irrational such as David Lynch (*Eraserhead* [1978], *Blue Velvet* [1985], *Lost Highway* [1997]) and for genres or films that celebrate antilogical and irrational narratives, such as rock music videos or Oliver Stone's *Natural Born Killers* (1994). But unlike these more popular representatives of mass culture, Buñuel was a true anarchist in spirit, whose art retains its biting, socially subversive edge untainted by commercialism. His body of work in this regard represents a major alternative to the norms and conventions of popular U.S. cinema.

Federico Fellini

Like the early work of his colleague Michelangelo Antonioni, Fellini's first films seemingly fall within the style of Italian neorealism. *The White Sheik* (1952), *I Vitelloni* (1953), and *La Strada* (1954) are realistic in their outward style but are so strongly allegorical as to infuse their narratives with a powerfully poetic and symbolic resonance. With *La Dolce Vita* (1960), Fellini turned his images away from the tradition of realism that had dominated Italian cinema since the mid-1940s and toward the stylized and fantastical filmmaking for which he would become famous. *La Dolce Vita* focuses on the professional and personal life of a journalist in Rome and opens with a series of long shots showing a statue of Christ transported by helicopter across the city— the statue and helicopter are a startlingly unexpected conjunction—and it ends with a fantastic sequence in which a huge, weird fish is captured by the city's inhabitants.

From this point on in his career, Fellini abandoned naturalism and realism to concentrate on fantasy and extravagantly embellished images. In *8½* (1963), for example, he explored the world of filmmaking with the self-consciousness that would become a hallmark of his cinema. In the film's story, a film director, Guido, who may represent Fellini himself, is creatively blocked, unable to complete his latest project, and he retreats into an adolescent world of dreams. The film ends with fantasy imagery in which Guido, imagining himself as a boy, directs performers in a three-ring circus.

Fantasy and Spectacle

Juliet of the Spirits (1965) continued this emphasis on the inner world of fantasy and dream, which Fellini achieved by distorting the exterior world of people and objects. Juliet (played by Giulietta Masina, Fellini's wife and frequent collaborator) escapes into a private world of hallucination to avoid the unpleasantness of her marriage to an unfaithful husband. The striking feature about Fellini's work, here as in his other films, is that Juliet's dreams are not so different in their visual style and emotional tone from the scenes depicting her daily life. Fellini's ability to give everyday reality a degree of weirdness and circuslike spectacle entails that Juliet's dreams are only slightly different from her waking reality, which, as Fellini renders it, is far from realistic. Compare, for example, two images from the film, reproduced below. In the first shot pictured here, Juliet reclines at the shore and watches a group of her neighbors arrive to frolic on the beach. Fellini films these neighbors so that they appear as odd figures in a strange procession, carrying an assortment of bizarre objects. The scene is like a hallucination; this, though, is Juliet's reality. In the second shot pictured here, Juliet dreams about a strange boat at sea and meeting a mysterious boatman on the shore. The visual style of the dream—its oddness and unreality—is not substantially different from the previous image drawn from Juliet's waking reality.

An Alternative to Hollywood Conventions

The special qualities of Fellini's cinema lie in his ability to transform the surfaces of everyday life, giving to them a strange, odd, circuslike appearance and atmosphere. Not surprisingly, as his career evolved, he turned toward overt spectacle and circus pageantry. *Satyricon* (1969) was a lavish but harsh view of ancient Roman decadence, and *The Clowns* (1970) took the circus as its subject matter. In 1974, Fellini examined his own youth in the autobiographical, extremely stylized *Amarcord*. Remembering episodes from his boyhood, he visualized them as a series of encounters with bizarrely configured people and places.

Juliet of the Spirits (1965)

Fellini's cinema transforms reality into spectacle and pageant. These images from *Juliet of the Spirits* representing fantasy and reality look identical. The odd promenade of beachgoers from Juliet's waking reality looks just as strange as her weird dream of a boat at sea with the top of a submerged man's head visible in the foreground. Frame enlargements.

Amarcord (1974)
A simpleminded man climbs a tall tree and refuses to come down, as friends and family members look on with anxiety. This anecdote is one of many moving, funny, and eccentric episodes in Fellini's nostalgic portrait of 1930s Italy, the period of his youth.

In subsequent films, such as *Casanova* (1976), *City of Women* (1981), *And the Ship Sails On* (1984), and *Ginger and Fred* (1986), Fellini continued to travel his unique path away from conventional realism and toward a world of exaggerated spectacle, circus atmosphere, and the subjective imagery of private dreams and hallucinations. Unlike Buñuel's work, though, which is extremely critical of conventional society, Fellini's extravagant imagery is more personally eccentric and lacks the sardonic, anarchic, antisocial impulses of Buñuel. Buñuel's dream imagery is subversive. Fellini's is personal and joyously poetic. The almost complete subordination of narrative to style in Fellini's films places his work far from the norms of Hollywood cinema. Fellini's style is radically antirealistic, his world on screen a personal pagent of spectacular and theatricalized characters.

Akira Kurosawa

Unlike the other international auteurs, Kurosawa's cinema does not represent an obvious break with the models of narrative and style in the U.S. cinema. Kurosawa's work does not display the austere, narrow emotional range of a Bergman, the anarchic, antisocial impulses of a Buñuel, or the delight in a fantastical circus atmosphere of a Fellini. But, in more subtle ways, Kurosawa's work does depart from some of the conventions of the U.S. cinema. Though he began making films during World War II in Japan, Kurosawa matured as a filmmaker in the postwar years with a series of urban dramas focusing on the physical, emotional, and spiritual conditions of life in a defeated and ruined nation. These films included *Drunken Angel* (1948), *Stray Dog* (1950), and *Ikiru* (1952).

Kurosawa found international acclaim with a series of vibrant, visually spectacular period films, many of which were set during the violent turmoil of Japan's sixteenth century. His period films include *Rashomon* (1951), an international classic about a rape and murder that is recalled in strikingly different terms by each of the four witnesses called to testify; *Seven Samurai* (1954), in which seven warriors defend a village of farmers against marauding bandits, a film that exerted a tremendous influence on the U.S. cinema and was remade in 1960 as a Western, *The Magnificent Seven;*

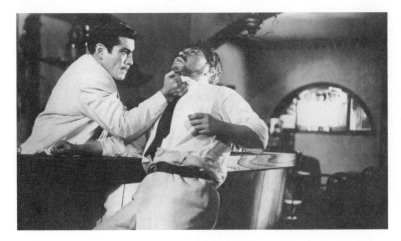

Drunken Angel (1948)
In *Drunken Angel* and other films of the postwar years, Kurosawa portrayed the efforts of a defeated nation to recover from the devastation of war. His treatment of gangsters and doctors and crime and sickness symbolized a recommended course of national recovery.

and *Throne of Blood* (1957), a widely admired version of *MacBeth* set during the civil wars in the sixteenth century. Kurosawa also adapted Shakespeare's *King Lear* as *Ran* (1985), set in the sixteenth-century period that has had such significance for him as an artist. Kurosawa's samurai film, *Yojimbo* (1961), inspired the line of spaghetti Westerns directed by Sergio Leone beginning with *A Fistful of Dollars* (1964), and his *The Hidden Fortress* (1958) was a major influence on George Lucas's *Star Wars* (1977).

Kurosawa's Cinematic Style

Kurosawa's filmic style includes a conjunction of elements—aggressive, montage editing and the long take—that are rarely found together. More typically, filmmakers will favor either montage or long takes, but Kurosawa has relied on their conjunction throughout his career. The battle scenes in *Seven Samurai* feature what was then an unprecedented use of rapid-fire editing to capture the ferocity of the battle, while in *Kagemusha* (1980), another samurai battle epic, Kurosawa opens the film with a static, 7-minute shot that holds on three characters who remain largely motionless for the duration of

Throne of Blood (1957)
Kurosawa is best known for his period films dealing with the samurai wars of the sixteenth century. Transposing Shakespeare to this setting, he made the acclaimed *Throne of Blood*.

Kagemusha (1980)
A static camera and a seven-minute shot provide the daring opening of *Kagemusha,* Kurosawa's epic about the end of the samurai era in Japan. Despite his fondness for scenes of physical action and the moving camera, Kurosawa also loves still, static compositions. He integrates movement and action with moments of quiet and contemplation as few other filmmakers have.

the shot. Kurosawa proved equally adept with movement (editing and moving camera shots) and with stillness (the frozen tableaux compositions of his long takes). More-over, beyond his use of montage, Kurosawa's editing shows a marked departure from the Hollywood norms of continuity cutting because, in many of his early films, he rarely repeats camera set-ups throughout a scene. Under the Hollywood system, filmmakers built a scene by repeating shots taken from familiar (i.e., previously seen) camera positions. This helped maintain continuities of character position and screen direction. Kurosawa's editing, by contrast, demands a continuing effort at perceptual reorientation from the viewer because the camera's angles of view are ever-changing.

In a scene from *Seven Samurai,* several farmers from the village come to town to hire samurai for protection against bandits. They spend the night at a run-down inn, sharing the room with some local ruffians who are contemptuous of the farmers and with a boastful, arrogant, but humiliated samurai. Instead of repeating camera positions, Kurosawa uses set-ups that offer novel and sometimes bewildering perspectives on the action. The scene contains 19 different camera setups and only 5 repetitions of a previous setup. Some of these repetitions, though, are deceiving because they begin with a familiar framing but then use camera movement to shift to a new position. In Kurosawa's later films—from *Dodeskaden* (1970) to *Madadayo* (1994)—he simplified his editing by filming with two cameras placed at right angles to one another and allowing each shot a long duration before making an edit.

Kurosawa's use of multiple cameras when filming, and his reliance on the telephoto lens, are other essential features of his style and point to important differences from the Hollywood cinema. In Hollywood's practice, scenes are restaged and reshot each time a new camera perspective is needed. By contrast, Kurosawa permitted the action of a scene to run through in its entirety and captured it using up to six cameras running simultaneously. He believed that he got better performances from the

Seven Samurai (1954)
Ferocious action is a Kurosawa hallmark. Rapid-fire editing, telephoto lenses, and moving cameras plunge viewers into the battle scenes of *Seven Samurai*.

actors this way, and it is a distinctly different approach to production from the U.S. system in which action is restaged for coverage by a single camera.

Kurosawa's use of telephoto lenses ensures that his images have a different visual appearance than those in the U.S. cinema. The extreme long lens that Kurosawa favored imposes a radical foreshortening on the representation of depth. Foreground and background areas of composition are compressed in ways that distort normal perspective. This minimizes the viewer's perception of spatial depth in Kurosawa's shots. In sum, while Kurosawa's films fall into familiar genres—police thrillers, medical dramas, battle epics—his unconventional methods of filming and editing and use of telephoto lenses clearly differentiate his work from the U.S. style. Nevertheless, his work has exerted tremendous influence on U.S. directors—Steven Spielberg, George Lucas, Martin Scorsese, Brian De Palma—because of his skill at filming and choreographing physical action. Kurosawa, for example, created the modern style of slow motion and montage editing, used everywhere in films today when showing scenes of violent action. The scene in *Seven Samurai* that shows the killing of a kidnapper is the classic textbook example of screen violence that showed virtually every modern filmmaker how to combine slow motion and dynamic editing to stylize violent death. While Kurosawa developed his own unique style as a filmmaker, his influence on Hollywood cinema has been profound and far-reaching.

Each of these auteurs—Antonioni, Bergman, Buñuel, Fellini, and Kurosawa—achieved international prominence during the 1950s and 1960s and created a body of work very different in theme and design from that of U.S. filmmaking. As such, their work demonstrates the extraordinary range of stylistic options that are available to filmmakers and the enormous flexibility of the medium of cinema. These directors created memorably stylized approaches to image and narrative construction. Their imaginative work demonstrates that cinema is infinitely powerful in its ability to reconfigure the visual and physical realities of daily life and to reshape, through image and narrative, the viewer's sense of self and world.

☐ CINEMA AND SOCIETY: THE NEW WAVE PHENOMENON

A second striking feature of the international cinema, and of film history in general, is the tendency for a new national film style to coalesce around a group of young filmmakers and critics who issue written proclamations about the need for cinematic alternatives and their intention of creating them. Thus, a **new wave** or a new direction and design within an existing national cinema is born. This section examines four of the most famous examples of the new wave phenomenon: Italian neorealism in the 1940s, the French New Wave of the late 1950s and 1960s, the New German Cinema of the 1970s, and Hong Kong cinema of the 1980s and 1990s.

Italian Neorealism

Neorealism exerted tremendous influence over Italian filmmakers throughout the 1940s and 1950s. Directors Antonioni and Fellini both had to work free of this influence before developing their own unique cinematic styles. Though it emerged in the 1940s and had peaked and declined by the end of the 1950s, neorealist style continues to be highly influential. Ermanno Olmi's *The Tree of Wooden Clogs* (1978), for example, is true to its neorealist origins in its simple, quiet, unsentimental focus on peasant life.

Goals of Neorealism

Neorealism developed as a reaction against the Fascist film style that typified Italian cinema under Mussolini. Mussolini had invigorated Italian cinema through construction of the vast national studio, Cinecitta, but films produced during the Fascist years came to be known derisively as **"white telephone" films.** They focused on upper-class characters in sumptuous surroundings, leading lives of leisure and decadence, allegedly spending most of their time talking on white telephones.

In 1942, critic and screenwriter Cesare Zavattini called for a new kind of film, equating entertainment films under the Fascists with perpetuation of a false consciousness and a false view of reality. Zavattini urged filmmakers to use the cinema as a medium for documenting and recording authentic social reality, rather than for creating glossy, if entertaining, fantasies. Zavattini urged filmmakers to show the everyday rather than the exceptional, to show things as they are rather than as they seem, to show the relation of the people to their society rather than to their dreams, and to show the common people, workers and peasants, rather than idealized heroes and wealthy, upper-class socialites.

In 1943, critic Umberto Barbaro coined the term "neorealism" to describe this approach to cinema. Luchino Visconti's *Ossessione* (1943), a dramatization of a U.S. crime novel, signaled a decisive break with the "white telephone" tradition. Visconti gave this tale of desire and murder a vivid national setting by capturing the bleakness and poverty of the contemporary Italian countryside. In 1945, Roberto Rossellini's *Open City* received international acclaim and marked the full emergence of the neorealist style. Portraying the efforts of an Italian resistance leader, a Communist guerrilla fighter, and an Italian priest to fight the Nazi authorities occupying Rome, *Open City* vividly illustrates the methods and techniques of neorealist filmmaking.

Neorealist Techniques

Neorealist filmmakers like Rossellini preferred to shoot on location rather than using artificial sets and to employ non- or semiprofessional actors. They also wanted to avoid intricate plots and fancy narratives. They believed that elaborate plotting and intricate storytelling (as in, for example, *Citizen Kane*) imposed an artificial structure on reality. *Open City* honors these techniques. The film was shot on location in Rome shortly after the Nazi occupation and tells a fairly simple story. Critics and viewers worldwide were stunned by the film's realistic evocation of a city ruined by warfare, crushed under the Nazis' authoritarian and cruel grip.

Like those of other neorealists, Rossellini's approach marked an explicit departure from the visual style of U.S. cinema and of Italian "white telephone" films. With their big stars and glossy production values, Hollywood cinema and the "white telephone" films offered escapist views of social reality for a country with an active peasantry struggling to emerge from the wreckage of war. Accordingly, the neorealists rejected the glossy production techniques of studio filmmaking.

The neorealists employed a casual, open style of composition instead of deliberate and complex framings. Characters moved in and out of the frame instead of being artfully arranged within the shot. Camera set-ups tended to be functional and basic. The neorealists avoided expensive equipment like booms and dollies and the extravagant camera movement these make possible. Such equipment and camera movement signal the vast resources of a film studio, and, hence, a kind of glossy manipulation and reworking of the raw social reality that the neorealists sought to document.

Lighting set-ups tended to be very spare and unadorned. The neorealists avoided the elaborate high-contrast and low-key lighting popular in U.S. cinema at this time because these designs required expensive studio resources and because they communicated the kind of glossy production values that neorealism aimed to avoid. As with lighting, composition, and camera movement, the neorealists used editing with restraint. They avoided montage as a way of achieving effects, believing it to be an inherently unrealistic structural device and overly manipulative of the viewer's response.

Using these simple approaches, neorealist directors concentrated on what was in the frame rather than on the properties of the image itself. In other words, unlike directors such as Alfred Hitchcock, Orson Welles, or Michelangelo Antonioni, neorealist directors did not wish to create images so complex and self-conscious that they called attention to themselves as artificial creations. Instead, they wanted to portray authentic subjects rooted in the conditions of postwar Italian society. Cinema techniques were to be unobtrusive and simply used as a means of capturing, rather than falsely transforming, these social realities. Neorealists emphasized the observational, rather than the transformative, capabilities of cinema.

Case Study: *Open City*

The philosophy of filmmaking that motivates these techniques is an ideal, a powerful one. In practice, a given filmmaker was likely to deviate from strict neorealism. Rossellini's *Open City,* for example, illustrates the application of neorealist principles as well as significant departures from them. Rossellini's use of non- and semiprofessional actors, authentic settings, a story rooted in Italian social reality and spare, unadorned camera techniques is consistent with neorealist ideals. To gain a sense of the gap between artistic ideal and the realities of actual filmmaking practice, though, it will be helpful to examine where the film also falls somewhat short of these ideals.

In *Open City* there are four significant stylistic departures from neorealist principles. First is the film's humor, which is clearly contrived as a way of manipulating viewer responses and modulating the emotional tone of the film. The priest, Don Pietro, although he is heroic and maintains a valiant resistance against the Nazis even unto death, is both the butt and source of comic episodes. Early in the film, playing soccer with a group of boys at his parish, he is bopped on the head by the ball. Later in the film, in its funniest scene, he smacks a garrulous old man on the head with a frying pan to shut him up so that Nazi soldiers, passing nearby, will not hear him.

The film needs the humor in these and other episodes because it is, otherwise, a terribly sober depiction of the costs of resistance and the valor of heroic sacrifice. By the end of the movie, most of the main characters have been murdered by the Nazis. The humor offsets the grimness of the picture and provides much-needed respite and relief, but it is, clearly, the result of aesthetic calculation by the filmmaker.

A second stylistic departure from the neorealist ideal is Rossellini's use of explicit religious symbolism. During the climax of the movie, Don Pietro and Manfredi, the Communist leader, are captured by the Nazis. In an attempt to break the priest and extract vital information from him, they torture Manfredi. During this brutal scene, the film draws a series of visual analogies with the suffering of Christ, even positioning Manfredi in a crucifixion pose. Elsewhere in the film, the Nazis murder the fiancée of an Italian resistance fighter. When Don Pietro cradles her body, Rosellini films this as a Pieta composition and stresses its importance by allowing the camera to

Open City (1945)
Don Pietro cradles the body of Pina (Anna Magnani) in an explicit Pieta composition that relates Pina's sacrifice to Christian iconography. The camera lingers on the composition to give it emphasis. Frame enlargement.

This powerfully expressive composition on the brink of Don Pietro's death places the viewer directly in the line of fire and emphasizes the priest's anguish and faith. It is an extraordinary image and is quite calculated in its design and effects. Frame enlargement.

linger on it. The composition's overt symbolism, which evokes Christian iconography, is a long way from any notion of naturalism or realism, strictly conceived.

Thirdly, the film employs a series of expressive, visually manipulative compositions. At the end of the film, as Don Pietro is about to be executed by a firing squad, the camera photographs the priest in the foreground while his Nazi executioners line up behind him in the distance. It is an extremely powerful, tense, and unsettling composition because it places the viewer in close proximity to the anxiety and suffering of the priest and also directly in the line of fire. It is clearly an artfully arranged image. An expressive composition like this is untrue to the neorealist ideal that a filmmaker should make minimal use of cinematic technique in ways that call clear attention to the artistry involved. Nevertheless, it is a very effective composition to use at this point in the film, effective not in terms of neorealist methods but in terms of good filmmaking. Rossellini the filmmaker, rather than Rossellini the neorealist, responded to the emotional needs of the scene by producing a camera set-up that conveyed the power and tragedy of Don Pietro's execution. The emotional response it arouses in viewers is appropriate to the subject matter.

Lastly, the editing in *Open City* tends at times to elicit overt emotional and intellectual associations that result from the filmmaker's manipulation of his materials and that are incompatible with realism, strictly conceived. Perhaps the most striking use of editing to make an editorial point lies in the sound mix employed during the torture sequence late in the film. While Manfredi is being beaten and burned by his interrogators, the Nazi officer in charge grows bored with the spectacle. He leaves the torture room to enter an adjoining chamber where a group of German officers lounges about a piano, partying. The lounge is a haven of culture and comfort. It contains the piano, fine furniture, drink, and expensive food. As the Nazi officer opens

Expressive sound editing overlaps piano music from the Nazi officers' lounge with the screams of their victims in the adjoining torture chamber. The sound dissolve enables Rossellini to make a political point about the relation between Nazi culture and death. Frame enlargement.

the door to cross from the torture chamber to the lounge, a sound mix dissolves the screams of the prisoner into the sound of the piano so that the two overlap.

Rossellini's point, here, is that Nazi culture has its basis in death. The musical performance in one room accompanies torture in another, and sound editing relates the two acoustically by having the sounds of one overlap the sounds of the other. The acoustical relation is intended to point to a political relation. Strictly considered, the technique is artificial, an imposition by Rossellini on the materials of social reality that he sought to observe and document. In practice, however, a filmmaker must balance artistic *ideals* against those artistic *effects* that can be obtained or are needed. Rossellini made the right choice here. The effect is subtle and cinematically sophisticated, and it does not intrude for long on the naturalistic style of the film.

The Legacy of Neorealism
Italian neorealism declined in the late 1950s, in part because Italian political culture became hostile to the populist worker and peasant-based visions of the neorealist filmmakers, but also probably due to the unrelenting seriousness of the pictures themselves. Nevertheless, neorealism remains of lasting historical and stylistic importance because it demonstrated, after years of studio filmmaking focused on wealthy characters and narrative fantasies, how powerful the cinema can be as an instrument for documenting social realities. Furthermore, it demonstrated how artistically effective the results can be when a filmmaker rejects the norms of studio style associated with make-believe narratives, and, through simplification of technique, tries to honestly represent social conditions. In this regard, neorealism goes to one of the medium's root properties; neorealist methods virtually define the medium's impulse toward realism and documentation. The legacy of neorealism, therefore, is powerful and fundamental: It defines

an essential approach to realism in the cinema and exerts a continuing influence on film-makers who want to use the camera to explore social conditions.

The French New Wave

Generational dynamics like those that characterized neorealism were at work in the emergence of the French New Wave in the 1950s. As in Italian neorealism, a novel film style emerged along two fronts—in theory and practice—and characterized a new generation of filmmakers.

Theoretical Foundation

Published in 1948, Alexandre Astruc's essay, "Le Camera-Stylo," signaled an important shift in critical thinking about the cinema. Astruc called for filmmakers to use the cinema as writers and painters have employed their mediums, that is, as a means of personal expression. He claimed that after years of essentially commercial existence the cinema would claim its right to be an art, like painting and the novel, of personal expression. Astruc employed the term **"the camera-pen"** to designate the work of a filmmaker who used the medium in this fashion.

An important center for much new thinking and writing about French cinema was the community of critics working for the film journal *Cahiers du Cinema,* cofounded by Andre Bazin in 1951. These critics included Francois Truffaut, Jean-Luc Godard, and Claude Chabrol, all of whom became, in a few years, important New Wave directors. In 1954, Truffaut published the essay, "A Certain Tendency of the French Cinema," which attacked the studio-bound, overly literary style of filmmaking, heavily dependent on plot and dialogue, which then prevailed. Truffaut claimed that a rededication to the importance of the image and a personal use of cinema was the corrective medicine needed to rejuvenate the artistry of French cinema.

In this essay, Truffaut also proclaimed a new policy of authors on the part of the journal *Cahiers du Cinema.* The journal's criticism would henceforth emphasize the unity of themes and visual structure in the films of auteur directors, those directors who functioned as an author influencing and guiding the design and organization of their films. The auteur director was the film's author, responsible for its artistic vision, its visual and narrative structure. This orientation became known as the **auteur theory** (see Chapter 11).

The French critics claimed that even in the Hollywood system, where the producer typically had the ultimate administrative authority over a film's production, important auteurs prevailed. These auteur directors included Alfred Hitchcock, John Ford, and Howard Hawks. Though they tended to work in established genres such as the detective film and the Western, their movies seemed to have strong recurring themes and signature visual elements. At a time when U.S. culture failed to regard cinema as an art or take its filmmakers seriously, the French critics helped to show Americans about the real artistry in Hollywood cinema.

Technical Features

Given their theoretical assumptions, it was to be expected that when the *Cahiers* critics put down their pens and took up cameras, their films would explore the medium in a highly personal and idiosyncratic way. Indeed, the style of French New Wave films, the first group of which premiered in 1959, was unusual, inventive, and experimental. French New Wave films employed innovative technology and a style that broke the rules of traditional French and Hollywood studio filmmaking. Among these new technologies were lightweight cameras that permitted the stylistic feature of location shooting. New Wave directors also employed very fast film stock that enabled them to shoot on location under lighting conditions that the studio filmmaker of previous decades would have found impractical or undesirable. With more flexible light requirements, they could shoot in a greater variety of physical environments.

Third, New Wave films employed Nagra tape recorders, which were distinguished by their light weight and sophisticated sound recording capabilities. The Nagra recorders enabled directors to employ direct sound, to capture environmental sources of sound on location, as opposed to creating a soundtrack in a recording studio during postproduction. Each of these technical features was extremely important in enabling New Wave films to break with traditional French and Hollywood studio style in which both sound and image were highly processed and refined via shooting under the controlled conditions of indoor sound stages. These features of style and technology distinguish the first group of New Wave films to arrive in theaters in 1959.

Initial Productions

Breathless   Jean-Luc Godard's *Breathless* was an homage to U.S. gangster movies, and particularly Humphrey Bogart, in a tale of a small-time gangster on the run from the police. Godard's edits were often ragged and abrupt and featured the revolutionary technique of jump-cutting. In the **jump cut,** portions of the action are left out, disrupting continuity so that the flow of action seems to break and jump from one moment to the next. In the film's early sequence, where the thief shoots a policeman, Godard uses several jump cuts to fragment continuity. These made a tremendous impression on viewers and critics.

Hiroshima, Mon Amour   Alain Resnais's *Hiroshima, Mon Amour,* the second of the three New Wave films to premiere that year, typified an even looser, more freewheeling approach to cinematic time and space. Exploring the love affair between a French actress and a Japanese architect in postwar Hiroshima, Resnais's film takes the viewer in and out of several different time periods and states of consciousness, with transitions that are abrupt and not always clearly marked. For example, in one of the film's most famous temporal juxtapositions, the French actress looks at her Japanese lover lying in bed. She glances at his hand, and this triggers a memory flashback, visualized on screen by an abrupt, quick image of the hand of her dying German lover in wartime France. The logic of the cut is psychological, as the actress's memories trigger the image, and the editing suggests the interpenetration of past and present, accessed through memory. As the film progresses, tracking shots exploring the architecture of postwar Hiroshima are intercut with similar tracking shots exploring the architecture of wartime France in ways that suggest the simultaneity of past and present, the existence of the past inside the present, within the minds of the characters.

The opening of *Hiroshima, Mon Amour* exemplifies its radical design. The film begins with a series of shots showing two bodies embracing and covered by what seems to be radioactive fallout. On the soundtrack, a man and a woman's voices engage in a poetic dialogue. She asserts the necessity of remembering the horrors of war and

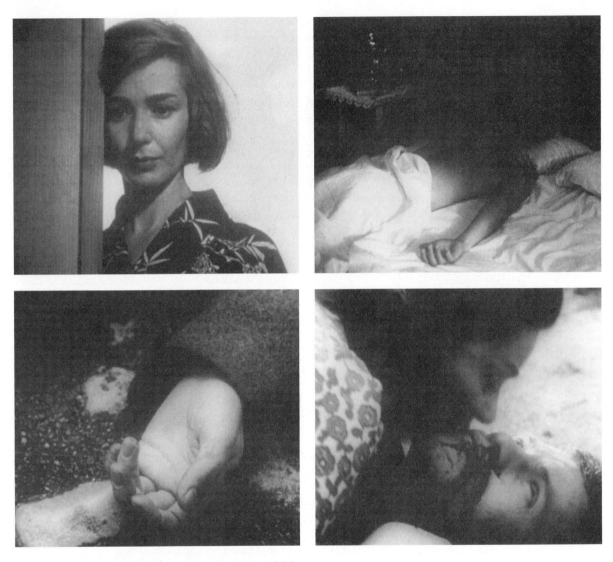

Hiroshima, Mon Amour (1959)

In *Hiroshima, Mon Amour,* time is fragmented and reorganized by memory and desire. Looking at the hand of her sleeping Japanese lover, the French actress recalls the twitching hand of her dying German lover years earlier in World War II. Resnais's film fulfills Astruc's call to use cinema to reveal the workings of human consciousness. Frame enlargements.

he counters by insisting that, in time, even memories of the most horrifying tragedies must fade and vanish.

Throughout this long, poetic dialogue, no fictional characters appear. The bodies embracing, covered with fallout, remain anonymous. The viewer cannot see their

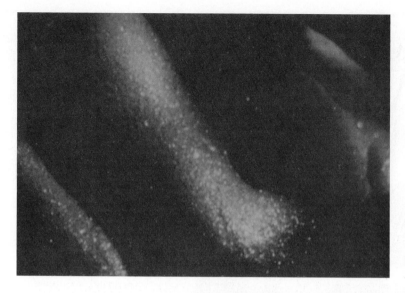

The poetic, metaphoric prologue visualizes the paradox of love in a nuclear age of mass destruction. Nuclear ash covers the entwined arms of embracing lovers. Frame enlargement.

faces, nor correlate them with the voices on the soundtrack. Instead of introducing characters within a narrative, the camera explores, in a series of hypnotic tracking shots, the streets and buildings of Hiroshima, the banks of the river Ota into which victims of the bombing fled following the firestorm, and the faces and gnarled figures of bomb survivors. By withholding the narrative and characters from the opening sequences of the film, director Resnais and screenwriter Marguerite Duras establish an overt, explicitly symbolic and metaphoric tone, enabling the film to articulate a philosophical interest in the effects of time on human memory.

The 400 Blows   Francois Truffaut's *The 400 Blows* was the third film of 1959 to announce the emergence of the New Wave. Truffaut's film is an unsentimental account of an adolescent delinquent named Antoine Doinel (played by Jean-Pierre Leaud), whose adventures Truffaut followed in four additional films over the next twenty years. Giving these films an unusual unity and coherence, Leaud continued to play Doinel, so that the aging of the actor and the character were perfectly correlated. *The 400 Blows* was shot on location in Paris and features very fluid editing, extremely quick transitions from shot to shot and scene to scene, and a lyrical energy and delight in location filming that distinguished the film from the set-bound studio productions Truffaut had criticized in his 1954 essay.

Instead of offering the clean narrative closure typical of French and Hollywood studio films, Truffaut's film concludes with a deliberately ambiguous ending. Eluding the authorities one last time, Antoine Doinel runs down to the beach and looks uneasily about. The film ends with a freeze frame of his anxious face, deliberately refusing a concluding statement about the character's fate and inviting the viewer to contemplate the ambiguities and uncertainties of life.

Later Careers of Truffaut, Godard, and Resnais   Each of these New Wave directors established long and prolific careers. Truffaut directed a wide range of films, including

The 400 Blows (1959)
Jean-Pierre Leaud as Antoine
Doinel in Truffaut's *The 400
Blows,* the first of several films
tracing the life of Doinel.

other New Wave classics like *Shoot the Piano Player* (1960) and *Jules and Jim* (1961) before embarking on a pair of Hitchcock-style thrillers in *The Bride Wore Black* (1967) and *Mississippi Mermaid* (1969). Truffaut continued his Antoine Doinel series with a contribution to the anthology film *Love at Twenty* (1962) and with *Stolen Kisses* (1968), *Bed and Board* (1970), and *Love on the Run* (1979). His *The Wild Child* (1969) and *The Story of Adele H.* (1975) are exquisitely mounted period films, and *Day for Night* (1973), one of his most popular pictures, is a loving valentine to the movie industry, a film about the making of a film by a movie director played by Francois Truffaut. His career and life were cut short by an untimely death from cancer in 1984.

Jean-Luc Godard became the most important and cinematically influential director of the New Wave. Godard's films, following *Breathless,* were ever more radical attempts to break down the normative conventions and styles of the commercial cinema. *Weekend* (1967), examined in previous chapters, was Godard's violent rejection of consumer society and his own acknowledged end to narrative filmmaking. *Le Gai Savoir* (1969) was an ambiguous visual essay on the effects of language, film, comic strips, and television on human consciousness and society. The film has no story. Instead, it focuses on two characters who meet in a television studio at night to reflect on images and language.

At the end of the 1960s, Godard joined a collective filmmaking group called Dziga Vertov and produced such pictures as *British Sounds* (1969), *Wind from the East* (1969), and *Tout va Bien* (1972) in which he explored the connections between images, cinema, and ideology in a politically forceful manner. As Godard's style became more radical, however, and his interest in a politically rigorous interrogation of the na-

Sauve Qui Peut LaVie (1980)
A signature Godard composition: a character posed before a declamatory background in *Sauve Qui Peut LaVie*. Godard uses such images as self-reflexive moments. Image and text contrast and contend with one another. The effect is often ironic and playful—Cain and Abel, cinema and video. The implied relationship is counterintuitive. If anything, video, and the alternate nontheatrical delivery systems of which it is part, will kill cinema (theatrical film).

ture of cinema became more pronounced, his films, not surprisingly, became more inward and withdrawn and their ideal audience smaller.

In the mid-1970s, Godard experimented with film/videotape combinations in such works as *Numero Deux* (1975) before returning to theatrical filmmaking with *Sauve Qui Peut* (1980) and other features, including the controversial *Hail Mary* (1984), a contemporary retelling of the Immaculate Conception that offended many Catholics, and a typically eccentric adaptation of *King Lear* (1986). Godard remains active, and if he is today no longer as prominent a filmmaker as he once was, his revolutionary films of the 1960s and 1970s are very important works and assure his place in cinema history.

In subsequent films, Alan Resnais continued to explore the effects of memory and time on human consciousness. *Last Year at Marienbad* (1961), scripted by Alain Robbe-Grillet, assaulted narrative with a story deliberately constructed like a labyrinth, mystifying the viewer as to time structure and narrative tense. In the film, a man tries to persuade a woman that they have met the year before at a posh resort. She denies this, and for the remainder of the film, they meet and remeet and have the same conversation in different settings and implied time frames. Clear, temporal referents and narrative causality break down in *Last Year at Marienbad*.

Last Year at Marienbad (1961)
Resnais aimed for a total ambiguity of time and setting and for the destruction of narrative in *Last Year at Marienbad*. The mysterious hotel is the real star of the film. The seductive tracking shots down the hotel corridors may have influenced Stanley Kubrick's camerawork in *The Shining* (1980). Frame enlargement.

In *The War Is Over* (1966) Resnais applied his interest in time and the effects of memory to a political framework, examining the past and present life of a middle-aged Spanish revolutionary whose ideals are called into question by a younger group of Parisian Leftists. *Providence* (1977) put the viewer inside the mind of a dying British novelist and studied the way memory and desire can reconfigure the realities of time and place. Resnais has remained active as a filmmaker, and in more recent films—*Melo* (1986) and *Smoking/No Smoking* (1993)—he continues to explore his interests in unconventional approaches to narrative.

Other New Wave Filmmakers

Other important French New Wave directors include Claude Chabrol, whose long career is virtually a variation on the works of Hitchcock. Chabrol's films include *Les Biches* (1968), *The Butcher* (1979), *Just Before Nightfall* (1971), and *Masks* (1987). Also associated with the New Wave are Louis Malle (*Murmur of the Heart*, 1971), Eric Rohmer (whose series of "moral tales" includes *My Night at Maud's,* 1967), Jacques Rivette (whose films explore the temporal limits of cinematic narratives, e.g., *Out One Specter* [1972] is a 4.5 hour condensation of a 13-hour original), and Agnes Varda (whose *Cleo from Five to Seven* [1962], *One Sings the Other Doesn't* [1977], and *Vagabond* [1985] explore, from a feminist perspective, the psychological and emotional landscape of women's lives in contemporary society).

Significance of the French New Wave

The French New Wave illustrates a fundamental dynamic in the history of film style, namely, a process of generational revolt, wherein a collective of young directors attempts to throw off the inherited styles and forms of the dominant cinema that confront them as they enter the industry. The results of their experiments rejuvenate the traditional industry that, in time, tends to absorb their work. This dynamic characterized Italian neorealism and appeared again in connection with the New German Cinema.

The remarkable success of New Wave visual and narrative experiments can be measured, in part, by their profound influence on U.S. cinema. In 1967, Arthur Penn's *Bonnie and Clyde* was a major commercial hit. Penn's freewheeling approach to direction and storytelling, his novel mixture of comedy and tragedy, slapstick and graphic violence, and the rapid montage editing and abrupt transitions supplied by editor Dede Allen were inspired by the rule-breaking of the French New Wave, which blended genres, moods, and styles in an often irreverent fashion and demonstrated that a more flexible and fluid film style could be enormously popular. Following *Bonnie and Clyde,* *Easy Rider* (1969) also showed New Wave influence, as did many U.S. films of the late sixties and early seventies, so different in their aggressively offbeat styles than mainstream studio films had been. The language of French New Wave filmmaking is now so pervasive a feature of modern film style as to be an almost invisible influence.

New German Cinema

During the 1960s a group of young filmmakers impatient with the inherited forms of the older, established German cinema pioneered a New German Cinema. As with Italian neorealism and the French New Wave, they announced their efforts by issuing manifestoes and proclamations that described the goals of the new approach.

Bonnie and Clyde (Warner Bros., 1967); **Easy Rider** (Columbia Pictures, 1969)
Influenced by the French New Wave cinema, *Bonnie and Clyde* and *Easy Rider* broke prevailing film styles in the American cinema with their freer, experimental approach to image design. Frame enlargements.

In 1962 at the Oberhausen Film Festival, twenty-six young directors signed a manifesto declaring a break with existing film traditions and the need to redefine German cinema. Among the signers of the Oberhausen manifesto were Volker Schlondorff (*Young Torless* [1966], *The Tin Drum* [1979] and, for U.S. television, *Death of a Salesman* [1985]), who became a major figure in the New German Cinema, and Alexander Kluge, whose *Yesterday Girl* (1966) established a certain continuity with the French New Wave by using jump cuts, a handheld camera, and printed title cards (like a Godard film), in telling a New Wave-style story of a young woman who drifts into a life of petty crime.

Other important directors associated with the emergence of the New German Cinema in the 1960s were Jean-Marie Straub and Daniele Huillet, whose work was among the most radical experiments at attenuating the emotional effects of narrative, and, indeed, of cinema itself. *Not Reconciled* (1965) and *The Diary of Anna Magdalena Bach* (1968) feature intentionally flat, unemotional acting, the use of direct sound, an unclear temporal structure, and, in the latter film, very long concert performances, with no audience shown, interspersed with brief narrative scenes.

Subsequently, Volker Schlondorff, with his wife Margarethe von Trotta, directed *The Lost Honor of Katherina Blum* (1975), which, accompanied by von Trotta's own *The Second Awakening of Christa Klages* (1977), examined women allied with political extremists in Germany's 1970s climate of terrorism and increasing state authoritarianism. The work of Agnes Varda in the French New Wave and von Trotta in the New German Cinema highlight the important contribution of women filmmakers in the contemporary international cinema. Varda's and von Trotta's feminist perspectives help shape an alternative social and ideological voice within their films, sensitive to the emotional, social, and political problems and place of women in contemporary society.

In the early 1970s, filmmaking in Germany was state-supported. Government television helped fund theatrical films, which were then shown on public television once their theatrical run had ended. This arrangement provided a major stimulus for production and for the emergence of auteur filmmakers because the government often sought to promote the work of directors whose work had a distinctive artistic style.

Fassbinder and the Politics of Melodrama

Among such filmmakers were Rainer Werner Fassbinder, one of the most prolific of modern directors. Fassbinder directed a series of politically charged **melodramas** inspired by the work of Hollywood director Douglas Sirk in the 1950s. Sirk's films included *Magnificent Obsession* (1954), *All That Heaven Allows* (1955), and *Written on the Wind* (1957), stylish melodramas about characters struggling with their desires and the verdicts that society cast on their desire. Fassbinder's *The Bitter Tears of Petra von Kant* (1972), *Fear Eats the Soul* (1973), and *Fox and His Friends* (1974) examined how power dynamics in personal relationships embody types of oppression found at large in society between established and stigmatized groups. *Fear Eats the Soul,* for example, portrayed the social prejudice an elderly widow incurs when she falls in love with a young Arab and marries him. This prejudice eventually infects their relationship. The Sirk influence was especially strong on *Fear Eats the Soul*, which was essentially a remake of *All That Heaven Allows.*

Fassbinder considered melodrama to be an effective vehicle for examining the political aspects of personal relationships because, in melodrama, a character's emotions, gestures, and behavior are so oversized and exaggerated that an intelligent director might use this material in a self-conscious way, making it a commentary on society, as Fassbinder felt Douglas Sirk had done in his Hollywood films. Fassbinder used melodrama's exaggerated emotional struggles and clear moral distinctions between hero and villain to describe how society, with its power hierarchies, influences

Fox and His Friends (1974) Fassbinder (left) performing in his *Fox and His Friends.* During his relatively brief career, Fassbinder worked at a fiery pace to complete an amazing 41 films in 17 years.

Aguirre, the Wrath of God (1972)
Klaus Kinski's Spanish explorer in *Aguirre, the Wrath of God* is one of many memorable madmen and lunatics who populate Herzog's films.

even the private sphere of personal life. In using Sirk's work as a template for his own, Fassbinder showed the blend of affection for Hollywood, and the critical distance from it, that was a distinctive feature of the French New Wave.

Herzog and Mystical Cinema

In contrast to Fassbinder's relentless interrogation of the ways that people will internalize the social power structure and live it out in their personal lives, director Werner Herzog tended to avoid depictions of social and political issues. Instead, his work celebrates mystical and antirational states of mind and modes of existence. In films like *Even Dwarfs Started Small* (1970), *Aguirre, Wrath of God* (1972), *The Great Ecstasy of Sculptor Steiner* (1974), *Every Man for Himself and God Against All* (1975), and *Heart of Glass* (1976), the characters are grotesques, supermen, mystics, or oddities.

Herzog's images aim not for social clarity, but rather for the evocation of mystery and the unknowable. The opening of *Heart of Glass,* for example, includes a long mystical prologue of clouds, mountains, and waterfalls accompanied by a poetic recitation on the dissolution and rebirth of the earth. The narrative that follows deals with a community that loses the secret for creating ruby-colored glass, a secret on which its social identity depends, and begins to disintegrate. The story is diffuse, scattered, and uses a cast of actors who were hypnotized. These hypnotic trances give the performances a weird and otherworldly tone that is well-suited to the film's mythological parable about dissolution and rebirth.

Like earlier New Wave filmmakers in Italy and France, Herzog had a historical sense of the cinematic traditions that influenced his work. He considered the expressionist films of the 1920s to be especially important, not just for his own work but for all of cinema history. He tackled this influence head-on by remaking one of the

Heart of Glass (1976)
Herzog hypnotized his actors in *Heart of Glass* to create some of the oddest performances in cinema. It was part of his cinematic pursuit of the poetic and mystical attributes of human life.

classic expressionist films, F. W. Murnau's *Nosferatu* (1922). Herzog's *Nosferatu* (1979) is lovingly rendered and reverent, with its horrific, rat-faced vampire a memorable evocation of Murnau's spooky original.

Wenders and Antinarrative Filmmaking

Fassbinder and Herzog represent the opposing poles of social criticism and mystical antirationalism in the New German Cinema. Between their extremes is the work of director Wim Wenders, whose movies focusing on wandering, drifting, alienated characters create a kind of collective antinarrative. Convinced that narratives construct misleading

Nosferatu (1979)
Herzog's regard for German expressionism led him to remake one of its classic films, F. W. Murnau's *Nosferatu* (1922), a version of the Dracula story. The remake is a loving and reverent homage to the art of the silent cinema and yet another evocation in Herzog's cinema of mystical landscapes. Frame enlargement.

versions of reality by imposing an artificial structure on the essentially disorganized nature of daily life, Wenders attenuates the narratives in his films with sustained attention on objects, silence, and states of dissociated consciousness.

The Goalie's Anxiety at the Penalty Kick (1971) focuses on the psychological disintegration of a soccer goalie, suspended from his job, who subsequently murders a woman and then drifts in a state of extreme psychological disengagement. The dissociation of the character is structurally described by a narrative that is loose, disconnected, and without apparent direction. By breaking down the narrative links between events, Wenders creates an antinarrative, a film composed of events that fail to cohere into a causally determined storyline. Similar in style, *Alice in the Cities* (1973), *The Wrong Move* (1974), and *Kings of the Road* (1976) constitute Wenders's "road trilogy" about drifting characters.

Wenders's other work includes a tribute to legendary U.S. director Nicholas Ray, *Lighting over Water* (1980), an attempt to make a U.S. studio film under producer Francis Ford Coppola, *Hammett* (1982), and *The State of Things* (1982), a bitter and sardonic reflection on his disappointing experience with Coppola. Wenders scored a major critical and box-office success with *Wings of Desire* (1987), about a melancholy angel (Bruno Ganz) drifting and watching over the city of Berlin who becomes fascinated by human beings. Longing to feel what they feel, he enters their world and falls in love with a young trapeze artist. The film inspired the Hollywood remake, *City of Angels* (1998). Unlike Fassbinder or Herzog, in some of his later work—*Until the End of the World* (1991), *The End of Violence* (1997)—Wenders shifted to the international filmmaking arena, using a Euro-American cast and crew. Cast members included Andie MacDowell, John Malkovich, and William Hurt, from the U.S. cinema, Fanny Ardant, a regular in Francois Truffaut films, and Marcello Mastroianni, a major Italian star and frequent Fellini collaborator. In this respect, he transcended his national origins as a practitioner of the New German Cinema to become an international auteur.

The Goalie's Anxiety at the Penalty Kick (1971) Wenders relentlessly focused on the alienation and mental breakdown of an unemployed goalie. For Wenders, telling a story was less important here than exploring a drifting, aimless, despairing state of mind. The film was one of Wenders's many antinarrative experiments.

Hong Kong Cinema

A New Wave amid Cultural Peril   The most recent instance of New Wave film-making emerging within a national cinema is the example of Hong Kong in the 1980s and 1990s. Hong Kong's film industry has long been a vibrant and prolific one, sustained by an avid moviegoing public. In terms of output, it is one of the world leaders in annual film production and exports, and its most powerful studios commanded regional markets along the Pacific Rim.

In the 1960s and 1970s, the Shaw Brothers Studio operated as a vertically integrated major, owning production facilities and theater circuits in Hong Kong, Singapore, and Malaysia and dominating these markets as well as those in Taiwan and Thailand. Furthermore, in the 1970s Hong Kong cinema attained significant overseas popularity, and found an international star in Bruce Lee, who starred in three martial arts movies made for the independent studio Golden Harvest. With *The Big Boss* (1971), *The Chinese Connection* (1972), and *The Way of the Dragon* (1972), Lee was poised for a huge career that was cut short by his sudden death in 1973.

Prior to the 1980s, Hong Kong movies were tied to more traditional forms of costume pictures, swordplay films, martial arts movies, musicals, and comedies. The work of the new filmmakers who emerged in the eighties—John Woo, Tsui Hark, Ringo Lam, and others—was aggressively experimental in its fusion of existing forms and traditions. Unlike the rigor and restraint of the other New Wave cinemas covered in this chapter, the Hong Kong movies are sensuous and sense-assaulting. Rapid-fire editing, swooping camera moves, ferocious violence, and an intoxicating fusion of reality and magic characterized the "anything goes" mode of contemporary Hong Kong cinema.

John Woo   The best-known figure, internationally, of the Hong Kong New Wave is unquestionably John Woo. His ultraviolent urban crime films, starring Chow Yun-fat—

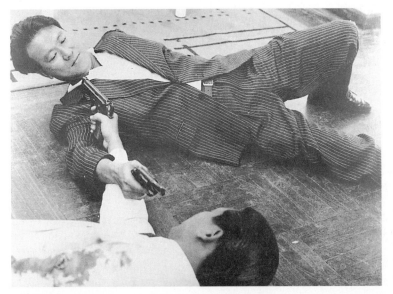

The Killer (1989)
The trademark John Woo face-off—intimate adversaries, guns to the head, locked into a prolonged showdown that triggers an apocalypse.

A Better Tomorrow (1986), *A Better Tomorrow II* (1987), *The Killer* (1989), *Bullet in the Head* (1990), and *Hard Boiled* (1992)—are a stylish fusion of Sam Peckinpah-style gun battles with choreography derived from martial arts and swordplay films. Woo's characters fly through the air, pirouette, turn somersaults, and perform other acrobatic moves, with guns blazing. Woo is fascinated by the choreographic possibilities inherent in this kind of action filmmaking, which leaves realism far behind, but he anchors the choreography with stories about strongly felt issues of honor, friendship, and loyalty and that feature a recurring motif of male antagonists bonding in a lethal mixture of regard and enmity.

Woo is an absolute master of action choreography, achieved with montage editing and multicamera filming, and the dizzying action ballets that he orchestrates are among the best work of this kind that cinema has produced. The abundant violence in his films functions as hyperkinetic spectacle, and its duration and ferocity can be startling even for today's jaded moviegoers. This violence reaches apocalyptic proportions in *Hard Boiled,* which portrays Hong Kong as a city out of control, impossible to rule, with dark forces of destruction poised to erupt and consume all. This sense of apocalypse was tied, as Woo has noted, to the country's reunification with China, which would occur a mere five years after the release of *Hard Boiled.*

In this regard, the violence in Woo's films has a metaphoric dimension, as the embodiment of a cultural sense of doom. But its masterful choreography helped make him a cult figure, as his stylish blood operas gained a strong international following. As many overseas directors had done before him, Woo used this fame as a means of entry to the Hollywood cinema. *Hard Boiled* was his last Hong Kong film. Following its production, he launched a Hollywood career that got off to a shaky start with *Hard Target* (1993) before finding considerable success with *Face/Off* (1997).

The bloody, urban crime films that Woo popularized were taken up by other filmmakers, including Ringo Lam (*City on Fire,* 1987; *Prison on Fire 1* and *2,* 1987, 1991; and *School on Fire,* 1988). In *City on Fire,* Chow Yun-fat plays a police informer who infiltrates a gang of jewel thieves but comes to feel conflicting loyalties toward the gang that befriends him and his police employers. The film ends in a bloody shootout and standoff that served as a model for Quentin Tarantino's *Reservoir Dogs* (1992). Lam's editing is not as flashy or aggressive as Woo's, but he rejuvenated the gangster and crime film with equal enthusiasm.

Tsui Hark   Other directors, most notably Tsui Hark, were embracing the martial arts, costume, and ghost story traditions, blending genres with abandon and bringing an ultra-fast pace, flamboyant camera moves, and aggressive editing to the material. Tsui Hark is one of the wittiest, most stylish and inventive producer–directors working in contemporary cinema. His *Once upon a Time in China* (1990)—its name an homage to Italian director Sergio Leone—inspired a long-running film series about folk hero and kung fu master Wong Fei-hung.

Tsui's *Zu: Warriors from the Magic Mountain* (1981) invigorated the swordplay film with generous helpings of fantasy special effects that show why he is sometimes called Hong Kong's Steven Spielberg. Set in 1913 China, *Peking Opera Blues* (1987) is a rollicking, high-spirited adventure yarn about three women—a revolutionary, a servant, and an aspiring Peking Opera performer—who become entangled in political

Peking Opera Blues (1987)
Political guerrillas disguise
themselves as Peking Opera
performers and elude the
authorities with spectacular
effect in Tsui Hark's outlandish,
rollicking adventure. Frame
enlargement.

intrigue. Tsui deftly mixes comedy, drama, acrobatics, breathtaking stunts, hairbreadth escapes, pageantry, and martial arts in a nonstop narrative marked with exuberance and unceasing invention. As does John Woo, Tsui shoots with multiple camera set-ups that enable him to cover the action from many angles and then edits this material so that each scene becomes a kaleidoscope of quickly changing compositions. Yet he never loses control of the material or his command of the narrative.

Tsui produced Ching Sui-Tung's *Chinese Ghost Story* (1987), which boasts a similarly exuberant, inventive syle. (Like many popular films, this one would run to several installments, all produced by Tsui.) A bill collector, Ning, falls in love with a beautiful ghost who is enslaved by an evil tree demon, and, aided by a maxim-spouting Taoist swordsman, Ning battles the demon to save his love so that she may be reincarnated. Beautifully shot, and edited at a dizzying pace, the film is, by turns, spooky, funny, touching, sad, and always flamboyant in its visual design and emotional appeal. In this regard, *Chinese Ghost Story* embodies the outstanding features of the New Wave Hong Kong cinema—filmmaking carried along by sheer enthusiasm for the medium and an embrace of popular, go-for-broke storytelling, features that demonstrate the symbiotic bond with the moviegoing public that made the national cinema in this period so vital.

Chinese Ghost Story (1987)
The ghostly Sian (Joey Wang)
awaits her human lover, who will
battle a thousand-year-old evil in
order to free her. This popular
blend of romance, spook story,
and martial arts inspired several
sequels and epitomizes the
enthusiastic, go-for-broke style
of the Hong Kong New Wave.
Frame enlargement.

By contrast, though, with the ostentatious and ornate styling of many Hong Kong directors, Ann Hui's *Boat People* (1982), about the plight of displaced Vietnamese, *Song of the Exile* (1990), about a mother–daughter relationship, and *Summer Snow* (1995), about an old man with Alzheimer's disease, are more quiet and nuanced works about the cultural issues of Hong Kong's self-identity and relations with mainland China.

China and the Ticking Bomb of 1997 These issues have been fundamental for Hong Kong's New Wave. Fueling this explosion of filmmaking energy and dizzying array of styles were intense cultural anxieties over the fate of the country. Hong Kong had been a British colony since the end of World War II, but Britain and China began a rapprochement, and in 1984, Britain agreed to hand over control of Hong Kong to China in 1997. Hong Kong's cultural anxieties about domination by China's authoritarian government were compounded by the Tiananmen Square massacre in 1989.

John Woo and other New Wave filmmakers stated that the approach of 1997 was felt like a ticking bomb, and the New Wave's content and style were understood metaphorically as embodiments of this tense cultural context. A recurring image in Woo's films is the standoff between hero and villain, with each holding a gun to the other's head. Like Woo's out-of-control characters, Hong Kong felt like a country with a gun to its head. Like the title of Ringo Lam's film and a recent book on the subject, it was a city on fire. These anxieties unquestionably influenced the often apocalyptic style of the films by Woo and Ringo Lam.

But beyond the volatile cultural and political atmosphere that helped fuel the New Wave, the significance of Hong Kong film in this period lies in the exuberance of its approach to popular storytelling and in its resistance to the cultural inroads that Hollywood imports were making throughout world markets. Its freshness and daring, anything-goes attitude were signs of a healthy cinema in touch with a movie-loving public, in contrast to the stale and derivative formulas characterizing many costly and overproduced Hollywood films. Moreover, the top box-office films in Hong Kong tended to be the domestic, homegrown productions, not Hollywood blockbusters. This reversal of the pattern that typically prevails in overseas markets was the sign of an energetic national cinema responsive to its indigenous audience and unique cultural challenges. Amid the globalization of so much contemporary film culture, this was a significant and impressive counterexample.

◻ IMPORTANCE OF THE INTERNATIONAL CINEMA

The New Wave phenomenon illustrates a continuing relationship between the norms of Hollywood cinema and the emergence of alternative national film movements. The work of neorealists, Truffaut, Godard, John Woo, and Tsui Hark, grows out of indigenous cultural and artistic traditions while also being aware of the norms of Hollywood filmmaking and the icons of the U.S. cinema. The global presence of Hollywood film elicits a series of explicitly formulated cinematic alternatives that chart new stylistic approaches while Hollywood, in turn, seeks to absorb the alternatives. John Woo, Tsui Hark, Chow Yun-fat, and martial arts star Jackie Chan have all tried to turn their Hong Kong fame into a successful Hollywood career, with Woo and Chan having had the greatest success.

This short survey of some key international filmmakers and movements can only begin to suggest the abundance of alternative styles and forms of narrative filmmaking. Third World political filmmaking, for example, in Cuba, Latin America, Africa, and China offers a vibrant embrace of revolution, a worldview very different from that of Hollywood film. East European films (produced before the breakup of the Soviet Union), working through metaphor and social allegory, offer a sustained critique of Soviet authoritarianism. The cinema thrives in India, the Middle East, Asia, and the Pacific rim. Films here are uniquely influenced by social norms and cultural frameworks that are very different from those that inform Hollywood production.

The availability of international films at local video stores and on cable television enables viewers to become citizens of world cinema and connoisseurs of the range of styles the medium offers. This chapter has sketched only a portion of this range. Many other filmmakers and styles await exploration, offering viewers an exciting and unpredictable social, cultural, and visual journey. International film can be a window onto the world, enlarging one's social horizon and establishing a context in which the Hollywood cinema becomes simply one reference point among many.

SUMMARY

Cinema exists within an international framework, the product of multiple cultures and nationalities. In this international framework, Hollywood filmmaking has been a global and dominant influence. The corporate structure of the U.S. industry, and its multinational reach, accentuates the impact of contemporary Hollywood blockbusters. While this results in some erosion of variety and diversity in the international cinema, as audiences clamor to see more films like the popular Hollywood blockbusters, one should not overstate or overemphasize this development.

Of greater importance is the flourishing of diverse artistic styles throughout film history. While Hollywood exports a certain kind of film to cinemas throughout the world, many filmmakers in other countries explore alternatives to the norms and style of Hollywood film. Cinema has an enormous creative potential for redefining methods of storytelling and image design. Periodically these coalesce around a national movement to revise film style or create new waves of film production.

As a part of this process, Hollywood both inspires and absorbs foreign influences. In Germany, Fassbinder pays homage to the works of his beloved Hollywood director, Douglas Sirk. Jean-Luc Godard works free of the Hollywood influence apparent in early works like *Breathless* to reach a point of extreme stylistic reduction and near-total rejection of narrative in films like *Le Gai Savoir*.

Hollywood draws foreign directors to its studios. Peter Weir, George Miller, and Paul Verhoeven all make highly successful and profitable films within the Hollywood industry, yet their work, like the work of other generations of émigré filmmakers in Hollywood, has subtly changed the style of U.S. filmmaking.

Film is a medium of enormous creative potential, and the huge range of film styles prevailing in the international cinema testifies to this potential. A sophisticated understanding of cinema requires an understanding of the importance of Hollywood filmmaking as well as knowledge of the work of filmmakers who are not a part of the

Hollywood model. This work should include the alternative narrative and image styles of Antonioni, Wenders, Resnais, and Godard, the psychological and spiritual focus of Bergman, the pageantry and spectacle of Fellini, the thrilling genre work of Kurosawa, the playful subversiveness of Buñuel, and the dedicated social visions of the neorealist filmmakers.

Virtually every reader of this textbook is an accomplished master at watching Hollywood films. To broaden that mastery by exploring alternative cinema styles, auteurs, and movements is to deepen the pleasure and excitement that movies can offer.

SUGGESTED READINGS

Peter Bondanella, *The Cinema of Federico Fellini* (Princeton, NJ: Princeton University Press, 1992).

Luis Buñuel, *My Last Sigh,* trans. Abigail Israel (New York: Knopf, 1983).

Timothy Corrigan, *New German Film,* rev. ed., (Bloomington: Indiana University Press, 1994).

Robert Phillip Kolker, *The Altering Eye: Contemporary International Cinema* (New York: Oxford University Press, 1983).

Paisley Livingston, *Ingmar Bergman and the Rituals of Art* (Ithaca, NY: Cornell University Press, 1982).

James Monaco, *The New Wave: Truffaut, Godard, Chabrol, Rohmer, Rivette* (New York: Oxford University Press, 1976).

Stephen Prince, *The Warrior's Camera: The Cinema of Akira Kurosawa* (Princeton, NJ: Princeton University Press, 1999).

Sam Rohdie, *Antonioni* (London: BFI, 1990).

Judy Stone, *Eye on the World: Conversations with International Filmmakers* (Los Angeles, CA: Silman-James Press, 1997).

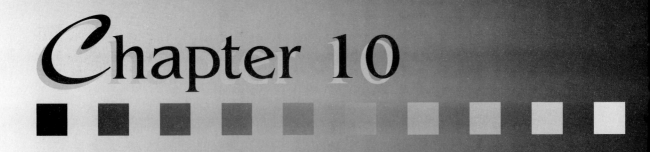

Chapter 10

Film Criticism
and Interpretation

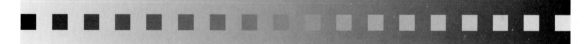

Chapter Objectives

After reading this chapter, you should be able to:

- explain what criticism is and what purposes it serves
- describe how communication signs are multidimensional
- explain the task of the critic and how criticism functions as rhetoric
- define and distinguish three basic modes of film criticism
- describe three stages in the creation of criticism
- explain the deductive method of criticism

- distinguish explicit or first-order meanings from latent or second-order meanings
- recognize critical interpretation as a strategic reorganization of a film's structure and meaning
- list and define three types of attributional errors
- learn how to develop a framework of interpretation
- learn how to create and practice film criticism

Key Terms and Concepts

criticism
polyvalence
sign
rhetoric
newspaper/television
 reviewing

general-interest journal-
 based criticism
scholarly criticism
identification
description
interpretation

deduction
latent meaning
framework of
 interpretation
attributional errors

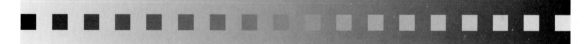

Previous chapters explored the ways that filmmakers create images and tell stories in the U.S. and international cinema. Once a film is completed, when the filmmaker's work is finished, critics and viewers take over, interpreting what they see and debating its meaning and merits. What is film criticism, and what is film theory? How are the two related? What purposes do they serve, and what pleasures do they offer? This chapter explores the nature of film criticism, and the next chapter examines film theory.

☐ WHY CRITICISM EXISTS

Whether carried out by casual viewers or by professional critics who are paid for their services, criticism and interpretation are necessary and inevitable. **Criticism** is the attempt to discover and interpret the meanings and intentions of the film or filmmaker that extend beyond a film's surface features. Like all forms of expresssed communication, these meanings are complex and multidimensional.

Rambo: First Blood Part II (1985) was the second of three films in which Sylvester Stallone played Vietnam warrior John Rambo. In the film, Rambo returns to Vietnam many years after the war to search for Americans missing in action who may be held in captivity. Prevailing against overwhelming odds, Rambo manages to rescue several and bring them home.

At the end of the film, exhausted by his heroic exploits and angry at the duplicity of U.S. government bureaucrats, Rambo delivers a speech in which he identifies himself as a spokesperson for all Vietnam veterans and announces that what they really want is simply for their country to love and honor them. "I want what they want and what every other guy who came over here and spilled his guts and gave everything he had wants—for our country to love us as much as we love it."

Rambo was a hit at the box office, and its extraordinary popularity would seem to indicate that the moviegoing audience responded positively to Rambo's heroics and to his plea at the end of the film that the United States accept its Vietnam veterans and acknowledge their honor. Many veterans, however, objected to the film and to Rambo's speech. Some were offended that Stallone tried to identify himself with them and wrap himself in their cause. They pointed out that Stallone never served in Vietnam, and they felt that their cause was poorly represented by a bloodthirsty and cartoonish character like Rambo.

These differing responses to the film illustrate the principle of **polyvalence,** the multidimensionality of its **signs** and their meanings. A popular audience seeking action

Rambo: First Blood Part II
(Tri-Star Pictures, 1983)
Does Sylvester Stallone's warrior, John Rambo, express old-fashioned American patriotism, or is the character a calculated attempt to cash in on Cold War politics? Film criticism provides the answers to this kind of question.

and spectacle enthusiastically embraced *Rambo;* these viewers found its action and spectacle to be acceptable representations of the Vietnam war. By contrast, many Vietnam veterans felt that the film and the character offered a grossly distorted portrait of the war. With regard to Rambo's speech at the end, is it a noble plea to honor Vietnam veterans or a cynical exercise in political opportunism calculated in terms of its likely box-office effect? It is the job of criticism and interpretation to answer such questions. Because film images and narratives are extraordinarily complex—are polyvalent—debates about their meaning are inevitable. Herein lies the function of criticism and interpretation: It helps to clarify these meanings and to resolve their ambiguity.

◻ THE TASK OF THE CRITIC

Film criticism does not mean that one criticizes a movie in the sense of pointing up its flaws or failed ambitions. Criticism is not a negative act. The critic tries to come to terms with the multidimensional meanings of a given film. The critic (1) teases out implicit or subtle meanings, (2) clarifies seemingly contradictory messages or values in a given film, and (3) creates a novel way of interpreting or understanding a film. This last function is the central act of criticism: the creation of a new interpretation that extends or deepens a viewer's appreciation of a film.

Criticism as Rhetoric

Film criticism is a form of rhetoric. **Rhetoric** is the skillful use of language with the aim of persuasion; the critic seeks to persuade the reader that a given interpretation of a film is right and true. There are two sources of pleasure in good criticism. The first derives from reexperiencing the film through the critic's descriptions and interpretations; the second derives from an engagement with the critic's use of language. Many people read criticism, not because they necessarily agree with the critic, but because they like the way that a particular critic writes or talks about the movies.

Because criticism is a rhetorical act, the critic needs to know how to write well, how to construct an argument, and how to select evidence and employ it carefully so as to persuade readers that the proffered interpretation is correct. Though it is primarily an exercise in rhetoric, however, criticism also has an empirical dimension because the critic must reference ideas against the evidence of the film. To be persuasive, interpretations should be grounded in a careful description and selection of evidence from the film under discussion. Misidentification or explicit attributional errors weaken the critic's argument and will lessen a reader's support for the interpretation that is being constructed.

Criticism in the Era of Blockbusters

Before we discuss the different types of criticism, it's worth pointing out that film criticism today exists in a state of crisis, undermined by the marketing practices of the film industry. The ideal goal of criticism is to lead the viewer to a deeper understanding of films and filmmakers. Until recently, influential critics had an opportunity to champion films and directors, to help build a consensus of opinion about their work, and bring viewers to it. In the 1940s, for example, James Agee, critic for *The Nation,* championed the later, unpopular films of Charles Chaplin (films such as *Monsieur Verdoux* [1947]) and helped to make a case for their merits. In the 1970s, *New Yorker* critic Pauline Kael used her influence to champion the unconventional films of directors Robert Altman and Sam Peckinpah.

By arguing that cinema was *important* artistically and culturally, Agee and Kael helped to create a film culture linking critics, viewers, and movies. Today it is very difficult for a critic to work this way. In previous decades, many films stayed in release for longer periods of time, giving critics time to champion their cause.

Today, there is so much product in distribution that individual films come and go very quickly, giving thoughtful critics little time to react and no time to create a culture with readers about film. Moreover, marketing pressure from the industry is enormous, and it tends to undermine the integrity of criticism by turning it into a form of advertising and promotion. The opening weekend box office makes or breaks a film, and this creates tremendous pressure on critics to blurb films, to write quotable copy that can be used in advertising. "One of the greatest films of all time!" "An action-packed extravaganza!"

This kind of criticism is really just a form of promotion and marketing. It provides little insight on a film. Unfortunately, criticism today is all too often a sales tool for the industry. The critic in a big media market who *consistently* gives bad reviews to the big blockbusters probably won't keep his or her job for very long. This erosion of the critic's function has accompanied an erosion of film culture. Mass media film criticism today is much more about promoting blockbusters than the idea that cinema can be an important medium culturally and artistically.

Criticism, then, doesn't exist in isolation. It is deeply affected by the nature of the industry whose products it covers.

☐ MODES OF CRITICISM

Film criticism differs greatly depending on where it is practiced and the audience to whom it is directed. Film criticism falls into three basic modes: newspaper and television reviewing, general interest journal-based criticism, and scholarly criticism. The objectives and implied audience differ for each mode.

Newspaper and Television Reviewing

Film reviews in the daily newspaper or as part of a television news or review program are probably the most familiar modes of film criticism. **Newspaper and television reviews** are prepared for a general audience; they perform an explicit consumer function. The reviewer answers the moviegoer's most basic and most immediate question, should I see this movie? Newspaper and television reviews are usually very short, and the reviewer must address this question right away. The reviewer typically does this by giving a highly personalized and subjective response to the movie. To do so, these

Harry Potter and the Sorcerer's Stone (Warner Bros., 2001)
The industry's marketing practices have helped to erode much contemporary film criticism. Because they are so aggressively advertised, many blockbusters are "critic proof"; they do well in their opening weekend regardless of how they are reviewed. Dependent on Hollywood's product and perks for their jobs, many movie critics go along by writing reviews that make good advertising copy. Think of how many times you have seen a film described as "One of the greatest films of this or any year!"

critics use terms that describe the intensity of their emotional reactions. If they like a film, they call it dazzling, stunning, hilarious, or sensational. If they don't like it, the film is a stinker or a bomb.

What the Newspaper/TV Critic Does
By concentrating so intensively on the issue of whether they liked or disliked a movie, these critics model a series of emotional responses to the movie under discussion. These responses enable viewers to decide whether they should see the film or not. If the reviewer is trusted and hated the movie, then the consumer knows to stay away from it. Sometimes, though, an inverse relationship prevails: Many moviegoers decide they'll probably like a movie if a given reviewer hated it.

In addition to providing a detailed description of their emotional reactions, newspaper and television reviewers also provide a plot summary of the film (without disclosing the ending—this is a cardinal rule in this mode of criticism) and a discussion of the stars who appear in the film. These, too, serve an explicit consumer function. People want to know what a movie is about before deciding to see it, and, typically, they seek out films that feature their favorite performers.

Finally, the newspaper or television critics may also include a brief statement of the film's general theme. Reviewers of *Dances with Wolves* (1990), for example, tended to stress how the film's noble and heroic portrayal of the Sioux constituted a reversal of traditional Westerns that presented Native Americans as savages and villains. This judgment, however, tended to overlook or disregard many Westerns that preceded *Dances with Wolves* that also offered a heroic and sympathetic portrait of Native Americans.

The thematic content of *Dances with Wolves* was hardly new or revolutionary, although newspaper and television critics tended to respond as if it were.

This example points to a general weakness with this mode of criticism. Because they emphasize their emotional responses and have to keep their review brief, newspaper and television critics usually do not provide a historical perspective on the films they discuss and are unable to clarify how those films may link to earlier works and traditions, as in the case of *Dances with Wolves*. The newspaper or television reviewer is also unlikely to provide much analysis or description of a film's audiovisual structure, of how a filmmaker employs the elements of editing, sound, or mise-en-scène.

Newspaper and television critics, then, typically concentrate on four things: a description of their emotional reaction to the film, a plot summary, a discussion of star performance, and a brief statement of the film's theme. Coverage of these areas enables the reviewer to serve the explicit consumer function of helping readers or listeners decide whether they should see the film.

General-Interest Journal-Based Criticism

General-interest journal-based criticism is that criticism that falls somewhere between newspaper and television reviewing and scholarly criticism. Reviewers for such literate but general-interest publications as *The New Yorker, The New Republic, The Village Voice,* and *The New York Review of Books* typically have more space in which to compose their reviews and do not face the same urgent consumer function as the newspaper or television reviewer. As a result, the general-interest journal critic can offer a more detailed and sophisticated portrait of a film's structure and messages.

Case Study: Pauline Kael

One of the best known general-interest journal critics was Pauline Kael, the reviewer for *The New Yorker* magazine from 1967–1991. During her tenure, Kael was an extremely powerful and influential critic, a passionate critic whose love for the medium was apparent in every review. She championed the causes of those films and filmmakers (Sam Peckinpah and Robert Altman, for example) that she admired, and she was a merciless opponent of those she deemed mediocre or inferior.

Last Tango in Paris   Perhaps her most famous review was her glowing rave for Bernardo Bertolucci's *Last Tango in Paris* (1972). Bertolucci's film about the affair between a young woman and an aging widower in Paris was extremely controversial in its day for its sexually frank content. Kael met the controversies head on in a spirited defense of the film in which she proclaimed that Bertolucci and Marlon Brando, its director and star, had altered the face of an art form.

In defending and promoting *Last Tango*, Kael went far beyond the immediate consumer function of the newspaper or television reviewer. She began the review by establishing what she considered to be the revolutionary character of this film, the degree to which it changed the face of its medium. She compared it to the premiere of Stravinsky's *The Rite of Spring* (*Le Sacre du Printemps*), a musical composition that she maintains was comparably shocking and unconventional for its initial audiences.

> Bernardo Bertolucci's *Last Tango in Paris* was presented for the first time on the closing night of the New York Film Festival, October 14, 1972; that date should become

Born on the Fourth of July (Universal Pictures, 1989)
For readers, one of Kael's great assets was the intensity of her opinions. She passionately embraced the films she liked and mercilessly condemned those whose artistry she found lacking. She championed the work of Robert Altman, Sam Peckinpah, and Martin Scorsese, and could be harsh toward films she didn't like, such as *Born on the Fourth of July*.

a landmark in movie history comparable to May 29, 1913—the night *Le Sacre du Printemps* was first performed—in music history. There was no riot, and no one threw anything at the screen, but I think it's fair to say that the audience was in a state of shock, because *Last Tango in Paris* has the same kind of hypnotic excitement as the *Sacre,* the same primitive force, and the same thrusting, jabbing eroticism. The movie breakthrough has finally come. Exploitation films have been supplying mechanized sex—sex as physical stimulant but without any passion or emotional violence. The sex in *Last Tango in Paris* expresses the characters' drives. Marlon Brando, as Paul, is working out his aggression on Jeanne (Maria Schneider), and the physical menace of sexuality that is emotionally charged is such a departure from everything we've come to expect at the movies that there was something almost like fear in the atmosphere of the party in the lobby that followed the screening. Carried along by the sustained excitement of the movie, the audience had given Bertolucci an ovation, but afterward, as individuals, they were quiet. This must be the most powerfully erotic movie ever made, and it may turn out to be the most liberating movie ever made, and so it's probably only natural that an audience, anticipating a voluptuous feast from the man who made *The Conformist,* and confronted with this unexpected sexuality and the new realism it requires of the actors, should go into shock. Bertolucci and Brando have altered the face of an art form. Who was prepared for that?*

*"Last Tango in Paris," © 1972 by Pauline Kael, from *For Keeps* by Pauline Kael. Used by permssion of Dutton, a division of Penguin Putnam Inc.

Kael's comparison of *Last Tango* with *The Rite of Spring* was a strategic rhetorical move. Stravinsky's composition, though initially attacked as ugly and offensive, is today regarded as a classic. By using it as a gauge for measuring the shock that *Last Tango* had aroused in its initial viewers, Kael helped to legitimize the film by favorably comparing it to an already established artistic masterpiece. In doing so, she left no doubts about the high esteem in which she held the film and about her belief in it as art.

Kael's use of Stravinsky illustrates one of the most important services the general-interest journal critic performs (and one that the brief format of newspaper or television reviewing does not permit), placing the film under discussion into a broad cultural and historical context. After briefly summarizing the film's plot, Kael explores in considerable detail the history of Brando's screen persona, how the film draws on it and exploits it, and the way Bertolucci's direction was influenced by traditions of French and Italian cinema. Her references here include films that many of her readers may not have seen. These include Jean Renoir's *La Chienne* and *La Bête Humaine,* Jean Vigo's *L'Atalante,* Luchino Visconti's *Ossessione,* and Roberto Rossellini's *Open City.*

> The colors in this movie are late-afternoon orange-beige-browns and pink—the pink of flesh drained of blood, corpse pink. They are so delicately modulated (Vittorio Storaro was the cinematographer, as he was on *The Conformist*) that romance and rot are one; the lyric extravagance of the music (by Gato Barbieri) heightens this effect. Outside the flat, the gray buildings and the noise are certainly modern Paris, and yet the city seems muted. Bertolucci uses a feedback of his own—the feedback of old movies to enrich the imagery and associations. In substance, this is his most American film, yet the shadow of Michel Simon seems to hover over Brando, and the ambience is a tribute to the early crime-of-passion films of Jean Renoir, especially *La Chienne* and *La Bête Humaine.* Léaud, as Tom, the young director, is used as an affectionate takeoff on Godard, and the movie that Tom is shooting about Jeanne, his runaway bride, echoes Jean Vigo's *L'Atalante.* Bertolucci's soft focus recalls the thirties films, with their lyrically kind eye for every variety of passion; Marcel Carné comes to mind, as well as the masters who influenced Bertolucci's technique—von Sternberg (the controlled lighting) and Max Ophuls (the tracking camera). The film is utterly beautiful to look at. The virtuosity of Bertolucci's gliding camera style is such that he can show you the hype of the tango-contest scene (with its own echo of *The Conformist*) by

Last Tango in Paris
(United Artists, 1972)
Pauline Kael's famous review of *Last Tango in Paris* used a carefully chosen rhetorical style to praise the film and placed it within a detailed film historical and cultural context. Newspaper and television reviewers cannot offer such comprehensive discussion. Frame enlargement.

stylizing it (the automaton-dancers do wildly fake head turns) and still make it work. He uses the other actors for their associations, too—Girotti, of course, the star of so many Italian films, including *Senso* and *Ossessione,* Visconti's version of *The Postman Always Rings Twice,* and, as Paul's mother-in-law, Maria Michi, the young girl who betrays her lover in *Open City.* As a maid in the hotel (part of a weak, diversionary subplot that is soon dispensed with), Catherine Allegret, with her heart-shaped mouth in a full, childishly beautiful face, is an aching, sweet reminder of her mother, Simone Signoret, in her *Casque d'Or* days. Bertolucci draws upon the movie background of this movie because movies are as active in him as direct experience—perhaps more active, since they may color everything else. Movies are a past we share, and, whether we recognize them or not, the copious associations are at work in the film and we feel them. As Jeanne, Maria Schneider, who has never had a major role before, is like a bouquet of Renoir's screen heroines and his father's models. She carries the whole history of movie passion in her long legs and baby face.

These comparisons with other films enable Kael to contextualize *Last Tango* within the traditions of cinema that have nourished Bertolucci and whose marks are apparent in *Tango.* The comparisons also enable Kael to display her own credentials as a sophisticated film critic whose horizons of cinema experience extend well beyond the present film under discussion. Notice how different this aspect of her reviewing is from the norms of newspaper and television reviewing, which mandate that the critic focus almost exclusively on the immediate film under discussion. Finally, Kael's lively writing style, and her willingness to champion the cause of films in which she believes, conveys her deep love for cinema and her joy in sharing that passion with readers.

The Merits of Journal-Based Criticism   In her long career, Pauline Kael exemplified the merits and virtues of the general-interest journal-based critic. She was witty, intelligent, informed about the history and culture of the cinema, and passionately in love with the medium. This breadth and depth of discussion, coupled with a lively writing style, typify the strengths of this mode of criticism. As a writer, Kael had the space necessary to explore her ideas in detail. Readers of her criticism were the beneficiaries, and her writing went well beyond the reviewer's immediate task of separating the good from the bad. Her essays capture broad aspects of film history and culture, and they dissect the spirit of the times in which the films were made. As important critical documents, they have been collected in several volumes representing the decades of her work.

Scholarly Criticism

Unlike newspaper and television reviewing or even general-interest journal-based criticism, scholarly criticism contains almost no focus on the consumer function of telling readers whether they should see the film or skip it. Instead, **scholarly criticism** explores the significance of a given film in relation to often complex issues of theory, history, or technology. It appears in such journals as *Film Quarterly, Cinema Journal, Screen,* and *Wide Angle,* and is written for an audience of scholars rather than general readers. Scholarly critics, therefore, use a more demanding and specialized vocabulary, accessible to scholars if not to general readers. Often using models of film theory to buttress their arguments, scholarly critics explore theoretical and historical questions rather than issues of merit, i.e., whether a given film is good or bad.

Case Study: *Dead Again*

Scholarly criticism is illustrated by this analysis of Kenneth Branagh's *Dead Again* (1991) that appeared in *Cinema Journal,* an academic publication read largely by university-trained film scholars and graduate students. The film's story is about the murder in the 1940s of Margaret Strauss, allegedly by her composer husband, Roman, and the consequences of that death many decades later. The authors of the essay analyze the film as an example of postmodernism, that is, as a film whose style and content are largely defined by reference to earlier traditions of film and literature.

> In the wake of numerous critical pronouncements concerning the nature and viability of postmodernism as a descriptive, critical, and political category, it seems appropriate to interrogate a current instance of popular filmmaking in order to test the viability of this discourse. In this essay, we look at *Dead Again* (1991), a film that might be deemed 'postmodern' through its deployment of numerous thematic, intertextual, stylistic, and self-reflexive strategies.*

The authors then go on to analyze in detail the numerous ways in which *Dead Again* quotes from the cinematic past.

> With its thematic focus on the past, *Dead Again* is a film that seems to encourage the audience to play with it, to identify its numerous allusions to other films, genres, and film stars. To analyze the narrative for its meaning would seem to violate the playfulness that the film seems to invite. The film defies classification according to a single generic mode. In the allusions to other works, we are given a mélange of different forms: crime detection, thriller, melodrama, and the occult. For Caryn James, this mixture is a hallmark of post-modern cinema. As she notes, such films "rejuvenate old genres . . . by being them and by mocking them at the same time." In *Dead Again,* the allusions to other works include most prominently Hitchcock's *Rebecca* (1940). The Gothic imagery associated with Manderley is reiterated in the image of the Strauss

Dead Again (Paramount Pictures, 1991)
Scholarly criticism of recent films, such as *Dead Again,* starring Emma Thompson and Kenneth Branagh, does not address consumer-oriented questions—Is this a good movie? Should I see it?—but rather explores in detail particular artistic, cultural, or theoretical issues. Frame enlargement.

*"*Dead Again* or A-Live Again: Postmodern or Postmortem?," by Marcia Landy and Lucy Fischer in *Cinema Journal* 33:4, pp. 3–10. Copyright © 1994 by the University of Texas Press. All rights reserved.

mansion. Furthermore, Roman and Margaret Strauss's portrayal, as well as that of Inga, the housekeeper, plays off the dominant characters in the Hitchcock film. In its adherence to the crime thriller genre, *Dead Again* resurrects incidents, character types, and conventions associated with crime detection and with aggression toward female victims in such films as *Dial M for Murder* (1954), *Frenzy* (1972), and *Psycho* (1960). There are also numerous allusions to images and characters from such thrillers as *Journey into Fear* (1942) and *The Stranger* (1946), especially to the elusive, deceptive, or malevolent identity of the male protagonist. British and Hollywood melodramas of the 1930s and 1940s are also referenced, including films such as *Gaslight* (Dickinson [1939] and Cukor [1944]), which involve questions of a woman's sanity. Like *Dead Again, Humoresque* (1946) and *The Seventh Veil* (1945) are melodramas that foreground musicians. The latter, starring Ann Todd and James Mason, closely parallels Branagh's film with its plot involving a pianist and her moody, domineering, and mysterious guardian. Through these allusions, *Dead Again* thus fuses the genres of crime detection, thriller, and melodrama. Furthermore, it effects another hybridization by conflating the woman's film with the male melodrama . . .

The allusions to other films and the conflation of genres are deployed in a number of ways: as clues for the audience, as narrative markers, as selective moments in history (and particularly in the legacy of representation), as an homage to the commercial cinema. The rather complicated collage of citations and genres upsets conventional expectations concerning plot and character. For example, the audience is bombarded with clues which might lead to an understanding of the diegetic past. Thus the beginning of the film with its montage of newspaper clippings involving the death of Margaret Strauss, the stages of Roman Strauss's sentencing, and the introduction of the newspaperman, Baker, would appear to present the film's enigma: was Roman Strauss guilty of murdering his wife? However, the opening scene of Strauss on death row invokes a sequence from Welles's script to *Heart of Darkness*, where the viewer witnesses events through the eyes of a condemned man. Furthermore, it also suggests Monsieur Verdoux's walk to death at the end of Chaplin's 1947 film, another story of a woman-killer. Knowledge of other filmic texts seems required to understand this one.

In the spirit of *Citizen Kane* (1941), the enigma turns out to be the nature of storytelling itself, involving the mystery of who is the keeper of knowledge. Whose story is this? Who is telling the tale and to what ends? Whose point of view are we invited to explore? The film inserts characters that resurrect the hermeneutics of *Citizen Kane,* especially in Strauss's whispered words to Baker (a descendant of Jed Leland), which invoke the puzzle of "Rosebud." In *Dead Again*'s hydra-headed interest in investigating and uncovering the past, it asks us to discern who is the narrator: the newspaperman, the hypnotist, or the doubled figure of Roman Strauss and Mike Church? The narrator is certainly not the tripled figure of Margaret and Grace/Amanda, played by Branagh's wife to quadruple the equation. These problems concerning narration would seem to underscore the film's indeterminacy and instability, a characteristic that we might consider as centrally identified with the postmodern.

This analysis is obviously very different from what a reviewer writing for a newspaper or general-interest journal would produce. First of all, it is not a review oriented to a potential consumer but is a detailed analysis of how the film is postmodern by virtue of its rich set of references to other works of film and literature. The authors provide minimal plot summary, only enough to make their analysis clear, and they are less interested in reaching a clear verdict about the quality of the film (the reviewer's

Citizen Kane (RKO, 1941); **Dead Again** (Paramount Pictures, 1991)
Scholarly criticism may attempt to clarify the cinematic traditions and influences that operate
on a film. Orson Welles's *Citizen Kane* influenced the visual and narrative design of *Dead
Again*. The wealthy composer in *Dead Again* has a striking emblem (the treble clef) on the
gate to his estate, just as Charles Foster Kane has (the letter K) in the earlier film. The
emblems are emphasized at similar points in each film's narrative. Frame enlargements.

eternal question of whether a film is "good" or "bad") than with explaining how it
works as a visual narrative that constructs a network of relationships with prior films
and directors.

Accordingly, the authors discuss in detail how director Branagh and the film play
off the work of Orson Welles, Charles Chaplin, and Alfred Hitchcock, and such specific films as *Citizen Kane, Rebecca, Gaslight,* and *Monsieur Verdoux.* The authors explore
these relationships with references to critical concepts of postmodernism, voyeurism,
psychoanalysis, and gender and genre issues. Instead of the consumer-oriented function of newspaper reviewing, or the part consumer, part analytic focus of general-interest
journal-based criticism, the emphasis here is entirely analytic and is geared to a smaller
audience of specialist readers familiar with the critical concepts and film references
employed in the essay. Note how the tone of the writing differs from Pauline Kael's
work, which compared *Last Tango* to other films and filmmakers. The scholarly tone
is less emotional than Kael's approach and is more analytic and informational.

The clearest indicator of the essay's specialized audience is the language the authors
use. It is densely packed with information, loaded with names, terms, and concepts, and
the authors do not always elaborate on their meaning or background because they assume
their readers are already knowledgeable in these areas. For these reasons, the essay's language might seem forbidding or excessively difficult to nonspecialist readers.

Scholarly criticism seeks to analyze how the narrative or audiovisual design of a
film works with reference to existing traditions of cinema or other arts and with ref-

erence to basic critical concepts or models of film theory. Unlike newspaper or general interest journal-based criticism, scholarly criticism performs virtually no consumer function. Instead, it appeals to specialized film scholars interested in expanding their knowledgeability of given films and filmmakers.

☐ CREATING CRITICISM

Whether one is writing for a newspaper, general interest magazine, or scholarly journal, there are three stages in the creation of criticism. These are the stages of identification, description, and interpretation.

Identification and Description

The critic **identifies** and **describes** passages or elements of the film that are relevant to the critical interpretation being developed. Identification and description generally occur together. Their purpose is to simplify and reduce the wealth of material in the film that the critic confronts. In this respect, they are strategic tools, enabling the critic to omit nonrelevant details. A verbal description of a visual sequence can be endless because of the huge quantity of visual, narrative, and behavioral cues present in even a few seconds of film. Critics, therefore, must limit the range and amount of material on which they will draw to build their **interpretation.** They do this by employing a deductive method.

Working Deductively

Case Study: *Psycho*

The critic works **deductively,** that is, he or she uses some general assumptions to guide the search for supporting evidence. Without some unifying assumptions, some sense of what to look for, a critic will find only disconnected bits of information. Suppose, by way of example, that a critic was developing an interpretation of Alfred Hitchcock's *Psycho*. Such a critic might wish to deal with the theme of voyeurism as Hitchcock develops it throughout the film. The idea of voyeurism, then, would become an assumption or goal organizing the search for evidence.

Norman Bates, the psychopathic killer, has a secret peephole in his motel office that he uses to spy on attractive women guests as they undress for bed. During one of the most intense scenes in the film, Hitchcock films Norman peeping through the hole in his wall, watching Marion Crane, whom he is about to murder, as she undresses before taking a shower. Hitchcock shows Norman's eye in close-up, peering through the peephole. Hitchcock then switches to a subjective shot, representing Norman's point of view, as the camera peers at Marion. The subjective shot aligns character viewpoint and spectator viewpoint in one voyeuristic moment. By identifying and describing this subjective shot, a critic can link it to the general theme of voyeurism that the critic will assert is central to the film and that guides the selection of details for analysis.

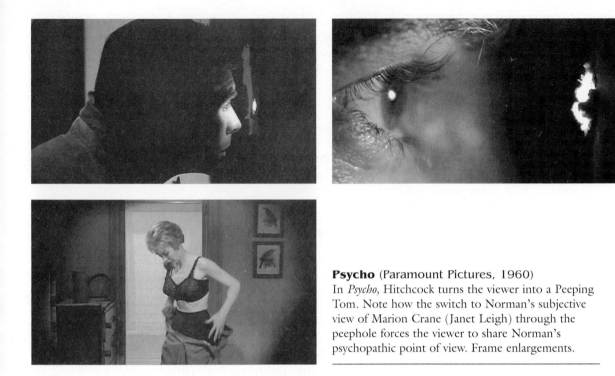

Psycho (Paramount Pictures, 1960)
In *Psycho*, Hitchcock turns the viewer into a Peeping Tom. Note how the switch to Norman's subjective view of Marion Crane (Janet Leigh) through the peephole forces the viewer to share Norman's psychopathic point of view. Frame enlargements.

Working deductively, the critic uses the general goals or premises of the criticism to guide a search for relevant material in the film. Refining and sharpening these goals enables the critic to efficiently identify useful material. The critic, for example, might refine the theme of voyeurism in *Psycho* by connecting it with Hitchcock's statements about why cinema appeals to its viewers. Hitchcock believed, and said, that cinema offers moviegoers pleasures that are essentially voyeuristic. In the darkened theater auditorium moviegoers permit themselves to see things they would ordinarily shun in daily life—sex, violence, aberrant or criminal behavior—and they derive pleasure from these experiences. Hitchcock believed that viewers are like the Peeping Tom, able to witness forbidden sights without being held accountable for what is seen and enjoyed.

Knowing these terms by which Hitchcock understood the cinema and its pleasures, the critic of *Psycho* could seek out aspects of the film's visual design that demonstrate Hitchcock's regard for the film viewer as a voyeur. The critic would emphasize the moment where Hitchcock makes the viewer share Norman's voyeuristic view through the peephole and would also select the film's opening scene, wherein the camera pans the skyline of Phoenix, Arizona, cranes down toward a hotel window, and then peeks in to glimpse a pair of lovers reclining on a bed.

Citing these shots, the critic could argue that Hitchcock visualizes explicitly voyeuristic behavior. The critic could suggest that the camera prowls to the window and then peers beneath the curtain to see the semiclothed lovers on the bed. The

Psycho (Paramount Pictures, 1960)
Hitchcock's camera explicitly simulates the movement of a prowling voyeur, drawing closer
to a darkened window, then peering inside to see two partially clad lovers in a bedroom.
Frame enlargements.

critic would be justified in labeling such a shot as a voyeuristic moment because the
movements of the camera seem to call to mind the actions of a Peeping Tom.

Notice the deductive method of proceeding. With an understanding of Hitchcock's equation of cinema and voyeurism, the critic selects details that illustrate this.
The Hitchcockian emphasis on voyeurism established an interpretive framework that,
in turn, provided selection criteria, enabling the critic to pick out relevant aspects of
visual design. The themes or ideas that the criticism seeks to establish—here, the idea
that *Psycho* exhibits a voyeuristic design—enable the critic to select relevant details
and to omit nonrelevant details.

Using Precise Terminology

The critic should carefully label those elements of film structure that are being identified. The camera's movement toward the window and then underneath the blind
needs to be identified and described as a moving camera shot and labeled as either a
tracking or crane shot. The camera movement is crucial for Hitchcock's effect. The
moving camera implies not just the prowling activity of the Peeping Tom, but also
the voyeur's progressive focusing of attention, the drawing closer to a private and
secret moment. Identifying and describing these features of camera movement are
key to linking this scene with the general theme of voyeurism that guides the criticism. Strong and precise description of the camera's movements integrates this scene
with the critical premise and strengthens the force of the critic's argument and its
effect on the reader.

In a similar fashion, the critic should recognize, and precisely describe, the use
of a subjective shot in the scene where Norman looks through the peephole at Marion Crane. This shot represents Norman's point of view and also the viewpoint of
the film's spectator. Good criticism would explore the implications of these aligned
viewpoints. What does it mean for Hitchcock to invite the film's viewer to share the

perspective of the central character, a psychopathic killer? What kind of relationship is Hitchcock suggesting exists between Norman and the film's viewers who share his space and his view of Marion?

By precisely identifying carefully selected details, and matching these details to the critical premise, the critic's descriptions become a part of the interpretation being developed. The interpretation grows out of the descriptions and seems to follow inevitably from them, provided the criticism is performed with sophistication and intelligence. When this is not the case, the reader will tend to feel that the critic is stretching things or trying to justify an interpretation that does not fit the evidence.

Interpretation

The third component of criticism, **interpretation,** is the assignment of meaning to a scene or film that it does not immediately denote. Based on the assumptions that guide the criticism, the critic searches for details and describes them in ways that support the interpretation that is being developed. As we have seen, a film's images and narratives are polyvalent: They express more than one thing or idea. A film's first-order meanings are those that are immediately expressed at a surface level by the characters, dialogue, and story. In general, criticism is the act of reorganizing these elements of a film to emphasize **latent** (or second-order) **meanings,** those that are not immediately expressed at the surface level of character and story. Critical interpretation is an act of uncovering latent meaning.

Revealing Latent Meaning

Case Study: *Natural Born Killers*
Oliver Stone's *Natural Born Killers,* one of the most controversial films of recent years, portrays the exploits of two mass murderers, Mickey and Mallory. They are

Natural Born Killers
(Warner Bros, 1994)
Oliver Stone said that this film was meant to be a satire of a modern media culture saturated with violence. Does the film work this way or does it become the very thing it wants to satirize? Does it critique violence or glorify it? It is up to the critic, and viewer, to decide.

young, in love with one another, and they enjoy killing people. The film opens with a graphic slaughter scene in a roadside diner, during which Mickey and Mallory stab, shoot, and dismember its patrons. After that, they embark on a cross-country killing spree that makes them famous. The media turn them into celebrities.

Stone said that the theme of the film "is that violence is all around us; it's in nature and it's in every one of us, and we all have to acknowledge it and come to grips with it." He said that the film was meant to be a criticism of the mass media's sensationalism and glorification of violence for profit. But is *Natural Born Killers* a criticism of contemporary culture or is it the very thing that it professes to attack, namely, a glorification of violence?

To answer this question, a critic must sort out the film's explicit and latent meanings. **Latent meaning** is indirect, implied by a film's narrative and audiovisual design. It is not immediately obvious or explicit.

In terms of the film's explicit meanings, Stone develops his critique of the mass media through the character of Wayne Gale (Robert Downey, Jr.), a cynical television journalist who wants to sensationalize Mickey and Mallory's crimes because it will be good for ratings. Stone also shows the empty-headed fans of the killers who are turned on by media coverage of their crimes.

On the other hand, however, many elements of the film operate in a latent fashion to counteract the goal that Stone described. Mickey and Mallory are the most attractive characters in the film, for example, and the couple's victims are unpleasant and repulsive, which makes it easier for the viewer to applaud their murder and enjoy the spectacle of slaughter.

Stone intercuts color and black-and-white 35mm footage with 16mm and 8mm film footage and video footage. He intercuts live action and cartoon images, and uses jump cuts and camera angles that lurch in a crazy, off-kilter fashion. This unusual style helps to make the violence hypnotic and fascinating. It becomes spectacle. The imagery is so aggressive and intense that it arguably overwhelms the clear point of view that Stone described as his goal for the film.

By citing these aspects of character and structure, a critic could suggest that *Natural Born Killers* becomes the very thing it pretends to attack. The film has apparently inspired several real-life killings by disturbed individuals seeking to emulate Mickey and Mallory. Faced with this history, the critic must decide whether it is irrelevant to the film itself or provides evidence that the movie's latent meanings are so powerful as to incite some viewers to act out their dangerous fantasies.

The film's explicit meanings (the setting, characters, and story) and the latent meanings (the audiovisual design that works to pump up the violence and make the killers attractive) create contradictions and ambiguities that criticism seeks to resolve. Doing so, the critic seeks to clarify a film's implicit, latent meanings. This is often a main goal of criticism.

Creating a Framework of Interpretation

As we have seen, a critic cannot build an interpretation without first having some organizing assumptions that tell the critic what to look for. To uncover latent dimensions of meaning, the critic employs **frameworks of interpretation,** the intellectual, social, or cultural frames of reference that a critic applies to a film in order to

WRITING FILM CRITICISM

Learning to write good film criticism can be easy to do. As a developing film critic, you can follow these basic steps (all of which assume that you have found a film to critique): Establish an interpretive framework, apply the framework, and draw interpretive conclusions.

Developing an Interpretive Framework

Start out by establishing a framework of interpretation to apply to the film. This framework will tell you what to look for in the film being critiqued. Without such a framework, criticism is impossible and deteriorates into an effort to patch together disconnected pieces of information. To develop a framework of interpretation, you

can research subjects or issues addressed by the film so that you can develop a basis for evaluating how the film treats them. You can view other films produced by the same director or movies by other filmmakers that deal with the same topic or genre. This will enable you to become familiar with a body of work that you can use to contextualize the film that you are critiquing.

Study some of the film theories discussed in the next chapter and try to apply them to the film. You should also read what other critics have said about the film because this will stimulate your thinking and help you generate ideas. It will also allow you to see how other writers have constructed their critical arguments.

Star Wars (Twentieth Century Fox, 1977) Good film criticism enhances one's understanding of a given film's design and expressive meanings. Indeed, the critic helps establish those meanings. With *Star Wars*, the critic could discuss the film's stylistic debt to early movie serials or the symbolic implications of the stark clash between good and evil at the heart of the narrative.

derive an interpretation of that film. Frameworks of interpretation guide the selection of relevant details for analysis. The critic interpreting *Natural Born Killers* as a glorification of violence needs to know something about the real-life crimes connected to the film. This might require additional, special research, but no critic can proceed without a framework of interpretation. Otherwise, the deductive process of criticism is impossible; without some framework of interpretation, a critic will

Remember, though, that the goal of criticism is to produce a novel or original interpretation, not to recycle someone else's ideas.

To develop a framework of interpretation, go beyond the film itself to develop a social, philosophical, aesthetic, or historical context that you can apply to the film. Two measures of good criticism are relevant here. Your interpretive framework should be rich and comprehensive, and it should fit the film to which you are applying it.

Application of the Framework

Once you know the kind of things you will be looking for, you then need to view the film at least two or three times. Search for material in the film that you can identify as a potential fit with the interpretive frame. Having found it, carefully isolate it from the rest of the film through a strategic description. This description will simplify and reduce the amount of film material it is necessary to work with. In other words, you needn't describe everything in a shot or scene, only what is relevant to the interpretation you are developing.

Each subsequent viewing should become quicker since you will become more efficient at finding and extracting the information you need. A VCR or DVD player is an excellent study tool because it permits freezing the action and repeating it as often as necessary to check for details. Search the film for key scenes, character interactions, aspects of narrative structure, and elements of audiovisual design that can be integrated with your framework of interpretation and used to support the argument you are developing. The other chapters in this textbook highlight many features of audiovisual design and narrative that you might wish to isolate for critical analysis. If it doesn't fit, don't force it. The people reading the criticism will know if the interpretations are false or unworkable for the film.

Remember to simplify the sequences discussed by eliminating unnecessary information. Precisely label all aspects of visual design, quote dialogue accurately, and spell character names correctly. A critic who fails to do this loses credibility.

Building an Argument

There is no single formula or method for constructing a critical argument. However, all the rules normally associated with good writing also apply to film criticism. You want to persuade the reader that your interpretation of the film reveals important patterns and layers of meaning that are not immediately apparent or explicitly conveyed during a casual viewing.

Be careful, therefore, to build your argument by clearly guiding the reader through all of the steps and stages of critical thought, from describing your initial critical premises to the citation of evidence and the statement of conclusions. Good writing is clear, connected, and forceful. Because criticism is a rhetorical act, the quality of the writing is as important as the quality of the ideas in swaying the reader to your positions. Finally, remember that good criticism is provocative. If your ideas are challenging, if the connections that you draw across the images and narrative episodes are novel and insightful, you will enrich the readers' understanding of the film and may even send them back for another, wiser viewing.

only find disconnected bits of information. To develop frameworks of interpretation, the critic needs to do much more than simply watch movies. The critic must be sufficiently well-read, educated, and cultured to possess numerous frameworks of interpretation that can be applied to films and that can nurture acts of criticism. The broader a critic's social and cultural frames of reference, the richer the criticism that is produced.

Attributional Errors

As a critic applies frameworks of interpretation to a film, selecting and describing details, and then assigning meaning to those details, the critic needs to be cautious about committing common attributional errors. **Attributional errors** can occur when a critic erroneously attributes an effect in film to a given creator. Common attributional errors stem from three sources. Two involve errors of intended meaning and the third involves errors of implied authorship. To some extent, these attributional errors are an inevitable part of criticism; they are inherent to a critic's work, which necessarily assigns meaning to aspects of film narrative and structure. The following discussion, then, is not meant to suggest that critics must avoid these errors at all costs; as noted, they probably cannot. But, by keeping in mind the attributional errors to which criticism is prone, the critic will be more cautious and deliberative and thereby produce richer and more rigorous criticism.

Errors of Intended Meaning   Two common types of attributional errors are those of intended meaning. Critics, by nature, assign meanings to films. However, not every effect or apparent design in a film is meaningful, understood in terms of the intentions of its creators. Sometimes filmmakers do things simply because they like the effect, not because they are trying to express a particular idea or feeling. In fact, unlike critics, filmmakers are often reluctant to speak or think self-consciously about the design implications of their work.

Easy Rider (1969) broke a lot of the rules of conventional studio filmmaking. Viewers instantly notice the flash cross-cutting (see Chapter 4) between scenes and remember this long after seeing the film. Viewers might legitimately wonder why the filmmakers employed this technique, and a critic might develop an interpretation in which flash cross-cutting becomes emblematic in some way of the film's view of society in the late 1960s or its themes of freedom and violence. Such an interpretation could be very interesting and might enrich one's understanding of the film, but the critic would commit an attributional error if he or she argued that the filmmakers employed flash cross-cutting with a particular intended meaning in mind.

The film's editor, Donn Cambern, admitted that the flash cross-cutting developed simply because it was an unusual way of handling scene transitions. Cambern described the origin of the flash cross-cutting by saying,

> "That came about in looking for a way to simply make a transition from one scene to the other. We literally had to experiment to find how long those cuts needed to be in order to convey the idea. . . . At first we said, 'Ah! We got something great here,' so we started pumping it every place. Speaking of redundancy, it got to be absolutely indulgent. I don't remember how many times it's used, but it's not that much. But people remember the technique."

As Cambern's remarks indicate, not every aspect of visual design has a particular meaning. Sometimes the effects themselves are their own end and provide the film-maker with sufficient incentive for executing the scene that way.

In addition, films are polyvalent in ways their creators never intended. Audiences see meanings that filmmakers may not or did not intend. Steven Spielberg intended the execution scenes in *Schindler's List* to horrify audiences. He did not want the vio-

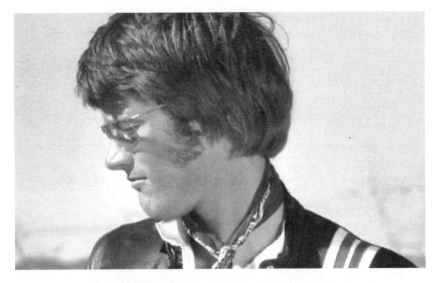

Easy Rider (Columbia Pictures, 1969)
Easy Rider broke many conventional rules of filmmaking, but not all of the film's visual techniques were meant to convey particular meanings. While critics search for meaning and tend to it in most features of a film's design, filmmakers themselves often work intuitively and may have very practical, rather than symbolic or expressive, reasons for shooting or editing a scene in a particular manner. Frame enlargement.

lence in such scenes to elicit laughter, but it did from at least one audience of high school students who apparently found the violence less than horrifying. Spielberg was fascinated by this and remarked that some modern viewers had become very desensitized toward screen violence.

A critic commits an attributional error of intended meaning when asserting that (1) some effect or scene has a specific intended meaning never expressly planned by a filmmaker or (2) some effect or scene has a specific meaning intended by a filmmaker that is expressly different from the meaning the filmmaker did intend. The first type of error attributes intended meaning to an effect that is without any such meaning, and the second type misrecognizes the intended meaning that is there.

Cinematic meaning, of course, does not derive solely from a filmmaker's intentions. This is an important point. Because filmmaking is such a collaborative art, viewers often cannot know what the intentions of a single artist working on a production may be. Viewers are free to interpret and derive meaning from films in their own fashion. Critics, though, often assert that specific elements of style have particular meanings intended by filmmakers. It is these assertions that may be vulnerable to the two fallacies discussed here. Note, however, that uncovering these errors typically requires documentation of a film's production history. This is true, as well, for the next error of attribution.

Errors of Assigned Authorship The third type of attributional error is an error of assigned authorship. Because filmmaking is such a collaborative process, it is often difficult to assign responsibility for a particular effect or aspect of visual design to an individual craftsperson. The color design of *Do the Right Thing* is the contribution of production designer Wynn Thomas working in collaboration with director Spike Lee and cinematographer Ernest Dickerson. The kaleidoscopic structure of *Annie Hall* owes as much to editor Ralph Rosenblum as it does to writer/director Woody Allen.

These cases are documented through interviews with the principal artists involved. With most films, the precise areas of collaborative influence remain undocumented. Accordingly, a critic almost never knows, for certain, who was responsible for what in a given film. Critics commonly attribute effects to the director. This is a kind of critical shorthand, a necessary, but somewhat misleading procedure. The director is merely one key player among many and should in no case be regarded as the sole author for all of a film's finished effects or design.

The Steps in Creating Criticism

Three steps are essential for creating good criticism. First, when viewing a film, the critic sees the potential application of a given framework of interpretation. The work of criticism is the application of this frame to the film. Before starting to build the interpretation, the critic may research more fully the interpretation that he or she seeks to apply. For example, if the critic is interpreting *Invasion of the Body Snatchers,* he or she might research the McCarthy period of the 1950s or the existence of documentation on the political attitudes, and specifically attitudes toward McCarthyism, of director Don Siegel, screenwriter Daniel Mainwaring, and other members of the cast or crew.

Second, armed with a fully elaborated framework of interpretation, the critic applies this framework to the film by selecting and describing relevant details, aspects of cinematic structure, and elements of the narrative that can be regarded as meaningful according to the framework employed. Quantity of evidence carries considerable weight here. The more evidence from the film the critic can isolate, the more aspects of its visual or narrative design that are integrated into the argument being constructed, the more persuasive the critical interpretation will be.

Third, by assigning meaning to these details, by placing them within the interpretational frame, the critic reorganizes the film's structure. The newly reconfigured film will seem inevitably to embody the meanings the critic has assigned to it. With the best criticism, these meanings become an enduring part of the film itself and help shape the context in which it is seen by new viewers.

SUMMARY

Film criticism is the use of language to impose a new organization on a film, its images, and narratives. Because it translates pictorial material into words, criticism is a rhetorical act, and it depends, for its persuasive effect, on the critic's language skills and intellectual sophistication. While a rhetorical act, film criticism includes an empirical dimension. By selectively citing details of audiovisual and narrative design, the critic reorganizes a film's structure to emphasize or draw out implicit meanings not apparent to a casual viewing. The critic employs a deductive method, applying an interpretational framework to the film and using it to guide the selection of details for analysis. These details are then integrated into the intrepretive framework, helping the critic build a novel interpretation of the film.

Criticism assumes a number of distinct forms. Newspaper reviewing is heavily consumer oriented, designed to answer the reader's question about whether a given movie is worth seeing. As such, newspaper criticism tends toward plot summary, descriptions of the film's characters, and the performances of stars in those roles.

The general-interest journal-based critic usually has more space to practice the craft. As such, this critic can go into greater detail about the artistic traditions to which a given film belongs and in detailing the particular visual and narrative style employed by a filmmaker. The consumer function, here, is less urgent. Scholarly criticism tends to be written for a community of scholars rather than the general reader. As such, it employs a specialized language and tends to draw on one or more distinct theoretical models.

A film's narrative and images contain multiple meanings. These are multidimensional and complex. As an example of this, any five people are likely to provide rather different accounts of what a particular film means. This is the condition that makes criticism necessary and enjoyable; criticism is the act of persuasively assigning one meaning to a film rather than another. Often, viewers feel that their experience of a film does not come to an end with the final credits. They want to kick the movie around in their heads a bit more or talk about it with friends to get a better understanding of what they think of the movie or how they feel about it. To do this, they might also read critical interpretations of the film, and, if the criticism is good, it enriches their understanding and experience and may even drive them back to the film for another viewing.

Because criticism, though, is rhetorical and because the multidimensional range of meanings in any film is vast, a critic's interpretation is likely to vary according to: (1) the forum—newspaper, general-interest journal, scholarly journal—in which it is performed, and (2) the particular theoretical model employed. The newspaper reviewer's assessment of a movie is likely to be rushed and clearcut. It's either a good movie or a bad one, one that viewers should see or avoid at all costs. The assessment of a general-interest journal-based critic is likely to be more measured, multilayered, and ambivalent.

The fact that a single movie can give rise to such a range of criticism and interpretation should not leave viewers feeling frustrated about the enterprise of criticism or doubtful of its usefulness. Instead, this is proof of the creative and conceptual richness of the cinema and of the many ways it addresses the audience. The critic reimposes meaning and psychological closure on the inherently ambiguous and provocative experience of watching a movie. This richness is cause for celebration and is one more reason for loving and embracing the medium of cinema.

SUGGESTED READINGS

David Bordwell, *Making Meaning: Inference and Rhetoric in the Interpretation of Cinema* (Cambridge, MA: Harvard University Press, 1989).

Pauline Kael, *Movie Love: Complete Reviews 1988–91* (New York: Plume, 1991).

Mark Crispin Miller, ed., *Seeing through Movies* (New York: Pantheon, 1990).

Jonathan Rosenbaum, *Placing Movies: The Practice of Film Criticism* (Berkeley: University of California Press, 1995).

Andrew Sarris, *Confessions of a Cultist: On the Cinema, 1955–59* (New York: Simon and Schuster, 1970).

Steve Vineberg, *No Surprises, Please: Movies in the Reagan Decade* (New York: Schirmer Books, 1993).

Chapter 11

Models of Film Theory

Chapter Objectives

After reading this chapter, you should be able to:

- explain the nature of film theory and the types of questions it investigates
- describe the characteristics, strengths, and limitations of realist models
- describe the characteristics, strengths, and limitations of auteurist models
- describe the characteristics, strengths, and limitations of psychoanalytic models
- describe the characteristics, strengths, and limitations of ideological models
- describe the characteristics, strengths, and limitations of feminist models
- describe the characteristics, strengths, and limitations of cognitive models
- select the most appropriate theoretical model for the particular type of questions that need answers
- understand that multiple theoretical perspectives are required because the cinema is multidimensional

Key Terms and Concepts

film theory
realist theory
deep focus cinema-
    tography
long take
perceptual realism

auteurist theory
psychoanalytic theory
voyeurism
taboo images
ideological theory
ideology

feminist theory
cognitive theory
perceptual processing
interpretive processing
eyeline match
schema

Our earlier chapters examined audiovisual design in the cinema and the viewer's contribution to the screen experience. A logical concluding point in this exploration of cinema is to examine the nature of film theory because theory tries to answer the question, what is cinema? **Film theory** is a systematic attempt to think about the nature of cinema: What it is as a medium, how it works, how it embodies meaning for viewers, and what kind of meanings it embodies.

This chapter examines six models of film theory that have crucially shaped the thinking of film scholars. These are the realist, auteurist, psychoanalytic, ideological, feminist, and cognitive models of film theory. Each model is especially good at dealing with some aspects of film style and the viewer's experience while being limited in its ability to deal with other aspects. Each model emphasizes certain aspects of the film medium and the viewer's experience at the expense of others. As a result, each model constructs a somewhat different portrait of the medium from the others.

☐ REALIST MODELS

This textbook has emphasized that the cinema has a double capacity. It both records and transforms the people, objects, and situations before the camera lens. Filmmakers use cinema as a recording medium to make pictures of the events, people, and situations in front of the camera, but they can also use the complex tools of their craft to manipulate the visual and acoustical design of their films. This tension within cinema between its recording functions and the power it gives filmmakers to stylize and transform reality poses a challenge for film theory when it attempts to locate a basis for realism and for realistic film styles. On which attributes of cinema should a theory of realism depend?

Elements of Realist Theory: Bazin

Theories of realism in the cinema look for points of correspondence between film images and the social, psychological, and physical realities before the camera. Typically, **realist film theory** restricts a filmmaker's manipulations of audiovisual design in order to honor and respect the integrity of the events and situations before the camera. Realist theory often implies that there is a threshold beyond which stylistic manipulation begins to falsify or distort the truths that the realist filmmaker pursues. Italian neorealists (Chapter 9), for example, aimed to define such a threshold by holding a filmmaker to the creation of relatively simply stories and the use of nonprofessional actors and real locations, the better to honestly record the social realities of postwar Italy.

Questions about the nature of social or psychological reality, where it properly lies, and how the cinema relates to it are extremely difficult problems. French theorist Andre Bazin offered an ingenious and famous solution. Composed in the 1940s and 1950s, his essays on cinema exerted an enormous influence on the French film critics writing for the journal *Cahiers du Cinema,* who would themselves later become film directors (see the section on the French New Wave in Chapter 9). Bazin based his theory on an ethical assumption about the nature of reality, and he suggested specific elements of film structure as the ones best suited for a realist style.

Ethical Components of Bazin's Realism

Realistic film styles for Bazin were those that respected and reproduced the viewer's experience of reality. Bazin felt that each person's perspective on the world was, to a significant degree, uniquely his or her own and differed from the perspective of others. In this regard, reality possessed an ambiguous quality. Different people viewing the same scene or situation would tend to extract differing interpretations of it. Bazin believed that filmmakers should develop a style that respected these ambiguities and that did not unfairly coerce or manipulate viewers into sharing a single, mass emotional response to the scene or film. He believed that filmmakers should employ techniques that honor and enhance the ambiguities of reality and give viewers room to develop their own interpretations and responses. These conditions would form the basis of a realist style.

Structural Basis for Bazin's Realism

Bazin suggested that particular elements of film structure were more or less suited to representing the ambiguities of reality and giving spectators freedom of response. Bazin felt that the techniques best suited for realism were **deep-focus cinematography** (where a great distance separates sharply focused foreground and background objects) and the **long take** (shots of long duration) in a style that minimizes the importance of editing.

Shots employing deep focus can create multiple areas of interest and activity within the frame, ranging in crisp focus from foreground to background. As a result, viewers have more to study in a deep-focus shot than in a more conventional shot that is organized around one main area of interest. In the shot illustration from *Citizen Kane* (1941), viewers might concentrate on Mrs. Kane and the banker in the foreground, on the father in the midground, or on young Charlie playing in the snow in the background, or they might scan all these areas in a manner and sequence that will differ from viewer to viewer. For Bazin, such shots are more ambiguous than shots composed using a narrow plane of focus because they afford viewers multiple ways of viewing and responding to the material in the frame. Used in conjunction with deep focus, long takes enhance this visual ambiguity by extending the deep-focus compositions in time. For Bazin, deep focus "brings the spectator into a relation with the image closer to that which he enjoys with reality. Therefore, it is correct to say that independently of the contents of the image, its structure is more realistic." By contrast, for Bazin "montage by its very nature rules out ambiguity of expression."

By minimizing editing, deep focus and the long take respect the wholeness and richness of space and reality. By contrast, montage fractures and divides this wholeness. For Bazin, therefore, it was incompatible with a realist style. Bazin criticized filmmakers who used montage to control the audience, manipulate their responses, and elicit mass emotional reactions. Montage-oriented directors who would fail Bazin's ethical basis for a realist aesthetic include such masters as Alfred Hitchcock and Steven Spielberg.

Psycho (Paramount Pictures, 1960)
Mass-emotion films, such as *Psycho*, fail Bazin's test of a realist film by provoking all spectators to share a uniform emotional response (fright, in the case of *Psycho*). Frame enlargement.

Using very brief shots edited at a frenzied pace, the shower sequence from *Psycho* achieved Hitchcock's goal of making the audience share a single, uniform response— scream with fright. Hitchcock said about *Psycho* that he wasn't interested in the actors or their performances or even the story, but only in using the elements of pure cinema, primarily editing, to make the audience experience a mass emotion. A similar strategy operates in Steven Spielberg's *Jaws* (1975), where editing, specifically cross-cutting, creates considerable suspense and terror about the shark's attacks. Like *Psycho*, *Jaws* is a mass-emotion film in which filmmakers use technique with brilliance and sophistication to ensure that all members of the viewing audience experience the same intense reactions.

This uniformity of response is precisely what Bazin wished to avoid. Montage editing has an inherit tendency to manipulate the viewer's response, and this placed it outside the ethical basis of his film realism.

Bazinian Filmmakers

Bazin praised the work of directors who employed deep-focus compositions and the long take. He greatly esteemed French director Jean Renoir (*The Grand Illusion* [1937], *The Rules of the Game* [1939]) for his use of deep-focus cinematography and for his tendency to employ camera movement rather than montage. *The Grand Illusion* contains a series of remarkably fluid camera moves and mobile framings. Rather than cutting to a new camera set-up, Renoir kept his camera and the actors in nearly constant motion, extending the length of his shots past the point at which other directors would cut and using deep focus to create multiple areas of activity within the frame. The resulting richness of his compositions was the essence of Bazinian realism.

Bazin also admired U.S. director Orson Welles. In *Citizen Kane* (1941), Welles filmed entire scenes in one or two lengthy shots. In the scene where Kane's parents make arrangements with a banker to raise him and to act as young Charlie Kane's guardian, Welles composed the scene in two shots. The action begins with a long shot showing young

Citizen Kane (RKO, 1941)
Deep focus in *Citizen Kane*. Young Charles Kane plays outside while his parents sign away control of his future to a banker. Note the crisp focus in foreground, mid-ground, and background. Frame enlargement.

Charlie playing in the snow and the camera pulls inside the window of young Charlie's home to reveal his parents and the banker. The camera tracks in front of his mother as she crosses from the window to a table to sign the papers, and Welles records this scene in an extraordinary deep-focus shot (see illustration). In the second shot of the scene, the camera is outdoors and tracks across the porch of the cabin to young Charlie in the snow, where the adults join him and announce his fate.

The two extended takes that compose this scene, running nearly four minutes, represent a clear stylistic alternative to the standard rules of continuity editing, which would mandate using first a master shot and then inserts matching action to the master. But instead of editing from shot to shot, Welles uses camera and character movement to change the compositions, effectively editing *within* the shot. As Bazin pointed out with respect to Welles's films, "dramatic effects for which we had formerly relied on montage were created out of the movements of the actors within a fixed framework."

The supreme example of a filmmaker who employs deep focus, rather than montage, to create rich compositions with multiple areas of interest is the French director Jacques Tati. In films like *Playtime* (1967), editing plays virtually no creative role at all. This comic film about the encounters of a bumbling Frenchman with a bewildering modern world of steel skyscrapers and plastic commodities is played out entirely in lengthy shots composed in deep focus where an amazing number of things are happening simultaneously within the frame.

Strengths of Bazinian Realism

Bazin's theory of realism has an extraordinary strength. It stresses the ethical contract that exists between a filmmaker and an audience, and it challenges filmmakers and viewers to think about the cinema's potential for unfairly manipulating its

The Evil Dead
(New Line, 1983)
Bazinian theory contains an ethical dimension—it seeks to honor each person's unique experience of reality. Films that are overtly manipulative of their viewers, or elicit prurient or sadistic impulses, do not achieve the ethical ideal that Bazin held for the cinema. Frame enlargement.

audiences. Bazin cited ample evidence throughout film history to support his argument that the ethically motivated filmmaker, seeking to respect the viewer's experience of reality, should avoid a style that is overtly manipulative and based in montage.

If Bazin was right that individuals' subjective experiences of reality are varied and that a basis for realist style lies in employing cinematic tools that respect this variety, then it follows that filmmakers who use cinema to manipulate audiences into holding socially objectionable reactions are engaging in an unfair or unethical exploitation of their viewers. Although Bazin wrote about film beginning in the 1940s until his death in 1958, his work has important implications in this respect for contemporary film. Among the most controversial of contemporary horror films are the so-called slasher films, such as *Scream, Friday the 13th, The Toolbox Murders,* or *Driller Killer,* featuring elaborate scenes in which a psychopathic killer stalks and murders attractive young women and men. These films typically use subjective shots to emulate the killer's viewpoint as he stalks and slaughters his victims.

Following Bazin, one could object on ethical grounds that this kind of stylistic manipulation is unnecessarily sadistic. It elicits only the most violent of desires from audiences and treats viewers with a measure of brutality, cruelly enforcing a limited range of socially questionable physical and emotional responses. For a Bazinian realist, such films fail to respect the integrity of each viewer and the uniqueness of his or her approach to reality. Bazin's theory of realism has much to say about the ethical contract that obtains between filmmakers and viewers and about the extraordinary potential for coercing emotions that filmmakers have at their command.

Weaknesses of Bazinian Realism

The major weakness of Bazin's realist aesthetic is that it exists as a potential, an ideal that is never fully realized in any given film. Some of the filmmakers Bazin cites as practitioners of deep focus or the long take also employ montage. *Citizen Kane* includes a number of celebrated sequence shots composed in deep focus, but it also employs some striking montages.

Very few films do without the expressive power of editing. In *Rope* (1948), Alfred Hitchcock tried to dispense with editing. Most of the shots in *Rope* run a full ten minutes. Hitchcock only cut when the camera ran out of film, and even then he went to great pains to disguise the cut by having it occur at moments when a character or some other obstruction blocks the camera's view. Hitchcock, however, found the practice unsatisfying, and he discontinued the experiment after *Rope*, recognizing that without editing he had very little ability to create dramatic and psychological rhythm and tempo. Few films representing a pure application of Bazinian principles exist.

A second weakness of Bazinian theory lies in its tendency to minimize the degree to which even deep-focus–long take cinematography can manipulate the viewer's perceptions. In Jacques Tati's *Playtime,* when Tati needs viewers to look at a particular area of the frame, he uses a sudden loud noise, a rapid movement, or a bright color to draw attention there. Even within the long take–deep-focus approach, filmmakers can still guide and influence viewer perceptions.

Other Realist Models

Although it has been extremely influential, Bazin's approach is not the only basis for a theory of film realism. In Chapter 7, we examined documentary realism, which offers filmmakers a method for documenting social conditions and events by minimizing the use of fictionalizing techniques.

Another approach to realism emphasizes the nature of the perceptual information found in cinema and its correspondence with the perceptual information people use in everyday life. This approach may be called **perceptual realism** because it locates a source of realism in cinema at the perceptual level. Film technique builds on a viewer's ordinary perceptual habits and ways of processing the visual and auditory world. Through lighting, sound design, and camera placement, filmmakers build sources of three-dimensional information into their images and can selectively emphasize these sources. As a result, film images look three-dimensional rather than as they truly are, a two-dimensional projection on a flat surface.

Wide-angle lenses, for example, emphasize depth cues. Near objects will appear larger in size than distant objects; this is an everyday perceptual cue that the eye and brain use to infer information about depth and distance. Wide-angle lenses exaggerate these size disparities, making near objects somewhat larger than they are and distant objects somewhat smaller. Thus, wide-angle lenses convey this kind of depth information with special vividness (and, as a result, are the basis for the deep-focus realism of Bazinian theory), in contrast to telephoto lenses, which tend to reduce these differences by magnifiying the size of everything in the frame. The appearance of depth and distance in the film image is thus a realistic perception because it utilizes the same information that is found in the three-dimensional world. (Though Bazin did not write in terms of perceptual science, its findings furnish a strong foundation to his theory.)

As with other theories of realism, however, perceptual realism encounters a challenge. Its elements are counterbalanced by the medium's transformative abilities. Cinema reconfigures, stylizes, and creatively distorts the correspondences between the screen world and the viewer's perceptual experience. An adequate understanding of cinematic realism, based on perceptual correspondences, must also acknowledge their limitations and the transformative properties of cinema that exist in tension with them. In sum, realism is a concept that must be carefully qualified when applied to the cinema because there is much about the medium that is patently unrealistic.

☐ AUTEURIST MODELS

Auteurist film theory studies film authors. Auteurist theory, accordingly, studies film as a medium of personal expression in which great directors leave a recognizable stylistic signature on their work. Auteur critics usually consider this author to be the director. The term *auteur* derives from the French word meaning 'author', and this model of criticism has become the most commonly employed and deeply ingrained method of thinking about film.

The French origins of auteur theory occurred in the 1950s when the critics for *Cahiers du Cinema* began to write director-centered film criticism and suggested that even in the Hollywood system a handful of auteurs produced great films. This was a controversial assertion because in the 1930s and 1940s, during the high period of the Hollywood system, directors were often hired functionaries who filmed the script as economically and quickly as possible and who answered to the film's producer. Nevertheless, the auteur critics suggested that John Ford, Alfred Hitchcock, and others were true auteurs by virtue of having a recognizable and consistent artistic style from film to film. By contrast with the 1950s, when the auteur theory first emerged, film directors today enjoy more prestige and public recognition as artists. In fact, many directors today achieve superstar status and even directors who have made only one or two films are allowed to place their name above the film title and claim possessive credit, as in "A Film By . . ."

Auteurist criticism developed among the French New Wave critics and then was imported to the United States in the 1960s. Today, director studies are among the most common forms of film criticism. They trace the style of key directors regarded as important artists and as the major creative influence shaping the materials and design of their films. Such directors include Akira Kurosawa in Japan, Ingmar Bergman in Sweden, Federico Fellini in Italy, and, in the United States, Alfred Hitchcock, John Ford, Francis Ford Coppola, Martin Scorsese, and many others.

Elements of Auteurism

An auteurist critic looks for consistency of theme and design throughout a director's films. In practice, this means that the critic looks at three correlated elements: cinematic techniques, stories, and themes.

Case Study: Alfred Hitchcock

In the case of Alfred Hitchcock, a director frequently studied from an auteur perspective, these consistent and recurring elements include stories about characters falsely accused of crimes (the "wrong man" theme, found in such films as *The 39 Steps, The Wrong Man, Strangers on a Train,* and *North by Northwest*) and visual elements such as cross-tracking shots, the subjective camera, high-angle shots, mirror imagery, and long stretches of film without dialogue but with an intensively visual design that Hitchcock called "pure cinema."

In addition, the critic developing an auteur study of Hitchcock might seek correlations between Hitchcock's upbringing and private life and the subjects and techniques of his films. An auteur critic might draw a connection between Hitchcock's intense relationship with his mother and the frequently recurring mother figures in the films, or between Hitchcock's Catholic upbringing and attendance at a Jesuit school and the narratives of guilt, sin, transgression, and crime so common in his films. Hitchcock's fascination with crime, his attendance of murder trials at England's Old Bailey Court, his visits to the Black Museum of Scotland Yard, his attraction to the suspense writer Edgar Allen Poe, and his fascination with celebrity killers such as England's famed John Christie, who buried the bodies of his victims under the floorboards of his house, would seem to have an obvious bearing on the films.

The auteur critic could also draw on anecdotes told by Hitchcock as a standard part of interviews, such as the imprisonment story about the time his father allegedly took him to a police station where Hitchcock was locked in a cell, then subsequently

Strangers on a Train (Warner Bros., 1951) In Hitchcock's moral universe, everyone is guilty of something, if not by deed then by thought. Accordingly, many of his films focus on a "wrong man" theme, with a character falsely implicated in a crime he did not commit. Guy (Farley Granger) is unwillingly drawn into a bizarre plot to murder his wife, and, though he does not commit the deed and even protests against it, he has harbored murderous thoughts about her. To suggest this moral guilt, Hitchcock frames him behind bars, with his face half in shadow. Frame enlargement.

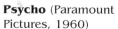

Psycho (Paramount Pictures, 1960) Hitchcock's lifelong fascination with crime certainly influenced his screen work. He studied the careers of England's famous murderers and helped create some of the screen's most famous villains. Norman Bates (Tony Perkins) in *Psycho* remains one of cinema's most chilling monsters. Frame enlargement.

released with a warning by the police that "this is what we do to naughty boys." By telling such anecdotes, Hitchcock encouraged the search for connections between his personal life and his films. He said, "I was terrified of the police, of the Jesuit fathers, of physical punishment, of a lot of things. This is the root of my work."

To the extent that the auteur critic can find consistent themes, stories, and audiovisual designs running through the body of a director's films, and can even tie these elements to the filmmaker's private life, the critic can argue that such a director is a true auteur whose films embody a personal and artistic vision.

Strengths of the Auteur Model

Auteur criticism has helped elevate cinema to the level of art in the eyes of critics, film-makers, and the general public. By stressing the uniformity and integrity of a direc-tor's artistic vision, the auteur critic argues in favor of a unified body of work. By doing so, the critic implies that film is more than just a business, a product manufactured for profit, or an ephemeral and diverting entertainment. By stressing film as an art, auteur criticism undeniably bolsters the power of directors relative to producers and other members of the production crew and has helped to legitimize the film medium.

Moreover, in many cases, the director *is* the catalyst of a production, the key crew member who synthesizes, directs, and helps guide the contributions of other per-sonnel. Production designers and cinematographers emphasize the need to subordi-nate their artistic vision and interests to the desires of the director in an effort to help the director get the results he or she wants. With many directors, therefore, it is le-gitimate to argue in favor of some degree of auteurism.

Weaknesses of the Auteur Model

The weaknesses of auteur criticism lie in its tendency to commit the attributional er-rors discussed in the last chapter. If one looks at enough films of any director, visual and narrative patterns will probably begin to emerge, but not all of these are mean-ingful, nor should they necessarily be attributed to the director. Filmmakers sometimes execute an effect simply because they like the way it looks or even, more mundanely, because they had to shoot or edit a scene a certain way due to uncooperative weather, the scheduling of in-demand actors, or simply running out of money. Many factors that influence the look of a finished film are things over which filmmakers have little or no control. Japanese director Akira Kurosawa was asked about his framing of a scene in *Ran* (1985), a film about samurai warfare in sixteenth-century Japan. Kurosawa's response says much about the realities of filmmaking. He replied that he had to shoot from the angle he used: Any other angle would reveal the Sony factory and airport nearby, incompatible with the film's period setting.

Even more damaging to the auteur critic's search for a sole author is the fact that film production is collaborative. It is often impossible to assign responsibility for an effect to a particular individual such as the director, even when the filmmaker in ques-tion is one with a readily recognizable style, such as Alfred Hitchcock. Hitchcock collaborated with the screenwriters on most of his films but mainly to guide the de-sign of the narrative and ensure that it afforded him opportunities to create interest-ing visual effects. Constructing a narrative from scratch and building it into an elegant finished structure was something Hitchcock did not do on his own, in the manner of a filmmaker like Woody Allen. He needed the services of accomplished screenwriters. The elegant charm and light spirit of *Rear Window* (1954), *To Catch a Thief* (1955), and *The Trouble With Harry* (1956) have an important point of origin in the scripts John Michael Hayes furnished for these films. Much of Hitchcock's other work lacks the unique spirit of his collaborations with Hayes, and this suggests that Hayes played a considerable role in shaping the style of these pictures.

Some of Hitchcock's finest films, such as *Notorious* (1946), about U.S. agents in-filtrating a nest of Nazi spies in Brazil, were shaped by decisive creative intervention

Vertigo (Paramount Pictures, 1938)
James Stewart, as detective Scotty Ferguson, hangs precariously, high above San Francisco, in *Vertigo*. In film after film, Hitchcock took his characters and viewers to the edge of the abyss and forced them to look at the darkness and chaos below. In doing so, he created a distinctive cinematic universe, but he did not work alone. He depended on the vital input of his collaborators. Hitchcock may be an auteur, but the cinema remains a collaborative medium. Frame enlargement.

from the producer. In the case of *Notorious,* producer David O. Selznick insisted again and again that the scripts from Hitchcock and his writers were not good enough and needed merciless revision. As was his custom, Selznick even offered specific suggestions for changing the characters and story situations. Only when the revisions satisfied Selznick was Hitchcock allowed to begin filming.

There is no effective way for auteurist criticism to deal with the problems posed by collaboration. The auteur critic detects consistent patterns across the body of a director's films and hopes that those things attributed to the director are, indeed, justified. In most cases, though, the critic attributes things on faith, without documentation in the form of interviews or written records about who on the crew did what. Many auteur critics respond to this problem by claiming that, by "Hitchcock," they mean not the private individual, but rather the body of films with their unified themes and visual designs. Accordingly, "Hitchcock" becomes a construction required by theory, referring to the films and not to the man. This stratagem is a way of dealing with the objection that a critic can never really know who is responsible for what in a film, and it corrects some, but not all, of the reasons for making the objection.

A final weakness of auteur criticism should be noted. In some cases, the critic's attempt to discover a unified body of work produces bias and distortion. Poor films may be elevated to the status of masterworks, and a critic may regard even a minor film by an auteur director as a greater work than an undeniably major film, such as *Casablanca,* by a nonauteur director (in this case, Michael Curtiz).

☐ PSYCHOANALYTIC MODELS

Drawing primarily from the writings of Freud and French psychoanalyst Jacques Lacan, **psychoanalytic film theory** emphasizes film's elicitation of unconscious sources of pleasure. For psychoanalytic critics, the film medium activates deep-rooted psychological, sometimes infantile and nonrational, desires and anxieties.

Elements of Psychoanalytic Models

Voyeurism

Psychoanalytic critics examine the way that cinema organizes and manipulates a viewer's pleasures and attraction to the screen spectacle. The cinema activates what psychoanalytic critics refer to as the "scopic drive" or **voyeurism,** a primary pleasure obtained from looking at things. In the cinema, the scopic drive provides viewers with voyeuristic pleasure derived from looking at characters and situations on screen.

Voyeuristic or scopic pleasures can be aroused in two ways by the cinema. In the first, cinema techniques, such as close-ups, draw the viewer's attention to aspects of the screen spectacle that arouse nonrational pleasures, often sexual ones. Psychoanalytic critics have examined the way that male directors will use long, lingering close-ups to examine the glamorous, sexy appearance and costuming of female stars, such as Marlene Dietrich or Marilyn Monroe, who embody male erotic desires.

Fetishizing the Body

Psychoanalytic critics describe Dietrich's elaborate costuming and ritualistic visual presentation in a series of films she made for director Josef von Sternberg (*Morocco* [1930], *Shanghai Express* [1932], *Blonde Venus* [1932], *The Scarlet Express* [1934], *The Devil Is a Woman* [1935]) as a kind of visual fetish. With lingering visual attention, the

---

Elaborately costumed and posed in the films of Josef von Sternberg, Marlene Dietrich becomes a point of concentrated visual focus, commanding the camera's attention and receiving its lingering gaze. (Paramount Pictures)

camera studies the precise outline, design, and appearance of Dietrich as an erotic object. While the Sternberg films enjoy a high critical reputation due to their exquisite artistic design, many less reputable films display the bodies of their performers in a fetishized fashion, a practice that includes male stars as well as female ones.

The glistening, well-defined muscles of Sylvester Stallone or Arnold Schwarzenegger command a great deal of attention in their action films. For psychoanalytic critics, this visual attention emphasizes the bodies of Stallone and Schwarzenegger as idealized sexual objects conforming to an exaggerated cultural ideal of male potency and power.

Through its framing strategies, then, film concentrates and organizes the visual attention of its audience around such erotically charged objects as the body of a Marilyn Monroe or a Sylvester Stallone. In doing so, films activate the spectator's pleasures in looking, voyeuristic in nature, and the spectator's scopic desire to possess an object through a controlling gaze.

Taboo Images

A second way the cinema can appeal to the voyeuristic pleasures of its viewers is by displaying **taboo** (forbidden) **images**. Films offer spectacles of sex and violence that excite viewers in ways they would deny in polite society. Viewers of *The Silence of the Lambs* eagerly spend time in the company of serial killer Hannibal Lecter, whereas in real life they would shun such a person. Unlike real-life violence, bloodshed and killing on screen give many viewers intense aesthetic pleasure. For psychoanalytic critics, the cinema's ability to excite viewers with spectacles of sex and violence illustrates its powerful appeal to an audience's primitive, nonrational, unconscious desires. Polite society restricts outward expressions of sexual or aggressive behavior, yet the cinema displays these in extremely arousing ways.

This elicitation of arousal has implicated cinema in controversies about the socially undesirable effects of viewing movie violence. Most popular films present violence as an exciting and attractive spectacle, which stimulates some members of the audience to act out their aggressive fantasies. A sequence in *The Basketball Diaries* (1995)

Rambo III (Carolco, 1988) Sylvester Stallone's engorged, glistening muscles in *Rambo III* add a sexual dimension to the film's violence, especially since they receive such extraordinary visual attention throughout the film. Male, as well as female, stars may function as erotic objects.

The Silence of the Lambs
(Orion Pictures, 1991)
Hannibal Lecter (Anthony Hopkins)
in *The Silence of the Lambs* exerts a
powerful fascination for viewers who
are repulsed by his monstrousness
yet attracted by his wit and intelligence. The special power such a
character has over viewers may
require a psychoanalytical explanation since it seems to contradict a
viewer's rational judgment that such
a person is evil and to be avoided.
Frame enlargement.

in which a high school student brings a gun to class and shoots his teacher and fellow
students has apparently served as the inspiration for similar real-world incidents. The
visual design of the sequence—the camerawork, compositions, lighting, and editing—
gives it a stylish appearance and accentuates its ability to arouse spectators. Most viewers clearly know the boundaries between real life and fantasy. Some, though, do not
and have difficulty controlling their violent thoughts and impulses. Intensive movie
violence can help stimulate these thoughts and impulses to the point that an individual

The Basketball Diaries (New Line, 1995)
In this notorious scene, a disaffected youth (Leonardo DiCaprio) guns down his classmates and
schoolteacher. The backlighting, tilted camera angle, flame-spouting gun, and black leather costume give the violence a stylish and artful appearance. The visual rhetoric makes it exciting and
appealing, thereby creating a problematic ethical relationship with viewers. Frame enlargement.

acts on them. In this regard, cinema can reinforce the irrational dispositions of some of its viewers. In a culture that is already heavily saturated with violent and aggressive messages, this can help increase the incidence of antisocial behavior.

Strengths of the Psychoanalytic Model

Psychoanalytic criticism emphasizes the complex ways that film arouses an audience's emotions and desires. These desires may not be conscious or fully understood by viewers, yet films can reach deep inside viewers' minds to influence the ways they understand their world, themselves, and their feelings. Sometimes the emotional response of an audience is so extraordinarily intense and concentrated, at such an unbearable pitch, that a psychoanalytic explanation seems warranted.

As an example, consider the opening of Luis Buñuel's and Salvador Dali's *Un Chien Andalou* (1928), which features one of the most horrific images in screen history. The scene leaves viewers shocked and gasping for breath, as if they had been hit in the stomach. In the scene, discussed in Chapter 9, a man (played by Buñuel) stands behind a seated woman. He pulls out a straight razor and opens her left eye. The film then cuts to a long shot of clouds slicing across a moon, as the audience breathes a sigh of relief, thinking that, as usual, the camera has turned away from something that promises to be too horrifying.

In the next moment, though, the filmmakers show what viewers most dread. The razor slices into an eye that pops and disgorges a blob of gelatinous fluid. This is an old movie, and violent images have a way of becoming less intense and horrifying over time. This, though, is not one of those cases. The image has a special, sustained power to disturb and nauseate viewers. Contemporary audiences recoil with the same intensity and disgust that viewers felt in 1928.

A psychoanalytic explanation can help here. As Freud suggested, among all the parts of the body that might potentially be wounded, people seem most sensitive about their eyes. Freud connected this anxiety to fears of castration. Whatever one might think of such a connection, Freud seemed correct in noting the special intensity of the nonrational, even instinctual, terror over the threat of wounds to the eyes. When an object or situation is so charged with emotional energy, psychoanalysis looks toward the unconscious for an explanation. The anxieties seem, in some way, to be fundamental and primitive components of human identity, and, for psychoanalytic theory, the unconscious is the most primitive part of the mind. Psychoanalytic theory, then, enables critics to ask about why certain film images seem so charged with emotion and about how, in such moments, the cinema provokes and intensifies the reactions of its audience.

Weaknesses of the Psychoanalytic Model

There are several weaknesses to psychoanalytically based criticism. The first is that psychoanalytic theory is based on ambiguous clinical data. The case studies, the analyses of patients' behavior and dreams that form the basis of the theory, are accessible as data only through the interpretations an analyst has placed on them. A scholar wishing to check the validity of psychoanalytic claims cannot do so by going back to the original patient, the original dream, or behavior. These can never be retrieved except through the analyst's published interpretations. The scientific status of psychoanalytic theory, therefore, is weak because the information on which the theory draws is either inaccessible or unavailable for re-examination. This means that psychoanalytic film theory must pretend to have a clinical basis that it, in fact, never does.

Secondly, it has a tendency to overextend itself, to be used as a means of explaining all dimensions of an audience's emotional response to movies. Psychoanalytic critics tend to see the cinema as a medium that plays on mainly irrational desires and irrational perceptions. On the contrary, though, many aspects of the viewer's response to movies are entirely rational and do not require special explanation with reference to the unconscious mind. Among these are the demands for reference and correspondence with experience that viewers expect from a photographically based medium like cinema.

Psychoanalytic theories emphasizing irrational states of mind and desire are best applied to certain categories of films rather than to all films. Horror films, for example, are especially deserving of psychoanalytic attention because of the way they activate primitive fears and anxieties and center on monsters and supernatural beings who, arguably, represent irrational terrors. Selectively applied to films that elicit exceptionally charged and nonrational responses from viewers, psychoanalytic theory can clarify the special qualities of these responses. Psychoanalytic theory is less useful as a means of explaining how all films operate.

☐ IDEOLOGICAL MODELS

Critics use **ideological film theory** to examine the relationship between movies and society and, specifically, how film represents social and political realities. An **ideology** is a set of beliefs about society and the nature of the world, involving assumptions and judgments about the nature of right and wrong, good and evil, justice and injustice, law and social order, and human nature and behavior.

Ideologies are systems and patterns of thought characteristic of a particular society or social subgroup. All societies or social subgroups contain ideologies, which people internalize by virtue of growing up in that culture or by gaining membership to that group or subgroup.

Societies contain multiple ideologies, and these are not always coherent or harmonious. Because of this, all societies are subject to ideological tensions and conflicts. Among conflicting ideologies in U.S. culture are the commitments to individual freedoms, on the one hand, and, on the other, the power of state and local governments to enforce law and maintain public order.

The ongoing controversies over gun control illustrate these conflicting ideologies. Proponents of gun control emphasize the need for government to ensure public safety by getting guns off the street. Opponents emphasize the individual right to own and bear arms. Such conflicts are very difficult to resolve and tend to arouse a great deal of emotion on each side, as the ongoing battles about gun control illustrate. Ideological conflict is a typical social phenomenon arising from the simple fact that not all of the belief systems that circulate through a society are compatible or consistent with one another.

Elements of Ideological Models

Ideological film critics study the ways film portrays society and gives voice to one or more social ideologies. The ideological critic often starts by describing certain social trends or habits of thought and then demonstrates how these are represented in given bodies of film. Ideological critics, for example, emphasize the way that many Hollywood Westerns, which portray Native Americans as villains and as obstacles to be removed, support traditional cultural beliefs about manifest destiny, the inalienable right of European settlers to claim the wilderness and divest Native Americans of their land.

Levels of Ideology

Social ideologies exist in films on either first- or second-order levels, that is, they are either explicit or implicit. *Rambo: First Blood Part II* (1985), about a super U.S. warrior who returns to Vietnam many years after the war and defeats the Vietnamese in battle, offers U.S. culture a kind of substitute and vicarious symbolic victory in a war the nation lost. By virtue of its explicit treatment of social, political, and historical topics, it is an overtly ideological film. Its story deals with anxieties about the role of the United States as a world superpower and with lingering questions about its defeat in Southeast Asia. As such, the images and narrative of *Rambo* are ideological in an immediate, explicit, first-order way.

Films that are ideological on a second-order level present social messages and portraits of society that are implicit, indirect, and subtle. Examples of second-order ideological films are *Back to the Future* (1985) and *Field of Dreams* (1989), both of which are intimately connected to the mood of the era in which they were produced, especially the nostalgic myth of a return to the past represented by 1980s political culture.

In *Back to the Future,* the hero, Marty McFly (Michael J. Fox) travels back in time, and Ray Kinsella (Kevin Costner) from *Field of Dreams* mysteriously recreates the past in an Iowa cornfield of dreams. Both characters meet their parents from the past and, by doing so, they reclaim their boyhood. An ideological critic would show how these narratives correlate with the political culture of the 1980s, particularly its nostalgic embrace of an ideal past and the folklore of small towns and close-knit communities that underlay the appeal and vision of the Reagan presidency.

Unlike *Rambo,* where the political ideologies are up front and out in the open, *Back to the Future* and *Field of Dreams* do not strike one immediately as political films. An ideological critic, however, could argue, correctly, that these films are closely entwined with the political culture of their period. As a result and despite their overt appeal as entertainment vehicles, they are ideological in a second-order, implicit, and indirect way.

Ideological Point of View

Just as films may be directly or indirectly ideological, they may also take up a variety of positions with respect to the ideologies they portray and the views of society developed in their narratives. Although a wide range of such positions exists, three main categories are the most important. Films can support established social values, criticize established values, or offer an incoherent, ambiguous, and unresolved presentation of social values. To describe the ideological position of a film, a critic must specify two things: the constellation of social values within the film and its attitude toward them, and, second, the social groups to whom those values belong.

Position One: Ideological Support   The first position—support for established social values—is illustrated by many contemporary war films, which take a very positive and
patriotic stance with respect to America's military forces. *Black Hawk Down* (2001),
for example, recounts the horrendous fighting in Somalia between a local warlord's army
and U.S. Marines. Consistent with war films since *Saving Private Ryan,* the depiction
of battlefield violence is graphic and intense. This violence, though, serves to emphasize the heroism, bravery, and determination of U.S. forces, qualities that the film stresses.

Like many contemporary war films, *Black Hawk Down* does not offer a political
perspective on the fighting. In fact, it avoids political analysis and, instead, offers a

---

Black Hawk Down (Columbia, 2001); **We Were Soldiers** (Paramount, 2002)
Many contemporary war films avoid dealing with the politics of war and questions surrounding the projection of U.S. power overseas. Instead, they take a close-up view of battlefield
violence and stress the bravery and patriotism of American soldiers. In *Black Hawk Down*
(a), Americans find themselves outgunned in Somalia but manage to prevail. In *We Were Soldiers* (b), Lt. Col. Hal Moore (Mel Gibson) prays with his children at bedtime while his wife
looks on approvingly. The film uses family and religion for ideological purposes, stressing that
virtue and patriotism are the essential meanings of the Vietnam War. Frame enlargement.

straightforward tribute to America's military by concentrating on the close-in details of hand-to-hand fighting.

More recently, *We Were Soldiers* (2002) portrays the courage and determination that enabled a battalion of 400 U.S. Army soldiers to prevail over 2000 enemy soldiers during the Vietnam War in 1965. The movie stresses the strong family and religious background of the main character, Lt. Col. Hal Moore (Mel Gibson). Many scenes show Moore at home and his devotion to family. He frolics with his kids, has heart-to-heart talks with them, and prays with them before bedtime. By giving family and religion such emphasis, the film scores ideological points. The character is defined in terms of a very positive vision of a good, moral life, and this moral framework is then transferred to the battle scenes in Vietnam, helping them to become a statement about American patriotism and bravery.

The major ideological effect of *We Were Soldiers* lies in the way that it erases all of the war's controversy, substituting for that a redemptive and heroic vision of American sacrifice. Toward this end, the filmmakers deleted a key scene placed at the end of the film in which, after the battle, Moore warns Pentagon officials that the Vietnamese will be a tough enemy, suggesting that a decision to pursue the war would be foolish. The scene added a very different point of view, one that was more critical of the war. It was, therefore, cut out. Consistent with many contemporary Vietnam War movies, *We Were Soldiers* portrays a controversial war by ignoring the controversy and emphasizing instead traditional elements of patriotism.

Because societies contain multiple communities and multiple ideologies, films might support social values that have currency within one community or subgroup but that are disdained or rejected by other groups. *Longtime Companion* (1990) examines the spread of AIDs in the 1980s by focusing on a small, closely-knit community of gay men in New York City. When released, the film was controversial because its affectionate, supportive portrait of gay life clashed with the value of groups convinced that gay sexuality is wrong or who blamed the gay community for the spread of AIDs.

Position Two: Ideological Critique   Films offering a genuinely critical view of established social values are less common in the U.S. industry than those that offer clear support for such values. Nevertheless, in the late 1960s, films such as *Easy Rider* (1969) and *The Wild Bunch* (1969) presented heroes who were outlaws or rebels dissatisfied with and struggling against what was then termed "the establishment." In *Easy Rider* and *The Wild Bunch,* audiences sympathized with the outlaws and not with mainstream society; the heroes' rebellion exposed the pettiness and intolerance of society. More recently, *Robocop* (1987) offered a savage critique of the social Darwinism that underlay 1980s economic policies, especially those cutting the social safety net from under the poor while revising the tax laws to benefit the very wealthy.

Outside relatively rare social satires like *Robocop,* critiques from a left-wing perspective are uncommon within the U.S. industry. By contrast, European filmmakers are much sharper in their political critiques. Italian director Gillo Pontecorvo, in *The Battle of Algiers* (1965) and *Burn!* (1969), critiqued the imperialism of France and England at the time of their empires in these films about heroic guerrilla struggles for revolution and independence. Furthermore, by implication, *Burn!* offered a cri-

Philadelphia (Tri-Star Pictures, 1994)
Commentators and critics argued over the ideological content of *Philadelphia*, which focused on the film's portrayal of a homosexual man (played by Tom Hanks) with AIDS. Some critics suggested that the film minimized the character's gay identity and sexuality in the interest of appealing to heterosexual audiences that have traditionally avoided gay-themed films. Frame enlargement.

tique of U.S. intervention in Vietnam. This kind of left-wing, socially critical film-making is virtually nonexistent in the U.S. industry.

The reasons are not hard to understand. Many millions of dollars are at stake in a film production today, and Hollywood is not eager to risk losing big chunks of its market with hard-edged social criticism. It is easier, and potentially more profitable, to reinforce existing ideologies than to challenge them in fundamental ways. *Starship Troopers* (1997) offers an instructive lesson in this regard. Director Paul Verhoeven and screenwriter Ed Neumeier tried to use the format of World War II propaganda films in order to equate war with fascism, but this critique was overwhelmed by the film's intense violence and bravura special effects. These made the film very marketable

The Wild Bunch (Warner Bros., 1969)
The savage violence of *The Wild Bunch* contained a powerful indictment of society. The film viewed society as being hopelessly corrupt, and its outlaw heroes were only slightly less bad than everyone else.

and more conventional and conservative by blunting the sharpness of its political critique of imperialism and militarism.

Position Three: Ideological Conglomeration   Radical ideological criticism is rarely found in the U.S. industry. Hollywood films more commonly assume a position of ideological conglomeration, that is, they contain a mixed set of appeals and social outlooks. This is an understandable result from the conditions of mass market production. Major studio films are designed for consumption by large, heterogenous audiences composed of diverse groups, communities, and subcultures. To appeal to these diverse groupings, Hollywood often puts, ideologically, a little of this and a little of that into a film. The resulting mix creates a sufficiently ambiguous product calculated to attract as many members of the target audiences as possible while offending few. Ideological conglomeration enables Hollywood to appeal to a multitude of different viewers.

The futuristic social satire, *Total Recall* (1990), portrayed ruthless corporations exploiting workers on a Martian mining colony and using the media back on Earth to camouflage and disguise political reality. Excessive product placements in the film undermined its social satire. *Total Recall* was 1990's product placement champion, the film that featured more placements than any produced that year. The anticorporate satire of *Total Recall* did not sit well with the continual corporate advertising carried by the product placements. By helping to tame the film's anticorporate satire, the product placements provided a greater degree of social familiarity and ideological comfort to viewers watching the movie's disturbing futuristic world.

In *Rambo III* (1988), set in Afghanistan following the Soviet invasion, Rambo's boss, Colonel Trautman (Richard Crenna), is captured by a brutal Soviet officer. Trautman offers the officer a history lesson, saying,

> "You know there won't be a victory. Every day your war machines lose ground to a group of poorly armed, poorly equipped freedom fighters. The fact is that you underestimated your competition. If you'd studied your history, you'd know these people have never given up to anyone. They'd rather die than be slaves to an invading army. You can't defeat a people like that. We tried. We already had our Vietnam. Now you're gonna have yours."

This speech is a clear example of a conglomerated ideological mix. It offers, surprisingly enough, a leftist analysis of the U.S. role in Vietnam, with the United States as the invading force crushing an indigenous people's desire for freedom. It then places this analysis in the service of Cold War perceptions of the Soviet menace in Afghanistan and employs the political terminology of the Reagan administration (the Afghan rebels as "freedom fighters," a term Reagan used to refer to the soldiers in Nicaragua, funded by the United States, who were opposed to the Nicaraguan revolution).

The resulting mixture of a left-wing analysis of the Vietnam War and right-wing, Cold War, anti-Soviet perceptions produces a conceptual mishmash in which the discourse becomes unintelligible and breaks down, even as its content is intended by the filmmakers to attract a diverse audience composed of both liberal and conservative members. Ideological conglomeration serves a strategic economic function in the film industry, enabling films to offer broad-based appeals to diverse and frequently conflicting social groups.

Narrative and Ideology

A final component of ideological film criticism should be noted. This is the close relationship that exists between narrative and ideology. Ideological film critics regard narrative as an especially good vehicle for ideology. A film's narrative shows a series of changes in a situation or a state of affairs and concludes by explaining how some condition has come about. By so doing, it can embody an ideological *argument*.

Fatal Attraction (1987), for example, tells a story about a happily married stockbroker whose casual adultery produces a nightmare for his family when the woman he is seeing turns out to be a violent psychopath. In telling a story that moves from the allure of casual sex and the excitement of adultery to terror and anxiety and concluding with the death of the female villain and the reunification of the family, *Fatal Attraction* constructs an argument about the importance of family and fidelity and about the violation of trust and love that can result from casual adultery.

Note, though, that this is an ideological argument, and that all of these categories—family, love, fidelity, adultery—are ones that the film constructs in the course of developing its argument. As such, one can quarrel with some of the definitions. Was it really necessary, for example, to turn the stockbroker's lover into such a monster? In the real world, adultery does not inevitably have such horrific and monstrous consequences. It is essential for the film's ideological argument, though, that these consequences ensue. They enable the film to invoke the importance of family and to conclude its ideological argument with a vision of family triumphant.

Strengths of the Ideological Model

Ideological criticism has the great strength of clarifying the multidimensional aspect of film content, especially the way that a given movie may reflect and embody diverse currents of social opinion and belief. Because many films are ideological in an implicit and second-order way, such criticism usefully uncovers otherwise unnoticed aspects of social meaning. Good ideological criticism prevents viewers from becoming too complacent, too naive about the way film can display and distort important social

Fatal Attraction
(Paramount Pictures, 1987)
Fatal Attraction builds its ideological argument about the sanctity of marriage and family through its narrative about a violent threat to the family of Dan and Beth Gallagher (Michael Douglas and Anne Archer). The film's ideology is conveyed by its narrative.

OLIVER STONE

With much thunder and rage, Oliver Stone revitalizes a left-wing political vision in mainstream U.S. cinema, although to call his vision left-wing is to give it perhaps more unity than it actually possesses. After serving in the infantry in Vietnam and subsequently studying filmmaking at New York University, Stone scripted several violent, pulp films (*Midnight Express,* 1978, *Conan the Barbarian* 1982, *Scarface,* 1983, *Year of the Dragon,* 1985) and directed a routine horror film, *The Hand* (1981).

In his second film as director, the remarkable *Salvador* (1986), he began to define his niche as a powerful, sometimes strident, critic of U.S. society and foreign policy. Completed during the Reagan era of the early and mid-1980s as a criticism of the administration's support for a brutal military regime in El Salvador, Stone's film is an act of political courage and commitment. Like most of his work, however, it is not without ambiguity and ambivalence. It skillfully dissects the duplicity of U.S. policy in El Salvador and the violence of the regime the United States supported, but backs away from acknowledging the peasant revolutionaries as a viable alternative. As a result, Stone cannot find any solution to the horrors he portrays, and his political engagement turns into despair.

Stone's next film, *Platoon* (1988), put him in the big leagues as a filmmaker. As an antidote to the comic book fantasies embodied by Sylvester Stallone's Rambo

Platoon (Orion Pictures, 1986)

Platoon was one of the most influential films of its decade. Avoiding Rambo-style heroics, it shows the war as a horrifically destructive event. The film mixes realism with religious symbolism, as in the Christian imagery employed in this shot showing an American soldier's death. Stone returned to the war in several subsequent films, but *Platoon* remains his best work on that subject. Frame enlargement.

character, Stone's film was hailed by veterans and critics as the most realistic portrait of the Vietnam war yet made. *Platoon* does have a surface realism, yet it also employs explicit religious symbolism and generic

and political realities. Ideological criticism keeps viewers vigilant against the egregious screen distortions of important social issues.

Weaknesses of the Ideological Model

The major weakness of ideological criticism occurs when a critic too quickly collapses different levels of meaning, moving too rapidly from the specificity of the film, the particulars of the characters and their situations, to the extraction of a more abstract and generalized ideological message. *Back to the Future* may be a key film of the 1980s,

narrative formulas. Its political view of the war is murky, but it portrays with great intensity the suffering and loss of U.S. soldiers.

Stone next applied his *Platoon* narrative formula—a young man torn between good and bad father-figures—to U.S. capitalism in *Wall Street* (1987), and then made one of his least popular but best films, *Talk Radio,* which powerfully portrays the free-floating popular rage and anxiety that threatens U.S. society and democracy.

A grandiose style and an increasingly strident tone mar some of his subsequent films. *Born on the Fourth of July* (1989) contains an extraordinary Tom Cruise performance as Vietnam vet Ron Kovic, but Stone's audiovisual style is unrelentingly bombastic. The viewer is pummelled by its grandiloquence and by a one-dimensional view of how young Kovic was brainwashed by macho, jingoistic U.S. culture, personified by John F. Kennedy in the period the film portrays.

Stone apparently revised his view of Kennedy for *JFK* (1991), which portrays a dovish president eager to withdraw from Vietnam and killed by Washington powers intent on prosecuting the war. While the film is structurally brilliant in its complex montage editing and clear summary of a mountain of assassination data, Stone weakens his case by building his argument on a speculative and unproven thesis that Kennedy was going to withdraw from Vietnam. As a result, the film occupies a muddy middle ground, neither a clear fiction, nor a responsible historical document.

Attacked by many media commentators for the conspiracy theories of *JFK,* Stone lashed back with *Natural Born Killers* (1994), an ugly account of two mass murderers whose crime spree is glamorized by the news media and who are portrayed as celebrities by reporters eager to promote the latest scrap of tabloid sensationalism. The film is a mishmash of disjointed MTV-style technique—flash cuts, off-kilter camera angles, jerky handheld camerawork, random pans, and other visual manipulations that exist for their own sake. The film glorifies and embodies what it pretends to attack: the violence and ugliness in modern U.S. society and its promotion via film and television.

Nixon (1995) is a surprisingly compassionate portrait of Richard Nixon's life and presidency, with a masterful performance by Anthony Hopkins in the role. *U Turn* (1997) is an unpleasantly violent film noir that returned to the disjointed and off-kilter style of *Natural Born Killers.*

Stone's films are vociferous, cinematically powerful attacks on the power structure in U.S. society. In carrying out this project, he is virtually unique among contemporary U.S. directors who generally prefer box-office returns to social messages. But Stone faces a quandary. U.S. society offers no clear left-wing alternatives to the system he opposes. As a result, he has no effective ideological position from which to speak and criticize and few alternatives that he can offer. It will be interesting to see, in his future films, how and whether he will work through this problem.

connected with the era's zeitgeist, but it should not be reduced to that. It is also a clever, multileveled comedy that speaks to its viewers in a variety of ways.

When an ideological critic pays scant attention to the particular and concrete details of a film's characters and story situations, in favor of a more abstract social message, it weakens the force and logic of the analysis. It may be that the ideological argument of *Fatal Attraction* is that sex is bad if it takes place outside of marriage, but the enormously complex concrete details of the film, and the intricacies of its narrative, should not be reduced to such an abstract and blanket statement. Sophisticated ideological analysis maintains a clear separation between these levels.

☐ FEMINIST MODELS

Critics use **feminist film theory** to discover and describe a distinctively female perspective on film, as well as those ways in which the cinema might be found uniquely pleasurable by female viewers. In practice, feminist models of criticism blend elements of psychoanalytic and ideological analysis. The psychoanalytic component is found in attempts to understand the ways that cinema arouses pleasure and desire in audiences and how this might differ on a gender basis. The ideological component is found in the efforts of feminist criticism to relate the depiction of gender in film to prevailing social attitudes, assumptions, and practices found in the general society of which film is part.

Elements of Feminist Models

Images of Women in Film

Feminist film criticism tends to assume two forms. The first is an analysis and description of the images of women in films that have been created largely by men. Many feminist critics examine the way that visual spectacle and the use of the close-up function in film to present women as visual and erotic objects for the contemplation of a male audience. For feminist critics, the extraordinary visual attention given to the bodies of stars such as Marilyn Monroe or Marlene Dietrich turns these performers into erotic objects for a male audience and into dehumanized elements of visual design.

Feminist analyses focus on narrative strategies as well as specifically visual ones. A feminist analysis of *Fatal Attraction* might concentrate on the fate of the film's nominal villain, Alex (portrayed by Glenn Close). A feminist critic could emphasize the way that the film ideologically constructs the character of Alex as a monster whose outrageous behavior toward the hero's family requires that she undergo an extraordinary amount of suffering and physical punishment to atone for her crimes.

Because the film presents Alex as such a monster, the feminist critic might reasonably suggest that *Fatal Attraction* regards female sexuality that is unconstrained by the institutions of marriage and family with a great deal of fear, suspicion, and loathing. Alex is an independent, single, aggressive, and very sexual woman. In the film, she is ideologically suspect because of these very qualities. By creating and then destroying this monster, the film offers a very traditional message about the ideal role of women as wives and mothers rather than as single professionals.

In recent years, feminist theory has investigated some of the prevailing gender roles assigned to men in commercial cinema. These investigations have included the phenomenon of the "hard-bodied" male action hero (Sylvester Stallone, Arnold Schwarzenegger, Jean-Claude Van Damme), a figure of great violence, exaggerated physical prowess, few words, and little introspection. Feminist theory asks about the ideal of "maleness" that such a figure embodies and its implications for ordinary men and women.

In recent films, women have assumed this character type. In *Lara Croft: Tomb Raider* (2001), Angelina Jolie plays the kind of muscle-bound action hero, blazing away with automatic weapons, that male action stars have long played. At the same time, a regressive, and perhaps even sexist, view of women comes through. Lara Croft can kick butt, but the camerawork and costuming play up her Barbie-doll figure, with outlandishly large breasts. Is this progress, a feminist critic might ask?

Lara Croft, Tomb Raider (Paramount, 2001)
Muscle-bound action heroes are now played by women, not just men. Lara Croft is comfortable with a variety of weapons and never met a man she couldn't out punch and out shoot. And yet the film gives great emphasis to her exaggerated Barbie-doll figure. Is this progress or merely the same old formula of a woman's body put on display in cinema? Frame enlargement.

Feminist Filmmaking

The second focus of feminist criticism is closely related to the first. It is the discovery of alternative feminist forms of filmmaking and images of characters. What difference does it make to a film's imagery and narrative if the writer and/or director are female, rather than, as is usually the case, male?

The feminist critic has a wide range of filmmakers and models of filmmaking from which to choose. The critic could examine the work of a director like Kathryn Bigelow, who specializes in the action genres traditionally associated with male directors. Her films include *Blue Steel* (1990), an urban police thriller, *Point Break* (1991), about a string of perfect bank robberies and the FBI agent sent to investigate, and *Strange Days* (1995), a futurist thriller about virtual reality. Because *Blue Steel* and *Point Break* are genre pictures, the feminist critic would be interested to uncover the minor variations that a director like Bigelow might create within these standard and traditional formats. Bigelow is an articulate filmmaker and a proponent of the view that women directors must not be ghettoized as makers of soft, sensitive films.

> "Conventionally, hardware pictures, action-oriented, have been male-dominated, and more emotional kind of material has been women's domain. That's breaking down. The notion that there's a woman's aesthetic, a woman's eye, is really debilitating."

Bigelow's films are indistinguishable, stylistically, from male-directed action pictures, and they prove that women can excel as filmmakers in precisely the kinds of material long claimed by men.

With regard to independent films, a feminist critic might emphasize that a female director can exert an important influence on productions that are not slotted into particular genres or targeted to be large crowd pleasers employing traditional formulas. Two such films are *The Piano* (1993) and *Orlando* (1993).

Case Study: *The Piano* and *Orlando*

The Piano, written and directed by Jane Campion, stars Holly Hunter (Best Actress Oscar-winner for the role) as a mute, Victorian, unwed mother who travels to New Zealand to fulfill an arranged marriage to an English farmer living there. Ada arrives in New Zealand accompanied by her child and her piano. The film explores her torturous reception as both a woman and an artist. She confronts a culture that is alien to her and places her into the most restrictive of sex roles, expecting her to be a dutiful wife to a well-meaning but insensitive and ultimately brutal husband (played by Sam Neill).

The most telling measure of his insensitivity is his refusal to transport her piano from the beach to their plantation home. Unable to speak or unwilling to do so for reasons that in the film remain mysterious, Ada's only form of communication with the world is her music. Denied this by her husband, who abandons the piano and who later mutilates one of her hands, Ada becomes progressively more alienated from her surroundings, sexually, emotionally, aesthetically. A feminist critic could emphasize the improbability of a male screenwriter or director demonstrating this degree of sensitivity to a woman's psychological and physical plight and such a complex metaphorical understanding of the close relationship between the social oppression of women and control over the rights to speech, art, and communication.

Sally Potter's *Orlando* (1993) examines the consequences of gender roles and how they affect the way people live their lives. Potter's film is adapted from a Virginia Woolf novel about a young man during the Elizabethan era who lives for over four centuries without aging but who mysteriously changes into a woman. Orlando, thus, experiences the world from the perspective of each gender. Living as both a man and a woman, Orlando comes to appreciate the uniqueness of each gender's role and how socially conditioned these roles are.

During the 1850s, Orlando has a brief but intense affair with an adventurer. She tells her lover that, if she were a man, she might not choose to die in battle for an uncertain cause, might find the price of death too high for freedom. "Would I then be a real man?" she asks. The lover replies that, were he a woman, he might not choose to live through his children and sacrifice everything for them. He might choose instead to travel abroad rather than having a family. "Would I then be a real woman?"

The Piano (Miramax, 1993) In *The Piano*, Holly Hunter portrays Ada, an unmarried mother coping with life in a rustic, remote New Zealand community. Written and directed by a woman, the film emphasizes Ada's viewpoint and treats the narrative's male characters as supporting, rather than lead, players. Frame enlargement.

he asks. The film looks at the basis of male and female identity and tries to uncover a deeper human identity beyond gender. When Orlando wakes up and discovers that he is now a woman, he looks into the mirror, sees a woman's nude body, and says, "the same person, no difference at all, just a different sex."

The Piano and *Orlando*, though popular, are philosophically and aesthetically distinct from male-directed productions. In the unique terms of their narrative and images, and in the political and philosophical perspectives brought to gender, its social definition and impact on sexuality, speech, and art, each film offers the pleasures of an alternative perspective in cinema and the importance of having female or feminist forms of filmmaking.

Strengths of the Feminist Model

Feminist criticism has made a major contribution to the understanding of how gender perspectives and gender biases influence film images about the world and the way narratives are organized to privilege male characters and experiences at the expense of strong female characters. To a large extent, this bias in favor of male experience results from the extraordinary power male filmmakers have long enjoyed relative to the much smaller number of women directors in charge of major productions. Because of this power, men have constructed images of women in films, and, for a feminist, these images necessarily say more about men than women. Accordingly, feminist criticism emphasizes the importance of women directors having an artistic voice in the world of cinema as a means of balancing the voices that male directors have long commanded.

Weaknesses of the Feminist Model

Gender is one of the many screens through which human experience is filtered, and, while it has a profound impact on the terms by which people live their lives, it is not the only means for ordering one's experience of the world or organizing the design of films. Sophisticated feminist criticism understands when best to apply accounts emphasizing gender differences and to what degree. The feminist sensibility behind *Orlando* or *The Piano* is more profound and enters more deeply into the design of those films than does the fact that *Blue Steel* or *Point Break* are directed by a woman. In the latter case, the weight of genre and traditional commercial formulas tends to minimize the distinctive contributions that a female director can make. As with all models of criticism, the feminist critic must develop a sensitive understanding of which material will most benefit from her (or his) distinctive tools of analysis.

☐ COGNITIVE MODELS

Cognitive film theory studies the ways viewers process and interpret visual and auditory information in film and how specific structural features may cue or invite particular kinds of interpretations. Cognitive film theory focuses on: (1) the viewer's perception of visual and sound information and (2) the ways that viewers organize and categorize these perceptions in order to derive meaning from a film. With its emphasis on

Moonstruck (MGM/United Artists, 1987)
Cognitive theory stresses how viewers perceive and interpret audiovisual information. Viewers give that information a higher-order level of meaning and structure than the images and sounds themselves convey. These two shots from *Moonstruck* illustrate the eyeline match. In terms of perceptual information, all a viewer sees are separate images of Cher and Nicolas Cage looking in different directions. But viewers organize the shots by inferring, across the cut, that the performers are looking at each other. This level of information is not in the images themselves; the viewer supplies it. Frame enlargement.

perceptually based interpretation and understanding, cognitive film theory derives many of its principles and assumptions from research in perceptual psychology, computer science, and communications. The cognitive film theorist is less concerned with developing an interpretation of the content of a specific film than with understanding how viewers in general process audiovisual information in order to extract meaning from films.

Elements of Cognitive Models

For cognitive film theorists, viewers understand visual and auditory information by using **perceptual** and **interpretive processing**. Perceptual processing refers to sensory perception by viewers. Interpretive processing refers to the higher-level interpretations that are placed on sense information. Let's consider how cross-cutting—a convention of continuity editing used to suggest that two or more events are occurring simultaneously—elicits both levels of response from viewers.

Understood in terms of perceptual processing, a viewer watching a cross-cut sequence sees a succession of shots flashing by on the screen as an alternating series. One series, for example, may show a swimmer desperately racing for shore while the other series shows a shark cutting through the water. Understood in terms of interpretive processing—the cognitive or active interpretational response to sensory information—the viewer draws an inference from the alternating series of recurring images. That inference is a presumption of simultaneous action, the assumption that the narrative lines presented in the cross-cut sequence are occurring at the same moment of time.

These two levels of processing emphasize the basic perceptual skills that the medium of cinema builds on as well as the viewer's contribution to the creation of meaning in cinema. The distinction between the terms highlights the difference between the actual on-screen audiovisual information and what a viewer attributes to that information. Cognitive film theory, therefore, studies the ways that specific audiovisual designs in cinema communicate information to the viewer who responds with an active interpretation. Another example can help to clarify this. A basic rule of continuity editing is the **eyeline match**. In terms of perceptual processing, a viewer watching a sequence cut using the eyeline match sees a series of close-ups or medium shots of actors oriented so that the directions of their gazes are in complimentary directions—one looks screen left, the other looks screen right. From the interpretive perspective, viewers respond to this editing code by inferring a relation of proximity and communication between the characters. The viewer infers that characters presented using the eyeline match are communicating with one another and/or are near each other.

Schemas

Attention to interpretive processing enables cognitive film theorists to examine the ways that a viewer's responses to film are guided by a series of **schemas** or frameworks of interpretation. A fundamental assumption of cognitive film theory is that viewers' responses to film are not strictly sensory-driven, that is, are not entirely explainable as immediate responses to the visual and auditory information contained in the film. Viewers bring to this information a large set of schemas, or frameworks of interpretation, that they have developed through personal experience in the world, as members of given cultures and societies, and as experienced film viewers.

Using schemas, a viewer can understand and interpret visual and narrative information in an extremely efficient and rapid fashion. To viewers familiar with science fiction movies—viewers whose experience in this genre has enabled them to develop an extensive set of interpretational schemas—a bright light on a character's face coupled with an awestruck expression instantly evokes the idea of an alien presence. Viewers familiar with Westerns will have schemas attuned to that genre. They know that a cowboy walking into a saloon will order whiskey, but seated around a campfire will prefer coffee. The more audience knowledge a filmmaker can assume, the more efficient is story presentation. Less needs to be explained.

Filmmakers often count on the existence of specific interpretational schemas in their target audience and design their films to exploit these schemas. The gender-bending villain in *The Silence of the Lambs,* who crossdresses and makes himself up to look like a woman, triggers an audience's cultural schemas regarding the acceptable range of gender displays and sexual behavior. The villain's flagrant violation of conventional schemas regarding proper gender display provokes, as the filmmakers intended, anxiety and disapproval from most audience members.

Why Film Is Comprehensible

In addition to studying the ways that audiences apply schemas to process visual and narrative information, cognitive film theory investigates the more general question of what makes film so comprehensible, accessible, and enjoyable to audiences worldwide. The answers provided by cognitive theory emphasize the correspondences that exist between film and a viewer's real-world perceptual and social experience. For the

The Silence of the Lambs
(Orion Pictures, 1991)
The cross-dressing villain in *The Silence of the Lambs* breaks cultural rules regarding proper gender behavior. The filmmakers count on this violation of a viewer's culturally influenced schemas to generate strong disgust and condemnation of the character. Frame enlargement.

cognitive theorist, film is comprehensible, accessible, and enjoyable because it builds many similarities between the means used to represent a world on-screen and the spectator's familiar habits of perception and social understanding.

Perceptual Correspondences   The viewer sees a three-dimensional world on the flat surface of the screen because the photographic images reproduce important real-world sources of information about spatial depth, about the location and distribution of objects in space, about volume, texture, and movement. Just as this information tells viewers where objects are located in the real, three-dimensional world, it provides the same information in the represented reality of a screen world. Today, many film images are created not with a camera but in the computer. Software programs routinely create this information to make the computer-created image look convincingly three-dimensional. Second, the codes of continuity editing used to build scenes create a consistent projective geometry within the represented three-dimensional world on-screen that is analogous to the viewer's own visual and physical experience. Throughout a scene edited using continuity principles, the screen coordinates of up, down, front, back, right, and left remain consistent, regardless of changes in camera position and angle.

Third, point-of-view editing establishes, for the viewer, easy narrative comprehension because the judicious use of long shot and close-up clarifies important narrative information and emphasizes characters' emotions. Viewers see everything they need to know and are given all the information they need in order to understand the narrative. Fourth, in the film image the viewer reads and understands the significance of characters' facial and gestural expressions, just as the viewer does with real people in daily life. Viewers are extremely good at decoding the meaning expressed on people's faces and through gestures, and they use these skills when watching a movie. Actors are professionals trained to mimic the range of gestural and facial cues significant within their culture so as to evoke the emotions typically associated with those expressions and gestures.

Pointing to these complex correspondences between the information contained in film images and the viewer's real-world perceptual habits and skills, cognitive film theorists persuasively explain why films are so easily understood by large numbers of people.

Social Correspondences   A second set of correspondences connects the screen world to viewers' experiential skills and knowledge. Viewers apply to the screen world many

Notorious (RKO, 1946)
The three-dimensional information contained in this shot from
Hitchcock's *Notorious* includes
the relative sizes of the men, the
converging parallel lines on the
floor, and the diminishing size
and spacing of the floor tiles.
These cues—which derive from
everyday visual experience—
establish the illusion of depth
and distance in the image.
Frame enlargement.

assumptions and judgments about people and proper role-based behavior that are
derived from social experience. These assumptions coexist with, and are modified by,
others that the viewer derives from narrative formula and genre. Characters in a horror film, for example, behave like viewers expect characters in a horror film to behave—
they always go down into that dark basement where a monster is lurking!—but these
behaviors must also correlate with dimensions of human experience that the viewer
finds credible or valid.

Research involving preschool children and adolescents indicates that a close relationship prevails between a child's developing stock of moral and ethical concepts
and his or her abilities to use these concepts to interpret character behavior in movies.
Very young children are likely to judge a character as good or bad depending on
whether the character looks attractive or ugly. Older children override such appearance stereotyping with more complex evaluations based on the moral or ethical content of the character's behavior.

Person perception, then, is a process that commonly underlies nonfilmic interper-
sonal and social experience and the inferences and evaluations viewers make about characters in movie narratives. Filmmakers draw from this important source of correspondence
in creative ways. The presentation of Hannibal Lecter in *The Silence of the Lambs,* the
film's stress on his wit, intelligence, and compassion for the heroine Clarice Starling as
well as his sadistic cruelty, complicates the viewer's desire to establish a stable moral
and ethical evaluation of that character. Viewers are attracted by his positive qualities
and charisma yet repulsed by his violation of normative human behavior.

Strengths of the Cognitive Model

The strengths of cognitive film theory are twofold. First, this model, unlike many of
the others, is research-based. The assumptions and principles of the theory are

There's Something About Mary (20th Century Fox, 1998) Cognitive theory helps explain why and how viewers readily understand cinema, but it is limited in its ability to explore the medium's emotional appeals. *There's Something About Mary* was a huge popular hit with audiences who delighted in its humor. Cognitive theory cannot fully explain such responses. Frame enlargement.

supported by empirical data, which make the theory directly testable, and, accordingly, give it a great deal of explanatory power.

Because of its empirical dimension, cognitive theory provides a strong foundation for understanding how viewers make sense of film images and narratives. Rather than relying on critical speculations that may or may not be applicable to real viewers, the cognitive theorist studies the perceptions and interpretations of actual viewers and is able to help clarify the factors that make film an intelligible medium for its audience.

Second, by providing explanations for the intelligibility of motion pictures, cognitive film theory provides an understanding of why the cinema has become so popular across cultures. Cinema provides viewers with an easily understood spectacle, and this helps ensure its enormous popularity throughout the world. If the motion picture medium was difficult to understand, it would never have become so popular.

Weaknesses of the Cognitive Model

The primary weakness of cognitive film theory is its relative lack of attention to the emotional components of the viewer's experience. Cognitive theory is extremely good at analyzing how viewers perceive and interpret audiovisual information in film narratives, but it has not proven to be as good at analyzing the complexities of a viewer's emotional responses. Interest in cognitive theory by film scholars, however, is a very recent phenomenon, and it may be that cognitive theory will yet have something to contribute in this area. At present, however, psychoanalytic models have more to say about the emotional components of film viewing.

A second weakness of cognitive theory should also be noted. It has relatively little to say about the transformative functions of cinema, the way films go beyond and imaginatively transform the boundaries of the viewer's experience. Films are not mere copies or mirrors of that experience; they reorganize and reconfigure it in complex ways. Moreover, the determinants of meaning in film are manifold. How a filmmaker manipulates structure, what a viewer brings to a film, and the visual and narrative traditions and genres in which a given film is located, all these are part of the elaborate mixture that produces meaning in film. Like all models of film theory, cognitive theory answers some questions and ignores others. The theorist must know when best to apply it and how.

SUMMARY

Because cinema is such a rich and powerful medium of communication, because it affects viewers' lives and their thinking about the world in so many ways, it is important to reach an understanding of what the medium *is*, independently of its existence in any given film. Film theories are systematic attempts to think about, and explain, the nature of cinema, how it works as a medium, and embodies meaning for viewers.

Because the cinema is multidimensional, no one theory has all the answers. Each theory is best suited to answering certain kinds of questions. Realist theory emphasizes the cinema's recording and documenting functions and the ability of filmmakers to use photographic images and naturalistic sounds to capture social realities existing before the camera. Theories of realism tend to define a threshold beyond which the cinema's transformation of social realities is regarded as fictitious, duplicitous, stylized, or distorted. To this extent, realist theories stress the ethical contract that exists between filmmaker and audience.

Realist models aim to establish difficult distinctions between the cinema's recording and documenting functions and its transformative abilities. It is often very hard, though, to know where these distinctions lie. Every camera position implies a viewpoint, and some degree of stylistic transformation of the raw material before the camera is inevitable. It is the job of realist theories to say how much transformation is too much.

Auteur theory stresses the human qualities of cinema and emphasizes that mechanically produced sights and sounds can be organized by artists into an aesthetically satisfying design. Auteurism insists that this mechanical, twentieth-century medium is capable, in the right hands, of producing art.

Psychoanalytic theory emphasizes the enormous potential of cinema to provoke emotional responses in its viewers that may be unconscious, primitive, nonrational, and even contrary to the behaviors polite society demands. Psychoanalytic theory is drawn to explain the highly charged poetic and emotional power of certain images and why they seem to exert such a hold over viewers.

As a medium seen by millions, cinema inevitably has a social impact, and its images and stories construct politically and socially charged views of the world. Ideological film theory uncovers the often subtle terms by which cinema codes its views of reality and, by revealing them, can give viewers control over them.

Feminist film theory reveals the gender biases at work inside the views of social reality offered by films made by men within an industry where power is still largely wielded by men. Images of women in film frequently have been defined by male filmmakers, and feminist theory looks for the alternative artistic and social voices of female filmmakers. Feminist theory reminds viewers that gender is one of the most powerful screens through which film images and stories pass and that male filmmakers may tend to organize those images and stories differently than female filmmakers.

Cognitive theories aim to provide answers to some of the most basic questions about cinema. Why is it intelligible to viewers? Why are many films so easily understood? How can a filmmaker facilitate an audience's understanding of shots, scenes, and stories? How do viewers base their interpretations of films on analogies with their own perceptual and social experience? Cognitive theory points to the ways in which cinema works as a medium of communication.

All of these theoretical models are important because motion pictures are never just one thing. Films offer portraits of the world that can seem realistic but that code and transform sociopolitical content into an emotionally powerful experience. Each theory provides a different point of entry for analyzing a film's design and its effects on viewers.

Film viewers should always keep in mind the extraordinary richness of the motion picture medium. It is what makes cinema such a challenging medium to study and one that is so powerful to experience. Hopefully, these chapters have indicated something of that richness. Equipped with this knowledge, you can embark on an exciting journey. A world of cinema—composed of films from different decades, countries, and genres—awaits exploration. Let intelligence and curiosity be your guides, and enjoy an incredible diversity of film experiences. It is easy to love the cinema. It gives so much back in return.

SUGGESTED READINGS

Dudley Andrew, *The Major Film Theories* (New York: Oxford University Press, 1976).

Andre Bazin, *What is Cinema?*, 2 vols., ed. and trans. Hugh Gray (Berkeley and Los Angeles: University of California Press, 1971).

David Bordwell and Noel Carroll, eds., *Post-Theory: Reconstructing Film Studies* (Madison: University of Wisconsin Press, 1995).

Diane Carson, Linda Dittmar, and Janice Welsch, eds., *Multiple Voices in Feminist Film Criticism* (Minneapolis, MN: University of Minnesota Press, 1994).

Molly Haskell, *From Reverence to Rape: The Treatment of Women in the Movies* (New York: Holt, Rinehart, and Winston, 1974).

E. Ann Kaplan, ed., *Psychoanalysis and Cinema* (New York: Routledge, 1990).

Annette Kuhn, *Women's Pictures: Feminism and Cinema* (London: Routledge and Kegan Paul, 1982).

Gerald Mast, Marshall Cohen, and Leo Braudy, eds., *Film Theory and Criticism: Introductory Readings*, 4th ed. (New York: Oxford University Press, 1998).

Stephen Prince, *Visions of Empire: Political Imagery in Contemporary American Film* (New York: Praeger, 1992).

Glossary

Additive Color Mixing   A system used for creating color on television where red, blue, and green lights are mixed together to create all other hues.

ADR   *Automated dialogue replacement* (ADR) is a postproduction practice in which actors re-record lines of dialogue or add new ones not present at the point of filming. Computer software enables proper synching of these lines with the performer's lip movements as recorded on film.

Aerial Perspective   A visual depth cue in which the effects of the atmosphere make very distant objects appear bluish and hazy.

Ambient Sound   The background sound characteristic of an environment or location. For a film like *The Last of the Mohicans*, set in a forest, ambient sounds include the rustle of branches and the cries of distant birds.

Anamorphic   Method of producing a widescreen (2.35:1) image by squeezing the picture information horizontally and stretching it vertically. This method is used for both theatrical films and for DVD home video formatted for 16 × 9 (widescreen) monitors or projection systems. Unsqueezing the picture information during projection or viewing produces the widescreen image.

Ancillary Market   All of the nontheatrical markets from which a film distributor derives revenue. These include home video, cable television, and foreign markets.

Angle of View   The amount of area recorded by a given lens. Telephoto lenses have a much smaller angle of view than wide-angle lenses.

Antinarrative   A narrative style that tends, paradoxically, toward eliminating narrative by employing lots of digression, avoiding a clear hierarchy of narrative events, and by suppressing the causal connections among events.

Aspect Ratio   The dimensions of the film frame or screen image. Aspect ratio is typically expressed in units of width to height.

Attributional Errors   Mistakes of interpretation that arise when a critic erroneously decides that some effect in a film has a meaning expressly intended by its creators or incorrectly assigns the creative responsibility for an effect to the wrong member of the production crew. Uncovering these errors typically requires documentation of a film's production history.

Auteur   A director whose work is characterized by a distinctive audiovisual design and recurring set of thematic issues. Auteurism is a model of film theory and criticism that searches for film authors or auteurs.

Auteurist Film Theory (Auteur Theory)   A model of film theory that studies the work of a film auteur (or author). Directors are generally considered to be the prime auteurs in cinema. Auteurist theory studies the films of a cinema auteur as works of personal expression.

Back Light   The light source illuminating the space between performers and the rear wall of a set. Along with key and fill lights, back light is one of the three principal sources of illumination in a scene.

Beta Movement   A perceptual illusion in which the human eye responds to apparent movement as if it were real. Because of this illusion, viewers think they see moving figures on a film or television screen when, in fact, there is no true movement.

Blockbuster   A hugely profitable film usually featuring a fantasy theme and a narrative heavily dependent on special effects.

Boom Shot   A type of moving camera shot in which the camera moves up or down through space. Also known as a *crane shot*, it takes its name from the apparatus—a boom or crane—on which the camera is mounted.

"Camera-Pen," The term used by Alexandre Astruc to designate the use of cinema as a medium of personal expression. The concept was a major influence upon French New Wave directors and their conviction that cinema was a director's medium (see **Auteur**).

Camera Position   The distance between the camera and the subject it is photographing. Camera positions are usually classified as variations of three basic set-ups: the long shot, the medium shot, and the close-up.

Canted Angle   A camera angle in which the camera leans toward screen right or screen left, producing an imbalanced, off-center look to the image. Filmmakers often use canted angles to capture a character's subjective feelings of stress or disorientation.

Cinematic Self-Reflexivity   A basic mode of screen reality in which the filmmaker establishes a self-referential audiovisual design. A self-reflexive film calls attention to its own artificially constructed nature.

Cinematography   The planning and execution of light and color design, camera position, and angle by the cinematographer in collaboration with the director.

Classical Hollywood Narrative   Type of narrative prevalent in Hollywood films of the 1930s–1950s and still popular today. The plot features a clear, main line of action (with subordinate subplots), marked by a main character's pursuit of a goal, in which the story events are chained in tight causal relationships. The conclusion cleanly resolves all major story issues.

Close-Up   One of the basic camera positions. The camera is set up in close proximity to an actor's face or other significant dramatic object that fills the frame. Close-ups tend to isolate objects or faces from their immediate surrounds.

Cognitive Film Theory   A model of film theory that examines how the viewer perceptually processes audiovisual information in cinema and cognitively interprets this information.

Composite   The joining together of a shot's digital effects and live action elements.

Composition   The arrangement of characters and objects within the frame. Through composition filmmakers arrange the visual space on-screen into an artistic design.

Computer-Generated Images (CGI)   Images that are created and designed using computer software rather than originating as a scene before the camera that is photographed. Sophisticated software enables digital artists to render textures, lighting effects, movement, and other three-dimensional pictorial information in highly plausible and convincing ways. Bearing this information, CGI can be married (composited) with live action photography to stunning effect, as the exciting interaction of real actors and CGI dinosaurs in *The Lost World* demonstrates.

Continuity Editing   As its name implies, continuity editing maximizes principles of continuity from shot to shot so that the action seems to flow smoothly across shot and scene transitions. Continuity editing facilitates narrative comprehension by the viewer.

Contrast   The differences of light intensity across a scene. A high-contrast scene features brightly illuminated and deeply shadowed areas.

Convention   A familiar, customary way of representing characters, story situations, or images. Conventions result from agreements between filmmakers and viewers to accept certain representations as valid.

Costumes   The clothing worn by performers in a film. Costumes help establish locale and period as well as a given film's color design.

Coverage   The shots an editor uses to bridge continuity problems in the editing of a scene. By cutting to coverage, rather than relying on the master shot, an editor can finesse many problems of scene construction and can improve an actor's performance.

Crane Shot   See **Boom Shot.**

Criticism   The activity of searching for meaning in an artwork. The critic seeks to develop an original interpretation by uncovering novel meanings inside a film.

Cross-Cutting   A method of editing used to establish simultaneous, ongoing lines of action in a film narrative. By rapidly cutting back and forth between two or more lines of action, the editor establishes that they are happening simultaneously. By decreasing the length of the shots, editors can accelerate the pace of the editing and imply an approaching climax.

Cue Sheet   A breakdown of a scene's action, listing and timing all sections requiring musical cues.

Cut   A type of visual transition created in editing in which one shot is instantaneously replaced on screen by another. Because the change is instantaneous, the cut itself is invisible. The viewer sees only the change from one shot to the next.

Deduction   The method by which the critic works, using the general goals of the critical model to guide the search for supporting evidence.

Deep-Focus Cinematography   A style of cinematography that establishes great depth of field within shots. Gregg Toland's cinematography for Orson Welles's *Citizen Kane* is a classic example of deep-focus composition.

Depth of Field   The area of distance or separation between sharply focused foreground and background objects. Depth of field is determined by the focal length of a lens. Wide-angle lenses produce deep focus or great depth of field, whereas telephoto lenses have a shallow depth of field.

Description   A stage in creating criticism wherein the critic fully describes those relevant features of narrative or audiovisual design on which the critical interpretation will be based.

Design Concept   The underlying creative concept that organizes the way in which sets and costumes are built, dressed, and photographed on a given production.

Deviant Plot Structure   A narrative whose design and organization fails to conform with viewers' expectations regarding what is proper or permissible.

Dialogue   One of the three basic types of film sound, it includes speech delivered by characters in a scene and voice-over narration accompanying a scene or film.

Digital Effects   The computer-designed components of a shot that may be composited with live action elements.

Digital Grading   Method of digitally altering image elements, such as color balance and saturation, contrast, gamma, and filtration. *O Brother, Where Art Thou?* was the first feature, shot on film, to be entirely digitized and then color-corrected in this fashion. Also called *digital timing.*

Digital Video   An increasingly accepted alternative to celluloid film, this format captures picture information as an electronic signal in binary code. Images captured on digital video look different than those captured on film, but, once in binary format, images can be stored and manipulated by computer programs for editing and special effects work.

Direct Sound   Sound that is captured and recorded directly on location. Direct sound also designates an absence of reflected components in the final recording.

Director   The member of the production crew who works closely with the cinematographer, editor, production designer, and sound designer to determine a film's organizing, creative structure. The director is generally the key member of the production team controlling and synthesizing the contributions of other team members. On budgetary issues, however, the director is answerable to the producer who has the highest administrative authority on a production.

Dissolve   A type of visual transition between shots or scenes, created by the editor. Unlike the cut, the dissolve is a gradual screen transition with distinct optical characteristics. The editor overlaps the end of one shot with the beginning of the next shot to produce a brief superimposition.

Diversification   A corporate structure in which a company conducts business operations across a range of associated markets and product categories.

Documentary   A type of film dealing with a person, situation, or state of affairs that exists independently of the film. Documentaries can include a poetic, stylized audiovisual design, but they typically exclude the use of overt fictional elements.

Documentary Realism   A subcategory of the realist mode of screen reality. The documentary realist filmmaker employs the camera as a recording instrument to capture events or situations that are transpiring independently of the filmmaker. Documentary realism is also a stylistic construction in that the filmmaker's audiovisual design imposes an artistic organization on the event that has unfolded before the camera.

Dolly   A type of movable platform on which the camera is placed to execute a tracking shot. Tracking shots are sometimes called *dollies* or *dolly shots*.

Editing   The work of joining together shots to assemble the finished film. Editors select the best shots from the large amount of footage the director and cinematographer have provided and assemble these in the proper narrative order.

Editor   The member of the production crew who, in consultation with the director, designs the order and arrangement of shots as they will appear in the finished film and splices them together to create the final cut.

Effects (sound)   One of the three basic types of film sound. Effects are all of the nonspoken, nonmusical sounds in a film (e.g., footsteps, breaking glass, etc.).

Emulsion   The light-sensitive surface of the film. Light sensitivity varies among film stocks. Fast films feature emulsions that are very light sensitive, requiring minimal light for a good exposure. Slow films feature emulsions that are less light sensitive, requiring more light on the scene or set for proper exposure.

ENR   Named for Ernesto N. Rico, this method of film processing retains a portion of the silver in film emulsion, which is normally removed during developing. This has the effect of making shadows blacker, desaturating color, and highlighting the texture and edges of surfaces.

Errors of Continuity   Disruptions in the appropriate flow of action or in the proper relation of camera perspectives from shot to shot. These errors may include the failure to match action across shots or to maintain consistent screen direction.

Establishing Shot   A type of long shot used to establish the setting or location of a scene. In classical continuity editing, establishing shots occur at the beginning of a scene and help contextualize subsequent close-ups and other partial views of the action.

Explicit Causality   The tight chaining of narrative events into a strong causal sequence in which prior events directly and clearly cause subsequent events. Characteristic of Hollywood filmmaking.

Expressionism   A basic mode of screen reality in which filmmakers use explicit audiovisual distortions to express extreme or aberrant emotions or perceptions.

Extras   Incidental characters in a film, often part of the background of a shot or scene.

Eyeline Match   The matching of eyelines between two or more characters who are engaged in conversation or are looking at each other in a scene, in order to establish relations of proximity and continuity. The directions in which the performers look from shot to shot are complementary. That is, if performer A looks screen right in the first shot, performer B will look screen left in the next shot.

Fade   A visual transition between shots or scenes created by the editor. Unlike the cut, the fade creates a gradual transition with distinct visual characteristics. A fade is visible on screen as a brief interval with no picture. The editor fades one shot to black and then, after a pause, fades in the next shot. Editors often use fades to indicate a substantial change of time or place in the narrative.

Fall-Off   The area in a shot where light falls off into shadow. Fast fall-off occurs in a high-contrast image where the rate of change between the illuminated and shadowed areas is very quick.

Fantasy   A basic mode of screen reality in which settings and subjects, characters, and narrative time are far removed from the conditions of the viewer's ordinary life. Fantasy characters may have super powers or advanced technology that lends them extraordinary abilities.

Feature Film   A film typically running between 90 and 120 minutes.

Feminist Film Theory   A model of film theory that examines the images of women in film and issues of gender representation.

Fetishizing Techniques   As emphasized in psychoanalytic film theory, these are elements of style that concentrate the viewer's attention for extended periods upon erotic imagery or material in a way that displaces other components of a scene or shot.

Fictional Documentary Realism   The style of a fiction film employing the techniques of documentary realism to create the illusion that it is a documentary. In such a case, the appearance of documentary realism is a fictional construction.

Fill Light   A light placed opposite the key light and used to soften the shadows it casts. Along with key and back lights, fill light is one of the three principal sources of illumination in a scene.

Film Noir   A cycle of crime and detective films popular in the U.S. cinema of the 1940s. Low-key lighting was a major stylistic attribute of this cycle.

Film Stock   Camera negative identified by manufacturer and number. Stocks vary in terms of their sensitivity to light, color reproduction, amount of grain, contrast, and resolution.

Film Theory   A philosophical or aesthetic model that seeks to explain the fundamental characteristics of the medium of cinema and how it expresses meaning.

Final Cut   The finished edit of a film. The form in which a film is released to and seen by audiences.

Flashing   A technique used to desaturate color and contrast from a shot and to create a misty, slightly hazy effect. Film stock is flashed by exposing it to a small amount of light prior to developing.

Flicker Fusion   Along with persistence of vision and beta movement, this is one of the perceptual foundations on which the illusion of cinema rests. The human eye cannot distinguish the individual still frames of a motion picture because of the speed at which they are projected. Flicker fusion designates the viewer's inability to perceive the pulsing flashes of light emitted by the projector. These flashes and the still pictures they illuminate blend together to produce an illusion of movement.

Focal length   The distance between the optical center of the lens and the film inside the camera. Lenses of different focal lengths will "see" the action in front of the camera very differently. See **Wide-Angle, Telephoto, Normal,** and **Zoom Lenses.**

Foley Technique   The creation of sound effects by live performance in a sound recording studio. Foley artists perform sound effects in sync with a scene's action.

Frame   The borders of a projected image or the individual still photograph on a strip of film. Frame dimensions are measured by aspect ratio.

Framework of Interpretation   The intellectual, social, or cultural frames of reference that a critic applies to a film in order to create a novel interpretation. It is the general intellectual framework within which an interpretation is produced.

General-Interest Journal-Based Criticism   A mode of criticism that falls between newspaper/television reviews and the highly technical, scholarly criticism. In this mode, the critic can offer a more detailed and sophisticated discussion of a film's structure and meanings than can newspaper/television reviewers.

Genre   A type or category of film such as a Western, musical, gangster film, or horror film that follows a set of visual and narrative patterns that are unique within the genre.

Gray Scale   A scale used for black-and-white cinematography that measures color intensity or brightness. Black-and-white film and the black-and-white video camera can differentiate colors only if they vary in degrees of brightness. The gray scale tells filmmakers which colors will separate naturally in black and white.

Greenscreening   Filming of live actors against a blank and colored (green) screen for subsequent compositing with digital elements.

Gross   The total box-office revenue generated by a film before expenses are deducted.

Hard Light   Light that is not scattered or diffused by filters or reflecting screens. Hard light can establish high contrast.

Hard-Matted   Method of producing letterboxed video transfers of widescreen films. The widescreen ratio is preserved for viewing on a 4:3 monitor by masking that part of the video signal that displays on the top and bottom of the monitor's screen and displaying the widescreen image in the unmatted area.

High-Angle   A camera angle usually above the eye level of performers in a scene.

High-Definition Video   Compared with standard video, which has 480 scan lines of picture information, hi def video has up to 1080 scan lines. The Sony/CineAlta HD24P format, which George Lucas used to shoot the latest installments of his *Star Wars* series, runs at 24 frames per second, like film, and carries a resolution of 1920×1080 pixels.

High-Key Lighting   A lighting design that minimizes contrast and fall-off by creating a bright, even level of illumination throughout a scene.

Historical Realism   A subcategory of the realist mode of screen reality. Historical realist films aim to recreate in close detail the manners, mores, settings, and costumes of a distant historical period.

Homage A reference in a film to another film or filmmaker. The climatic gun battle on the train station steps in Brian De Palma's *The Untouchables* (1987) is an homage to Sergei Eisenstein's *The Battleship Potemkin* (1925), which features the famous massacre on the Odessa steps.

Hue One of the basic attributes of color. Hue designates the color itself. Red, blue, and green are primary hues. They are not mixtures of any other color.

Identification A stage in creating criticism wherein the critic selectively identifies those aspects of the film that are relevant for the critical argument being developed. The identification of selective film elements enables the critic to simplify and reduce the wealth of material in the film.

Ideological Film Theory A model of film theory that examines the representation of social and political issues in film.

Ideology A system of beliefs characteristic of a society or social community. Ideological film theory examines the ways in which films represent and express various ideologies.

Implicit Causality The loose sequencing of narrative events. Narrative causality is minimized, and the viewer's sense of the direction in which the story is moving is weaker than it is in films that feature explicit causality.

Implied Author The artistic perspective implied and embodied by a film's overall audiovisual design.

Intensity A basic attribute of color. Intensity measures the brightness of a hue.

Internal Structural Time The dynamic tempo of a film, established by its internal structure (camera positions, editing, color and lighting design, soundtrack). Perceiving this internal tempo, viewers label films as fast or slow moving, yet internal structural time never unfolds at a constant rate. It is a dynamic rhythm. Filmmakers vary the tempo of internal structural time to maintain viewer interest.

Interpretation The goal of criticism. By examining a film's structure, a critic assigns meaning to a scene or film that it does not immediately denote.

Interpretive Processing The viewer's attribution of meaning to audiovisual information, as distinct from perceptual processing, which is the purely perceptual response to this information. Film viewing involves both components. Understood in terms of perceptual processing, a viewer watching a cross-cut sequence sees a succession of shots flashing by on screen as an alternating series. Via interpretive processing, the viewer attributes a representation of simultaneous action to the alternating series. This attribution is not a meaning contained within the images themselves. It is the viewer's contribution.

Iris An editing transition prevalent in silent cinema. A circular mask closed down over the image (an iris out) to mark the end of a scene or, alternatively, opened up (an iris in) to introduce a new scene.

Jump Cut A method of editing that produces discontinuity by leaving out portions of the action.

Key Light The main source of illumination in a scene usually directed on the face of the performer. Along with fill and back lights, it is one of the three principal sources of illumination in a scene.

Latent Meaning Meanings that are indirect or implied by a film's narrative and audiovisual design. They are not direct, immediately obvious, or explicit.

Leitmotif A recurring musical passage used to characterize a scene, character, or situation in a film narrative.

Letterbox A method of formatting wide-screen motion pictures for video release. Black bars mask the top and bottom of the frame, producing a wider ratio picture area in the center of the frame. While the aspect ratio of a letterboxed video image closely matches the original theatrical aspect ratio, the trade-off is a small and narrow image as displayed on a television monitor.

Limited-Release Market The theatrical distribution of independent film, typically on a smaller scale than the release market for major studio productions.

Linear Editing System Until the latter 1990s, editors worked on celluloid film, with the footage in their workprints derived from camera negative. Using a linear system, the editor searched for material by running footage from beginning to end and joined shots sequentially, one after another. Such editors were in physical contact with actual film, unlike those using nonlinear systems who access an electronic signal via a keyboard.

Live Action Those components of a special effects shot or scene that were filmed live before the camera.

These elements may then be composited with digital effects.

Long Shot   One of the basic camera positions in which a camera is set up at some distance from the subject of the shot. Filmmakers usually use long shots to stress environment or setting.

Long Take   A shot of long duration, as distinct from a long shot, which designates a camera position.

Low-Angle   A camera angle usually below the eye level of performers in a scene.

Low-Key Lighting   A lighting design that maximizes contrast and fall-off by lighting selected areas of the scene for proper exposure and leaving all other areas underexposed.

Majors   The large studio-distributors that fund film production and distribute films internationally. Collectively, these companies constitute the Hollywood industry. They are Columbia Pictures, Warner Bros., Disney, MGM/UA, Paramount, 20th Century Fox, and Universal.

Master Shot   A camera position used by filmmakers to record the entire action of a scene from beginning to end. Filmmakers reshoot portions of the scene in close-up and medium shot framings. Editors cut these into the master shot to create the changing optical viewpoints of an edited scene. When used to establish the overall layout of a scene or location, the master shot can also double as an **establishing shot.**

Matched Cut   A cut joining two shots whose compositional elements strongly match. Matched cutting establishes continuity of action.

Matte   A painted landscape or location that is composited with the live action components of a shot. Mattes were traditionally done as paintings on glass, but many contemporary films use digital mattes created on a computer. Matte can also refer to a mask that is used to block or hide a portion of the frame, as when producing a widescreen image in theatrical projection. See **Soft-Matted, Hard-Matted.**

Medium Shot   One of the basic camera positions in which a camera is set up to record from full to half-figure shots of a performer.

Melodrama   The predominant dramatic style of popular cinema, emphasizing clear moral distinctions between hero and villain, exaggerated emotions, and a narrative style in which the twists and turns of the plot determine character behavior.

Method Acting   An approach to screen performance in which the actor seeks to portray a character by using personal experience and emotion as a foundation for the portrayal.

Miniature   A small-scale model representing a portion of a much larger location or building.

Mise-en-scène   A film's overall visual design, created by all of the elements that are placed before the camera. These include light, color, costumes, sets, and actors.

Montage   Used loosely, *montage* simply means "editing." In a strict sense, however, *montage* designates scenes whose emotional impact and visual design are achieved primarily through the editing of many brief shots. The shower scene from Hitchcock's *Psycho* is a classic example of montage editing.

Motion Control   Cinematography in which the camera's movements are plotted by computer so that they can be replicated when designing the digital components of the shot.

Motion Parallax   Also known as **motion perspective,** the term designates the changing positions of near and far objects as the viewer or the camera moves through space.

Motion Perspective   The change in visual perspective produced by the camera's movement through space. The visual positions of objects undergo systematic changes as the camera moves in relation to them. Camera movement will produce motion perspective but a zoom shot will not.

Music   One of the three basic types of film sound. Film music may include the score that accompanies the dramatic action of scenes as well as music originating on screen from within a scene.

Negative Cost   Accounting term for the expenses incurred by a film production, excluding the cost of advertising and publicity.

Neorealism   A filmmaking style that developed in postwar Italian cinema. The neorealist director aimed to truthfully portray Italian society by avoiding the gloss and glitter of expensive studio productions, emphasizing instead location filmmaking, a mixture of non- and semiprofessional actors, and simple, straightforward visual technique.

Newspaper/Television Reviewing   A mode of film criticism aimed at a general audience that performs an explicit consumer function, telling readers whether or not they should see the film being reviewed. Film reviews presented as part of television news or review programs also belong to this mode.

New Wave   A new stylistic direction or design appearing within a national cinema in the films of a group of (usually young) directors who are impatient with existing styles and seek to create alternatives.

Nonlinear Editing Systems   Computerized editing on digital video. This system gives editors instantaneous access to any shot or scene in a film and enables them to rapidly explore different edits of the same footage. Once a final cut has been reached on the digital video footage, the camera negative is then conformed (edited to match) this cut. Unlike an editor using a linear system who would actually handle film, the nonlinear editor uses a computer keyboard to find shots and join them together.

Nonsynchronous Sound   Sound that is not in synch with a source visible on screen.

Normal lens   A lens of moderate focal length that does not distort object size and depth of field. The normal lens records perspective much as the human eye does.

Off-Screen Sound   A type of sound in which the sound-producing source remains off-screen. Off-screen sound extends the viewer's perception of a represented screen location into an indefinite area of off-screen space.

180-Degree Rule   The foundation for establishing continuity of screen direction. The left and right coordinates of screen action remain consistent as long as all camera positions remain on the same side of the line of action. Crossing the line entails a change of screen direction.

Open Matte   Formatting of 1.85:1 aspect ratio films for the television/home video ratio of 4:3 by transferring the film full frame without the matting that was used during projection in theaters.

Ordinary Fictional Realism   A subcategory of the realist mode of screen reality. Such films feature a naturalistic visual design, a linear narrative, and plausible character behavior as the basis for establishing a realist style.

Pan   A type of camera movement in which the camera pivots from side to side on a fixed tripod or base. Pans produce lateral optical movement on-screen and are often used to follow the action of a scene or to anticipate the movements of performers.

Pan-and-Scan   A method of formatting wide-screen motion pictures for video release. Only a portion of the original wide-screen image is transferred to video. A full screen image appears on the video monitor, but it represents only a portion of the original wide-screen frame.

Parallel Action   An editing technique that establishes multiple, ongoing plot lines and simultaneous lines of action. Editors generally use the technique of cross-cutting to establish parallel action.

Perceptual Correspondence   Those properties of cinema that duplicate the visual information that viewers encounter in the everyday world. These include information about object size, light and shadow, movement, and facial expression and behavior as signs of emotion and intention.

Perceptual Processing   The film viewer's perceptual response to audiovisual information, as distinct from interpretive processing, which is the active interpretation of that information. Film viewing involves both components. The viewer sees color, depth, and movement (perceptual processing) in cinema and may attribute particular meanings to those perceptions (interpretive processing). Understood in terms of perceptual processing, a viewer watching a cross-cut sequence sees a succession of shots flashing by on-screen as an alternating series. Via interpretive processing, the viewer attributes a representation of simultaneous action to the alternating series. This attribution is not a meaning contained within the images themselves. It is the viewer's contribution.

Perceptual Realism   The correspondence of picture and sound in cinema with the ways viewers perceive space and sound in the real, three-dimensional world.

Perceptual Transformation   Those properties of cinema (e.g., a telephoto lens or a simultaneous zoom and track in opposite directions) that distort or alter the visual information that viewers encounter in the everyday world or that create completely novel visual experiences that have no basis in real-world experience. An example of the latter would be the high-speed bullet effects used in *The Matrix*.

Performance Style   The actor's contribution to the audiovisual and narrative design of a film.

Persistence of Vision   A characteristic of the human eye in which the retina briefly retains the impression of an image after its source has been removed. Because of persistence of vision, viewers do not see the alternating periods of light and dark through which they sit in a theater.

Phi Phenomena   The many different conditions under which the human eye can be fooled into seeing the illusion of movement. Beta movement is one of the phi phenomena.

Pictorial Lighting Design   A lighting design that does not aim to simulate the effects of an on-screen light source. Instead, the design moves in a purely pictorial direction to create mood and atmosphere.

Pixel   With reference to computer-based images, a pixel is the smallest unit of a picture capable of being digitally manipulated. The sharpness or resolution of an image is a function of the number of pixels it contains. High-end computer monitors, used in sophisticated film effects work, may have 2,000 pixels per screen line.

Plot   The order and arrangement of story events as they appear in a given film.

Point of View   The perspective from which narrative events are related. Point of view in cinema is typically third-person perspective, although filmmakers routinely manipulate audiovisual design to suggest what individual characters are thinking or feeling. Point of view in cinema can assume a first-person perspective through the use of voice-over narration or subjective shots in which the camera views a scene as if through the eyes of a character.

Point-of-View Shot   See **Subjective Shot.**

Polyvalence   The attribute of having more than one meaning. Motion pictures are polyvalent because they possess multiple layers of meaning.

Postdubbing   The practice of recording sound effects and dialogue after principal filming has been completed. *ADR* is the contemporary term for postdubbing. In the case of postdubbing dialogue, the technical challenge is to closely match the

rerecorded dialogue with the performer's lip movements in the shot.

Postproduction   The last stage of filmmaking, following the shooting and sound recording of scenes, that includes the editing of image and sound and finalizing of digital effects.

Practical (light)   A light source visible on a set used for exposure.

Preproduction   The stage of filmmaking that precedes the shooting and sound recording of scenes. It is the planning and preparation stage.

Previsualization   Any of a number of methods by which filmmakers try to visualize a shot before actually exposing film in the camera. Storyboards are a form of previsualization as are various software programs that will model a set as seen by different camera positions and lenses.

Producer   A production administrator who hires a director and supervises a film's production to ensure that it comes in under budget and on schedule. While directors work under a producer, in practice producers generally allow directors considerable creative freedom.

Production   The stage of filmmaking that includes the shooting and sound recording of scenes.

Production Design   The planning and creation of sets, costumes, mattes, and miniatures according to an overall concept articulated by the production designer in collaboration with the director.

Production Track   The soundtrack as recorded at the point of filming. The final soundtrack mix included on release prints to theaters includes portions of the production track along with a great deal of sound created in postproduction.

Production Values   Those elements of the film that show the money invested in its production. These typically include set designs, costumes, locations, and special effects.

Product Placement   The appearance of products on screen as part of a film scene. These appearances are advertisements for which the merchandiser pays a fee to a product placement agency. Film production companies derive revenue from these fees.

Product Tie-Ins   Products marketed in conjunction with the release of a blockbuster film. For example, a

Jurassic Park video game. These products often bear the logo or likeness of characters in the movie.

Psychoanalytic Film Theory   A model of film theory that examines the unconscious, sometimes irrational, emotional, and psychological relationship between viewers and films or between characters within films.

Real Author   The actual flesh-and-blood author of a film, as distinct from the implied author, the artistic perspective embodied by a film's overall audiovisual design.

Realism   A basic mode of screen reality. Ordinary fictional realism, historical realism, and documentary realism are subcategories of the realist mode.

Realist Film Theory   A model of film theory that seeks to explain how filmmakers may capture, with minimal distortion, the essential features of real situations and events, or, in the case of fictionalized events, how filmmakers may give them an apparent real-world status.

Realistic Lighting Design   A lighting design that simulates the effects of a light source visible on-screen.

Realistic Sound   Sound that seems to fit the properties of a real source. In practice this is an elastic concept because many sounds that seem to be realistic are, in fact, artificial and derive from sources other than the one that is designated on-screen.

Rear Projection   A technique for simulating location cinematography by projecting photographic images of a landscape onto a screen. Actors are photographed standing in front of the screen as if they were part of the represented location.

Reflected Sound   Sound that is reflected off surfaces in a physical environment before being captured by the microphone. By manipulating characteristics of sound reflection, sound designers can capture the physical attributes of an environment.

Rental   Accounting term for the revenues returned to a film distributor.

Rhetoric   The use of language to persuade and influence others. Film criticism is a rhetorical activity.

Room Tone   A type of ambient sound characterizing the acoustical properties of a room. Even an empty room will emit room tone.

Rough Cut   The film editor's initial assembly of shots in a scene or film before the editing is tightened and perfected in the fine cut.

Running Time   The amount of real time it takes a viewer to watch a film from beginning to end. Most commercial films run between 90 and 120 minutes.

Saturation   A basic characteristic of color. Saturation measures color strength and is a function of how much white light is mixed into the color. The more white light that is present, the less saturated the color will seem to be.

Schema   This term derives from the psychology of perception and designates a mental category or framework used to organize information. Applied to cinema, it helps explain the function of devices like the master shot, which provides viewers with a schema or map of a location and the characters' positions within it. Viewers use the visual schema provided by master shots to orient themselves to changing camera positions and to integrate partial views of a scene provided by close-ups.

Scholarly Criticism   A mode of criticism aimed at a specialized audience of scholars, employing a technical, demanding vocabulary, and exploring the significance of given films in relation to issues of theory or film history.

Screen Reality   The represented reality depicted by a fictional film. Screen reality is established by the principles of time, space, character behavior, and audiovisual design as these are organized in a given film.

Sequence Shot   A long take whose duration extends for an entire scene or sequence. Such a scene or sequence is accordingly composed of only one shot and features no editing.

Sets   The controlled physical environment in which filming occurs. Sets may be created by blocking and lighting an area of ground outdoors or by building and designing a physical environment indoors.

Shading   A visual depth cue in which gradations and patterns of light and shadow reveal texture and volume in a three-dimensional world and can be used to create a three-dimensional impression on a flat theater or television screen.

Shot   The basic unit of film structure, corresponding to the amount of footage exposed in the camera from the time it is turned on until it is turned off.

Shots are visible on-screen as the intervals between cuts, fades, or dissolves.

Shot-Reverse-Shot Cutting   A type of continuity editing generally used for conversation scenes. The cutting alternates between opposing over-the-shoulder camera set-ups showing each character speaking in turn.

Shutter   Device inside the camera that regulates the light reaching the film. In a film projector, the shutter functions like an on/off switch, regulating the light reaching the screen to produce beta movement and critical fusion frequency.

Sign   In communication theory, that which embodies or expresses meaning.

Soft Light   Light that is diffused or scattered by filters or reflecting screens. Soft light creates a low-contrast image.

Soft-Matted   The use of mattes during projection to mask the top and bottom of the film frame and produce a widescreen (1.85:1) image.

Sound Bridge   Sound used to connect, or bridge, two or more shots. Sound bridges establish continuity of place, action, or time.

Sound Design (Designer)   The expressive use of sound throughout a film in relation to its images and the contents of its narrative. Working in conjunction with the director, the sound designer supervises the work of other sound personnel.

Sound Field   The acoustical space created by all the speakers in a multichannel, surround-sound system.

Sound Hierarchy   The relative priority given to dialogue, effects, and music in a given scene. In most cases, dialogue is considered the most important of these sounds and rests atop the sound hierarchy.

Sound Montage   A type of sound editing that conjoins many discrete sound effects and sources.

Sound Perspective   The use of sound to augment visual perspective. Sound perspective often correlates with camera position. In a long shot reflected sound may prevail, whereas in a close-up direct sound may prevail.

Soundstage   The acoustical space created by the front speakers in a multichannel, surround-sound system.

Speech   Dialogue spoken by performers playing characters in a narrative.

Spotting   A collaborative process between the director and composer during which they spot or identify passages in the film that require musical scoring.

Star   The highest profile performer in a film narrative. Stars draw audiences to theaters and establish intense personal relationships with their publics.

Star Persona   The relatively fixed screen personality of a star.

Story   The entire sequence of events that a film's plot draws on and references. The plot arranges story events into a given order, which may differ from the story's proper chronology.

Story Time   The amount of time covered by the narrative. This may vary considerably from film to film. The narrative of *2001: A Space Odyssey* begins during a period of primitive prehuman ancestry and extends into the era of space travel, while the narrative of *High Noon* spans, roughly, 90 minutes, closely approximating that film's running time.

Structure   The audiovisual design of a film. The elements of structure include the camera, lights and color, production design, performance style, editing, sound, and narrative.

Subjective Shot   Also known as a **point-of-view shot.** The camera's position and angle represent the exact viewpoint of a character in the narrative.

Subtractive Color Mixing   The method for creating color in film. Magenta, cyan, and yellow dyes combined in color film produce all other hues.

Super 35   Widescreen format that captures a 2:1 aspect ratio image on the camera negative. This image is then typically cropped to 2.35:1 for theatrical release and to 1.33:1 for full-frame home video release.

Supervising Art Director   During the classical Hollywood era, this was the head of the art department who supervised art design in all the films under production at a studio.

Supporting Player   A performer in a secondary role who does not receive either the billing or the pay of a major star. Many performers first establish themselves as supporting players before they become stars.

Surprise   A narrative technique used to jolt or startle the viewer. Creating surprise depends on withholding crucial narrative information from viewers, whereas creating suspense depends on providing viewers with necessary information. Showing the audience the bomb under the table before it goes off will create suspense. Not showing the bomb before it goes off will create surprise.

Surrealism   Influenced by Freudian psychoanalysis, this art style aims to appeal to the viewer's subconscious and irrational mind by creating fantastic and dream-like images. David Lynch's *Blue Velvet* is a surrealist film.

Suspense   A narrative technique used to create tension and anxiety in the film viewer. Creating suspense depends on revealing rather than withholding narrative information. Showing the audience the bomb under the table before it goes off will create suspense. Not showing the bomb before it goes off will create surprise. Unlike suspense, surprise depends on withholding information from the audience.

Synthetic Sound   Artificially designed sound that does not match any existing source. The sounds of the light sabers in the *Star Wars* films are examples of synthetic sound.

Taboo Images   Imagery depicting forbidden or disturbing subjects, often of a sexual or violent nature.

Technical Acting   An approach to acting in which the performer thinks through the requisite gestures and emotions and then exhibits them. In contrast to method acting, the technical actor does not look to personal experience as a basis for understanding the character.

Telephoto Lens   A lens of long focal length that distorts object size and depth of field. Telephoto lenses magnify the size of distant objects and by doing so compress depth of field and make them appear closer than they are.

Temp Track   A temporary musical track usually derived from an existing film that a director uses early in production to show the composer the type of musical composition he or she wants.

Thematic Montage   A style of editing that draws an explicit comparison between two or more images, as when Charles Chaplin compares workers and sheep in a pair of shots at the beginning of *Modern Times*.

Tilt   A type of camera movement in which the camera pivots up and down on a fixed tripod or base. Tilts produce vertical movement on screen and are often used to follow action and reveal detail.

Tracking Shot   A camera movement in which the camera physically moves along the ground to follow action or to reveal significant narrative information. Tracking shots can be executed by pushing the camera along tracks, by attaching the camera to a moving vehicle such as a car, or by using a handheld Steadycam mount, in which case the camera operator runs or walks alongside the action. Tracking shots are sometimes called *dolly shots*, after the "dolly" or movable platform on which the camera is sometimes mounted.

Translite   A photographic image, enlarged and backlit, this is one of the basic tools of production design, used to simulate a large, scenic view in the background of a set.

Typage   The manipulation of a screen character's visual or physical characteristics to suggest psychological or social themes or ideas.

Unit Art Director   In the classical Hollywood studio system in the 1930s and 1940s, the unit art director oversaw the creation of sets and costumes for a given production. The unit art director worked under a studio's supervising art director who supervised set and costume design on all of the studio's productions.

Visual Effects Supervisor   Member of the production crew who oversees the design of a film's special effects.

Voice-Over Narration   Dialogue spoken by an off-screen narrator. This narrator may be a character reflecting in voice-over on story events from some later point in the narrative or, as sometimes occurs in documentary films, the narrator may exist independently of characters in the story.

Voyeurism   A basic pleasure offered by cinema, derived from looking at the characters and situations on screen.

Wavelength   The characteristic of light that corresponds to color. Colors are visible when white light is broken down into component wavelengths.

White Telephone Films   Derogatory term for the glossy studio films produced by Cinecitta, Italy's national studio, during the Mussolini period.

Wide-Angle Lens   A short focal length lens that exaggerates depth of field by increasing the size of near objects and minimizing the size of distant objects. Because they can focus on near and far objects, wide-angle lenses can capture great depth of field.

Widescreen Ratios   Any of a large number of aspect ratios that exceed the nearly square, 1.37:1 ratio of classical Hollywood film and 1.33:1 ratio of conventional television. Widescreen films must be reformatted for video release using methods of letterboxing or panning-and-scanning.

Wipe   An editing transition prevalent in earlier decades of sound film. A hard- or soft-edged line (generally vertical) traveling across the frame marked the border of the outgoing and incoming shots. Although wipes are rare in contemporary film, George Lucas used them extensively in *Star Wars Episode One: The Phantom Menace* to evoke the style of old movie serials.

Zoom Lens   A lens capable of shifting from short (wide-angle) to long (telephoto) focal lengths. Using a zoom to change focal lengths within a shot produces the impression of camera movement, making it seem as if the camera is moving closer to or farther from its subject.

Index